The Effective Presidency

LESSONS ON LEADERSHIP FROM JOHN F. KENNEDY TO BARACK OBAMA

Erwin C. Hargrove

Paradigm Publishers
Boulder • London

Copyright © 2014 Paradigm Publishers

Published in the United States by Paradigm Publishers, 5589 Arapahoe Avenue, Boulder, CO 80303 USA.

Paradigm Publishers is the trade name of Birkenkamp & Company, LLC, Dean Birkenkamp, President and Publisher.

Library of Congress Cataloging-in-Publication Data

Hargrove, Erwin C.
  The effective presidency : lessons on leadership from John F. Kennedy to Barack Obama / Erwin C. Hargrove. — Second edition.
    pages cm
  Includes bibliographical references and index.
  ISBN 978-1-61205-434-6 (pbk. : alk. paper)
  1. Presidents—United States—History—20th century. 2. Presidents—United States—History—21st century. 3. Political leadership—United States—History—20th century. 4. Political leadership—United States—History—21st century. 5. United States—Politics and government—20th century. 6. United States—Politics and government—21st century. I. Title.
  JK516.H255 2014
  973.92092'2—dc23

                                                                        2013025813

Printed and bound in the United States of America on acid-free paper that meets the standards of the American National Standard for Permanence of Paper for Printed Library Materials.

Designed and Typeset by Straight Creek Bookmakers.
18 17 16 15 14   1 2 3 4 5

Contents

Preface

This book compares ten successive presidents according to their contributions and their mistakes in the stream of American history. My attention is on the decisions and actions of presidents in historical contexts and in the institutions within which they worked. One may generalize about the ability of individual presidents, in comparison with others, in varying historical contexts. This is a challenge to both political scientists and historians to compare presidents and find generalizations about when they may make a difference in history.

Much of my work on the presidency has had a normative cast. I have always been concerned with the uses and abuses of power in the presidency, in constitutional terms, and in regard to truth telling and deception. Leaders of strong ambition and talent are called to be president, often in difficult times. But they may also create false crises, and we must always be ready to withdraw our mandate from them. The study of the personality and character of presidents, which is often seen as an uncertain sidebar in presidential studies, is a central normative question.

Three of my friends in Nashville have read each chapter of the book as it was being written and have given their advice in detail. I have used them as sounding boards for clarity and persuasiveness of writing, and they have been invaluable in their help. They are Jacque Voegeli, an American historian who also provided his expertise, and Jack May and Clay Bailey, businessman-lawyer and attorney, respectively. The idea for this book grew out of an undergraduate seminar in the Vanderbilt history department that I taught in the spring of 2004. The course went so well that I decided that it might become a book, and I am grateful to the good students in that seminar. My writing has always been helped by my teaching.

Charles O. Jones, Stuart E. Eizenstat, and Alonzo L. Hamby read the manuscript for the press and gave both detailed advice and a broad critique, which helped me to raise the theoretical themes of the book beyond the separate profiles of presidents. Jennifer Knerr has been a creative, constant, encouraging friend as editor. The book is much better because of her advice. Finally, my wife Julie always smoothes my life and is the wind at my back as I work.

The Effective President

With the election of Barack Obama, the first African American president, in 2008, expectations of presidential greatness soared. After a first term filled with both great successes and disappointing setbacks, such expectations have become more moderate and a sense of pragmatism has taken over.

American political legend celebrates presidential "greatness" as the key to progress in American history. We have had a few "great" or "near great" presidents by general acknowledgement: Washington, Lincoln, and Franklin Roosevelt as "great" with less agreement on the "near greats": Jackson, Theodore Roosevelt, and Truman usually make the list. The implicit definition of "great" in these assessments covers three things: (1) extraordinary political talent, (2) historical opportunities for creative leadership, and (3) a lasting contribution to American history. A few "worst" presidents always make the list: Buchanan and Harding, because they faced intractable problems or were incompetent.

How does one assess the other presidents? Few meet the criteria of greatness, but we lack a standard for effectiveness and often measure our president against the great ones. I suggest that we define an effective president as a national leader who makes the most of his or her political opportunities. The effective president is able to find that area of the politically possible and act to achieve that goal. The effective president may also stretch what is possible by his or her leadership. All presidents cannot and need not be great, but we hope that most would be effective.

1

Effectiveness also extends to the ability to face and resolve national problems and move the country past old problems to new ones. Problems must be defined and redefined continually in American democracy, and this is the primary task of presidents. Our ideal should not be that of the great, heroic leader who transforms history in broad new directions, like Lincoln or Franklin Roosevelt. Such leadership comes only in great national crises. We require leaders who continually remind us of who we are and where we might go.

Popular expectations yearn for greatness. The candidates for president in any given election cycle always seem to fall short of such expectations because, as Shakespeare depicts King Henry V saying before the battle of Agincourt, without "ceremony" the king is "but a man." Candidates, without the mantle of office, are just men and women.

The desire for presidential greatness in the twentieth century was strong during two world wars and a severe depression. This desire was sustained by the progressive interpretation of American history in which presidents are the heroes of reform and spokesmen for the nation against a parochial Congress. Franklin Roosevelt was the implicit model against which his successors were compared. Leave aside the fact that his second term was a seeming failure and that he lost his grip on affairs toward the end. His halo effect is seen in the ways in which his successors have been seen to fall short of his great political skill. Dwight Eisenhower was parodied for lacking Roosevelt's skill, even though evidence of his very different talents is now apparent.

It was not until Ronald Reagan invoked Roosevelt as his model president and proceeded to reveal political skills not unlike FDR's that conservatives, who had stood outside the progressive myth, began to understand the power of the presidency. Republican politicians now invoke Theodore Roosevelt as an icon.

However, the conservative celebration of presidential centrality and power differs from the progressive one. There is greater emphasis on the power of the president to govern alone, free of the constraints of Congress, the bureaucracy, and the higher courts. This course follows from the logic of Republican presidential politics that, since Richard Nixon, has sought to create a partisan realignment in which the Republicans would be a majority party. Democratic majorities in the Congress were simply in the way. The imperative to centralization in the executive was extended by President George W. Bush, assisted by a compliant Republican Congress. The shift to the executive may have gone too far. Progressive presidents respected constitutional checks and balances and the spirit of politics within them in a way that President Bush did not. One may wonder whether the demand for presidential "greatness" was a guiding force in the Bush presidency and whether our constitutional institutions were well served.

Our three truly great presidents—Washington, Lincoln, and Franklin Roosevelt—served in times of national crisis. Leaders of high talent were required. Many other presidents have achieved much without national crisis.

We must also face the brute fact that some presidents with the personal ambition to be great have at times brought disaster by overreaching from their ambition. The Vietnam war and Watergate, with two flawed presidents, Lyndon Johnson and Richard Nixon, raise this possibility. Such presidents confused their personal ambitions with service to the nation. There is peril in an obsession with greatness.

The test of the effectiveness of presidential leadership must be shifted from the ideal of solo artistry to the question of how well a president is able to resolve policy problems in concert with Congress, the parties, administration, and the courts. Presidents do most often provide the lead in addressing policy problems.

But this can be done effectively only in concert with others, because otherwise the achievements will be hollow. We move forward as a nation together and great policy achievements require great consensus. By the same token, policy problems are resolved, not solved. We necessarily move forward incrementally.

Even when massive policy shifts have occurred, as in the New Deal, presidential leadership must build coalitions to win effectively, and always with an eye to the limits that politics will permit.

In the 2008 and 2012 presidential elections, candidates of the partisan camps promised different moons. But the nation was not well served. The problems that confront the nation—war, a runaway budget, Social Security and health care financing, disparities in income, global warming—are so immense that candidates dare not ignore them. Yet the challenge of facing such problems is so difficult that effective candidates and the president who is chosen would do best to promise only new departures, new down payments on the problems we face. The public will respond positively if the directions are clear and the costs are reasonable in the short term. Presidential leadership should seek effectiveness rather than greatness.

Woodrow Wilson wrote that a president was free "to be as big a man as he can" in our constitutional system. This has been the implicit standard for greatness. We lack clear standards for effectiveness short of greatness. The purpose of this book is to help us think about such standards. They are not likely to be uniform because historical circumstances, problems, and presidents differ.

Sidney Hook, a distinguished American philosopher, makes the distinction between "eventful" and "event-making" political leaders. The former are leaders who make differences at the historical margins. Their actions make a difference, but history has prepared the way. The decisive choices made by such leaders are consistent with the temper of the times and the collaboration of others. But they are not simply followers. Their actions or inactions may be decisive in an important issue. Harry Truman's decision to drop the atomic bomb on Japan was a crucial decision, but he made it in concert with his advisers.

The "event-making" leader, in Hook's words, is "the eventful man whose actions are the consequences of outstanding qualities of intelligence, will, or character rather than the accident of position" (1943, 154). Extraordinary talent is at work. Both eventful and event-making men may appear at "forking points" in history, but the event-making leader helps create the fork in the road. His extraordinary qualities free the path from opposition and increase the odds for success. This leader does not act alone. He or she needs lieutenants and the unified support of a political coalition. Once in power such a leader may act quite independently, but a political machine provides support, often uncritically.

Hook does not draw a sharp line between the two types in real life. A given leader may be eventful in some respects and event-making in others. He does not recommend event-making leaders for democracies. They may be creative but also destructive. Eventful leaders may be constructive or weak. Effectiveness is not guaranteed. Lenin and Hitler were event-making leaders for Hook. There is no mention of Gandhi, and he wrote before Nelson Mandela. But Hook insists that democracy must be on guard against men who would be heroes, citing the Chinese proverb that "the great man is a public misfortune." Heroes in history are usually those who make war, conquests, revolutions, and crusades. But even if great leaders are good men, democracies should be suspicious, because sooner or later the event-making leader will threaten the democratic process. He may violate the principle of majority rule when he thinks the majority to be wrong, and he may resist the slowness of democratic institutions when he believes the majority to be right. The majority may be wrong, but a true democratic leader must accept the fact and work to create a new majority by persuasion. But an event-making leader may become a demagogue who seeks to fool the public. He reveals contempt for democracy, even for his own followers. The greater his faith in himself, the stronger the issue to which his heroic vision drives him, the greater threat he is to democracy. He sees himself as the "indispensable instrument of his vision." This kind of leader continually presses for greater personal power, and delegated powers are dangerous. Democracies need great leaders with authorized powers, but they must be ready to take power back. Democracies must not glorify their leaders after they are dead, and they should praise the teachers, like Jefferson and Whitman, more than politicians. Genuine heroes exist in all walks of life and this must be acknowledged in the mythology of democracy.

Since 1961 we have had four event-making presidents: Lyndon Johnson, Richard Nixon, Ronald Reagan, and George W. Bush. The others have been eventful: John Kennedy, Gerald Ford, Jimmy Carter, George H. W. Bush, Bill Clinton, and Barack Obama. Each of the event-making presidents was creative and achieved much, but they each overreached in untoward ways. The eventful presidents varied greatly in the skills they brought to their tasks but there were strands of effectiveness throughout. There is not a sharp dividing line between the two kinds of presidents in practice, except for the one fault of reaching too far beyond appropriate limits.

The understanding of the presidency among political scientists has shifted across time among three approaches. Clinton Rossiter, a Cornell University political scientist, and James McGregor Burns, a major American scholar of the presidency, idealized the benefits of powerful presidents. Rossiter in *The American Presidency* (1956) was critical of Dwight Eisenhower for his passivity. Burns took Franklin Roosevelt to task in *Roosevelt: The Lion and the Fox* (1956) for being too little lion and too much fox. Both authors worked within the progressive tradition that celebrated a strong executive supported by majoritarian politics. Richard Neustadt, the leading presidential scholar in the second half of the twentieth century, was also a progressive, but his book *Presidential Power and the Modern Presidents* (1990) asked presidents to be skillful bargainers rather than heroic leaders. Neustadt understood American government to be one of "institutions sharing powers" and his ideal president had to know how to wring bargains out of fragmented institutions. No sooner had Neustadt's model become orthodoxy than the nation suffered the war in Vietnam and the scandals of Watergate. Trumpets sounded against "the Imperial Presidency" from many quarters. The abuse of authority through secrecy and illegality took center stage. The critiques were split between those, such as Neustadt, who held Johnson and Nixon personally accountable, and others who saw the national security state as a threat to the constitutional regime.

The two transition presidencies of Gerald Ford and Jimmy Carter gave way to the decisive leadership of Ronald Reagan, the moderate leadership of George H. W. Bush, the bargaining presidency of Bill Clinton, the assertions of power by George W. Bush, and the search for balance with Barack Obama. We have had a kaleidoscope of presidencies without any dominant pattern and uncertain standards for leadership.

Political scientists working today have not asked questions about the proper limits of presidential power. Most contemporary studies deny that presidents may be too powerful. Studies such as those of George Edwards, a contemporary student of the presidency, in *At the Margins: Presidential Leadership of Congress* (1989), see the president at best as a "facilitator" of policy agreement rather than a "director" who can tell Congress what to do. Presidents may make a difference, but at the margins. Most work on the presidency today by political scientists focuses on these marginal differences in presidential leadership, whether of Congress, bureaucracy, or public opinion. The individual political skills of presidents are seen as perhaps important but not that important. This finding is to be expected if one examines large numbers of cases using statistical methods. Some scholars, such as Theodore Lowi, a prominent scholar of American politics, in *The Personal President* (1985), would deny the importance of individuality in presidents in favor of explaining the actions of presidents according to the institutional roles they play.

This book widens the scope and changes the debate. The central question is whether individual presidents may make important differences in history. I forsake the search for empirical generalizations based on statistical analysis of a large number of cases and ask about the most important things each president attempted. One or two major achievements or failures can tell us a lot about a given president and the history he creates. The inquiry must be pursued through historical narratives in order to place each president in context and ask if he or she made a difference. Burns was critical of FDR as a fox because he wished for more of the lion's roar. On the other hand, Roosevelt achieved much as a fox, and it may be that eventful presidents are able to achieve much, in concert with democratic politics, without running the risks of overstepping their powers. Franklin Roosevelt was both an event-making and an eventful president and his ability to know when to be one and not the other, as he read democratic politics, was his great talent.

We require a framework for helping us make the distinction between eventful and event-making presidents. Individual presidents may be studied comparatively in the stream of American history, as Stephen Skowronek, a Yale University political scientist, and Aaron Wildavsky and Richard Ellis have shown. Changing political resources and opportunities for and constraints on action matter greatly in what presidents may achieve. But the political abilities of individual presidents also matter a great deal. It is therefore possible to generalize about the relative importance of individual talent in presidents to ask about effective leadership and the conditions under which it is effective.

The relationship between leadership and the historical context is dynamic. Creative leadership may be reinforced by favorable conditions, or overcome such conditions. Inept leadership may be helped by favorable events or be swamped by them. Many historical patterns are set by the past and are not easily—if at all—changed. But because not everything is determined, we must always be looking for contingencies, or forks in the road, in which presidents may make a difference. According to Hook, a contingency is a situation that is logically necessary and whose nonexistence is not logically impossible. But not everything about a contingent event is novel. The intelligence and will of leaders may make a difference, but historical constraints are always present. Skillful leadership understands that fact, and political realism is thus crucial to effective leadership. Hook introduces a moral dimension to leadership in believing that moral possibilities are present in contingent events. Moral leadership consists of identifying the possibilities of moral clarification and education within the prevailing historical framework. We ask of our ten presidents what differences each of them made in history and the relative importance of individuality in presidential achievement and failure. Presidents vary in their abilities and in the opportunities before them with varying results. One must ask several questions to carry out this analysis:

Context and Contingencies

What was the historical context in which each president worked? Such contexts are not uniform but vary across different areas of politics and policy and change over time. But no matter, the possibilities for creative action are either reinforced or constrained by historical context. No president is a hero in history who makes a difference all by himself. One must always ask under what conditions was leadership reinforced or constrained? What historical contingencies might a president discern and act upon to make a difference? Lyndon Johnson saw the possibilities for domestic reform in the wake of Kennedy's death and exploited that reality for success with Congress. Ronald Reagan saw the crumbling character of the Soviet regime more clearly than his advisers and acted accordingly. Mistakes may follow such leaps to opportunity. Johnson took the nation into a war that was bitterly regretted, but he may have been constrained by domestic politics and the commitments of previous presidents. George W. Bush took the nation to war in Iraq, and questions about the prudence of his actions are the central issue of politics today. It is often difficult to tell prescience from foolhardiness or arrogance.

Talents and Skills

What personal attributes and political skills do presidents bring to bear as they seek to act creatively in contingencies? How well do they match their purposes to the realistic possibilities for action in the context in which they work? Talented politicians must balance purpose and prudence if they are to be effective. This may be a crucial difference between lions and foxes, and the distinction is at the heart of our inquiry. An array of skills is required for effective leadership. Discernment of opportunity is a special kind of cognitive skill. Politicians feel their way into problems and situations and often see sets of possibilities that emerge as they act. The most effective politicians are able to read people and situations realistically. An understanding of the historical context and how to act strategically and tactically within it is crucial.

Did He Make a Difference?

What creative actions and achievements result from the exercise of skills in historical context? This is the most difficult analytic task, and it is not possible to give definitive answers. Lyndon Johnson took the nation to war in Vietnam, but explanations as to why he did so abound, and careful analysis of alternative hypotheses against the evidence is required. Ronald Reagan helped to bring the cold war to an end, but a good part of the credit should go to Mikhail Gorbachev, the Soviet leader with whom he worked. I try to answer such questions as best I can, always leaving the debate open and considering alternative explanations. I avoid asking about the long-term consequences of presidential actions, for example, the effects of tax cuts or civil rights laws. It is enough to describe what presidents do to achieve them.

Each chapter of this book explores the leadership of a given president according to these questions. The narratives of each chapter are representative of the patterns of leadership in each presidency. The final chapter asks about how presidents are able to use their skills to make a difference according to historical conditions. Under what conditions does individual talent make a difference? Are some talents more effective than others and, if so, why?

We then ask the question that inspired this study. How has American constitutional government fared in the modern presidency? As the reader may have anticipated, I believe that we need effective eventful presidents most of the time and should be suspicious to those presidents with ambitions for greatness.

This study is a blend of history and political science, in that narrative is joined to comparative analysis. The history begins with John F. Kennedy and works through the continuities and discontinuities of politics and policy across time. We see what each president inherited and then passed along. Narrative thus gives us a good sense of changing resources and constraints on action. One must read a given chapter according to what came before to fully understand the historical context in which a given president worked. The joining of narrative and comparative analysis is a union of two disciplines that should be joined.

When the second term of Barack Obama's historic presidency comes to a close, we will look ahead to the next major milestone in presidential history: the advent of the first female American president. Whenever that occurs, we can expect that the combination of narrative and comparative analysis will continue to enlighten, and that the touchstones of context and contingencies, talents and skills, and making a difference will continue to serve as reliable gauges of presidential effectiveness.

BIBLIOGRAPHY

Burns, James Macgregor. *Roosevelt: The Lion and the Fox.* New York: Harcourt, Brace, 1956.

Clinton, Hillary Rodham. *Living History.* New York: Simon and Schuster, 2003.

Edwards, George C., III. *At the Margins: Presidential Leadership of Congress.* New Haven, CT: Yale University Press, 1989.

Ellis, Richard, and Aaron Wildavsky. *Dilemmas of Presidential Leadership from Washington through Lincoln.* New Brunswick, NJ: Transaction Books, 1989.

Hook, Sidney. *The Hero in History: A Study in Limitation and Possibility.* New York: John Day, 1943.

Lowi, Theodore. *The Personal President: Power Invested, Promise Unfulfilled.* Ithaca, NY: Cornell University Press, 1985.

Neustadt, Richard M. *Presidential Power and the Modern Presidents: The Politics of Leadership from Roosevelt to Reagan.* New York: Free Press, 1990.

Rossiter, Clinton. *The American Presidency.* New York: New American Library, 1956.

Skowronek, Stephen. *The Politics Presidents Make: Leadership from John Adams to George Bush.* Cambridge, MA: Belknap Press of Harvard University Press, 1993.

Wayne, Stephen J. *Personality and Politics: Obama For and Against Himself.* Washington, DC: CQ Press, 2011.

CHAPTER ONE

John F. Kennedy

A Cautious Reformer

Each president enters office within streams of historical events that he did not create but must confront. The task of leadership for a president is to manage events so that some of those streams are responsive to his touch. Of course some of this work is the manipulation of appearances. That can be harmful if it is based on falsehood, but it can also be fruitful if the momentum toward achievement is enhanced. John F. Kennedy was fortunate in the timing of his domestic presidency. The years from 1953 until 1966 were a period of partisan debate about the purposes of government in which the flow of progressive reform became stronger and stronger. The crest of the wave began to rise just as the young president was killed and his successor became the president of the achievement that Kennedy might have been.

The election of Dwight Eisenhower in 1952 brought eight years of clear, responsible debate between the two parties about the purposes of American government. Democrats advocated the use of government to enhance both opportunity and security in health, education, and welfare. Eisenhower accepted the New Deal accomplishments by creating a new federal Department of Health, Education, and Welfare. Republicans did not deny the existence of social deficits, but they feared excessive federal spending and its effects on the economy and overgrown bureaucracy might do more harm than good as it bludgeoned its way into the federal system. Eisenhower sought balanced budgets, a sound dollar, and low inflation. Democrats thought it possible for government to stimulate the economy for dynamic growth according to new economic theories. During the second Eisenhower administration, Democratic reformers developed a number of new ideas in social and economic policy that became the intellectual capital for Kennedy's "New Frontier."

The grain of history was not so beneficent in international affairs. Kennedy's inaugural address dealt only with foreign affairs and it issued a challenge to the Soviet Union to the effect that the United States would seek peace with strength; certainly not a new idea, but from a new president. The idea of containment of the Soviet Union in its satellite states in Eastern Europe and of adventurism in third-world nations abroad, derived from the Truman administration, was accepted by Eisenhower. However, Democrats had become convinced that Eisenhower was too passive in competition in the nuclear arms race with the Soviet Union and that he had also pared back the army so that it would be difficult to deal with limited wars around the globe. Kennedy had campaigned on the existence of a "missile gap" and called for the development of army "special forces" to deal with brushfire wars. The gap turned out to be a myth, but the latter provided confidence that the United States might fight limited wars more effectively, a belief that was to be proved wrong in Vietnam.

Kennedy won the 1960 election primarily because of the three recessions that had taken place in Eisenhower's second term. He won only by a hair and was hindered by his Catholicism. The television debates with Vice President Richard Nixon boosted his public approval and were a harbinger of the politics of personality that he was to bring into the White House. The Democrats suffered a net loss of twenty-one seats in the House of Representatives, and it was apparent that the victor lacked a mandate, except perhaps for a more active government at home and abroad. Opinion polls from 1953 on had shown increasing support for Democratic ideas about federal aid to education, health insurance for the elderly, full employment, and, outside the South, civil rights, although to a lesser degree. But Kennedy lacked the votes in Congress to enact his New Frontier programs because of the large number of conservative Southern Democrats. When one subtracts that group of politicians, he had about a five-person majority in the House. The new president thus had a limited mandate without the requisite support to carry it out. Had he been able to enact his programs, he would have probably won public support for them because public opinion follows the actions of government as much or more than it leads government. The rhetorical leadership that he did provide for almost three years helped nudge the public in his direction.

THE MAN

Kennedy was a natural leader who taught himself to be a politician. He probably would not have chosen a political career had not his older brother, Joe Jr., been killed in World War II. Joe Jr. was the future president in his father's eyes. Jack forced himself to campaign for the House of Representatives in Cambridge, Massachusetts, in 1946, dragging his bad back from wartime injuries up tenement stairs night after night to meet voters, invoking the names of his Kennedy and Fitzgerald grandfathers, old-time Boston politicians. Once in the House, and then in the Senate in 1953, he was not a particularly effective legislator. Congress is for workhorses and policy entrepreneurs, and Kennedy saw himself as a potential statesman. He had met many world leaders when his father was ambassador to Great Britain before World War II and had observed others in a brief career as a journalist after the war and during his service in Congress. His primary interest was in foreign affairs. His commitments to Democratic domestic policies were casual, but once nominated, he accepted the ideas of reform that had been gestating during the Eisenhower years. He envisioned himself an actor on an international stage. One of his favorite plays was Shakespeare's *Henry V,* and he particularly liked the young king's stirring speech to his troops before the battle of Agincourt. But his romanticism was chastened by a detachment and sense of irony, which was his saving grace as a politician. He never permitted himself to be captured by any one idea, adviser, or lieutenant. Nevertheless he was able to convey idealism in both foreign and domestic policy, which, over time, was a source of great popular support. Its effect was certainly as strong as the superficial celebrity that he and his wife enjoyed. But the sense of irony and the detachment were always present. He always felt that he should be leading, and his most politically creative moments occurred when he was trying to break out of traps and boxes.

His advisers agreed that he was only interested in ideas if they were useful for immediate decisions. His mind was sharply analytical, and he could see to the heart of a problem quickly. Neither theories nor planning interested him, so he lived in the short run, often to his detriment. He ran a freewheeling White House staff and was a poor manager of policymaking. He would often give assignments to whoever was in the Oval Office without thought about possible executive crossed wires.

His best moments were when he was actually in charge, and his lowest moments were when he had lost control, although he would not relinquish it for long. He was capable of turning events around in a creative way. This adaptive ability matched the emerging historical context of increasing demands on government for social action. Such skill was not apparent when he became president, and perhaps he did not himself know of his own creativity, but he learned what he could and must do if he wanted to be an effective president in the act of trying.

Every Democratic president wishes to be another Franklin Roosevelt, but the conditions are seldom favorable. It is not at all clear that Kennedy thought of himself as an event-making leader like FDR. His personality and the political context within which he worked were much more congenial to efforts at creative eventful leadership, in which purpose and prudence were balanced.

DOMESTIC POLICY

Kennedy's legislative initiatives for federal aid to education, Medicare, and other social programs did not include civil rights. He felt that he needed southern Democrats in Congress to pass his programs because so many were committee chairmen by seniority. He lacked the votes to pass big programs, and the measures that did pass—such as an increase in the minimum wage, urban renewal, economic aid to distressed areas, and job training—were modest in their objectives.

Federal aid for teachers' salaries and school construction foundered on the question of whether Catholic schools should be considered. The Catholic bishops thought it only fair, but the idea ran up against claims that aid would violate the constitutional separation of church and state. Members of Congress were so divided on the question that nothing was done. Government health insurance for people sixty-five and older had strong public support. But the American Medical Association strongly opposed it and mounted a vigorous negative advertising campaign. The measure was defeated in the Senate and then bottled up in a House committee. The "conservative coalition" of Republicans and southern Democrats was too strong.

Kennedy preferred to work with foreign policy and had little taste for sitting down with congressional leaders to persuade and bargain. In fact, he was deferential to many of them because he had not been in the group that ran the Senate and he seldom asked individuals to help him with bills. He respected their need to represent their constituencies. He saw his job as educating the public for the need for major reforms and, in his last year, saw the possibility that he easily would defeat Senator Barry Goldwater, a very conservative Republican from Arizona, in 1964, carry in new Democrats, and thereby win congressional support for reform. He eventually began to understand that problems of chronic unemployment, inner-city poverty, racism, and crime were all related to persistent poverty. He had first discovered poverty when campaigning in West Virginia and never forgot it. After reading a summary of Michael Harrington's book about poverty *The Other America* (1962), he asked Walter Heller, the chairman of his Council of Economic Advisers, to develop a plan to attack poverty. The plan was first presented to President Johnson in January 1964, and his enthusiasm carried it to passage that year. The politics of the civil rights movement created a popular base for a poverty program at its enactment in 1964, a base that Kennedy had just begun to develop before his death.

Economic Policy

Kennedy was not specific in his campaign about how he would get the economy "moving again." The Joint Economic Committee of Congress had published studies before the election that called for tax cuts and temporary deficits, which would create demand and revive the economy, while making up deficits. The ideas were derived from the theories of the British economist John Maynard Keynes that dominated academic economics at the time. However, Kennedy knew very little about economics. The task force on economics during the campaign, chaired by Paul Samuelson, the eminent economist, had suggested a temporary $5 million tax cut in the first year, but Kennedy would not have it. The Republicans would eat him for lunch, he said, if he suggested a budget out of balance. His own Democratic leaders in Congress did not like the idea, so he promised a balanced budget to Congress in January 1961. He had asked Walter Heller, from the University of Minnesota, to chair the Council of Economic Advisers, without any clear idea of what Heller might do for him. Heller was a Keynesian economist who set about to educate the president. Kennedy's political and policy aides were, for the most part, lawyers who did not think much of economists. But Heller was able to show the usefulness of economists as his staff wrote critical assessments of spending proposals that came to the White House from the departments that ran against the purposes of the president. Heller began to write the president memoranda explaining what temporary tax cuts could do to stimulate the economy. Eisenhower had left an economy free of inflation but with much unused capacity in capital and labor, and Heller contended that tax cuts would not be inflationary and would lead toward greater capital investment, full employment, and increases in public purchasing power. Heller's ideas were not much liked in Congress or even the administration, but he was useful in unanticipated ways. For example, when Kennedy proposed to increase taxes for new military expenses during the period of Soviet threats to close off Berlin in 1961 and 1962, Heller invoked the aid of Paul Samuelson to meet with the president and other administration officials to argue successfully that a tax increase would only increase the likelihood of a recession.

Heller later remembered that as the economy did not grow and the stock market dropped, Kennedy began to fear the possibility of a recession as he ran for reelection. He began to listen, and Heller later reported, "One had this marvelous sense that he was getting it."[1] Kennedy also began to see that economic growth would help pay for his social programs. His last remark to Heller before he went to Dallas was that Heller would get his tax cut to pay for Kennedy's social programs.

The president gave a speech at Yale in June 1962 arguing that economic policy issues should no longer be ideological questions about the sanctity of balanced budgets, because economic policy alternatives were best assessed in technical and pragmatic terms; tax cuts could help the economy without harming it. Congressional and business opinion did not respond favorably to the talk. Even so, in August the president proposed a $13.5 billion tax cut, phased over time, to increase private investment without an increase in domestic spending, but said nothing about it in the fall campaign. He wanted Republicans to hold their fire. When the tax cut was introduced in January 1963, 72 percent of the public polled opposed it, if it would lead to an unbalanced budget. Kennedy helped himself to win by persuading Treasury Secretary Douglas Dillon, a Wall Street banker, to lead the fight in Congress. Dillon hoped to combine tax reform with the cuts and successfully persuaded a number of important businesspeople to go along. The chairmen of key committees were not easily persuaded, and the House passed the measure, but action was held over until 1964 when President Johnson was able to persuade the Senate. Kennedy, ever careful, had turned to Heller because he wanted to be a president who led despite his natural caution. This was creative eventful leadership. A failure to pick up the mantle here might have been corrected by Johnson, but Kennedy was able to sense new possibilities in linking tax cuts and domestic reform programs.

Civil Rights

The story here was the same as in other areas of domestic policy. Caution and temporizing gave way to leadership in response to political change and the ambitions of the president. Kennedy had little personal knowledge of the lives of black people when he became president and saw their demands as increasing his other problems. He also wanted the political support of the white South. He had won all but three southern states in 1960 and needed the support of Southerners in Congress for his social programs, although they, in turn, did little for him. At the same time, he appointed a number of black people to his government, created a commission on equal employment opportunity, and introduced a bill to limit literacy tests in voter registration. He hoped to balance the competing claims of Southern whites and blacks without antagonizing either because he had strong support from both populations. He was afraid that boldness on behalf of civil rights would split the Democratic Party and weaken his reelection possibilities. Civil rights problems were given to Attorney General Robert F. Kennedy, who tried to balance the contradictions. Civil rights law was weak at the time and the Justice Department worked primarily through the courts on issues of blatant discrimination, particularly in higher education.

"Freedom Riders" invaded the South to be beaten up in bus stations with axe handles. Federal marshals, sent by the Justice Department, could not protect the riders or prevent violence against black churches. The president stayed in the background while his brother negotiated with Southern bus companies, railroads, and airports to desegregate their facilities. The first dramatic event requiring strong federal action occurred in the fall of 1962 when James Meredith tried to enroll in the University of Mississippi. A federal court ordered that he be admitted, but Ross Barnett, the governor of the state, resisted until it came to the point where a white mob attacked federal marshals sent to protect Meredith as he registered. Kennedy was forced to send the army from Memphis to protect the marshals. He urged the cause of law and order, but it was apparent that he might not be able to straddle both sides for long.

The reality fully came home to Kennedy, and perhaps the nation, when Martin Luther King launched a drive against segregation in Birmingham, Alabama, one of the most segregated cities in the nation. Civil rights demonstrators were met in the streets by phalanxes of police with fire hoses and attack dogs. King sent children into the battle and they were attacked. The country saw it all on television, and many people were sickened. Just as a brokered truce between Birmingham businessmen and civil rights leaders was made, black mobs rushed into the streets in response to bombs set off at the homes of civil rights leaders. Kennedy was under heavy pressure from Martin Luther King to act and began to fear the possibility of black revolution. He decided that he had to do something and gave a nationally televised speech in June 1963 in which he spoke of justice for African Americans as a moral requirement and called for a civil rights law to protect their rights.

Kennedy knew the political costs of such action. Republicans were growing stronger in the South. White backlash to school desegregation was strong in his native Boston. George Wallace, the Democratic governor of Alabama, was threatening to enter northern presidential primaries. Kennedy declined in the polls, primarily among Southern whites. Approval of his presidency had been high, up to 70 percent or more, sometimes falling temporarily. But it fell to 50 percent in May 1963. Support went up after his speech but fell again in the fall. Congress did not act until Lyndon Johnson pushed a civil rights bill through in 1964. But Kennedy acted anyway. As a Democratic president he had to be true to the ideals of his party.

Kennedy's domestic presidency was a preparation for what came afterward with Lyndon Johnson. Kennedy was a blend of detachment and action in his political personality. He held back, from prudence, if the time did not seem right. This was the case with most domestic policy. His temperament matched the objective political situation. But when opportunities and contingencies opened, he could seize the day because the whole drift of Democratic politics required action.

FOREIGN AFFAIRS

The new president inherited and accepted the standing American policies of "containment" of the expansive drives of the Soviet Union beyond its own immediate sphere. Kennedy followed earlier Democratic critics in insisting that all U.S. force should not be put in the nuclear basket, especially after Premier Nikita Khrushchev of the Soviet Union called for "wars of national liberation." Kennedy and his advisers set about developing a policy of "flexible response," by which they meant alternative ways to deal with various forms of aggression. This was a reaction against Eisenhower's disavowal of the United States fighting limited wars. Khrushchev's speech was taken very seriously in Washington and the actions of nationalist revolutionaries in the undeclared quiet war between communist North Vietnam and the somewhat democratic South Vietnam, an American ally, were seen as a pertinent example of a war of national liberation. In fact, Khrushchev made the speech to impress the Chinese that the Soviet Union was just as revolutionary as China. But the speech had consequences far beyond its intentions. Kennedy and his advisers took it very seriously and, in due course, came to see the defense of South Vietnam as a staging ground for defense against wars of national liberation.

Kennedy had asserted the existence of the "missile gap," but when his own secretary of defense let it slip to the press that none existed, the president disowned him. Kennedy's fear that the United States would fall behind in a nuclear arms race actually caused his administration to begin a 150 percent increase in nuclear weapons—a race that, of course, the Soviets joined. As a part of his policy of flexible response, Kennedy also called for the development of "special forces" in the army who would be able to fight in guerrilla wars, despite the opposition of the army, which preferred conventional warfare of massed troops of infantry and artillery. Kennedy's foresight was ignored by the army in Vietnam to its own detriment.

The historian John Lewis Gaddis points out a contradiction within Kennedy's foreign policy. Policymakers believed, on the one hand, that communism was a monolithic force and that all communist nations would act alike. This denied growing evidence of the Soviet-Chinese rift. It was assumed that if the government of North Vietnam was communist, which it was, then it would not only seek to conquer South Vietnam but all of Southeast Asia, with communist China lurking in the background. On the other hand, the United States wished to create a world of diverse nations free from communist threat, but this would allow the possibility of independent communist nations. Kennedy never reconciled the contradiction.[2] Just as important, according to Gaddis, the United States could not afford the appearance of weakness or defeat anywhere in the world because "appearances contribute to reality." The strategy of containment thus had to be worldwide.

Kennedy and Khrushchev

Nikita Khrushchev had climbed over the backs of his rivals to the top of the greasy pole of the Soviet government by 1961. The hallmark of his career had been his capacity for unpredictable dramatic action, as when he denounced the crimes of Stalin in a speech to communist leaders in 1956. As Kennedy entered office, Khrushchev was hopeful of a rapprochement with the United States so that he could reduce military expenditures in favor of investments in agriculture and industry. The Soviet economy, contrary to his public claims, was foundering. His biographer, William Taubman, describes how Khrushchev felt the Chinese at his back and pressure from his colleagues to score victories abroad and success at home and says that in such tight situations he was "defenseless against his own weaknesses."[3] Khrushchev decided that Kennedy was a weak leader because he had not used U.S. forces to win when Cuban exile forces foundered on the beaches of Cuba during the Bay of Pigs incident in early 1961. He began to threaten publicly that he would sign a peace treaty with the East German government that would nullify the rights of the American, British, and French occupation forces in West Berlin in the middle of communist East Germany. East Germans were fleeing to the West through Berlin by the thousands, and the government of East Germany was pressing Khrushchev for action.

Kennedy accepted Khrushchev's invitation to meet in Vienna in June 1961, in hopes that trouble spots around the world, such as Laos and Berlin, might be resolved through reasoned diplomacy. He was warned either not to go or to be very careful. Senator Mike Mansfield feared that the meeting would be only "a slugfest with words." Kennedy hoped that he could reason with Khrushchev. In fact, the meetings were very difficult for Kennedy. He had little experience with bellicose Russians. Khrushchev took the initiative to berate the president about U.S. policies, and as Kennedy tried to warn against miscalculations by either side, Khrushchev pummeled him with outrage. For example, when Kennedy asked him to hold back from acting on Berlin, the Russian was furious, berating Kennedy for his actions toward Cuba. He could not believe that Kennedy would refrain from using American force in Cuba and therefore felt free to threaten him on Berlin. Khrushchev threatened to sign a peace treaty with East Germany in six months and told Kennedy that if he wanted war he could have it. Kennedy had assumed that his charm would work on Khrushchev and it did not. He later told *New York Times* reporter James Reston that "he beat the hell out of me." He resolved that he would have to prove his toughness to Khrushchev.

Kennedy saw Berlin as an opportunity to implement the policy of "flexible response." He announced to the nation in July that U.S. military forces in Berlin would be strengthened, called reserve units to active duty, and asked Congress for more money for the military. Eighty-five percent of those polled in a national opinion survey were ready to risk war over Berlin. Khrushchev was bluffing because he did not intend to fight in Berlin, but he did not believe that Kennedy would fight either. His ultimate practical solution was to build a wall to keep East Germans in and take some of the pressure off himself. But he still pressed the Berlin issue. Kennedy had been totally unprepared for dealing with aggressive Russians. He was naïve in thinking that reason, divorced from power politics, might hold sway. He had to learn the hard way. But he did face up to Khrushchev on Berlin and perhaps backed him down.

Two Cuban Cases

Kennedy had some difficulty finding his feet as a manager of foreign policymaking; indeed, it is not clear that he ever found it. Two cases are usually cited as his learning experience. The decision making about the Cuban exile invasion at the Bay of Pigs in eastern Cuba is rightly seen as a disaster, because it was managed poorly. But Kennedy learned from his mistakes and applied the lessons to his management of the Cuban Missile crisis.

The Bay of Pigs. The new president reappointed Allen Dulles as director of the Central Intelligence Agency (CIA). Dulles provided political cover as a Republican. Dulles soon after presented Kennedy with a plan for the invasion of communist Cuba by Cuban exiles, who were being trained in secret Central American camps by the CIA. Eisenhower had approved the training, but not an invasion plan. Kennedy had campaigned against Eisenhower's seeming failure to do anything to combat the dictator Fidel Castro and his communist regime. He was therefore in a political trap when Dulles approached him. He had promised to do something. The CIA planners were the kind of people Kennedy liked—smart, quick, bent on action. But they misled him with several false assumptions that could not easily be tested because of the secrecy of the operation. The CIA assumed that once the exiles had established a beachhead, a popular uprising would overthrow Castro. Castro's army and air force were said to be weak. The U.S. role would be kept secret, even though U.S. ships would carry the exiles to the beaches. All of these assumptions were false. Neither the State Department nor the CIA's intelligence analysts knew of the plan. Kennedy asked to have the invasion site moved to be less conspicuous, and there was a swamp between the new landing site and the mountain retreat route. No one told the president. He insisted that there would be no overt U.S. role, but the CIA failed to tell the exiles that—to their later dismay.

Discussions within the top foreign policy team were closely held because of secrecy and had an ad hoc quality with few hard questions posed. Kennedy felt trapped by the existence of the Cuban exile army. They could not just be turned loose in the United States with all the adverse publicity that would follow. He wanted the plan to succeed and remove Castro from his list of problems but without anyone knowing of an American role. He did not know much about the CIA and did not understand that its intelligence people, who were excluded from operations, might have helped him. The Joint Chiefs of Staff approved the plan but failed to tell the president that the United States would have to join the military action for it to succeed. The secretary of state, Dean Rusk, opposed the plan but feared to oppose the president, whom he did not know well. The secretary of defense, Robert McNamara, was busy elsewhere. Robert Kennedy warned dissenters off.

The action was a disaster. Castro knew of the plan, met the invasion on the beaches, and captured most of the exiles. Kennedy publicly took responsibility. McGeorge Bundy, the assistant to the president for national security, wrote a trenchant critique of the decision process for the president. But Kennedy's first response was to blame the CIA, the Joint Chiefs, and bureaucracy in general. He was the problem, and the president's responsibility is to make bureaucracy work for him. Kennedy's failure had been to close off discussion of the plan prematurely.

The Missile Crisis. A CIA study had informed the president of Soviet nuclear inferiority and he decided to disclose that information publicly, thinking that it would chasten Khrushchev over Berlin. It had just the opposite effect. Khrushchev was deeply and publicly embarrassed. His promises of a great success for the wheat crop also proved to be empty. He was desperate for a dramatic action and hit on the idea of placing long-range missiles in Cuba, not only to protect Castro, which he thought important, but also to reduce the imbalance of nuclear power with the United States. He would announce the existence of the missiles once they were installed, perhaps at a meeting of the United Nations in November 1962. William Taubman, Khrushchev's biographer, writes that Khrushchev had no plan should the United States discover the missiles and challenge him. He was an adventurer and gambler who actually believed that U.S.-Soviet relations would be improved by his actions. As U.S. surveillance from the air detected the shipment of missiles to Cuba during the summer of 1962, Khrushchev lied to Kennedy, claiming that they were only defensive and of very limited range. Kennedy should have made very clear to Khrushchev much earlier that he would not tolerate offensive weapons in Cuba, but he did not. This was being eventful to a fault, just following along. The president's advisers did not think that the Russians would ever send offensive weapons out of their country. As the congressional election campaign heated up during the fall, Republicans charged that the missiles going to

Cuba were offensive and the CIA began to suggest that this was more than likely. Kennedy warned Khrushchev not to put offensive missiles in Cuba, but it was too late. Their discovery from the air in early October produced a crisis of thirteen days.

The president convened a small group of top officials, who met secretly to advise him on what to do. It was an Executive Committee of the National Security Council, thereafter called the Excom. Its members consisted of cabinet officers, expert advisers (including the military), and experienced outsiders like former secretaries of state and defense. He had learned from the Bay of Pigs about shortcomings in a decision process. Therefore he pressed the group to develop and assess all possible alternative actions. The possibility of a direct private challenge to Khrushchev or an appeal to the United Nations, without a resort to a military response, were ruled out for fear that the ensuing delay would permit the Russians to fully install the missiles. Early enthusiasm for an air strike to destroy the missiles lost out when it was not clear whether they could all be found. The military wanted an invasion after an air strike. The idea of a naval blockade to keep Soviet ships away from Cuba eventually surfaced and Kennedy accepted it with the possibility of air strikes and invasion still on the table. This model of "flexible response" was later invoked in the Vietnam war. Kennedy wanted to leave Khrushchev a way out. His speech to the nation warned that any Cuban missile attack on any site in the Americas would be met by a U.S. nuclear attack on the Soviet Union. He was risking nuclear war to prevent it. The Soviet ships did turn back. Secret negotiations through the Soviet embassy in Washington led the president to say, but not promise, that he would never invade Cuba and to suggest privately that in due course obsolete NATO missiles in Turkey would be withdrawn. The crisis ended, and the missiles were withdrawn. Kennedy rode high in the public opinion polls. But the top military and foreign policy hawks felt that he had missed an opportunity to eliminate Castro and humiliate the Soviets.

Neither Khrushchev nor Kennedy had understood the other. The two elite cultures were too disparate. James G. Blight, a scholar of the missile crisis, argues that the fear of nuclear war during the crisis had a powerful impact on Kennedy and his secretary of defense, Robert McNamara, and, one presumes, on Khrushchev. Kennedy had always been worried that war might come from miscalculations like the one Khrushchev had made and had tried to warn him at Vienna, only to be rebuffed. The missile crisis was the prelude to the coup that removed Khrushchev from office in 1964.

Two Crises Reexamined

The social psychologist Irving Janis compared the Bay of Pigs and the Cuban Missile Crisis according to the concept of "group think." Put simply "group think" means that an implicit consensus so binds a group of decision makers to unspoken assumptions that they fail to examine possible flaws in their assumptions, with policy mishaps as a result. Such closed-mindedness is more likely when the decision makers are placed under great external pressure to act. He sees this process in decision making before the Bay of Pigs. The president could have pushed with hard questions far more than he did. His new lieutenants were feeling their way in office, were not really brought into full discussions, and wished to follow their new leader. This is all true, as the postmortem critiques suggest, but there is one problem. There was no group, because the president did not create one. Without a group, there cannot be "group think." Kennedy factored out dissent all by himself. One could attribute this to his executive style, but Kennedy did not want dissent. He wanted to act, with as much secrecy as possible, to get Castro off the map of American politics.

Janis saw the missile crisis as an exemplary case of how to avoid "group think." When he convened the Excom, Kennedy ruled out a diplomatic solution like going to the United Nations or sending a secret message to Khrushchev. He said that the missiles had to come out in short order, but did not tell the Excom what to do, asking them instead to develop alternatives that might be debated. Janis saw a discussion process of very high quality in which options were put forth, discussed, knocked down, and rediscussed. New information was sought at every step, and the execution of the blockade was carefully planned in advance.

There was no formal agenda, and everyone was encouraged to talk freely. Kennedy stayed away while choices were being developed so as not to inhibit open discussion, especially as deputies were less inclined to challenge their superiors if he were present. There was a general feeling of equality in the group. Kennedy himself established this by giving no one preferred treatment. The way in which he stood up to the members of the Joint Chiefs of Staff, who wanted to bomb and invade, emboldened others. Dangers were explored for each of the alternatives posed, and there was no false sense of security. People often changed positions during the discussions and felt free to do so. Soviet motives in placing the missiles in Cuba were a mystery, and there was much speculation but no stereotyping of Khrushchev and his colleagues. The president relied heavily on Llewellyn Thompson, a Soviet expert and recent ambassador to the Soviet Union, who knew

Khrushchev well. Kennedy, in particular, wanted to leave Khrushchev a way out, believing that in the long run the Soviet leader and his colleagues would be reasonable. Fortunately, Khrushchev believed the same thing to be true of Kennedy and, in the course of the crisis, the two men each came to have empathy toward each other.

Ernest May and Philip Zelikow, who edited an excellent transcript of the meetings, believe that if someone else had been president there might have been a different outcome. There might have been an air strike, for example, before other choices had been fully examined. Kennedy had put that idea on hold when McGeorge Bundy, his national security assistant, suggested that he do so. The meetings, as seen in the transcripts, were inherently disorderly. There was no time for papers setting out thoroughly researched options. All alternatives had to be discussed on the fly in the meetings, but it was possible to return over and over to each one until a final judgment was made. Reasoning was not guided by historical analogy because the situation was unprecedented. Discussion dealt with the problem at hand.

James Blight points out that in the Excom the hawks were willing to take risks because they thought the prospects of success were high. The doves wanted action that minimized risks and still achieved minimal goals. The hawks weighed probabilities, and the doves considered possibilities. Kennedy's closest advisers were doves. Hawks felt responsible to shape events in a major way. Doves wished to stabilize the situation. The doves were prudent and better at coping with this uncertainty than the hawks. Kennedy was a dove in his prudence.[4]

Was Kennedy's management of the missile crisis eventful or event making? The great importance of the event does not give the answer. Had he chosen air strikes and an invasion of the island to remove the Castro government, that might have been recognized as event making. But he did not do that, preferring to be cautious and feel his way to an accommodation. This was eventful leadership at its best. He recognized the danger of war and prevented it. A less skillful eventful leader might have managed the process less well and not overcome the stalemate. Hook sees the event-making leader as relying on his superior skill, will, and intelligence. Kennedy did this here, but along eventful lines. Eventful leadership is not always skillful or effective. Success is not guaranteed from either kind of leadership.

Kennedy failed at the Bay of Pigs and succeeded in the missile crisis. His virtues in the latter case were intelligence, detachment, and judgment. He did not so much manage the process as guide it. He asked hard questions and gradually felt his way to a decision. But this was different from knowing how to manage the decision-making process in the government as regularly constituted, as we see from the case that follows.

Vietnam

Kennedy could never find out what was happening in South Vietnam. He felt obligated to defend the republic of South Vietnam but could never find the means to implement policy intelligently. His haphazard style of executive decision making may have contributed to his confusion through the failure to seek out alternatives in a systematic way. Eisenhower had made the United States the guarantor of the republic of South Vietnam after the Geneva conference of 1954 divided the country into two, with North Vietnam governed by communist nationalists. Initially, the government of South Vietnam faced only the Viet Cong, domestic guerrillas who were only communist in part and only loosely linked to the North. President Ngo Dinh Diem of South Vietnam, who had been placed there by Eisenhower, was an autocratic ruler who relied on his brothers in high places to help him keep order in a very diverse country, which was in no sense democratic. Elites were Catholic, most people were Buddhist, and other religious sects had strong support. Diem was so insecure politically that he used his army to protect his position as much as to fight the Viet Cong.

The history of the Korean War, in which the United States fought communist aggression to a standstill, had a powerful implicit influence on American policymakers in the Eisenhower, Kennedy, and Johnson administrations. The Chinese entered the war on the North Korean side and loomed over Asia after the truce. The doctrine of containment of communist aggression was thus applied to the Far East. It took the popular form of an image of the "domino theory," in which if one country in Southeast Asia fell to communism the rest would fall, through aggression, in due course. The defense of South Vietnam was the linchpin. Khrushchev's commitment to "wars of national liberation" was focused on Vietnam, and after Vienna, Kennedy increased the small number of U.S. military advisers in South Vietnam as one place in which he could counter Khrushchev. He publicly subscribed to the domino theory.

His approach to Vietnam embodied a contradiction. South Vietnam could not be allowed to go communist. Yet it was not clear that the South Vietnamese government could defend itself. American policymakers failed to face that contradiction until the point that the United States began to do most of the fighting in 1965. Kennedy began the strategy of incremental escalation by increasing the number of U.S. military advisers to the government of South Vietnam, but he could not find out what was happening in such a faraway country. An initial mission in November 1961 reported that President Diem did not want American troops fighting his war unless the North Vietnamese were to invade. He did agree to take military advisers, however, and Kennedy sent about 2,000. This continued to the point that there were 16,000 advisers in Vietnam when Kennedy died. American policymakers did not fully understand the nature of the Diem regime and kept trying to tie military help to promises of reform of a corrupt administration. Diem always promised and never honored the promises. Kennedy privately told Arthur Krock, a columnist for the *New York Times* and a family friend, that he doubted the domino theory, did not think Americans could fight in Asia, and that he saw the split in the country as a civil war. He also told aides that he could not afford the domestic consequences of a defeat in South Vietnam. He rejected the warning that Vietnam could become a bottomless pit for the United States by insisting that he would never let that happen. The government of North Vietnam might have been willing to negotiate an agreement in which South Vietnam was governed by a coalition government of the Viet Cong and others for ten years. Kennedy and his advisers could not permit that because they believed in containing communism, especially in supposed wars of national liberation. But the president could never get a consensus among his advisers about what to do, particularly as American military advisers were drawn more and more into directing the combat operations of the South Vietnamese army, which was a weak fighting force. One must ask why the president did not undertake the kind of hard policy analysis with key advisers that he had used with the Excom in the Cuban Missile Crisis. Kennedy did not do this well except in crisis situations, and Vietnam was a slow crisis. For the most part, the public was in the dark about what was going on, and Kennedy complained to publishers when their reporters wrote stories of military failure. In early 1963 he told Senator Mike Mansfield that if he withdrew before the 1964 election, he would probably lose. He could only pull out later, he said.

Politics seemed out of control in South Vietnam as Diem attacked and destroyed Buddhist temples when their leaders challenged him. Buddhist monks burned themselves alive for Americans to see on television. The Viet Cong strength in the countryside grew rapidly. Kennedy gave two television interviews in September 1963 in which he said that he believed in the domino theory, but that the South Vietnamese would have to win their own fight. The catalyst for full American commitment came with the assassination of President Diem in a military coup on November 1, 1963. The coup was carried out with the full complicity of the Kennedy administration, even though the U.S. military in Vietnam opposed the American ambassador, Henry Cabot Lodge, who favored it. The president had been persuaded of the necessity of recognizing the leaders after a successful coup attempt, but he never imagined that Diem would be murdered. The result of U.S. support for the coup was an even greater commitment to South Vietnam. Robert McNamara wrote much later that neither before nor after the coup did the U.S. government explicitly confront the basic question of whether a stand in Vietnam was in the American national interest. He remembered that Kennedy "failed to pull a divided U.S. government together."[5] Before he went to Dallas to meet his death, Kennedy told Michael Forrestal, a White House assistant, to organize a full study of every possible option for the United States in Vietnam, including how to get out. His close friend Charles Bohlen remembered that Kennedy was "totally out to sea about what to do in Vietnam."[6]

One cannot know what Kennedy would have done. Waiting until after the 1964 election might have provided an opportunity to withdraw, but the situation was much worse politically and militarily in Vietnam at that later date than in late 1963. Kennedy was certainly skeptical about military promises and commitments. The trick was to find a way to withdraw with minimal domestic political damage and not to appear to be "soft on communism." Perhaps Kennedy would have been trapped by U.S. commitments and domestic politics. Or perhaps he would have found a way to act creatively. Charles Bohlen, an experienced diplomat and Soviet expert, wrote of Kennedy after his death: "There was an unknown quality about Kennedy, despite his realism, that gave you the infinite hope that somehow or other he was going to change the course of history."[7]

CONCLUSION

How does Kennedy measure up in terms of our questions about presidential leadership?

Context and Contingencies

The grain of history was favorable to domestic policy reform as Kennedy entered the White House. Much of the Democratic policy agenda had been developed by congressional policy entrepreneurs, assisted by policy advocates and scholars, during the late Eisenhower years. This gave Kennedy a program to campaign on in 1960 even though he was a cautious reformer.

He hoped for a grand reelection victory that would permit the enactment of his social programs, an unusual event for second-term presidencies, but the nation was ripe for reform. He was a laggard on civil rights until politics pushed him to act. He was a classic eventful leader.

Talents and Skills

Kennedy's strength and weakness was his detachment. He could not be stampeded into rash action, but he held back out of political caution.

And yet, he also wanted to be a decisive leader and did rise to the occasion in the missile crisis and on civil rights. There might have been more of this in a second term. His hold on the public was a genuine achievement. He could articulate ideals that inspired a generation and for which he is still remembered. He lacked a sufficient majority in Congress to pass his reform program. He was a president of preparation who paved the way for his successor to enact large reforms.

He was not knowledgeable about bureaucracy and appears to have learned little, nor did he ever develop effective ways of managing the executive processes that he needed to control to do his job. The Excom in the Cuban Missile Crisis was a small ad hoc group that he led well. But he often seemed lost in working with larger organizations, as seen in his frustrations about Vietnam.

Kennedy always sought to find the balance between purpose and prudence, and did perhaps better than any president in this study. Vietnam would have been the acid test, but he was not ready to face it when he died.

Did He Make a Difference?

Kennedy was eventful rather than event making. But he contributed to support for domestic reform and for sanity and prudence in the cold war. His talents and historical possibilities reinforced each other. He reached for new possibilities in civil rights and the test ban treaty and would have been an effective reforming president in a second term. However, his following the drift in Vietnam may have undermined those very possibilities without the exercise of courage that would go beyond prudence.

Effectiveness

Kennedy was, without doubt, an effective president. He could read the political lay of the land perceptively, and even though he was cautious by temperament and belief, he wanted his presidency to succeed as a place of leadership and knew when it was necessary to go beyond caution with leaps of faith. In fact, his ability to inspire others permitted such leaps. It is difficult to assign his responsibility for the eventual failure in Vietnam. He felt trapped by the dilemma but contributed to it by agreeing to the overthrow of Diem, which trapped him even further. One cannot say whether he would have found a way out of the trap. He had the ability to do so, and perhaps the political latitude, but he did not live for him and us to find out.

BIBLIOGRAPHICAL ESSAY

James L. Sundquist in *Politics and Policy, the Eisenhower, Kennedy and Johnson Years* (1968) describes how policy entrepreneurs among the Democrats in Congress, assisted by policy experts, developed the intellectual capital that made up the New Frontier ideas for programs. He also reports how public opinion gradually moved in support of such ideas before and after Kennedy was elected, but makes clear that the Congress as a whole was not ready to act. The two most recent Kennedy biographers, Richard Reeves, *President Kennedy, a Profile of Power* (1993), and Robert Dallek, *An Unfinished Life: John F. Kennedy 1917–1963* (2003), give us full portraits of the private man and the politician. Dallek is inclined to idealize Kennedy, and Reeves presents a less favorable picture of the man. Together they provide a good balance. Michael Beschloss has written a very rich account of the Kennedy-Khrushchev relationship from beginning to end in *The Crisis Years: Kennedy and Khrushchev, 1960–1963* (1991). And John Lewis Gaddis, the preeminent cold war historian, places historical events within a superb analysis of the theory of containment and the policy of "flexible response" in *Strategies of Containment* (1982). Peter Wyden has written the best account of the Bay of Pigs events, *Bay of Pigs: The Untold Story* (1979). James Blight and Peter Kornbluh have edited a rich discussion with participants of the invasion story, *Politics of Illusion* (1997). Richard Neustadt and Ernest May help explain how Kennedy's lack of understanding of the CIA handicapped him in *Thinking in Time: The Uses of History for Decision Makers* (1988). Tim Coates's edited book of primary documents on the Bay of Pigs and the Cuban Missile Crisis brings the events to life. See *The Cuban Missile Crisis, Selected Documents from the Administration of John F. Kennedy, January 1961–November 1962* (2001). Ernest May and Philip Zelikow edited the transcripts of the meetings of the Excom during the missile crisis and their analysis is astute. See *The Kennedy Tapes: Inside the White House during the Cuban Missile Crisis* (2002). Sheldon M. Stern has written a very fine analysis of the transcripts of the missile crisis, in which he portrays the interplay of strong views among Kennedy's advisers and the president's continual search for a reasonable solution despite strong arguments for more military action. See *Averting the Final Failure: John F. Kennedy and the Secret Cuban Missile Crisis Meetings* (2003). James Blight is very persuasive that Kennedy and McNamara were strongly and rationally motivated by fear that a miscalculation on either side could lead to nuclear war, although both men had a number of fallback positions short of such a war and would have used them. See *The Shattered Crystal Ball: Fear and Learning in the Cuban Missile Crisis* (1990). William Taubman's biography of Nikita Khrushchev, *Khrushchev: The Man and His Era* (2003), explains how Khrushchev would act recklessly without forethought but also makes clear how Khrushchev also wanted a détente of sorts with the United States. Irving Janis derived the concept of "group think" from the small group theory of social psychologists. It has merit, but one problem inherent in such experiments is that factors outside the group, which actors within the group must take into account, are ignored in the theory. See *Victims of Group Think* (1972). Alexander George refined the approach in his ideas of "multiple advocacy" and the conditions for optimal decision making in *Presidential Decision Making in Foreign Policy: The Effective Use of Information and Advice* (1980).

Allen Matusow's *The Unraveling of America, A History of Liberalism in the 1960s* (1984) gives a skeptical account of the merits of the early New Frontier legislative achievements. James Sundquist's *Politics and Policy: The Eisenhower, Kennedy, and Johnson Years* (1968), gives a full account of the relations of Kennedy and Congress against a national political background. John Kingdon's theories of the conditions for effective policy entrepreneurship apply to the Kennedy and Johnson years. See *Agendas, Alternatives, and Public Policies* (2d ed. 1995). Walter Heller described working with Kennedy in detail in Erwin Hargrove and Samuel Morley's edited book of interviews with past chairmen of the Council of Economic Advisers, *The President and Council of Economic Advisers* (1984). Herbert Stein supplies a useful moderately conservative corrective. There are many accounts of Kennedy and civil rights. Carl Brauer has written a good history of Kennedy and civil rights in *JFK and the Second Reconstruction* (1977). A very useful publication is Jonathan Rosenberg and Zachary Karabell, eds., *Kennedy, Johnson and the Quest for Justice: The Civil Rights Tapes* (2003).

The road to Vietnam has been richly described by George McT. Kahin in *Intervention: How America Became Involved in Vietnam* (1986). Leslie Gelb, with Richard Betts, links Vietnam policymaking to conditions of politics in *The Irony of Vietnam: The System Worked* (1979). David Kaiser's more recent book on the war and its prelude draws on primary sources for a rich account, *American Tragedy: Kennedy, Johnson, and the Origins of the Vietnam War* (2000).

The Gallup polls show Kennedy to have been a popular president for most of his time in office. He knew how to invoke a "rally round the flag" response from the public during foreign policy crises. The public supported his domestic policy ideas except for civil rights until his last year when Northern and Southern opinion split and reduced his support on that issue.

CHAPTER TWO

Lyndon B. Johnson

A Force of Nature

Lyndon Johnson became president with dignity in the face of tragedy. His composure and assurance to the American people that he was in charge and knew how to be president was a gift to the nation in a time of popular uncertainty after the violent death of a young president. This was Johnson at his best and as he wished to be. He was determined to be a leader of a great national consensus. Kennedy, in his last year, was nurturing a climate for reform in winning business and congressional support for his tax cut, advocating civil rights legislation, and hoping to change a few votes in the Senate for Medicare after the House had passed the bill. The House had also passed the civil rights bill. Carl Albert, the Democratic majority leader in the House, told an interviewer for the Johnson Library in 1969, in response to a question about whether the Kennedy legislative program was stalled in Congress in November 1963: "I didn't have that feeling. Actually, we were just getting ready to move in a big way."[1]

Opinion polls showed support for Medicare, civil rights legislation (in the North), and aid to education. Congressional constituency polls revealed favorable responses to reform ideas. Republican constituencies gave majority support for civil rights, aid to education, and even Medicare, until Republican congressional leaders opposed the bill in 1963. One cannot know what

Kennedy would have been able to achieve in 1964 but certainly President Johnson saw the rising tide and was determined to exploit it for all it was worth. Johnson is often given credit for securing passage of the tax cut, the civil rights bill, and the war on poverty in 1964 in the same Congress that had opposed Kennedy. We will see his undeniable skill in action. But the tide was moving in a direction that Kennedy would also have exploited. However, Johnson did not stop there. He was a force of nature in his determination, sometimes expressed to others, that he wanted to be the greatest president of all time. His standard of greatness was to pass as much reform legislation as possible. He eased into the presidency as an eventful leader, but deliberately used his ability and personality to be an event-making leader.

THE SENATOR

Johnson entered the Senate in 1949 and became the minority leader in 1951 with the support of Senator Richard Russell, the unspoken dean of the Southern delegation. When the Democrats won control of Congress in 1954, he became the new majority leader and led that majority until he became vice president in January 1961. The task of any Democratic leader was to try to create unity among Northern liberals and Southern conservatives on domestic issues. Men close to Johnson reported that he sought more than practical unity; he wanted to heal the historic tensions between North and South as much as possible. The structure and the culture of the Senate fitted his consensus aspirations perfectly and he honed his style of leadership accordingly. The traditions of unlimited debate and maximum latitude for individual senators to amend legislation, block appointments, and in general give personal courtesies to other senators had made the Senate a kind of "club" in which new senators deferred to their elders, and seniority in committees favored the longtime Southern members and chairmen. Johnson developed a system of creating coalitions by catering to the needs of each senator, with implied and real sanctions if cooperation was resisted. His first task was always to know every individual Democratic senator as well as possible; not only his desires, but also his or her strengths and weaknesses. He was an astute psychologist who could work with a person once he could "calibrate" him or her. This approach was often seen when he was president in his uncertainty about advisers whom he could not "calibrate." Trust and confidence from Johnson came with a positive calibration. He did not believe in creating a process of open discussion in the Senate but lined up the votes according to his soundings. This habit carried over into his presidency, especially in domestic policy. Foreign policymaking required group discussion, but Johnson was not particularly good at managing debate.

Aside from his persuasive and tactical abilities, the two most important things to know about Lyndon Johnson were his unquenchable idealism to do good and the personal insecurity that drove him to achieve. The night that Kennedy was killed, according to House majority leader Carl Albert, Johnson told Texas congressman Homer Thornberry, a very close friend, that he was going to forget his political career and to call the shots as he saw them as president.[2] Johnson had been an enthusiastic New Dealer in the Roosevelt years, but as Texas became richer after World War II, his idealism took a back seat to his political need to serve the interests of the oil and gas barons who ran the politics of the state. Northern liberals never fully trusted him, even as he became president. But when the black civil rights leaders asked the president in a meeting in the Oval Office why he was taking the lead on the civil rights bill, Johnson answered, quoting Martin Luther King, "free at last, free at last." He was now president of all the people. Numerous friends reported that he wanted to be the greatest president ever, greater than Roosevelt, and by this he meant legislative accomplishment. White House economists used to laugh when they saw Wilbur Cohen, the secretary of health, education, and welfare, coming into the White House. He was going to persuade the president to add something to a task force recommendation that had not been recommended. Johnson would always give in. When asked about this story years later, Cohen smiled and said, "Well, they were right."[3] The point is that Johnson had no prejudices and wanted to help everyone get a leg up on life. His language was terrible; he would talk about helping "nigras." But he wanted to help them. Ambition to be the greatest president by doing the greatest things was all one piece.

Johnson believed that he could pass major legislation every year and drove Congress until his last day. His domestic policy aide Joseph Califano wondered, in his oral history interview at the Johnson library, whether the president had not at times lost sight "that laws were not ends in themselves," and added that Johnson couldn't accept that he "couldn't do it all."[4] Paul Conkin, historian and Johnson biographer, writes that Johnson was "not open to tragic experience," so that by 1968, as he left the presidency, he was a "stumbling giant."[5]

Johnson's source of self-esteem was politics. He saw losing elections as worse than death and got sick before every election he ran in Texas; the strain and fear of losing was too much. On August 25, 1964, just before his nomination by the Democratic convention, Johnson read George Reedy, his press secretary, a statement that he was going to make withdrawing from the presidential race. This was during a most successful legislative year. Johnson read from his statement: "Our country faces grave dangers. These dangers must be faced and met by a unified people under a leader they do not doubt … I am not that voice or that leader." He went on to say that the South, the North, and the Negroes would not listen to him. Negroes would never follow a white Southerner. He cited the criticism of the *New York Times* and the *New York Herald Tribune,* which were critical of the Democratic platform. Reedy responded to him that it was "too late." It would just be giving the country to Barry Goldwater, the Republican presidential candidate. Johnson said that he did not care, and added: "I have a desire to unite people, and the South is against me, and the North is against me, and the Negroes are against me. And the press doesn't really have an affection for me." He cited a British journalist who had written that he was a "textbook caricature of a fast-dealing politician." Johnson told aides not long after this conversation that his critics thought that he wanted great power, but "what I want is great solace and a little love. That's all I want: Love, a little love."[6]

Johnson changed his mind, but his uncertainties about himself as president were extraordinary. On November 4, 1964, after his great victory over Senator Barry Goldwater, Republican from Arizona, Johnson called Edwin Weisl Sr., a New York attorney and longtime friend and adviser, to complain about press comments that people had voted for him as the lesser of two evils, describing him as a country "buffoon" who was "full of corn." Lady Bird and their two daughters visited so many states in which they received tremendous ovations. "I had the greatest affection that had ever been demonstrated before." He blamed Bobby Kennedy and his group for saying that "nobody loves Johnson." He asked Weisl, who was well connected with media leaders in New York City, to get the story of Johnson's successes out to the public. He complained that his critics denied that he had won a mandate in the election, and said that he would not be able to pass legislation against Republicans and Southern Democrats in Congress. Even FDR, in 1936, never won by as much in New York as he had. Weisl tried to reassure the president, but Johnson asked for an advertising and media campaign to celebrate him and his achievements. "How the hell do we create this image?" The conversation trailed off into more distrust of Robert Kennedy and more self-pity.[7] And yet Johnson was to have the most creative legislative year in 1965 of any president since Roosevelt.

In March 1965, when her husband was riding high as president with congressional success and popular support, Mrs. Johnson wrote in her diary that Johnson was in a "fog of depression," and added, "If you're enjoying what you do, you don't get tired no matter how hard you work. And if it's frustrating and full of uncertainties, you use up energies struggling against what you have to do…. But Lyndon feels chained right here and it's having a corrosive effect on his personality."[8] We are familiar with the kind of person who, no matter how much he or she achieves, still wants more success, because the need is insatiable and unconscious. There was emptiness in Johnson that only political success could fill, and to stave off the emptiness he had to keep striving, and with volcanic energy. By the same token, he could not abide political enemies or unhappy constituents.

Some of Johnson's insecurity was social. He had attended a state teacher's college in Texas, and saw himself as a provincial in the cosmopolitan world of his advisers. Yet he used those advisers and respected them. He could never understand why the nation seemed to love the Kennedys and not him. One associate once told him, when the question was posed, that he was "not lovable." But, as Paul Conkin sees it, Johnson was working "under the shadow of a dead god" (172). It is important to ask how Johnson's insecurities shaped his actions as president. His talents and idealistic ambitions were strongly apparent in his work. Personal insecurity fed the talent and ambition, but usually constructively. The ambition to do everything was perhaps fed by insecurity. His defensiveness about the U.S. role in Vietnam was surely a sign of insecurity, but the initial escalation of the war may have been Johnson the consensus leader. We will explore these psychological dimensions of action as we go along.

Leadership Style

George Meany, the leader of the AFL-CIO, remembered that Johnson called him the day after Kennedy was killed and invited Meany to the White House the next day. Johnson told the diverse group assembled that day that he wanted to be "the best president the country has ever had." Meany knew, of course, that Johnson would rely on him for help in Congress.[9] The new president made similar early calls to civil rights leaders, and old New Deal and congressional friends. The message was the same—I am your only president. I will be a reform president. I will need your help. He was less declarative and folksier with Southern senatorial friends, telling them how much he loved them and asking after their wives. He wanted everyone on board.

Johnson relied heavily on his knowledge of the individual members of Congress, particularly in the Senate. Joseph Califano reports that as policies were being developed, before final decisions were made about what to send up to the Hill, Johnson would sometimes tell aides to go talk to senator X or congressman Y. On the education bill he might say to go talk to Senator Wayne Morse about a point: "See what he thinks about it because if he doesn't like it it's never going to see the light of day, it will never get out of a subcommittee.... Something would stick in his memory.... You'd go up and see Morse. Even if you didn't understand exactly why he wanted you to see him, at the time you saw him you understood."[10]

Johnson understood from the beginning that he would have to work through colleagues and lieutenants in leading Congress. It would be a violation of congressional prerogatives and pride for him to intervene personally in persuasive efforts on every bill with a large number of members. It was also impossible because of the numbers. He did use the telephone and private meetings to persuade individuals, especially senators, to go with him. He kept close track of the progress of bills in committees and actions on the floor of each house and insisted on daily reports from his legislative assistants, to which he often responded with advice from experience. For example, Califano wanted to leak a report on the Model Cities bill before its presentation to Congress in January 1966. He feared that reporters would not understand it without background. Johnson refused without saying why. When a later bill barely passed, the president told Califano that a leak would have defeated Model Cities because members would have seen the cost—better to surprise them.

Journalists made a good deal about "the Johnson treatment," often illustrated by photographs of the president leaning over into the faces of congressional leaders. Most stories were vague about what the "treatment" consisted of, but the implication was of strong-arm methods. In fact, Johnson's skill was in personal persuasion, backed by the force of his personality. His longtime friend and adviser, Washington lawyer James Rowe, remembered: "He was face to face, as persuasive a man as you ever met, more persuasive than anybody I ever met. And he was a dangerous man in that sense. He could convince you that black was white if you gave him enough time."[11]

Carl Albert remembered that some members of the House thought that Johnson was an arm-twister but that "his great talent was his tenacity." He wouldn't turn loose and never stopped. One bill passed, and he wanted another. Johnson knew how to appeal to the idealism of members of Congress. Hale Boggs, a Democratic leader in the House, remembered that the knowledge that Kennedy had wanted his programs to be passed helped unify the party for Johnson's leadership in 1964. A telephone conversation with Senate minority leader Everett Dirksen about the 1964 civil rights bill, which he could not pass without Dirksen's contribution of Republican votes, showed this appeal: "We don't want this to be a Democratic bill. We want it to be an American bill. . . . I saw your exhibit at the World's Fair, and it said 'the Land of Lincoln.' So you're worthy of the Land of Lincoln. And the man from Illinois is going to pass the bill, and I'll see you get proper attention and credit."[12] Johnson used his talents to be an event-making leader in working with Congress in 1964. Kennedy might have won on some issues but Johnson's clean sweep was, in large part, due to the force of his personality.

The Great Society

At the close of the Johnson administration, his cabinet presented him with a scroll listing the legislative accomplishments by year, 1963 through 1968. The list contained 208 laws. One could sift through to estimate which bills had passed easily as part of the normal routine, for most presidential legislation passes in a bipartisan matter. But the great volume was surely Johnson's doing. Right up to the end, he would call the majority leaders and ask them to pass bills. One swath from 1967, for example, cites Air Pollution Control, Partnership for Health, Social Security Increases, Age Discrimination, Wholesome Meat, Flammable Fabrics, Urban Research, and Public Broadcasting.

The words "Great Society," were first used in a speech at the University of Michigan on May 22, 1964. Johnson had used the phrase, and variations of it, in a good many statements before, but he had been urging his speechwriter, Richard Goodwin, to pull all his ideas together in one speech. The theme of the speech, intended to distinguish it from the New Deal and Kennedy's programs, was to create a society with full opportunities for all people, with special attention to poverty and race discrimination. Johnson deliberately did not talk in terms of redistributing wealth from the better off to the poor. He was asking the middle classes to help the poor to help themselves. Of course, the most popular programs, such as Medicare, helped all citizens, but Medicaid for the poor was also slipped into the legislation.

Leadership of Congress

The three important achievements of 1964—the tax cut, civil rights bill, and the war on poverty—received varying degrees of White House preparation. The intellectual and political work for the tax cut had been well laid by Kennedy. The civil rights bill, which focused on the desegregation of public accommodations, was designed in the Justice Department and was well understood. The war on poverty, in contrast, was developed in ad hoc ways, without much intellectual foundation and very little under-standing of the causes of poverty and how best to deal with it. Congress was hardly consulted as the bill was pushed through, with the result that when the program later ran into trouble, Congress had no investment in it. The other two programs were more effective both for intellectual and political reasons.

Economic Policy

Walter Heller, chairman of the Council of Economic Advisers (CEA), remembered that Johnson was more dependent on economic analysis from the council than Kennedy had been. But he only "learned enough about the central issues and facts to make intelligent decisions ... but wasn't interested in going beyond that." Politics took over. Gardner Ackley, Heller's successor as CEA chairman, recalled that Johnson was not interested in economic reasoning. He wanted alternative choices and would try them out on dif-ferent people, inside and outside government. Eventually he learned that he could trust his economists to give him the economic facts, but would not listen to political advice from them. Ackley learned from experience that good advice was of no help to the president unless he could find a way to act on it politically.[13]

The way for passage of the tax cut in 1964 had been cleared in the House and Senate, but Johnson saw a roadblock in Senator Harry Byrd, chairman of the Senate Finance Committee. In a dramatic gesture, which Walter Heller called a "masterful charade," Johnson invited Byrd to the White House for breakfast and extracted a promise to hold hearings on the bill and to take a vote and let it go to the floor if Johnson kept the federal budget at $100 billion or lower. It actually came in at $97 billion. Then when things were going fine, Everett Dirksen introduced an amendment to the bill to reduce excise taxes, which would have reduced federal revenue by over $400 million. Johnson went into action and in a period of hours persuaded his friends on the committee, such as Richard Russell and Russell Long (senator from Louisiana), to defeat the amendment, which they did by one vote. Johnson's telephone conversations that afternoon showed the persuader at work:

> To Senator Abraham Ribicoff, of Connecticut, who was dragging his feet: "Goddammit, you need to vote with me once in a while, just one time.... The Democrats are going to be a miserable failure in the eyes of the whole country." He wanted the committee to meet and vote but Ribicoff protested that the opposition was strong and Johnson retorts: "No, it's not. No it's not

… if you'll help us we'll have it over, and I'll appreciate it and I'll remember it … don't let Everett Dirksen screw me this way…. You just work it out. Don't say how. I don't give a damn about the details."[14]

Johnson told Harry Byrd that it was not consistent for Byrd to lose $450 million in revenue when they are both trying to get the budget down. Byrd promised to help and the president said, "Help me, Harry, help me."[15]

The Revenue Act of 1964, without excise cuts, passed on February 26, 1964. But Dirksen came back with excise tax cuts later in the year. In a telephone conversation he asked the president to consider a water project for southern Illinois. Johnson looked into it and told Dirksen the next day that the Army Corps of Engineers would look favorably on it. In the first conversation Johnson told his friend:

> "Now you're not going to beat me on excise taxes and ruin my budget this year." Dirksen pleads the pressure of trade associations, and Johnson tells him to put it through the House because the Senate will not let him write a bill on excise taxes, which Dirksen admits. After Johnson calls Dirksen back to tell him that the Corps of Engineers will look favorably on the water project he added: "So don't you tell anybody now that you've got a back door to the White House but you go up there and don't kill my godamn tax bill tomorrow. Quit messing around in my smokehouse."[16]

One sees Johnson using the force of his personality to trade on old friendships here, something that most presidents cannot do. Nor could he do it in many cases, and he did not try.

Civil Rights

Lyndon Johnson wanted to get race problems off the back of the South for the sake of justice but also to bring the South fully back into the nation. He believed that the appeal had to be moral. Once he was president, Johnson told Senator Richard Russell that Russell had to get out of his way, that he would run over him to get a civil rights law. Russell warned that it would cost him the South, and the president replied that he would gladly pay that price. He also told Everett Dirksen that he did not have enough Senate support to vote down a Southern filibuster, with the implication that he would need Dirksen's help. A long courtship of Dirksen had begun. Go to work on Dirksen, he told Roy Wilkins, chairman of the NAACP. He called Walter Reuther, head of the United Autoworkers Union, and asked him to "stiffen the spine" of Democratic majority leader Michael Mansfield on imposing cloture on Senate debate against a filibuster. His relations with Russell stayed good during the entire legislative struggle from January to June. Dirksen and Russell talked throughout about when votes would be taken, with Johnson listening and prodding in the background. Johnson told Humphrey: "You and I are going to get Ev. It's going to take time. We're going to get him.… You get in there to see Dirksen. You drink with Dirksen. You talk with Dirksen. You listen to Dirksen."[17]

The central focus of the bill was on the desegregation of public accommodations. But there were also provisions for protecting voting rights, allocation of federal funds to enhance school desegregation, and forbidding discrimination in employment. Administration leadership was formally assumed by Attorney General Robert Kennedy, working closely with Humphrey, Mansfield, and Dirksen, with Johnson in the background. He made calls, held meetings, counted heads. The House bill arrived on the Senate floor on March 9, 1964, and Russell began the filibuster immediately. Dirksen added a number of harmful amendments; he did not wish to appear to be too compliant. But Johnson would permit no amendments; he wanted the House bill. In due course Dirksen gave up and told Humphrey that the bill would pass. He could deliver enough Republican votes. Larry O'Brien, head of the president's legislative staff, later said that Dirksen had no alternative but to cooperate. There was too much support for the bill, in Congress and among the public. House Republicans, who had gotten in early and did not want to see their bill compromised, also pushed the Senate. The filibuster was defeated on June 9 and the Senate passed the bill by 71 to 29 on June 19. Western Democrats and Republicans were the key to victory, and Everett Dirksen had made it possible. Johnson had appealed to his moral and patriotic sense. The new law had a solid footing in the politics of the country that would carry it through into the future, although Johnson began to worry immediately about black militancy and hoped that there would be a cooling-off period. As he was signing the bill on July 2, Johnson told White House assistant Bill Moyers "I think we just delivered the South to the Republican Party for a long time to come."

Johnson had pushed so hard for the tax cut and civil rights laws in part because his eye was on reelection. He would say that if the bills did not pass, "I'll go to the country with nothing." He expected Richard Nixon to be his opponent and saw a hard fight ahead. But just as he needed victories, a backlash on civil rights emerged. Alabama governor George Wallace entered the Democratic primaries in 1964 and won respectable numbers of votes from white blue-collar voters. Opinion began to shift that maybe Johnson was doing too much for black people too fast and precipitated a white backlash, which gathered strength throughout the rest of his presidency.

But this was not a problem during the dramatic events in Selma, Alabama, in March 1965, which led to the passage of the voting rights bill with the president's leadership. In January Johnson asked acting attorney general Nicholas Katzenbach to prepare a voting rights bill and discuss it with civil rights leaders. However, the president saw little chance of passage that year. He told Martin Luther King Jr. that he would get a voting rights law but not that year. But King and his colleagues in the Southern Christian Leadership Conference were impatient and not prepared to wait. They decided to create a provocation and chose Selma, Alabama, as the spot. Less than 1 percent of black people in Selma were registered to vote. Demonstrations were begun in February. King was put in jail and then released. He later met with Johnson and sensed that the president's enthusiasm for civil rights action was weak. King saw that he needed to tap public outrage. On March 6, a march of black citizens from Selma to Montgomery to register to vote took place. Johnson had sent two federal mediators to Selma to try to mediate between civil rights leaders and Selma officials, but the civil rights leaders did not want mediation; they wanted an incident. Johnson had pressed Governor Wallace to keep order, but the response was tepid. As the marchers began, a bunch of burly state troopers rushed at them, knocking them down and beating them with billy clubs. The nation saw it on television, and it was played and replayed.

Two days later Johnson announced that a new bill would be sent to Congress. He spoke to Congress on the evening of March 16 with a national television audience. Johnson wrote in his memoir that he wanted to use "every ounce of moral persuasion the presidency held.... And I wanted to talk from my own heart, my own experience." His words were so moving that all knew the bill would easily pass: "We cannot, we must not refuse to protect the right of every American to vote.... We have already waited more than a hundred years and more and the time for waiting is gone.... It is not just Negroes but really all of us, who must overcome the crippling of bigotry and injustice." He concluded with the words of the civil rights movements, "We shall overcome."[18]

The Senate passed the bill 77 to 19, and the House passed it 333 to 85. From that point forward Southern politicians, Democrats all, began to court the black vote at home. Few of them could oppose the legislation, because the right to vote could not be openly challenged. The bill passed so easily because the dramatic events and full media coverage of them influenced Congress, but also because of Johnson's moral leadership. He seized the moment to act after holding back out of prudence. I have argued that prudence is a cardinal quality in a political leader, and Johnson, as a realist, understood that. But prudence is not necessarily abandoned when the opportunity for great achievement presents itself, as was the case with civil rights. Johnson sought no more than the legal rights that were due to all Americans.

The War on Poverty

Keynesian economic theory brought answers to the problems of slow economic growth, but offered uncertain benefits to the poor if they were not already integrated into labor markets. They had to be able to take advantage of new opportunities, which their poor education and insufficient skills might not permit. John F. Kennedy had asked Walter Heller to work up an antipoverty plan, which Johnson embraced as "my kind of program." The initial idea was not tied to the civil rights movement or exclusively to black populations. There were a lot of poor white people. Johnson did not want any program to be redistributive. It was to appeal to the middle-class ideal of self-help. He wrote in his memoir that his aides warned him against the dramatic declaration of a "war" on poverty. The country was middle class and no one represented the poor. Yes, he said, but I will represent them. It was another opportunity for the new president to make his own mark. He told his economic advisers that "any problem could be solved." He records that he deliberately used the word "war" to rally and inspire the nation. There were also good political reasons for a new approach. Blacks were migrating north. The old city machines could not control them. He wanted black people to be included in the war to keep them in the Democratic camp.

Johnson launched a rhetorical campaign with key members of Congress, labor leaders, mayors, and other potential constituencies. The public was not mindful of poverty, but he was going to make them pay attention. He had little idea what should go into such a program, only telling Heller and the head of the Bureau of the Budget that he wanted a national program, not just a few little projects. He overrode prudence here because it was all too much of a rush without careful thought about how the program might realistically work. When he selected Sargent Shriver, the head of the Peace Corps, to direct the new program, he told him "The sky's the limit. You just make this thing work. I don't give a damn about the details."[19] Johnson wanted an innovative program but would initially commit only $500 million to it. He had just put through his tax cut and could not go beyond the $100-billion budget that he had promised for 1965. He knew that he did not want the old-line federal departments to run the program and resisted efforts by the departments of Labor and Health, Education, and Welfare to subsume it into their existing programs.

The core idea at the center of the new plan was "community action," in which local boards representing the poor would apply for federal grants to develop ad hoc programs for their poor, including the coordination of the work of local federal agencies. So many ideas had flooded the White House from the agencies that the Bureau of the Budget hit on community action as a device for coherence. The idea had originally come from experiments planned by the president's committee on juvenile delinquency in the Kennedy administration. Local action groups were to be independent of federal bureaucracy and big-city political machines to plan their own programs. But the experiments had not been tested by 1964. The Department of Labor also wanted job-training programs, so the Job Corps, to run training camps for disadvantaged youth, was put in the bill but not in the department. Then, in rapid order, Head Start for preschool children, a domestic Peace Corps, and other small programs of assistance were tacked on. It was not a coherent package, nor was there any theory about the causes of and remedies for poverty. It was all put in a new Office of Economic Opportunity in the Executive Office of the President.

Johnson and Shriver did not want a lot of debate about the bill, which the president first described in his State of the Union message in January 1964. He insisted on immediate hearings, fearing that delay would permit opposition to mobilize. Southerners feared that it was a cover for integration, for example, in the Job Corps. So Johnson persuaded Representative Phil Landrum, a Democrat from Georgia, to sponsor the bill. Republicans were excluded from the markup session in the House committee. Hard questions about what the programs would do in their actual implementation were shoved aside, if raised at all. There was also no public demand for the program, so it had no clear constituencies, even among those to be helped. In fact, the program was to create interest groups where they did not exist. The Senate first approved the bill without much discussion in July, and the House followed soon after. Congress was not expert in how to fight poverty and deferred to the administration, which had papered over issues with rhetoric. Republicans opposed it and never stopped trying to kill it in practice.

Johnson told Bill Moyers that he thought of the poverty program as similar to the National Youth Administration and the Civilian Conservation Corps of the New Deal, which were work programs for unemployed youth. Neither he nor anyone else foresaw that the community action programs in the cities would challenge federal and local officials about old programs that kept the poor dependent. The new generation of black militants in the civil rights movement began to move into community action. But no one, including Johnson, wanted a militant movement. The program was to be a bootstrap operation in which individuals were to work their way up. Even though the programs were small and weakly funded, they had been so overblown in White House rhetoric that there was a credibility gap, which the press loved to dramatize. By 1966 Johnson had lost heart. The Vietnam war was taking more of his time. The Bureau of the Budget began to cut back funding. Opinion polls showed that the great majority of middle-class white people still blamed the poor themselves for their problems.

Johnson made the difference in the legislative passage of the tax cut, the civil rights bill, and the war on poverty. The winds of politics were certainly at his back, but few presidents are likely to have his great knowledge of Congress and the principal personalities in it or to have perfected strategies of leading congressional politicians. Johnson was surely unique. The backlash on civil rights was to be expected, but the new laws were firmly on the books. The tax cut stimulated economic growth, but Keynesian theory requires the government to raise taxes to ward off inflation when times are good. Johnson waited until 1968 to do so, but by then it was too little and too late to prevent the roaring inflation inherited by his successors. The problem was that he wanted both the Great Society and the war and could not find a way to pay for them both. The antipoverty program was poorly designed, had no underlying theory about the causes of poverty, and only the poor as its constituency. Johnson had said "don't worry me about details," and the results were bad.

The 1964 Election

The political scientist Clinton Rossiter understood that Lyndon Johnson would win the 1964 election, but added that Barry Goldwater, the very conservative senator from Arizona, was the only Republican who could possibly beat him. Match this to Goldwater's remark that, as far as he was concerned, New York City could be sawed off the continent and sent out to sea, and you see Rossiter's insight.[20] The Republican Party was moving south and west, and Goldwater was the first politician to see it.

Goldwater was nominated through the actions of young Republican activists in state conventions and a dramatic victory over Governor Nelson Rockefeller of New York in the California primary. It was a straight fight between Eastern Republicans who had dominated presidential politics and insurgent westerners, with southern support. Goldwater voted against the

Civil Rights Act, went to Tennessee and suggested that the government sell the Tennessee Valley Authority, attacked agricultural subsidies while speaking in the farm belt, spoke against the idea of Medicare in Florida, and attacked the poverty program and welfare. He called for victory in the cold war, suggested using atomic weapons to defoliate trails in North Vietnam, and advocated giving NATO tactical nuclear weapons. Alabama governor George Wallace entered primaries and did well in Wisconsin and Maryland, but Goldwater asked him to withdraw, fearing that he would lose the South if Wallace stayed in, and Wallace complied. Johnson barnstormed the country to large, excited crowds. He got credit for unifying the nation and for his great legislative talent. He wanted to keep Vietnam out of the campaign and ran as a peace candidate against his opponent's militancy. Johnson promised that American boys would not go to Vietnam because "Asians should fight Asians." He derided Goldwater's extremism in domestic and foreign policy.

More Government

The president won 61 percent of the popular vote in the 1964 election, losing only Mississippi, Alabama, South Carolina, Louisiana, and Georgia (the states with heavy black populations), and Arizona. He brought large Democratic majorities into Congress, 68 to 32 in the Senate, and 295 to 140 in the House. The gain of 37 Democratic seats in the House meant that he would be able to carry out his legislative proposals. The power of the "conservative coalition" of Southern Democrats and Midwestern Republicans that had held since 1938 was broken. Key committee chairmanships in the House were in friendly hands. Johnson assumed that he had a mandate for more Great Society programs. It was assumed that his programs would pass. Certainly, there was no great public opposition. A mandate on the war, if one had been given, was to avoid drastic military action.

It is not possible here to describe all the programs that passed in the next three years. Among the most important measures was the passage of the Elementary and Secondary Education Act, which provided federal funds to state and local school systems for special educational programs for disadvantaged children. A major breakthrough came with the passage of Medicare, a program of health insurance for Americans over sixty-five and its companion, Medicaid, for the very poor. Public broadcasting for radio and television was created, regulation of pollution to protect the environment was enacted, and innumerable urban and health assistance programs were passed. A Model Cities program was passed in 1966 that created centers for urban planning and development for major cities, but it was spread too thin, poorly funded, and robbed the poverty program of resources. Johnson drove the Congress hard the entire time, despite the loss of the seats gained in the House in the 1966 congressional elections, which he had predicted. He knew that his capital in Congress would diminish in due course, but he never gave up. Voters liked the Great Society legislative programs even better after they were passed than before.

Some political scientists discounted the importance of Johnson's leadership in 1965 and 1966 because of the large Democratic majorities in Congress. He was also not as personally involved as he had been in 1964. But they failed to see that the president orchestrated the process in a way that no one else could. He had the votes, but large majorities could also be unruly. Johnson knew how to anticipate such difficulties and ward them off in advance. It was Johnson who pushed hard for a compromise between secular education associations and Roman Catholic educational leaders to work out a plan by which federal money would go to students in parochial schools rather than to the schools themselves. He worked the ropes personally on the passage of Medicare, overseeing every step in the congressional process, shaming medical leaders to support the bill, and personally meeting with many members of Congress. The addition of thirty-seven new Democrats in the House made a difference, and Senator Goldwater may have contributed more to that result than the president. The new members knew their careers depended on the president's success, and he led them accordingly. His personal skills and the political context were reinforcing. Even after the Democrats lost a number of seats in 1966, Johnson kept driving them.

Johnson intended the Great Society programs to be for the good of all citizens and therefore not to be radically redistributive, in which some were to gain and others lose. The least popular programs, directed to poverty, had the more severe problems of implementation and legitimacy. Johnson wanted to be a consensus leader to pull people up and tear no one down. He was guilty of rhetorical excess—for example, in his promises to end poverty—but this was perhaps politically necessary. The character of presidential politics in America demands that reform proceed on faith, because we never know enough to act otherwise when politics is favorable to action. Critics of the failures of implementation of Johnson's programs forget this reality. Still, the mishaps of the poverty program damaged the reputation of the entire Great Society and strengthened the Republicans in time.

The ultimate problem of the Johnson presidency was that, after its great triumphs, the political center would not hold. Reform was exhausted, and much of the public tired of it. We will see this in the transition from the Johnson to the Nixon administration. A watershed developed in which politics could be redefined in different directions. This would perhaps have happened in gradual and measured ways had there been no war. Johnson's efforts to take a middle path in conducting the war failed, and much else went down with it.

THE VIETNAM WAR

The central question is why Lyndon Johnson decided to send large numbers of American forces to fight in South Vietnam in July 1965. One must be careful about attributing motives. People do not always fully know why they act as they do, and they usually act for multiple reasons. Reasons are often given later as rationalizations after the fact. This is not to say that we do not act from purpose and reason, but that we may not fully understand our purposes and actions, or the environment in which we act. This simple fact makes it inherently difficult to understand the motivations of others, especially in regard to past actions. The actions of presidents cannot be explained by their personalities alone, or by the political opportunities and constraints that confront them, or by the historical stream in which they act. They most often seek coherence among these complex factors. Close acquaintance with a president's preferred ways of action—for example, Johnson's preference for consensus on a center path—may permit the development of propositions to set against the always incomplete evidence.

Early Days

A few days after he was sworn into office, Johnson met with his advisers, including Henry Cabot Lodge, the ambassador to South Vietnam who had returned to Washington. He told them that he was not going to lose South Vietnam; he was not going to be the president who saw Southeast Asia go the way of communist China. Nor, he said, did Congress favor any such development. These were very rash statements that Johnson need not have made, but he wanted everyone on board. Robert McNamara wrote later that Johnson told them to win the war, but added that they were never able to show him how "at acceptable cost or acceptable risk."

Johnson's dilemmas were clear to him at the outset. He would not withdraw and he was reluctant to fight, and there seemed no other possibility. For the next year and a half he would struggle with indecision, hiding his uncertainties from his advisers, and thus from historians and biographers. For the longest time he hoped that assistance to the government of South Vietnam would be sufficient. His temporary recourse was to urge McNamara to tell the South Vietnamese to take the offensive against the Viet Cong guerrillas in the South. North Vietnamese forces had not yet crossed the border in force. He told his advisers that he had to win an election before he could address Vietnam. He was only a "trustee" for Kennedy. This was a good buffer against the Joint Chiefs of Staff, who wanted to bomb North Vietnam, mine its harbors, and even use nuclear weapons if China were to intervene. He considered going to Congress for a resolution of approval of his actions in South Vietnam, but was warned off by William Fulbright, chair of the Senate Foreign Relations Committee, for fear of creating a "war fever." There was no sense of urgency among politicians, nor any public awareness of a problem. Johnson was also worried that the passage of the civil rights bill in 1964 might be delayed if he acted either to reduce or increase U.S. commitments abroad. He was counting on his legislative proposals to get him elected in the fall. In May he told McGeorge Bundy that another Korean war was in the offing, but that he did not think that South Vietnam was worth fighting for and yet one could not run from the communists. A long telephone conversation with his friend Richard Russell, chair of the Senate Armed Services Committee, on May 26 was guarded on his part, but Russell knew his own mind. The South Vietnamese would not fight, he said, and the United States could not fight well there. China might enter the war in that case. There must be a middle ground somewhere. Johnson said that his advisers warned against falling dominoes in Southeast Asia if North Vietnam won, but he did not think that the American people wanted a war. Russell expressed a lack of confidence in McNamara, who felt that he had to solve every problem. He did not think that Southeast Asia would be lost if the United States left South Vietnam. Russell had never been in favor of intervention in Vietnam. But, Johnson asked, wouldn't a president who withdrew be impeached? Russell answered: "We're in there and I don't know how in the hell you tell the American people you're coming out. They'll think that you'd just been whipped.... It'd be disastrous." But, he added, people would understand a negotiated agreement as in the Korean War. Johnson said that he did not think that the public favored intervention in Vietnam, but everyone he talked to wanted to go in and he feared that the Republicans would attack him for inaction.[21] This is the language of a fearful eventful politician.

The situation was worse by mid-1964. The North Vietnamese were assembling large units to send south. One government after another was toppled by coups in the south. There were seven governments altogether in 1964. Barry Goldwater, the Republican candidate for president, was advocating using nuclear weapons to defoliate trails between the two Vietnams, and mining the harbors in the north. Johnson had to find a public position.

He seized the opportunity in August when North Vietnamese torpedo boats attacked two American destroyers that were on intelligence missions in the Gulf of Tonkin inside northern waters. Johnson would have ignored the first attack but at the report of a second attack resolved on action. There is still question whether the second attack occurred, and Johnson knew of the uncertainty, but he took advantage of the event to ask Congress to pass a resolution that had been written much earlier and was waiting for a pretext. The Gulf of Tonkin resolution gave congressional support to the president to resist aggression in Southeast Asia by whatever means necessary. The Senate passed the resolution by a vote of 88 to 2 and the House by 416 to 0. The fact that the ships were on intelligence missions was deliberately not disclosed. Johnson's guide to action here was similar resolutions that Congress had given President Eisenhower for the defense of Taiwan and Lebanon. He did not want to be out in front alone. Senator Fulbright, his agent, assured the Senate that Johnson would return to the Senate if more drastic action were required.

The real significance of the resolution was political. Johnson could show his firmness in Vietnam so that Senator Goldwater could not attack him as weak. He could also represent himself as the prudent candidate against Goldwater's militant language. At one point during the campaign, he announced that no American boys would fight in Vietnam, saying, "Let Asians fight Asians." He spoke out against bombing North Vietnam, even as military planners were at work on a bombing plan. Eighty-five percent of the public supported the Gulf of Tonkin resolution. Johnson had his cake and ate it, too.

The Road to War

After the election, uncertainty persisted all around in the administration about what to do in Vietnam, with the exception of the military, who wanted to throw in all their guns. Reports from the field were bleak about the fighting will of the army of South Vietnam. It did not seem reasonable even to consider withdrawal from the area when things were going so badly.

Bundy, McNamara, and Rusk were inclined to stronger actions. Senators Mansfield and Russell and Vice President Humphrey argued against precipitate action, on grounds that bad policy would create bad politics for the president. Johnson continued to temporize. Johnson was skeptical of the efficacy of bombing North Vietnam, as urged by the high military, but he did heed the argument that bombing might stiffen determination in the South to fight. It was a short-run expedient. Bombing of North Vietnam began in February 1965 as reprisal for attacks on American installations in the South. Rolling Thunder, a sustained campaign that lasted for three years, finally began in early March initially against limited military targets. It was to have little effect on the infiltration of North Vietnamese forces into the South. In February, before the decision to bomb was made, Vice President Humphrey wrote the president a memo in which he predicted increasing political trouble at home for the president if the American role in the war were increased, because the effort would surely not go well. Public support would decline as casualties increased just as in the Korean war, and this was what happened. But Johnson was so angry that he shut Humphrey out of key decisions on the war for several months. Humphrey had to go on the public stump in defense of the president before Johnson relented.

Johnson reluctantly sent marine units to South Vietnam in February and March to protect American air bases. He then sent Army Chief of Staff Harold Johnson to Vietnam in March, and Johnson returned with a prediction that it would take 500,000 American troops in the country to save it. The shock was so great that the advice was not heeded, according to Secretary McNamara. By the end of May there were 50,000 troops in South Vietnam and Congress had voted a $700 million supplemental appropriation. General William Westmoreland, the commander of American forces, asked permission to use American troops in combat in support of the army of South Vietnam, and Johnson agreed. By June, Westmoreland had approval to use his forces independently. By then General Nguyen Ky and Nguyen Van Thieu had seized the control they were to keep until 1975 and were asking for more American help.

Robert McNamara wrote many years later that the United States should have withdrawn from South Vietnam either in 1963–1964 or early 1965. There was no political stability in South Vietnam, and the regime could not defend itself. He faulted himself for not raising fundamental questions about American interests at those critical junctures. However, McNamara was a manager, recruited from the Ford Motor Company because he knew how to run an organization. He knew little of the history of Vietnam. His job was to implement other men's plans. At the time he did everything he could do to muzzle the dissent of George Ball, the under secretary of state, who kept writing memos to the president urging him to cut his losses, stabilize combat at a lower level, and negotiate a peace agreement even if it meant the gradual loss of South Vietnam to a coalition government with home-grown communists. McNamara, the problem solver, would have none of it.

In June, General Westmoreland made a request for the infusion of Ameri-can soldiers up to a level of 175,000 by the end of 1965. North Vietnamese troops were flooding in. The army of South Vietnam was losing battles. Hard decisions had to be made. McNamara reports that in the weeks that followed, attention was entirely on coping with the short run. There was no real analysis of the consequences of decisive military action. McNamara was sent to Vietnam in July to develop alternatives for the president and, on his return, recommended sending 175,000 to 200,000 troops and calling up 325,000 army reserve troops. He saw this as preferable to withdrawal or doing more of the same. The United States might not win the war but it could perhaps force the North Vietnamese to negotiate.

The crucial meeting was on July 21. George Ball had written a memo opposing McNamara's plan and William Bundy, assistant secretary of defense, had written a memo that called for limited reinforcements to West-moreland with reassessment at a future date. McGeorge Bundy advised the president that he would want to hear Ball out, reject his position, and then address the other alternatives. Johnson gave Ball his day in court twice, invit-ing him back for an afternoon meeting to state his case more fully. Ball must be quoted because he saw the future more fully than anyone in the room:

> We cannot win, Mr. President. This war will be long and protracted. The most we can hope for is a messy conclusion. There remains a great danger of intrusion by the Chinese. But the biggest problem is the problem of the long war.
>
> The Korean experience was a galling one. The correlation between Korean casualties and public opinion showed support stabilized at 50 percent. As casualties increase the pressure to strike at the very jugular of North Vietnam will become very great. ...
>
> There is the problem of national politics. Every great captain of history was not afraid to make a tactical withdrawal if conditions were unfavorable to him. The enemy cannot be seen in Vietnam. He is indigenous to the country. I truly have serious doubts that an army of westerners can successfully fight orientals in an Asian jungle. ...
>
> The least harmful way to cut losses in SVN is to let the government decide it doesn't want us to stay there. Therefore we should put such proposals to the GVN that they can't accept. Then it would move to a neutralist position.

I have no illusions that after we were asked to leave South Vietnam, that country would soon come under Hanoi control....

If we wanted to make a stand in Thailand, we might be able to make it.[22]

The president asked Ball if the United States would not appear to be a "paper tiger" for withdrawing and Ball answered that a worse blow would be to be defeated by guerrillas.

No one in the meeting supported Ball. William Bundy wrote later that he wished that he had done so. McNamara carried the day. Johnson seems to have finally decided to go forward after a weekend meeting at Camp David with McNamara, Clark Clifford (a close friend who opposed intervention), and others. Clifford later remembered that Johnson thought that an infusion of 100,000 more men might encourage North Vietnam to negotiate. Senator Mansfield wrote Johnson on July 23 advising him not to call up the reserves or ask Congress for a new resolution. Opposition would flare and the domestic legislative program would be hurt. Mansfield was opposed to escalation on the merits and a few days later wrote a second letter signed by several senior senators of both parties—all friends of the president—urging prudence. However, when the president had the congressional leaders in to talk, all except Mansfield favored the actions he was about to take. Even Senator Russell got on board. Johnson presented himself as acting with moderation on a middle path.

George Ball predicted much that would happen but he could not solve the president's short-term political problem by giving him a politically feasible way to dampen down the American effort or withdraw altogether. The time for a graceful withdrawal, if it had ever existed, was long past. Johnson's delay of discussion and action in 1964 accompanied the continuing deterioration of effective government in South Vietnam. McNamara later wrote that every one of Ball's hard questions should have been analyzed along the way, but he resisted any such effort at the time. Johnson seems to have been much influenced by a memorandum from Dean Rusk, who argued that withdrawal from Vietnam would damage U.S. credibility around the world with the inference that the Americans would not support their allies. Such a failure would open the door to other aggression and might lead to a larger war. Johnson's advisers all believed this to be true, and George Ball was simply out of step.

Johnson announced his decision at a midday press conference on July 28. He would send 75,000 troops, up to a level of 125,000. This was in continuity with existing policy, he said. He did not want public discussion.

McNamara reports that he and the president were hoping that the new infusion of forces would drive the North Vietnamese to negotiations, permitting a short war. The reserves were not called up, and Congress was not asked for more money. Johnson said that he did not want to arouse Republican war hawks in open debate. He was also concerned that Soviet leaders not get involved, because he was trying to limit conflicts with the Soviets in Europe and elsewhere. He was promoting an East-West trade bill and a nuclear nonproliferation treaty.

Johnson certainly papered over the hard facts of the costs of war, then and later, but he was trying to protect his social programs and also avoid domestic pressures to enlarge the war. He wrote in his memoir that he would act no differently in July 1965 if he had it to do again. Congress would not have given him a tax increase to pay for the war. Funds were increased for Great Society programs every year thereafter, and if he had asked for tax increases, Congress would have cut the programs instead. The war took only 8 to 10 percent of the federal budget, which was less than in the Korean conflict. He forgot to add that Truman persuaded Congress to raise taxes that time. Johnson did not ask for a tax increase until 1967, and one was finally passed in 1968, which was too little and too late to curb inflation. He would not agree to cuts in his domestic programs in return for a tax cut. It was too much to ask.

Public opinion polls gave Johnson latitude without overwhelming support. In July 25 percent favored withdrawal, 24 percent favored escalation, 16 percent favored the present course, and 33 percent did not know what to do. These were much like the early figures in the Korean War.

The reader will remember that Mrs. Johnson was worrying that her husband was working harder at getting his programs passed by Congress and enjoying it less during the early months of 1965. The same emotions surfaced during July. Bill Moyers, who was very close to the president, saw outbursts of near "paranoia" as Johnson obsessed that sending more troops would destroy his presidency. Dean Rusk told Moyers of a similar concern. Richard Goodwin consulted a psychiatrist about Johnson after the president said that he was going to destroy all dissenters, many of whom were communists. One cannot easily assess these reports. Johnson's decisions were rational in terms of both his policies and his politics. We know that he did not like crossroads and fateful decisions because they could be divisive and lead to conflict. Johnson wanted consensus and surely sensed trouble ahead. Perhaps his own sense of his psychological integrity was threatened.

Explanations

The four explanations below emphasize different factors but they are not mutually exclusive. The fourth alternative draws on the previous three:

1. Johnson and his advisers believed that South Vietnam must not be lost because American influence and credibility in the world would be weakened. The domino thesis applied only to Southeast Asia, but concern about wars of national liberation was of worldwide scope.
2. Johnson did not encourage analysis and debate about policy choices at any point along the road from late 1963 to July 1965. He behaved as he had as Senate leader, separating his advisers and keeping his choices to himself. The argument is that if he had encouraged analysis and debate, he might have questioned some of his basic premises. He might also have taken advantage of opportunities to withdraw from the potential war before he was trapped by prior decisions.
3. Johnson was trapped by domestic politics, which would not permit him to leave South Vietnam but would only support a limited war. In this perspective the American involvement in Vietnam was caused by the commitments of the three previous presidents, which had become givens in domestic politics.
4. Johnson was a completely political man and eventful leader who sought coherence among politics and policy and organized policy-making processes, with the goal of consensus. He did not have the imagination or vision that would have been required to challenge the received wisdom about Vietnam inherited from his predecessors. This explanation draws on the other three without any sense that policy was determined. The president made the policy.

Beliefs

Presidents Eisenhower, Kennedy, and Johnson all worried that Southeast Asia would be lost to communism if South Vietnam were to fall. There was even talk of needing to defend India, the Philippines, and Japan. The precise reasons why the dominoes would fall were never clear. North Vietnam might dominate Laos and Cambodia, but would this reach to Thailand. Burma, or down to Malaysia? No persuasive analysis was ever presented. A larger fear was that if the United States were to fail to defend allies in the world, its credibility would suffer in the larger cold war. There is no doubt that Johnson and his advisers believed this.

Yuen Khong, a foreign policy scholar, contends that the Korean conflict provided the most persuasive historical analogy for policymakers.[23] President Truman had deliberately fought a limited war from 1950 to 1953 for limited objectives, which permitted Eisenhower to negotiate a limited peace in 1953. North Korea was denied the conquest of South Korea. By the same token, Johnson tried to avoid Truman's mistakes. Truman had not asked for congressional approval of his use of American forces to defend South Korea, having taken the issue immediately to the United Nations. Truman also ignored Chinese threats that they would fight if allied forces crossed the Yalu River into North Korea. Johnson was therefore sensitive to any recommended action that might provoke China. A limited war fitted Johnson's style of politics, but the analogy was not very good. The Soviets and Chinese were not so deeply involved in Vietnam as in Korea. There were no dominoes to fall in the first war except South Korea. North Korean aggression was more overt than North Vietnamese action. The Geneva treaties of 1954 had called for subsequent nationwide elections, which the government of South Vietnam, with American blessing, refused to hold, knowing that it would lose. The government of South Korea and its army were far more competent than in the South Vietnamese case. The greatest difference, however, to the White House, was that Vietnam was seen as a war of national liberation inspired by the larger communist nations. This belief was added to the Korean analogy to make it more persuasive. However, Johnson must have understood at the outset that the American people would not tolerate a long war. Disenchantment with the stalemated war elected Dwight Eisenhower in 1952. So Johnson appears to have hoped for a short war in which the North Vietnamese were forced to the negotiating table. He did not look at history closely enough.

JOHNSON'S EXECUTIVE STYLE

The argument here is that Johnson continued to act as a Senate leader when president. Fred Greenstein and John Burke, two presidential scholars, make the most persuasive case.[24] Johnson consulted widely, often one on one, and held policy decisions close to his chest until he was ready to act. Collegial discussion in which ideas competed was not part of his repertoire. The discussions of July were not about whether to go but how far to go. He would intimidate and shut out critics, as he did with Humphrey and Fulbright. But he listened to Russell, Mansfield, Ball, and others, along the way. But there was no careful analysis of the consequences of choices at critical forks in the road: sending marines to guard airfields, strategic bombing of rural North Vietnam, or the possibility of a long ground war in July 1965. The failure of the French to win over the rebel armies was dismissed without serious analysis. Knowledge of Vietnamese history was virtually nil, especially about the long rivalry between Vietnam and China. Johnson's advisers did not serve him well. Bundy was as much an advocate as he was a guardian of the president's choices. McNamara was ignorant of Vietnam, knew little of military strategy, and saw himself as a manager who could move the war machine in the directions the president wished. Dean Rusk, having been at Oxford in the 1930s and assistant secretary of state for the Far East during Korea, was a rigid advocate of defense against encroachment of one nation against another. The three worked hard to keep George Ball away from the president and to prevent meetings in which Ball's dissent was openly discussed.

Robert McNamara completely recanted in his 1995 book.[25] He reproached himself for resisting Ball's attempts to open up debate. For example, he had complained at the time that one Ball paper—which he, Bundy, and Rusk had savaged in a meeting with Ball—was not well staffed. Ball had to work alone on it without State Department help. McNamara later wrote that the paper should immediately have been given a thorough staff analysis and taken to the president. He and Rusk had resisted any such meeting with the president at the time for fear that dissent would widen, and Bundy had complied. McNamara acknowledged that the domino theory was never analyzed for its validity. He blamed himself for the failure to analyze the idea of fighting against guerrillas in jungles using conventional armed forces as in Korea and World War II. He could not understand, in retrospect, why he had not challenged the idea. He recalled that the president had kept military and economic advisers away from each other, not wishing for there to be discussion about the costs of the war. These are hard insights from a man who considered himself an expert in policy analysis. McNamara eventually lost confidence that the United States could prevail in Vietnam and made that clear to the president in 1967. In due course he was sent to the presidency of the World Bank. One of his strong attributes was loyalty to the president, not only to Johnson but also to the office. He could not bring himself to resist accepted policy until the end.

Richard Neustadt and Ernest May, writing as advocates for the uses of history for policy analysis, found Johnson wanting. He slid into decisions, perhaps with personal agony, but without sufficient forethought. Doers like Johnson and his advisers are not inclined to reexamine their implicit assumptions because they must make decisions under the pressure of time and events. Historical analogies are thus helpful for organizing their thinking and, once in place, are not easily challenged. A conscious effort must be made to challenge consensus. The focus is usually on facts or competing interests and less on guiding concepts. Neustadt and May think that a few studies, for example, of the French experience, might have provided a caution. Humphrey's memo to the president predicting domestic turmoil from a long war was dismissed crudely. A good analysis would have asked Johnson where he would be in 1968 in comparison to where Truman was in 1952. But busy, practical men are in competition with each other, fear to yield, and have great self-confidence. Neustadt and May know this and hope for analysis only at the margins. No one in the White House did this analysis for Johnson perhaps because he did not want it done.

The hard, unanswerable question is whether better policy analysis could have caused Johnson and his lieutenants to question their own assumptions. It seems unlikely given their strong beliefs, which, in fact, precluded further analysis. Was the president the key here? His style did not help. Nor was he a man who made a big investment in the content of policy, as we saw with the development of the Great Society. Had he pursued hard questions, his top advisers surely would have responded.

Domestic Politics

Burke and Greenstein claim that Johnson was not constrained by politics in late 1964 and early 1965. He had just won an election with 60 percent of the popular vote as the peace candidate. Public opinion about Vietnam was uncertain, and certainly confused. Few members of Congress had taken hard-and-fast views, and many were skeptics about the American commitment. Johnson might have been able to reduce the American role in the civil war had he attempted to do so. The answer to that, of course, is that Johnson did not want to do that. He always regarded withdrawal or neutralization in favor of the Viet Cong and North Vietnam as signs of failure.

The counterargument is that domestic politics did not give Johnson such latitude. Leslie Gelb and Richard Betts, prominent political scientists, argue that the political system "worked" before, during, and after Johnson's presidency in that the long-standing policy of containing communism was followed, elite and popular opinion accepted compromise in that a middle path was taken in pursuing the war, and all important views were considered without illusion about the odds for success.[26] All five presidents, from Truman to Nixon, were constrained by the requirement to contain communism, and any deviation might be punished politically, so they feared. Democratic politics are not congenial to unpopular action in the short term in order to achieve long-term goals. Thus, Johnson's inability to extricate the United States at key turning points was due less to the failure of analysis than to domestic politics. Johnson had to delay for all of 1964, he thought, in order to be reelected. He could not risk an uproar in Congress in that year over Vietnam for fear that passage of the domestic programs that would win reelection for him would be denied. The same constraint held for the first half of 1965, as the education, health, and civil rights bills were working their way through Congress. It was not so much what people thought about Vietnam but about what Republican opposition to a diminished role in Indo-China might do to his programs. Politicians worry most about latent opposition, and thus they avoid risks. By July 1965 the president was trapped by the consensus he had reaffirmed. He then became the prisoner of a war he could not afford to lose but could not win. Johnson believed that the supposed "loss" of China to communism in 1949 had poisoned American domestic politics since that time, leading to Republican charges of communists in government and softness on communism at the top. He feared critics on the right far more than critics on the left because they could ignite the public more easily. His objective was always defensive: not to "lose" South Vietnam. It was never to win the war. He fought the military off, time and time again, when they wanted to bomb northern targets that he thought might widen the war.

Johnson's awareness of the trade-offs between too much and too little war required him to stay in the center. They also required him to muffle his intentions in order to keep both hawks and doves off balance. This means that his policies often seemed contradictory, which they were. He had to tread what he thought was a narrow path. Gelb and Betts are correct to say that the political system worked because the politics and policy of the center were adhered to throughout. But could the center have been changed? Neustadt and May report that their students had difficulty writing a speech for Johnson to have given in July 1965 justifying nonintervention in Vietnam. The politics were difficult. This brings us to our final insights.

Johnson the Political Man

Lyndon Johnson's actions were all of a piece. He always believed that his task as a politician was to win agreement among contending parties. Johnson sought coherence among his beliefs, his management of advisory processes, and domestic politics. That search, in each case, was to discover a potential consensus and then seal agreement. This was his greatest skill, and effective politicians play to their skills. But skills also have deficits. Johnson was not a policy expert who wanted to learn about details. He probed his advisers, listened to his former congressional colleagues, took soundings of opinion, and then wove it all into politically feasible positions. He could expand consensus, as he did in civil rights legislation and other domestic programs, but the historical tide was running with him in these cases. The Vietnam situation was far more volatile, and therefore his words and actions lacked the coherence of his domestic agenda.

Each of the prior three explanations takes us only part of the way. This is because Johnson's beliefs, management style, and political craftsmanship were mutually reinforcing. But no one theory by itself can fully explain the larger picture. Johnson was a brilliant broker politician who knew how to find unity in disagreement. At times he could transcend brokered agreements into creative moral leadership. Vietnam was not such a case. He was not the man to call for a complete reexamination of the American role in Southeast Asia. He was a man of the center. But the story that follows is of the center failing to hold.

Was Johnson an event-making or eventful leader in regard to Vietnam? He could be said to have been eventful in his failure to challenge a political consensus that South Vietnam must be defended. He did not want to face the hard politics of Republican criticism were he to withdraw or try to negotiate without fighting. He remembered how the supposed "loss of China" had weakened Truman's presidency. But he also should have been mindful of how the military stalemate in Korea damaged Truman. He seems to have persuaded himself that the United States could prevail in Vietnam. To admit otherwise was to admit failure, something Johnson could not do. His very identity was at stake. He therefore took the leap into the void and thereby became an event-making president in aspiration who overreached and ultimately lost his effectiveness.

Chronology of the War

The American army and marines fought well on the ground from 1966 to 1968 and were able to defeat North Vietnamese forces on numerous occasions, but armies and supplies kept coming in from the north, and by 1968 there was only a military stalemate, which the North Vietnamese could sustain longer than the Americans. Johnson's stance did not change as he held to a middle path between hawks and doves, seeming to veer more against hawks, including the Joint Chiefs of Staff, who would escalate, without yielding to the demands from the peace movement to withdraw.

Johnson also became more defensive. He derided critics and stopped meeting with them, calling many of them communists. The war became a matter
of personal vindication. He would spend meetings in the Oval Office on
other topics lamenting his lack of support on the war. He continued to fear
that the Kennedys were out to get him especially after Robert Kennedy
was elected to the Senate in 1966 and turned against the war. There were
numerous reports that his top advisers were afraid of him and therefore
kept their ideas to themselves.

By 1967 Robert McNamara knew that he had miscalculated. On May
19 he wrote the president a memo in which he said that there was no prospect for either victory or negotiation. He recommended that only small
increments of forces be sent to Vietnam with a ceiling eventually placed
on the number. The army of South Vietnam should be pushed to do more
fighting. Bombing should be restrained and a political settlement should
be sought. The memo angered Johnson, and the Joint Chiefs of Staff fired
back their own paper recommending the invasion of the North as well as
Laos and Cambodia, and bombing of railroads from China. McNamara
then prompted a CIA report to the effect that the bombing was not effective
in preventing infiltration and that the domino theory could be questioned.
Johnson never showed the report to anyone.

McNamara tried again in a memorandum to Johnson on November
1 in which he called for a cap on ground forces, a halt to bombing, and
gradual shifting of the brunt of fighting to the South Vietnamese. This
was the "breaking point" with Johnson, who sent him to the World Bank
soon after.

On January 31, 1968, during the Tet New Year pause in fighting, the
North Vietnamese attacked a large number of cities in the South in hopes of
driving the Americans out. The fighting was intense for a month and made
dramatic television pictures as cities seemed to be consumed by flames. The
North sent in 84,000 men and lost about half that number. Their army was
decimated and the offensive was a failure. But the impression in the United
States was one of shock and realization that the United States had not found
a way to win the war. In the aftermath, General Westmoreland requested
an additional 200,000 troops with the support of the Joint Chiefs and the
opposition of Secretary McNamara, who was still in office. Johnson asked
Clark Clifford, the secretary of defense designate, to assess alternatives, and
a team went to work.

By this time the Democrats were deeply divided between hawks and
doves. Liberals in Congress openly attacked the president on the war and
called for less spending for the military and more for social programs. An

antiwar movement developed outside party politics. Democrats were divided, and Republicans grew more hawkish, insisting that Johnson listen to the military and win the war.

Public support for Johnson declined from just under 75 percent in mid-1965 to less than 50 percent in the spring of 1968. Tet was the shock that finally turned the public against the war as it was being fought, although many of the negative responses called for escalation to victory. Senator Eugene McCarthy, a critic of the war, almost defeated the president in the New Hampshire presidential primary in early March and many of his supporters were hawks. After McCarthy's victory, Senator Robert F. Kennedy entered the presidential race as a dove. Opinion in the middle was disappearing. Johnson began to realize that he could not meet Westmoreland's request and sustain the war as he was fighting it. Nor was he willing to escalate. Westmoreland's request was rejected. Richard Russell told the president that there could be no increased appropriations for the war unless the fight was taken to the North dramatically. The CIA experts on Vietnam confirmed that the war was being lost. Dean Rusk, the one adviser whom Johnson had always fully trusted, came up with a plan to keep U.S. armies in place, stop the bombing, and negotiate. There appears to have been a good deal of open debate within the White House in the spring months of 1968. Johnson was now listening because he saw that the political environment had changed.

He withdrew from the race for the presidency in a speech to the nation on March 31, 1968. He said that he hoped that his withdrawal would permit him to have a free hand, apart from presidential politics, to negotiate with the North Vietnamese and he called on them to do so. They agreed on April 3, and negotiations were planned to begin in Paris. Fifty-seven percent of the public gave the president their approval. Johnson had wanted a consensus that would not hold.

CONCLUSION

How does Johnson measure up in terms of our questions about presidential leadership?

Context and Contingencies

The times were ripe for the domestic reform idea that had been developing in the 1950s and Kennedy's short presidency. Kennedy would have been a reform president had he lived and been reelected. The opportunities for leadership were there for Johnson. Vietnam was another matter. There was a legacy but no policy and seeming intractability. The contingencies were stark: withdraw or increase the commitment.

Talents and Skills

It is unusual for a president to have the great personal knowledge of congressional leaders and the institutions that Johnson enjoyed. If knowledge is a skill, he had it in profusion and he used it to the maximum. He knew how to read people and situations and was a political realist in understanding how far he could go in wringing support from Congress. He was also a master at persuasion and intimidation.

He was much less sure of himself in foreign policy and perhaps relied too much on his advisers, all of whom had impressive credentials. Can we say that he was prudent? He was in the sense that he fought a limited war and tried to stay in the center of politics and policy. But he was not prudent in his refusal for the longest time to admit that he was fighting a losing game.

Did He Make a Difference?

Johnson was both event making and eventful. He followed the paths set by Kennedy in domestic and foreign policy, especially until he was elected in his own right. And yet he brought personal ambition for greatness and great ability to his work that Kennedy lacked, and as a result, he achieved more than Kennedy would have done in domestic policy.

Historians will debate whether Johnson was swept into war in 1964 and 1965 by the confluence of events that could not be reversed. It would have taken great political courage to have scaled down the American role in Vietnam from 1963 to 1965. He was clearly more skeptical about the commitment than any of his advisers except George Ball. But he went ahead. Any departure from established policy in Vietnam might have threatened the continuation of the Great Society. The Great Society was Johnson's claim to greatness and to event-making stature. But the most important measures had passed by mid-1965. Johnson might have tempered both the domestic program and the war. He had promised that American boys would not fight in Vietnam in 1964. But he was a realistic politician rather than a prudent one. He wanted too much of everything, and vainglory overrode prudence. Once the war was fully underway, he engaged in deception about how it was going and closed himself off from criticism. He could not stand the thought of opposition, but he eventually lost his presidency as a consequence.

Effectiveness

Johnson was a supremely effective president in domestic policy. He knew how to work the Congress to get what he wanted because of years of experience in doing just that. The sheer force of his virtuosity captured the imagination of the American people and ensured his election in 1964.

There will be much debate among historians as to whether he lost his political touch in regard to Vietnam. He tried to be politically astute by fighting a limited war, concealing the costs, and overstating the case for war rhetorically. He eventually became trapped by his own rhetoric. Judgment is dependent upon the initial commitments made. Once Johnson was on the military path, with all the forces that set in motion, at home and in Vietnam, it was very hard for him to reverse himself. He was not a man to admit failure. One must judge him to have been an ineffective president in regard to Vietnam, not only because his initial decisions to intervene may have been flawed, but that he persisted in them until forced to reverse himself at the very end.

BIBLIOGRAPHICAL ESSAY

The best general biography is by Robert Dallek, *Flawed Giant, Lyndon Johnson and His Times 1961–1973* (1998). He captures Johnson's boldness and richness of personality, seeing deficiencies of personality and yet accepting Johnson's great achievements. Doris Kearns's early biography, *Lyndon Johnson and the American Dream* (1976), based on her personal experience with Johnson in the White House and as one of the authors of his presidential memoir, has been criticized for being too psychoanalytic in her analysis of the legacy of his childhood. I do not share this criticism. No matter what the causes in his early life, Johnson was a tortured man who was desperate to be loved and who sought love all his life. She captures the tragedy of this fact very well. Paul Conkin has written a very workmanlike biography, which explains Johnson's political nature quite well. See *Big Daddy from the Pedernales: Lyndon Baines Johnson* (1986). Robert Caro's *Master of the Senate* (2002) on Johnson as the Senate leader continues Caro's critical assessment of Johnson the man seen in the previous volumes. But he does describe and acknowledge Johnson's legislative genius in the passage of the 1957 civil rights bill. Joseph A. Califano Jr.'s *The Triumph and Tragedy of Lyndon Johnson, The White House Years* (1991) is a portrait more than a biography, but he gives us the man he worked with and admired with level accuracy. Johnson's own presidential memoir, *The Vantage Point, Perspective of the Presidency 1963–1969* (1971), which he oversaw rather than wrote, does a very good job of explaining how he felt about his leadership and decisions.

There is some rationalization after the fact, but the reasons that Johnson gives for his actions are surely what he understood them to be at the time. However, he took out all the color, despite the pleading of his ghostwriters.

The two volumes of Johnson telephone conversations edited by Michael Beschloss are invaluable for filling in the facts in particular episodes and in the descriptions of how Johnson worked with members of Congress, particularly the Senate, and his immediate associates. See *Taking Charge* (1997) and *Reaching for Glory* (2001). A future volume covering all of the Vietnam years will surely be similarly rich. The oral histories in the LBJ Library at the University of Texas, *Oral Histories of the Johnson Administration*, overseen by Robert Lester, are extremely rich. Jonathan Rosenberg and Zachary Karabell have edited a superb analysis of telephone calls and conversations of Kennedy and Johnson policymaking on civil rights, along with a very good narrative, in the first volume of the series of presidential recordings to come from the Miller Center of Public Affairs at the University of Virginia. See *Kennedy, Johnson, and the Quest for Justice: The Civil Rights Tapes* (2003). William Doyle, *Inside the Oval Office* (1999), and John Prados *The White House Tapes* (2003), add other material of value.

Bruce Altschuler has written the best book about public opinion surveys and Johnson. See *LBJ and the Polls* (1990). Benjamin Page and Robert Shapiro have depicted the relation of changing public opinion about the Vietnam War to Johnson's actions. See *The Rational Public: Fifty Years of Trends in America's Policy Preferences* (1992). Lawrence Jacobs and Robert Shapiro have added to this analysis in an article showing that Johnson persisted in policy despite negative public opinion. See "Lyndon Johnson, Vietnam, and Public Leadership: Rethinking Realist Theory of Leadership," *Presidential Studies Quarterly* (September 1999).

The literature on domestic policy is too vast to be mastered so I cite only the few books that were most helpful to me. Erwin Hargrove and Samuel Morley's interviews with Walter Heller, Gardner Ackley, and Arthur Okun, Johnson's chief economists, are firsthand descriptions from expert participants. The book is *The President and the Council of Economic Advisers* (1984). Herbert Stein's history of economic policymaking, *Presidential Economics, the Making of Economic Policy from Roosevelt to Clinton* (3d rev. ed. 1994) is very good. James L. Sundquist's analysis of the relations of politics to policy, *Politics and Policy: The Eisenhower, Kennedy, and Johnson Years* (1968), carries the reader from Kennedy through Johnson expertly. Sundquist's edited depiction of the war on poverty, *On Fighting Poverty: Perspectives from Experience* (1969) and the study by David Zarefsky, *President Johnson's War on Poverty* (1986), set out the events clearly. Theodore Lowi supplies a trenchant criticism of the whole idea in *The End of Liberalism: The Second Republic of the United States* (2d ed. 1979). Good descriptions of civil rights politics and legislation are provided by Hugh Davis Graham, *The Civil Rights Era: Origins and Development of National Policy 1960–1972* (1990). Charles and Barbara Whalen, *The Longest Debate: A Legislative History of the 1964 Civil Rights Act* (1985), Robert Loevy, *To End All Segregation: The Politics of the Passage of the Civil Rights Act of 1964* (1990), and Russell Riley, *The Presidency and the Politics of Racial Inequality* (1999), are the best examples from a limited literature on the passage of civil rights legislation. Eugene Eidenberg and Roy D. Morey describe the making of educational policy in *An Act of Congress: The Legislative Process and the Making of Education Policy* (1969), and Theodore Marmor understands the passage of Medicare very well. See *The Politics of Medicare* (2d ed. 2000). Gareth Davies records the passage and decline of Great Society liberalism in *From Opportunity to Entitlement: The Transformation and Decline of Great Society Liberalism* (1996).

The literature on the Vietnam War is so great that one must work from the leading books, most of which supply primary sources as evidence. George McT. Kahin provides the best description of early commitments and gradual escalation up to the key 1965 decisions in *Intervention: How America Became Involved in Vietnam* (1986). David Kaiser covers the same ground, drawing on rich primary sources, in *American Tragedy: Kennedy, Johnson and the Origins of the Vietnam War* (2000). John Lewis Gaddis applies his analysis of the containment doctrine to Kennedy's and Johnson's choice in *Strategies of Containment* (2d rev. ed. 2005). John Burke and Fred Greenstein do the best possible job of analyzing Johnson's management of decision-making processes in *How Presidents Test Reality: Decisions on Vietnam, 1954 and 1965* (1989). David Barrett questions their thesis that Johnson manipulated his advisers in *Uncertain Warriors: Lyndon Johnson and His Vietnam Advisers* (1993). Richard Neustadt and Ernest May suggest in *Thinking in Time: The Uses of History for Decision Makers* (1986) that better policy analysis might have permitted hard questions to be raised that were, if asked, certainly not pursued. Leslie Gelb with Richard Betts in *The Irony of Vietnam: The System Worked* (2000), present the thesis that Johnson was trapped by domestic politics. Yuen Khong explains how the Korean analogy was uppermost in the mind of decision makers in *Analogies at War* (1992). Frederik Logevall presents a very interesting analysis of Johnson's fear of humiliation, personal and political, to explain the escalation in 1965 in *Choosing War: The Lost Chance for Peace and the Escalation of War in Vietnam* (1999). Robert McNamara's gigantic mea culpa stretches across two books *In Retrospect: The Tragedy and Lessons of Vietnam* (1997) and *Argument without End* (reissue 1999). David Di Leo in *George Ball: Vietnam and the Rethinking of Containment* (1991), and James Bill, *George Ball: Behind the Scenes in U.S. Foreign Policy* (1997) describe how George Ball saw the flaws in McNamara's approach to Vietnam policy that McNamara later acknowledged.

CHAPTER THREE

Richard M. Nixon

A Tragic Hero?

Aristotle's definition of a "tragic hero" was a great man who fell from a lofty position by virtue of a fundamental flaw in his character. King Oedepus in Sophocles's play, who gradually acknowledged unknown crimes in his own history, was such a hero even though he lost his power. Nixon fell from power because of flaws in his character, but he was not a fully "tragic hero" because he never acknowledged his flawed character or his crimes.

Kennedy, Johnson, and Nixon belonged to the political generation that believed that the United States could solve its problems. The nation had come through depression and war successfully, and the world seemed to beckon the achievement of what was often called the "American Century." These three presidencies shared a unique political era in which optimism gave way over time to uncertainty and, at the end, confidence in American institutions and their missions declined. But much was achieved domestically. Kennedy advocated the reforms that Johnson enacted and Nixon consolidated. It was a series of healthy political adjustments. By the same token, the tensions between the United States and the Soviet Union were brought from a high point to more of a modus vivendi as Nixon left office. The war in Vietnam was the tragedy of the time. The active American role began and ended in this period, and popular politics both empowered and ended the commitment. But the trauma to the nation continues to this day.

Richard Nixon entered the presidency as the liberal consensus on reform and intervention abroad was already broken. There was an opportunity for the construction of a Republican national coalition as Barry Goldwater had first envisioned in 1964. Nixon saw this more acutely than any other national politician. His 1968 run for the presidency appealed to the "silent majority" of middle Americans who felt that they had been left behind in the expansion of government on behalf of the poor and minorities, and who resented the new politics of protest and the counterculture of radical lifestyles among the young. The Democratic base in the South was eroding, and many blue-collar workers were angry about special treatment for minorities. Neither Nixon nor Hubert Humphrey, the vice president and Democratic candidate, had a plan to end the war beyond promising to do it, but at that point it was Johnson's war and Humphrey had difficulty breaking loose on his own.

The election did not produce a mandate. Nixon won 43 percent of the popular vote to Humphrey's 42.7 percent. George Wallace, the demagogic governor of Alabama who ran as an independent, won 13.5 percent and carried five Southern states. It was clear to Nixon that to be reelected, he needed to win those Wallace votes. His initial obstacle was the comfortable Democratic majorities in both houses. It took time, but the new president eventually created a political strategy behind a program of his own in domestic and foreign policy. He would seek stability in relations with the Soviet Union, and eventually China, in hopes of securing help in ending the war in Vietnam. He would reduce American commitments abroad in a realistic fashion. At home, he would consolidate and rationalize the programs of the Great Society. It was a promising start from a moderate Republican. The potential was there for a significant eventful presidency. The Johnson administration had begun to consider the consolidation and simplification of Great Society programs that Nixon was to continue. The economic "stagflation" that Nixon inherited required post-Keynesian remedies that any president would have attempted. The war in Vietnam had somehow to be ended. Continuity underlay policy aside from political rhetoric. Nixon himself had always been harsh in partisan rhetoric but more or less mainstream in domestic and foreign policy.

Biography

Richard Nixon's childhood was emotionally impoverished. His father, Frank Nixon, a self-employed grocer in Whittier, California, was a man of violent temper from whom Richard learned to stay away for fear of the strap. His mother, Hannah, spent much of her time nursing two ill brothers, for a time in Arizona, both of whom died as boys. Nixon later told a biographer that she only kissed him once. She never told anyone that she loved them, but he added, "she didn't have to." Bryce Harlow, a senior adviser to the president and an experienced observer of politicians, told the journalist Tom Wicker that Nixon as a young person "was hurt very deeply by somebody.... Hurt so badly he never got over it and never trusted anybody again." Henry Kissinger told Wicker: "He would have been a great man, had somebody loved him."[1]

One cannot discover the origins of this hurt, but out of it he developed a strong ambition to make his mark and be someone in the world. It was more than just the common ambition to rise from the lower middle class. He wanted to be an important historical figure. After he lost the race for the governor of California in 1962, he told a New York law partner that one must live a life of "great purpose" and must never give up that purpose. At the time, after two successive defeats, he was planning to run again for the presidency. It was the only place where he could put his stamp on history. He never liked popular politics but saw it as a means to larger ambitions. After he left the wartime navy, he found his vocation in an invitation by Whittier businessman to run for Congress in 1946 as a Republican. He also found a style that worked politically—that of attack. Charging that his incumbent Democratic opponent was "soft on communism," he easily won and was carried into a newly Republican Congress. His voting record was moderate, and he was an internationalist. But his reputation came with appointment to the House Un-American Activities Committee. The matter at hand was an investigation of Alger Hiss, a one-time high State Department official who denied that he had passed secret documents during the war to Soviet spies. Nixon did the hard work on the committee of finding the evidence to prove Hiss to be guilty of perjury. This made him a hero among Republican conservatives, but anathema to many liberals in public life who had stood behind Hiss and saw his prosecution as a witch hunt. Nixon was unfairly grouped with Republican demagogues who were tearing apart the Truman administration in search of communist spies.

Nixon's defeat of Representative Helen Gahagan Douglas for the Senate in 1950 was again characterized by false charges of communist sympathies.

After only a brief Senate career, he became Dwight Eisenhower's vice president. His principle job was to campaign for Republicans while the general president stayed above politics. He contributed little to policymaking, but his voice appears to have been one of moderate pragmatism.

Personality

After his defeat in the 1960 presidential election, Nixon wrote a memoir, *Six Crises*, in which he described how he had handled difficult political crises. The events were described as crises because they were episodes of personal testing: the Hiss case, the challenge to his possession of an expense fund from businessmen disclosed when he was a vice presidential candidate, Eisenhower's heart attack when he was vice president, an impromptu debate in a model American kitchen with Khrushchev in Moscow, an attack by rampaging students on his car in Venezuela, and the 1960 presidential campaign. These events were not really crises, but this was less important to him than his way of handling them. He described his effort to get control of his emotions, the self-discipline required to achieve calm, coolness in action, and then the emotional letdown following success. It is a picture of a man who is uncertain of himself and must exercise great self-discipline in order to enter the fight. It is not a picture of acting emotionally in a crisis. Nixon was often charged with that, but, even though he easily flew off the handle and issued extreme orders that he never expected to be obeyed, his response to decisions was cool and calculating, but almost always after a period of inner turmoil.

This account will focus on two Richard Nixons: the one who wished to be an important historical figure, and the one who was unable to trust other people. The first is most important for understanding his policy leadership. Although Nixon had not been a policy innovator, he burned to be one. He wanted to be an event-making leader to satisfy his need to be someone of great achievement and overcome his insecurities. The second factor is crucial for understanding his self-destruction in what came to be called Watergate, but which was foreshadowed in earlier actions. In both aspects of his nature, Nixon always seemed to be searching for an equanimity that he could not find. His greatest triumphs were never enough and were followed by periods of darkness in which he projected his own inner unhappiness onto others. He had to win but it was never enough. He could not appease his unconscious demons.

The President

Nixon's first interest was foreign policy, and he traveled the world in the years out of office and thought much about new possibilities. He saw clearly that the United States could not intervene all over the world to protect small nations from aggression or turmoil. America must attempt to create a stable balance among major world powers that might permit a lessening of foreign adventures on all sides. He wanted Soviet help with North Vietnam and had long thought that China should be brought into the international order from its isolation. He did not foresee an elegant new world order at first, but acted slowly step by step until, at the end of the day, he could talk of "détente," meaning a period of stability in world affairs. He acted opportunistically as he went along. His primary goal was to end the U.S. role in the war in Vietnam. He knew that his chances for reelection depended on it. But he was not simply willing for the United States to withdraw, as many were demanding. Such withdrawal, in his view, would weaken American credibility with allies and the major powers and make it more difficult for him to lead from strength in the world. There was nothing new here; he was carrying Johnson's standard.

Nixon had hoped at the outset that domestic policy could be delegated to cabinet officers with little involvement on his part. He wanted to make bold moves, perhaps heroic actions, and these are seldom found in domestic affairs. President Charles de Gaulle of France once contemptuously described domestic policy as having to do with "the price of milk" and Nixon liked to compare himself to Winston Churchill and de Gaulle as an actor on the world stage. In his first months as president, he told his chief of staff, Bob Haldeman, as Haldeman's diary reports it: "He feels he should be more aloof, inaccessible, mysterious, i.e. de Gaulle feels overexposure detracts from impact. Shouldn't be too chummy."[2] But as time developed, he came to see a major role for himself as a domestic policy leader. His political goal was to fashion a new Republican coalition, and his domestic policies were congruent with that purpose. He would not reject the Great Society, but would tighten its programs and set limits—for example, in civil rights and welfare. He would attempt to reduce the authority of Congress and the federal bureaucracy over social programs and transfer responsibility to the states and localities.

Domestic Policy

Nixon told his speechwriter, William Safire, that Republicans were supposed to manage things after the Democrats broke new ground, but "we have bigger things to do." He often referred disdainfully to Ohio State football as "three yards and a cloud of dust." He wanted to throw the long ball. This matched his conception of himself as a dramatic leader. This attitude was not consistent with his hope that domestic policy could be delegated, and he learned early on that a domestic program would have to be stimulated and overseen by the White House. His two senior White House advisers, Arthur Burns, a Columbia University economist, and Daniel Patrick Moynihan, a Democrat from Harvard, clashed repeatedly—the one advising consolidation and management, the other suggesting new policy initiatives. As policy advisers floundered in disagreement, he eventually charged his White Housed counsel, John Ehrlichman, with coordinating the development of domestic policy. Ehrlichman's job was to make sure that all points of view got through to the president. Nixon would seal himself off from people, because he could not bear to face and have to settle personal conflicts, but he did not usually seal himself off from ideas. He liked to learn about debates on paper, send his ideas back on memos, and deal with others through key lieutenants. He handled legislative strategy the same way, so one cannot find an active face-to-face or persuasive president in stories of legislative politics. His role was strategic rather than tactical. He did not have the personal skills that would permit him to persuade and bargain. He did not respect members of Congress and met with members, including the leadership, as little as possible, relying on a few staff people to manage congressional relations.

Nixon did not have a great deal of confidence that government could solve social problems, and often said so privately. His first impulse was to attack the Great Society programs head on, but Moynihan persuaded him that the result would be a political firestorm.[3] Moynihan suggested that the president take a year to develop a new domestic program, but Nixon records that "I wanted action." Nixon's advisers had done a number of studies about reform of the national system of welfare, and Nixon saw an opportunity.

Welfare Reform

The New Deal program of Aid to Families with Dependent Children was intended as a temporary measure to cope with unemployment during the depression of the 1930s. But it grew and grew after World War II, especially in families without fathers—in part because welfare was denied to families with unemployed husbands. This contributed to the break up of families and made the problem worse. There were also a large number of intact families best described as "working poor" who could barely make it in the economy. Welfare had never been popular because of the American work ethic that deprecated malingerers and loafers. But as numbers of the unemployed and working poor grew, the conservative economist Milton Friedman invented the idea of the negative income tax in which the government would make payments to all people below a given poverty line whether working or not. Sargent Shriver had recommended the idea to Johnson, but organized labor opposed such a low-wage idea and favored increasing minimum wages. U.S. Secretary of Health, Education, and Welfare Wilbur Cohen, also opposed it, arguing that social programs could be legitimate only if they were universal and thus favored increases in Social Security benefits.

Nixon might not have taken up the issue, but Pat Moynihan, a longtime advocate of reform, intrigued the president's imagination with the example of Benjamin Disraeli, the nineteenth-century British conservative prime minister. Disraeli was known for stealing reform ideas, such as expansion of the voting rolls, from the opposition liberals and calling them his own, taking the political credit. The idea of "Tory men and Whig measures" appealed to Nixon because it was a surprise and a way to "throw the long ball." The growth in the number of welfare recipients put the issue on Nixon's desk. Taxpayers resented welfare. Governors had to pay the costs. Johnson's policy analysts had begun to explore new ideas, and some of them stayed to help formulate what became a welfare reform proposal. The result was a bill sent to Congress in October 1969 that included a minimum standard for welfare payments for needy adults and children in all states. The federal government would bear the cost. Social work bureaucracy that administered welfare at all levels of government was to be considerably reduced. The basic idea was distrust of bureaucracy and a belief that people could spend their money better than government could do it for them.

A number of different plans had gone into the mix. Moynihan had made his mark in the Johnson administration with his paper on the erosion of the black family and the consequent economic hardship that followed. The uneven standards of welfare payments by the states were a target of a preelection task force led by Richard Nathan. Arthur Burns opposed the plan in favor of a program of federal revenue sharing to the states so that governors might pay for welfare. He predicted that a guaranteed payment to all low-income people would expand the welfare rolls at great expense. But Nixon wanted the plan because it was bold and also because he needed the support of moderate and liberal congressional Republicans for his policy of gradual withdrawal from Vietnam and the new relaxed guidelines for desegregation of Southern schools. However, the plan had fatal political flaws. The large majority of states with payment levels above the proposed federal standards did not like the reduced federal support.

Southern members of Congress valued cheap labor in their region and were not about to act to help bring black people out of poverty. Organized labor wanted higher minimum wages and guaranteed jobs for the unemployed and feared that the plan might undermine existing wage levels. The National Welfare Rights Organization feared that it would lose its constituency if poor people were better off. Northern blacks did not see that they would be better off and might be worse off. Last of all, many liberal reformers, including church leaders, were ready to believe the worst about Richard Nixon. They were easily persuaded by arguments that Nixon meant to reduce welfare levels all round. Republican conservatives were not going to give away taxpayers' money to the poor, who ought to be able to pull themselves up by their own hard work. The plan fell between stools of right and left with not enough people in the middle prepared to take risks to try something really innovative.

Nixon did not help in his television address on August 8, 1969, in which he introduced the plan. He used conservative language for fear of a popular reaction against the increase of welfare. There was no mention of expanding welfare rolls. He expounded the work ethic, promising the reduction of welfare. "What America needs is not more welfare but more workfare." He distorted his own plan to make the public think that welfare and work were opposites, when in fact the program would combine the two. He also promised that no benefits would be lowered, which was inconsistent with a national standard. He tried to obscure the contradictions within his own plan between adequacy of income and the need for work incentives. If guaranteed income were too high, there might be less incentive to work. But income had to be high enough to prevent the return to welfare. It proved to be difficult to find the right balance. The public response was positive, with 65 percent of a national sample telling a Gallup poll that they supported the plan.

The president's proposal threw both congressional conservatives and liberals into confusion, splitting each camp. Moderate to liberal Democrats and Republicans got behind the plan. Die-hard conservative Republicans and Southern Democrats were opposed. Wilbur Mills, the chairman of the Ways and Means Committee, and John Byrnes, the ranking minority member, supported the plan, and Burns was able to rally enough House Republicans to vote with reform Democrats for the bill to pass the House on April 16, 1970. Nixon provided little personal leadership. His aides reported that he would talk with members but was reluctant to ask for their votes. He relied heavily on Bryce Harlow, his congressional assistant, who knew the House well, and Gerald Ford, the Republican minority leader.

The Senate was a different story. Russell Long, the chairman of the Senate Finance Committee, a Democrat from Louisiana, never let the bill out of committee. He wanted strict work requirements without increasing the cost of existing programs. The White House had assumed that the more liberal Senate would pass the bill, but the Southerners were not about to do this. The Finance Committee eventually killed the bill, and efforts to revive it by amendments to other legislation failed. By November when the bill was finally killed, public support had vanished. Governors and mayors were the beneficiaries of Nixon's own program of general revenue sharing and needed the money less. Arthur Burns's own cautious idea had become the eventual reality.

Nothing happened for a time, and then in 1972 Democratic presidential candidate George McGovern proposed a $1,000 annual payment to every citizen by the federal government. Nixon saw more political benefit in attacking McGovern than in promoting his Family Assistance Plan and would not cooperate with Democratic senators who were trying to revive his plan. McGovern eventually dropped the idea after it was ridiculed, but welfare reform had seen its day. The public had always wanted cuts in welfare more than assistance to low-income people. In the end politicians were unwilling to make the unpopular choice of helping the poor and also expanding the coverage and cost of the program. It was difficult to explain and it went against the grain of the American work ethic. Neither Nixon nor his liberal opponents were prepared to educate the people about what might be gained. Nixon's effort at event making was not accompanied by a strong personal commitment on his part.

However, failure was not complete. Congress created new income benefits for the elderly, blind, and disabled by additions to the Social Security Act in 1972, in addition to the initiation of cost-of-living increases for Social Security recipients. The program of food stamps for the poor was expanded. Social welfare spending as a whole went from $55 billion in 1970 to $132 billion in 1975. Federal subsidies for the purchase of homes by the poor were created. The Nixon administration cooperated with congressional Democrats during Nixon's first term to do all this.

Revenue Sharing

One response to the frustration of legislative politics was to seek ways to send money directly to the states, in the form of general revenue sharing, and to consolidate Great Society social programs with a number of specific categorical missions into broad block grants in a given policy area, and send them to states for implementation. Both Congress and the federal bureaucracy would be largely bypassed in the process. Walter Heller, chair of Johnson's Council of Economic Advisers, had suggested general revenue sharing of surplus dollars from taxes with the states, but Lyndon Johnson was not about to take money from starving social programs at the end of his tenure. A Nixon task force recommended block grants to the states for social programs with latitude for their local implementation. Arthur Burns liked the idea, but Nixon thought that it lacked political sex appeal. However, as welfare reform languished, John Ehrlichman revived the idea at the same time that Nixon's economists were telling him that the economy needed a fiscal stimulus. The president began to see revenue sharing as preferable to increasing funds for categorical programs in different policy areas. He therefore proposed a program of general and special revenue sharing. The states were to receive general funds to use as they wished. Block grants for education, urban development, transportation, job training, rural development, and law enforcement were also proposed. Few strings were attached to the latter. Nixon did not tell his cabinet about the proposal for fear of opposition. No department head wants to lose control of his or her programs.

These ideas went against the grain of the "interest group liberalism" that grew out of the Great Society categorical programs. Members of Congress, both Democrats and Republicans, guarded these programs jealously for the benefit of their constituents. There was fear in Congress that governors and mayors, the political rivals of members of Congress, would use such funds for their own political benefit. Organized interest groups were even more vociferous in defense of categorical programs.

General revenue sharing eventually passed Congress, but special revenue sharing block grants did not receive a full hearing until late in the Nixon and early Ford administrations. Congressional Democrats then collaborated with the White House to create block grant programs in employment training and social services in which the federal government set goals, with minimal regulation, and provided evaluation research to help providers at the local level. There was a continuity of these ideas with the dissatisfactions of overregulated social programs from the Great Society. It was a smooth and useful transition in the political logic of federal programs. Welfare reform and revenue sharing were all of a piece for the simplification of bureaucratic programs. It was a search for a middle ground, which followed the collapse of Johnson's centrist coalition, but Nixon had to form ad hoc congressional coalitions. Nothing was automatic. It was effective eventful leadership.

A Continued Search for a Republican Center

Two other major policy strategies in Nixon's first term were in environmental policy and civil rights. In both cases Nixon reached beyond his own personal beliefs, which were quite conservative, to hybrid conservative/liberal policies and politics. The results were somewhat better than with welfare reform.

Environmental Policy

Nixon had never been interested in the environment and believed that most people did not care about it. But the national movement to protect the environment and limit pollution had surged in the Johnson years, and Nixon had to face the fact. New legislation had been developed and passed in Congress to ensure clean air and water. Senator Edmund Muskie, a Democrat from Maine and a likely contender for the presidential nomination in 1972, was the chief entrepreneur for environmental regulation. Nixon could not fight Muskie openly in such a popular cause, and indeed he joined him. On the advice of his own council on executive reorganization, he carried through the creation of the Environmental Protection Agency in 1970 to administer most of the recent environmental laws. On the same council's advice, the Bureau of the Budget was legally transformed into the Office of Management and Budget, with greater attention to departmental and agency management of programs. This included new authority to test proposed regulatory programs against cost-benefit analyses so that regulation did not reach in cost beyond expected benefits. This was intended as a check on excessive regulation. For example, why push for 100 percent pure water, when 95 percent clean water would protect the public? Nixon, as a good Republican, was less than enthusiastic about regulation if it impaired economic development. He vetoed the Clean Water Act because it provided for many more waste treatment plants than he thought necessary. It was the pork barrel overflowing. Congress overrode the veto, and Nixon impounded the appropriated funds—a practice that he continued with other legislation until he lost in the federal courts.

Nixon's commitment to a clean environment was uncertain at best. He detested "extreme environmentalists," as he called them, but most environmental policy did not interest him and he deferred to John Ehrlichman's environmentally friendly recommendations. One sees the same pattern as with welfare reform. Nixon was all for innovation so long as the costs did not get out of hand. Republican conservatives were always shouting in his ear. He really had no party base behind him and had to work, sometimes at cross-purposes, with Democrats who saw his environmental policies as only half measures.

Civil Rights

Nixon had supported the civil rights laws of the 1960s. But he won the Republican nomination with the support of Senator Strom Thurmond of South Carolina and other Southern conservatives, who might otherwise have gone to Ronald Reagan. Thus, as president Nixon had to balance his own values with his political necessities. He chose a middle course in which he told the South that he was required as president to enforce court orders of school desegregation, but that he was opposed to the busing of school children to force integration. In 1968, 68 percent of black children in the South were in all-black schools, as opposed to 40 percent in the nation. But in May 1968 the Supreme Court gave the federal government the authority to cut off funds to school districts that lagged in de facto desegregation. The Justice Department was authorized to bring suits against such districts. Robert Finch, Nixon's first secretary of health, education, and welfare (HEW), was anxious to broaden the Republican appeal to minorities and assembled a liberal team in HEW to enforce the new policy. His Office of Civil Rights then issued orders to five Southern states to speed desegregation. This led to a conflict with John Mitchell, the attorney general, who wanted to win the Southern states for the Republicans. He moved to take over enforcement through Justice Department suits rather than administrative orders. Mitchell thought the adverse publicity would be less and that Southern governors were more likely to yield to the courts. Nixon sided with Mitchell. He particularly wanted the support of Mississippi senator John Stennis on particular defense matters at that time. White House aides invoked polls that revealed a popular fear across the nation that the administration was moving too fast on school desegregation. Nixon had offered federal funds for teacher training and school construction to facilitate Southern school desegregation. He got little political credit for his achievement and did not really want it because it conflicted with his goal of winning the South for himself and his party. He told Haldeman in the chief of staff's words: "Wants me to tell the staff P is a conservative, does not believe in integration, will carry out the law, nothing more."[4] On more than one occasion he asked Congress to pass laws forbidding mandatory busing of children across district lines in the search for integrated schools. He saw busing as unwarranted social engineering and predicted that it would cause more harm than good. This was certainly the view of many white parents who turned to private education, especially church schools.

Nixon faced the fact that the civil rights laws of the 1960s were unassailable in the courts. Affirmative action in employment and compensatory education in the schools for blacks were followed by the claims of women's groups and minorities of many kinds, including the disabled. It was a tide that Nixon could not stem as the courts shifted from the protection of individuals to group rights. He was not an opponent of these trends necessarily, but he did need to straddle contradictions to protect his own political base. This was apparent in the development of a policy for minority employment opportunities.

One creative experiment was the Philadelphia Plan, which promoted the hiring of minorities in the building trades. Lyndon Johnson began the plan and it was picked up by George Schultz, the secretary of labor who was a University of Chicago business economist and for whom Nixon had a high regard. Moynihan saw the plan as a companion to welfare reform, because it would provide jobs for those working their way off welfare. He saw the chronic unemployment of young black males as a ticking time bomb. The industrial unions had begun to desegregate, but the craft unions were often closed father-to-son lodges. The plan required federal contractors to set goals for hiring minorities in order to win contracts. Civil rights laws would not permit hiring quotas. But affirmative action would, thereby becoming part of civil rights law on a case-by-case basis. The plan was developed for Philadelphia and then extended to nine cities. Nixon saw it, in part, as a way to divide unions (which would oppose it) from civil rights activists, and thus split Democrats.

Contractors were to set their goals by percentages rather than absolute numbers. Thus, in five years blacks were to be 12 percent of workers in the building trades in Philadelphia. Contractors chose the targets and relied on the unions for compliance. But the federal General Accounting Office opposed the plan because targets were said to be disguised quotas. The Congress could never develop a coherent position because of conflicts between unions and civil rights adherents among Democrats. The National Association for the Advancement of Colored People (NAACP) attacked the Philadelphia Plan for relying on contractors and unions. They wanted federally imposed regulation and attacked Nixon because "hard hat" construction workers had supported his actions in Vietnam. He was accused of pandering to them. Again, the search for a middle way in policy faltered.

The Philadelphia Plan eventually proceeded but never with the scope that had been envisioned for it.

Taking Stock

Nixon's search for a middle way in domestic policy had to be a process of muddling through. The Democrats controlled Congress. The "conservative coalition" did not understand what he was trying to do with his hybrid measures. Nixon was attempting to move the country in a more conservative direction by shifting the political center somewhat to the right. At this point he gave up on Congress and decided to try to shape policy through executive authority. In 1971 he sent Congress a proposal for consolidation of all federal departments into a basic four categories: human resources, natural resources, economic affairs, and community development. The idea had been recommended by the Ash Commission on government reorganization. The idea was to create greater consolidation across programs in given policy areas, simplify government, and permit greater presidential control. Congressional jurisdictions in committees and subcommittees would also be reduced as programs were consolidated. Congress saw this, and the idea did not even receive committee hearings. Nixon was searching for ways to reduce the power of both Congress and the bureaucracy. This move toward the "administrative presidency" revealed Nixon's frustration with checks and balances. He wanted to govern from the top without the messy politics of give and take and compromise. This was clear in economic policymaking and the crucial decisions that he made.

Economic Policy

Nixon did not like economic science one bit. Murray Weidenbaum, a close economic adviser, remembered how the president's eyes would glaze over during economic policy discussions.[5] It all seemed so hopelessly incremental. He inherited a bad situation. The economy was overheated when Nixon entered the White House. The rate of inflation was 4.7 percent, the highest since the Korean War. Unemployment was low at 3.3 percent but wage increases were averaging 6.5 percent, and the nation had an adverse balance of foreign trade.[6] Nixon and his economic advisers knew that inflation had to come down but he was not about to risk the unemployment that he thought had cost him the 1960 election. The members of his Council of Economic Advisers were moderates who wished to move gradually against inflation without too much disruption. The chairman,

Paul McCracken, told the cabinet in a meeting just before the inauguration that the best way to reduce inflation was to restrict demand and bring
prices down slowly by tight federal budgets, and restricting the supply of
money through the Federal Reserve Board. He also recommended that
Nixon extend the 10 percent surcharge on income and corporate taxes
begun by Johnson. The hope was that inflation would level off as the
economy continued to grow. The difficulty in practice was that inflation
went up and not down in 1970 and 1971 as the productive side of the
economy weakened. The first signs of "stagflation"—simultaneous inflation
and unemployment—were emerging.

Herbert Stein, who succeeded McCracken in 1971, saw the administration caught in a period of transition in economic theory and practice.
The Johnson tax cuts had stimulated the economy into growth and higher
revenues. But the political will to fight the inflation that came with prosperity, and war, was weak. Economic theory had no remedies for "stagflation."
Prices and wages were high and neither business nor labor believed that the
government would risk a recession to bring them down. No one wanted to
take the drastic steps necessary to cool off the hot economy. The Kennedy/
Johnson economists had believed that they could "fine tune" the economy
into balance between inflation and recession by alternately balancing tight
with loose budgets, depending upon the danger at the time. This would
not work for Nixon because the drastic action required to bring down inflation might cause a recession, and stimulation of the economy to prevent
recession would only add to inflation. Nixon appointed Arthur Burns as
chairman of the Federal Reserve Board in 1969 but with reservations about
what Burns might do to fight inflation. His parting comment was "You see
to it: No recession." As Burns began to tighten the money supply, Nixon
directed Charles Colson, a master of "dirty tricks" in the White House, to
put out the false rumor that Burns had asked the OMB for a 50 percent
salary increase. This was untrue, and it revealed a pettiness and distrust of
others in the president.

Congress began to press for an "incomes policy" in which the administration would set up guidelines for prices and wages that business and labor
would be encouraged to follow. Nixon's economists had no confidence in
voluntary guidelines, which had failed under Johnson. George Meany, still
head of the AFL-CIO, was opposed to guidelines because the real wages
of workers had fallen with inflation. Nixon was busy cultivating Meany as
part of his plan to bring workers into the Republican camp. So he hesitated.
In 1970 the president had read a book by Richard Scammon and Benjamin
Wattenberg called *The Real Majority*, which posited that the blue-collar

vote was the key to an electoral swing between the parties. As unemployment rose in 1971 Nixon's popularity declined, and he grew more and more dissatisfied with his economic advisers. He found help in John Connally, a Texas Democrat and longtime associate of Lyndon Johnson, who had been secretary of the navy and governor of Texas. Connally was appointed secretary of the treasury and placed in charge of economic policy. Connally was a tall, handsome man who exuded confidence and power. Kissinger believed that Connally's self-assurance was Nixon's Walter Mitty image of himself. The president made it clear to his economic team that Connally was to lead it and be the public voice, and he soon developed the kind of one-on-one relationship with Connally that he worked out with Kissinger in foreign policy.

Connally's first bold step was to attack the unfavorable balance of trade by blaming foreign governments for protectionism. The CEA economists were unhappy, fearing that he would try to raise barriers to trade. But Connally had been persuaded within the Treasury Department that a devaluation of the dollar would increase exports and create more jobs. He was thinking politically in terms of fostering Nixon's new Republican coalition. The CEA still favored a steady policy of balancing inflation and recession, with some thought about devaluation of the dollar. But by August 1971 Herb Stein reported that the clamor was for a "nonfattening hot fudge sundae."[7] Nixon turned to Connally and asked him to develop a plan of action. Nixon required the forcefulness of a Connally to bring him to hard decisions. He later wrote that he was unprepared for Connally's boldness. But Connally, like the president, liked the "big play."[8]

The first idea was to detach gold from the dollar. The British had asked that £3 billion be converted into gold for their own purposes, and this caused fear of a run on American gold. Foreign nations held more American securities than could be redeemed by the gold in Ft. Knox. A dollar freed from gold would find its natural level in world markets. The entry of foreign goods into American markets would also be taxed and taxes on business were to be cut. Finally, wage and price controls would be imposed temporarily until economic growth could catch up with reduced inflation.

The larger economic team was hastily convened at Camp David for the weekend of August 13, 1971, and everyone was sworn to secrecy. Connally set out the plan, and no one raised hard questions. He had offered a decisive way out of unresolved quandaries. No expert economic or bureaucratic staff was present, nor had there been any preparatory staff work. No one asked how large the tax stimulus should be or its effect on the deficit. No questions were raised about how the new international economic system would look like once the postwar system of currencies pegged to the dollar vanished. The question of how to administer the freeze and when to stop it was not fully addressed. Nixon was not interested in such details.

The president announced the new policy on August 15, 1971. There was to be a ninety-day freeze on prices and wages overseen by an administrative board, the convertibility of the dollar into gold was suspended, there would be a 10 percent charge on all imports, a 4 percent cut in federal spending, the repeal of a 7 percent excise tax on cars, and an increase in personal income tax exemptions. The stock market jumped seventy-five points the next day, and the public approved by wide margins. But George Meany and organized labor were opposed. Nixon had to give up his hopes of bringing labor into his coalition as he acted to win reelection in the short term. In the fourth quarter of 1971 the inflation rate fell to less than 3 percent. Unemployment was 6 percent, but Nixon then accelerated spending in 1972 by 10 percent to bring it down. The Federal Reserve also expanded the money supply by 9 percent.

Critics accused Nixon and Arthur Burns, who was now the chairman of the Federal Reserve Board, of deliberately pumping up the economy in order to win the 1972 election. There may have been an element of truth in this. On the other hand, Stein thought that everyone failed to see the strength of the inflationary tide. They were trying to stimulate the economy without inflation but lacked the economic expertise necessary to know when and where to stop. No one could have predicted the inflation of worldwide food prices, or the boycott against the United States of oil producers in 1973 over unhappiness with the U.S. support for Israel in the Six Day War with Egypt. In retrospect Stein and McCracken thought that it made sense to cut the dollar loose from gold, but that wage and price controls were a mistake. The economy would have come into balance in time. Stein understood public unhappiness with an unstable economy, but also saw that no one made an effort to educate the public about the trade-offs inherent in economic policy. But Nixon was running for president. His economic policy was electioneering rather than either eventful or event making. He took some quick fixes to win an election and leave the legacy of stagflation to his successors.

FOREIGN POLICY

Nixon was determined to be a great statesman in foreign policy. He knew that the cold war had to be scaled back and that China had to be brought into normal international relations. He saw himself as a strategic thinker, and in this sense, event making. And the historical opportunity was ripe. But he was not sure how to create his grand vision and felt his way step by step as he addressed his primary problem: the war in Vietnam. Nixon was determined to secure the withdrawal of U.S. forces from Vietnam with "honor" rather than to permit the fall of the government of South Vietnam. He counted on the Soviets to help him with the development of a new U.S.-Soviet relationship. The word eventually coined for the new relationship was "détente," meaning stability and predictability in world politics. Neither Nixon, nor Henry Kissinger, his agent in foreign policy, was a "Wilsonian" who sought to expand democracy or human rights through American foreign policy. They were "realists" who sought stability in an imperfect world with a balance of power among the United States, Western Europe, the Soviet Union, Japan, and eventually China. Nixon also conceived of U.S. support for smaller, regional powers that might, as U.S. allies, keep the peace in their areas—thus the U.S. encouragement of Iran and Pakistan to develop military strength. An element of cold war thinking remained in the unwillingness of the United States to accept communist adventures in the third world.

Nixon at Guam announced part of this worldview on July 25, 1969, at a press conference. His idea eventually came to be called the Nixon Doctrine. He asserted that the United States government would help those third-world nations threatened with external aggression or internal revolution if they were able to fight effectively for themselves. U.S. help would no longer involve direct intervention as in Vietnam, but would be economic, logistical, and material.

The announcement was impromptu, without any preparation and without the foreknowledge of either Kissinger or the State Department. The president did not want to get bogged down in debate and staff studies. The difficulty with the doctrine was the uncertainty of knowing which nations could help themselves and which could not, and which ones were more or less important to the American place in the world.

Kissinger was attuned to the Nixon Doctrine because he had disparaged the uncritical pragmatism of U.S. foreign policy, which had made commitments abroad without clear criteria. Once such commitments were routinized in the national security bureaucracies, they were difficult, if not impossible, to root out. So both he and the president believed that nothing innovative could be achieved with the full participation of either the state or defense establishments. Nixon always distrusted people and organizations that he could not control, and Kissinger was anxious from the first day to establish his primacy over William Rogers, the secretary of state, and Melvin Laird, the secretary of defense. Kissinger drew up rules, approved by Nixon, for the structure and procedures of the National Security Council. Kissinger himself was to chair most of the key committees, including a committee of deputies on which their bosses did not serve. He had operational authority over the Central Intelligence Agency and could issue orders within the key departments without the knowledge of the department heads.

Nixon always intended to be his own secretary of state but never made it clear to Rogers that Kissinger would be his principal adviser and the implementer of policy. He was not sure of Kissinger at the outset, but they were such a match intellectually and temperamentally that in time Kissinger became the first among seeming equals. Early meetings of the National Security Council did not go well when Rogers and Laird disagreed with the president. After the North Koreans shot down an American plane, Nixon and Kissinger wanted to retaliate with force but the others argued against it. The president held back but he was going to have no more of that. He found it very difficult to overrule his chief associates in person. Eventually, he relied on his chief of staff Bob Haldeman and Kissinger to convey his decisions to others. Discussions were often staged even though Nixon had already made up his mind. Nixon thought strategically but benefited from Kissinger's ability to conceptualize Nixon's own incomplete ideas. But Nixon necessarily made the strategic decisions with Kissinger on hand as his tactician. Nixon was more of a risk taker than Kissinger, always looking to throw the long ball. Kissinger's signal contribution to détente was the idea of "linkage," in which agreement with the Russians would depend upon good behavior on issues important to the administration. Thus, to get an arms limitation agreement and new opportunities for trade, the Soviets were expected to help constrain the North Vietnamese and be constructive in steps underway for a new agreement on the status of Berlin. It was perhaps naïve to think that carrots and sticks could control the Soviet leaders. Nor could the president control the American government as he wished, for example, when Congress made trade with Russia contingent on increased Jewish emigration from the Soviet Union to Israel.

Nixon made clear to the Soviet ambassador, Anatoly Dobrynin, that he should deal directly with Kissinger on important matters, rather than with the secretary of state. Dobrynin made the first overture of the possibility of arms reductions talks, and Kissinger oversaw that effort to completion. By the same token, when the Chinese indicated that they would welcome an emissary of the president in a secret visit to China, Kissinger was the one who went. All of this was done in secret. Nixon did not want political debate about his major foreign policy initiatives. He was an actor on a world stage, not a politician who lived by bargaining. Secrecy and back channels were the best way to get things done.

The Soviets

Leonid Brezhnev was struggling for dominance among his colleagues after the dismissal of Nikita Khrushchev and he made improved relations with the United States his program. By 1969 the Soviets had achieved nuclear parity with the United States, for which Brezhnev wanted recognition. The Soviet economy was doing poorly. The nation was technically backward, industrial management was poor, agriculture was failing, and consumer goods were shoddy. Brezhnev hoped that increased trade would bring new technology and stimulate Soviet industrial management to improve. He was also anxious for the impending treaty about Berlin in which West Germany would accept the legitimacy of East Germany. The Americans would have to agree to this.

Nixon and Kissinger accepted the reality of nuclear parity and did not challenge it. Arms reductions as such were not that important to them. Nixon wanted help with Vietnam, but also recognized that a successful negotiation of the Strategic Arms Limitation Treaty (SALT) would enhance his domestic political position.

China

After the Soviet Union forcibly put down the revolution in Czechoslo- vakia in 1968, the Chinese leaders began a campaign to support Eastern European communist regimes to oppose Soviet "imperialism." Mutual military build-up along the borders accelerated, and the Soviet press talked of nuclear strikes on Chinese missile sites. Chinese leaders were therefore looking for a counterbalance to the Soviets, just as Nixon was thinking of the same idea in reverse.

Washington responded to diplomatic probes from Beijing, and talks were begun in Warsaw. The State Department was not happy with opening relations with the Chinese communists because of the long-standing U.S. commitment to Taiwan, the last haven of the nationalist Chinese, who had fled the mainland after the communists came to power in 1949. As a result, the State Department was excluded from the White House back-channel communications with Chinese leaders. In December 1970 Chou En-lai, the Chinese premier, invited an American visit to China in 1971 during which preparations would be made for a visit by Nixon in early 1972. Henry Kissinger secretly visited Beijing from Pakistan in July. The ostensible topic for discussion was the status of Taiwan, which Beijing insisted was part of China. Kissinger agreed that the United States would reduce its military support for Taiwan and publicly embrace a "two nations, one China" policy, with the implication of eventual reunification to be worked out by the parties themselves.

After Nixon publicly announced Kissinger's trip and his own plans to visit China, it was hailed at home as a political master stroke, with praise that only Nixon, the longtime anticommunist, could have created domestic political support for such a bold move. His own visit to China in February 1972 was a television feast for the American audience. Despite the fact that the United States had fought a war with China in Korea from 1951 to 1953, there was a strong residual American liking for China, derived from multiple missionary efforts, the alliance of World War II, the large number of Chinese who had studied in American universities, and much favorable fiction by American authors about the Chinese and their history.

The Chinese government promised to caution the North Vietnamese but did nothing about it until 1972, when it became apparent that the peace treaty to be signed would permit North Vietnamese troops to remain in South Vietnam. Then the Chinese told Hanoi to come to agreement because they could win the civil war once the Americans left. So Nixon really got little help. There were limited tangible results from the rapprochement, but it began a series of events in which American-Chinese contacts were rapidly expanded in terms of diplomatic postings in both capitals, increased visits and exchanges by private groups, Chinese students in American universities, and eventual full diplomatic recognition with President Jimmy Carter. Nixon deserves credit for his boldness and, as we will see, the new tie with China may have helped him as leverage with the Soviets. However, in his private thoughts Nixon could not be satisfied with his success. After returning from China, he told Haldeman: "He feels Henry [Kissinger] isn't getting across on the PR standpoint on the P's handling of the situations in China. He says the main thing for us in China is the P's position as a big league operator. He's done it for years. The unusual world statesman capability, the personal qualities of the man. He wants to refer to this as a classic battle between a couple of heavyweights, each with his own style."[9] Presumably the other heavyweight was Mao. Nixon's self-image was event making, but he deserved it in the ways in which he pulled China into the world and eventually worked out a "détente" with the Soviets. These were major achievements.

Strategic Arms Limitation Treaty (SALT I)

The Johnson administration had begun to talk with Soviet leaders about arms reduction, until the suppression of the uprising in Czechoslovakia necessarily delayed any talks. Nixon had promised that the United States would achieve military superiority during the campaign, and Melvin Laird, the new secretary of defense, was ready to begin the development of new weapons. However, Nixon was afraid that Congress would cut defense rather than support development, particularly with unhappiness over the continuing war in Vietnam. He and Kissinger hit on the idea of "sufficiency" of American weapons in parity with Soviet strength. Both sides had first- and second-strike capability. The sensible thing to do was to try to stabilize parity. Nixon was not interested in the details of arms control and gave Kissinger great discretion in negotiations. Neither man thought that an agreement on parity would stop the development of future weapons, and large loopholes for that purpose were left in the treaty as finally negotiated. The negotiations were conducted along parallel tracks: the official teams who met regularly in various European cities and the back channel conducted in Washington by Kissinger with a small team of advisers through Dobrynin, who was in continuous contact with Moscow. Of course, the official Soviet negotiators knew of the Kissinger efforts and were often confused about the American position. Their American counterparts were often in the dark without knowing it. Experts in these matters have suggested that Kissinger made a number of errors as he negotiated the final agreement in Moscow in May 1972 with the official American team sitting in Helsinki and prevented from traveling to Moscow. The more important point is that Nixon and Kissinger did not mind the flaws in the SALT agreement. In particular, the Soviets were left free to place multiple warheads on their large intercontinental ballistic missiles, because the Pentagon wanted to do the same. But the treaty was still a great breakthrough, and Nixon could and did claim the credit in a dramatic return from Russia by night and an address to Congress and the nation about his achievement. This dramatic trip, following the drama of China, as good as elected Nixon in 1972. SALT I was oversold, which was apparent when Secretary Laird thereafter asked Congress for the B-1 bomber, MX missiles, and Trident submarines. But the president approved the proposals, saying that he must negotiate SALT II from strength.

Détente Appraised

Détente was a set of possibilities for future cooperation, which could not be guaranteed. Nixon received little, if any, help with Vietnam. Linkage did not work because the Soviet leaders began a new series of adventures in the developing world, which continued into the Ford, Carter, and Reagan years. Cuban troops were used as proxies in civil wars in Africa; the Soviet influence with Arab states continued; Marxist regimes in Somalia and Ethiopia were encouraged; and, of course, Afghanistan was invaded in 1978.

Nixon was completely consumed by the Watergate scandal from early 1973 until his resignation in August 1974, and these kinds of issues were left to Kissinger, now secretary of state. Kissinger rushed from one crisis to another on an ad hoc basis. His greatest achievement was securing a cease-fire between Egypt and Israel in 1973 after Egypt had made a military strike. He was able to secure Soviet cooperation in that effort and nullify Soviet influence in the region to some extent. He laid the foundations for the eventual gesture of peace to Israel by President Anwar Sadat of Egypt. The peace agreement between Israel and Egypt worked out by President Carter in 1978 drew on Kissinger's success. Any further analysis of Kissinger's role in détente must wait until a look at the Ford presidency, in which Kissinger continued as secretary of state.

Peace with Honor

Nixon told his cabinet that the United States would be out of Vietnam within a year. He was counting on Soviet support. His goal was the long-term survival of the government of South Vietnam. In his thinking, the collapse of that government would weaken American credibility with the major powers and U.S. allies around the world. It would be a sign that the United States would not keep its commitments. Whether the commitment was a good one in the first place did not matter to him, even as domestic protest made that very claim. But he knew that he could not attempt to defeat North Vietnam militarily by escalating the war. Neither Congress nor the public would stand for that. Yet he had latitude because public opinion was divided about what to do, as was congressional opinion, which reflected public divisions. Nixon had to balance his actions between the extreme hawks, who would escalate, and doves, who would withdraw immediately without concern for the government of South Vietnam. Many Democrats had turned away from the cold war ideas of containment of communism that they had taken into Vietnam and had become the peace party—but without clear ideas about the kinds of power the United States should try to exercise in the world. They simply wanted out of Vietnam.

Nixon made an early secret proposal to the government of North Vietnam, which called for the mutual withdrawal of American and North Vietnamese armies from the south followed by elections of a new government in South Vietnam. The offer was rebuffed with the demand that the Americans should depose the existing South Vietnamese government in favor of a coalition government in which communists would predominate. As this effort failed, Nixon and his advisers, especially Secretary Laird, fell back on the idea of a gradual withdrawal of U.S. troops from the south, complemented by U.S. help in strengthening South Vietnamese forces and the use of U.S. air power to hold forces from the north in check. Laird, who was anxious to reclaim budgets lost to the war, gave the name "Vietnamization" to the policy. The great uncertainty was whether the army of South Vietnam was up to the task, given a high rate of corruption, numerous incompetent officers, and the lack of a will to fight, as seen in the high number of desertions.

His opponents never gave Nixon a chance. When Kissinger was given an honorary degree by Brown University in the spring of 1969, a large number of people in the audience turned their backs. The action reflected hostility to the president. Popular protests in the fall of 1969, especially on university campuses, were robust but not violent. The protests demanded withdrawal without regard for the consequences. Nixon strengthened his domestic political position against protest with a nationally televised speech on November 3, 1969, in which he promised that Vietnamization would continue and appealed to the "silent majority" of America to trust his willingness to achieve a peace with honor. Sixty-eight percent of a national sample of the public approved, and both houses of Congress voted resolutions of support. The appeal was similar to his overture to a domestic coalition of "forgotten Americans." However, Nixon knew that he faced formidable opposition among congressional doves, the universities, and the *New York Times, Washington Post,* and the major television networks. He increasingly came to see such critics as not only hostile to him personally but unpatriotic and an obstacle to peace. He told Haldeman: "In this period of our history the leaders and the educated are decadent. Whenever you ask for patriotic support they all run away: the college types, the professors, the elites, etc.... When you call on the nation to be strong on such things as drugs, crime, defense, our basic national position, the educated people and the leader class no longer has any character and you can't count on them. We can only turn for support to the noneducated people."[10] He went on to say that he thought the Democrats would nominate an "ultraliberal" in 1972 and that was the chance for him to appeal to labor and the uneducated.

In the spring of 1970, the president saw a threat to the withdrawal of U.S. troops from the south by the existence of North Vietnamese command posts and supply depots on the Cambodian border not far from Saigon. Such outposts near Saigon could delay Vietnamization by attacking across the border. Americans had been secretly bombing the Cambodian borders, with the acquiescence of the Cambodian government, which did not want foreign troops in its territory. The bombings were kept secret, because otherwise the Cambodians would have to denounce the violation of their neutrality. Nixon was under pressure at home. The Senate had denied him two Supreme Court appointments, and the North Vietnamese were refusing to negotiate. He needed a bold move and found it in the decision to send U.S. and South Vietnamese armies into two spots within Cambodia where it was thought command posts might be located, although there was debate about their location. Nixon duplicated his familiar routine of preparation for crisis. He slept poorly and watched the movie *Patton* about General George S. Patton, a flamboyant hero of the Second World War, a number of times. He summoned his reserves of energy, steeled and calmed himself. Both Rogers and Laird opposed the decision because of military uncertainty and the risk of domestic disruption over seeming extension of the war. But Kissinger was with the president. Nixon explained his decision to the nation after the incursion had begun, but his speech was a disaster. He thought that he could repeat his successful "silent majority" speech, but he was mistaken. What might have been explained as a limited military strike to protect Vietnamization was converted into a maudlin self-dramatization about how the United States would not permit itself to be humiliated and that he would rather be a one-term president and do the right thing than see the United States act "like a pitiful helpless giant." He had personalized a limited military maneuver into a test of confidence in himself, perhaps to himself.

The worst of it was the aftermath. Campuses exploded all over the country. In early May, four protesting students at Kent State University in Ohio were killed by poorly led National Guard troops called to the campus to keep order. Congress was in an uproar as the Senate passed a resolution to withdraw troops from Cambodia by the end of June. Students at Stanford attacked their own university, throwing rocks and breaking large plate-glass windows on the central campus. The faculty at Brown University met to decide whether exams might be suspended so that students might campaign against the action. Students listened to the debate by loudspeaker out on the lawn, and any expression of defense of the president within was howled down with anger by faculty and students. There was an element of mass hysteria to it all, but Nixon had made himself a target, and his opposition saw him as virtually evil. He did promise to withdraw the troops in June, under congressional pressure, but in talking with his aides told them to "build up the president" to show how tough and resolute he had been. Compare him to General de Gaulle, he said. He told Haldeman that his decision had been more difficult than Kennedy's in the missile crisis and walked into a senior staff meeting and told them not to worry about being tough. He was as melodramatic as his opponents.

The Cambodian operation discovered weapons and supplies, but the command posts were not found. Critics later charged that the incursion extended the war to Cambodia, but the North Vietnamese had already sent forces into the interior of the country. A civil war began there in earnest between the government of Cambodia, the North Vietnamese, and their seeming allies, the Khmer Rouge communist revolutionaries. The country was later plunged into disaster by the Khmer Rouge victory, the desolation and mass murder it inflicted, and the eventual successful North Vietnamese defeat of the Khmer Rouge.

Nixon withdrew a large number of troops in June and September. In November 1970 he softened his proposal to the North Vietnamese, suggesting a cease-fire of both armies in place in South Vietnam after a treaty was negotiated, but the North still wanted the head of President Thieu of South Vietnam. Early in the year Kissinger had begun secret negotiations in Paris—parallel to the official talks—with top North Vietnamese officials. They had been suspended after the Cambodian action and later resumed. The winter and spring of 1971 was a depressing time for the president. A South Vietnamese offensive in Laos failed miserably. Kissinger was now suggesting at Paris that Thieu would resign before an election and run on his own, but this was met coldly. The Russians and the Chinese were urging North Vietnam to make an agreement with forces in place, but both were still sending supplies, and Hanoi would not budge. In February 1971 a Harris poll showed Senator Edmund Muskie, a Maine Democrat and vice presidential candidate in 1968, leading Nixon by a few points. The margin widened by May. However, the opening to China and the announcement of Nixon's visit in 1972, followed by disclosure that he would visit Moscow for the SALT talks in the same year, buoyed his public support.

The Moscow trip was threatened when North Vietnam launched a spring 1972 offensive designed to defeat the southern army. Nixon responded with massive air power directed against troops in the field as well as against Hanoi. He also ordered the mining of the harbors of the port of Haiphong, an important source of military supplies for the North. He feared that the Soviets would cancel the May summit and thought of doing it himself before they could. Vietnam was more important to him. But John Connally, who was brought to Washington to advise the president, argued against cancellation, insisting that the Soviets wanted the summit even more than Nixon did. It worked. The Soviets went ahead with plans and evidently never considered canceling the summit. But Nixon had taken a risk with the Soviets and openly defied Congress, which was moving slowly toward the idea of cutting off funds for the war. Nixon told aides that his mistakes had been made when he did not follow his own instincts: "The country can take losing the summit, but it can't take losing the war."[11] He wrote a memo to Kissinger saying that "We have the power to destroy his (enemy's) war-making capacity. The only question is whether we have the will to use that power. What distinguishes me from Johnson is that I have that will in spades," adding that they would fail only if the bureaucracies failed them.[12] Nixon wrote in his diary, paraphrasing Winston Churchill: "One can have a policy of audacity, or one can follow a policy of caution, but it is disastrous to try to follow a policy of audacity and caution at the same time. It must be one or the other. We have now gone down the audacious line and we must continue until we get some sort of a break."[13]

The Moscow summit was a success with the signing of the SALT treaty, as well as a treaty to limit ABMs, designed as defensive weapons against incoming missiles, to one or two sites in each country. Nixon believed that the ABM treaty had prevented a war in the buildup of defensive weapons. The professional military were not happy about SALT, and word reached Nixon in Moscow that the political consequences at home might be bad if he signed the treaty. His response was to say "the hell with the political consequences." A treaty would be made "on our terms."[14]

Withdrawal from Vietnam

After a major North Vietnamese offensive failed in March 1972, the North Vietnamese decided that they would be better off working out an agreement in Paris before, rather than after, the election, because Nixon might prolong the war afterward. Nixon had responded to the offensive with heavy bombing of the north. At the time, Kissinger remarked to the president that even if the United States had to withdraw from Vietnam without a settlement, he could claim credit for the honorable withdrawal of 500,000 troops from that country, and the war would be over—to much relief at home. Nixon reported "I considered the prospect too bleak to even contemplate." He told Kissinger: "The foreign policy of the United States will have been destroyed and the Soviets will have established that they can accomplish what they are after by using the force of arms in third world countries."[15] Defeat was not an option.

Negotiations in Paris began to be fruitful in the early fall. Kissinger was ready to settle with a cease-fire in place, the return of prisoners of war, and President Thieu's stand down before an election. Agreement on these terms was made in Paris in October with Nixon's approval. But President Thieu was ignorant of the terms of the agreement. He balked when told and continued to balk in the rudest and most offensive manner possible. One can hardly blame him. Thieu made a long list of reservations and asked that they be presented to the North Vietnamese in Paris. The president did not need an agreement to win the election and thought that he might obtain better terms later, and he was not yet ready to abandon Thieu. There was concern that a new Democratic Congress in January would shut down the war, and the president asked Kissinger to try for a modified agreement that would respond to some of Thieu's objections. Meetings in Paris in November resolved most issues, except for Thieu's demand that the two armies be largely separated by a demilitarized zone. Meetings in Paris in December could not resolve the question. The North Vietnamese would make no concessions to Thieu. On December 14, Nixon gave the order for severe and prolonged bombing of industrial and military targets in North Vietnam by fleets of B-52 bombers for a two-week period. The harbors of Hanoi and Haiphong were again mined. It is possible that the bombing was intended less for the North Vietnamese than to reassure Thieu. It was accompanied by guarantees in writing from Nixon to Thieu that U.S. air power would be used decisively to punish any North Vietnamese violations of the truce to come. Nixon had no authority to make either secret or public commitments of this kind but assumed that he would still be president to honor the commitments. What Congress might have to say was beside the point to him. The North Vietnamese finally relented, and a peace treaty was negotiated and signed in January on terms agreed to in October, but without Thieu's major reservations. President Thieu signed the treaty with a gun to his head, very reluctantly, after Nixon told him that he would sign it whether Thieu did or not.

Assessment

The hard question is whether the 1973 treaty terms could have been achieved in 1969 as critics charged. Some kind of agreement probably could have been worked out for a coalition government in South Vietnam with communists represented and Thieu out of the picture. But Nixon would not agree to this.

Critics argue that the South Vietnamese regime was corrupt and unable to defend itself and that a face-saving retreat early on might have produced a "decent interval" before the government fell. This was what actually happened in 1975, when North Vietnamese armies conquered South Vietnam.

The question turns on what might have been achieved by Nixon and Kissinger in negotiation for a "decent interval." But they did not want that and never considered it. Whether it could have been achieved is an irresolvable question. Whether Nixon could have engineered such a peace without tearing his own party apart is also a hard question. He chose not to even try. His larger purpose was to build a new Republican majority coalition. The peace people were not Nixon's people. It may very well be that an earlier peace might have prevented Watergate, because without the war Nixon might not have taken the extreme measures to destroy his critics that were attempted in Watergate.

It seems unlikely that an early retreat from South Vietnam would have weakened U.S. prestige in the world, as Nixon believed. The protracted war did a great deal to damage U.S. prestige, since we were floundering in what many thought was a tragic error of our own making. Certainly the violence with which Nixon fought the war is difficult to justify in terms of the limited results achieved. The American role in Vietnam was the first American experience in "nation building" and it failed. Eisenhower and Dulles took the crucial historical turning points in their creation of the Diem regime, and Kennedy's decisions to buttress that regime with active American military help was another step that was difficult to reverse. This was nation building. Nixon and Kissinger may have fooled themselves into believing that the government of South Vietnam could be a healthy state that could defend itself, although most of the evidence was against that assumption. There were no good choices along the long road in and out of Vietnam.

THE ELECTION OF 1972

We must backtrack at this point to discuss the presidential election, because Nixon's great triumph created a path for his self-destruction. As he prepared for the election, Nixon wrote in his diary: "The American leader class has really had it in terms of their ability to lead. It's really sickening to have to receive them at the White House as I often do and hear them whine and whimper and that's one of the reasons why I enjoy very much more receiving labor leaders and people from middle America who still have character and guts and a bit of patriotism."[16]

This was the spirit in which he fought the election. He wanted as large a majority for himself as possible in order to create what he called "a New American Revolution," in which he would forgo the compromises of his first term to establish his personal authority over both Congress and the executive branch to reduce the powers of the federal government at home, except in matters of national security, which belonged, in Nixon's view, solely with the president. His model for the American presidency was the French presidency of Charles de Gaulle, which stood above politics as the arbiter of the nation. To that effect, he amassed a war chest of millions for his own campaign and contributed very little in money or effort to Republican races for Congress. He established a separate campaign organization, the Committee to Reelect the President. The idea of the president as party leader was completely abandoned. Friendly critics at the time argued that Nixon was surely going to be isolated once he had won the election. He had been disappointed with congressional Republicans, felt sympathy for Southern Democrats, and had discussed forming a new conservative party, but the idea was not practical. He had suggested to Republican politicians that John Connally run with him as the vice presidential candidate, but Connally, a former Democrat, was not acceptable. Nixon told the journalist Theodore White that if he ran as a Republican, the party would pull him down to its level. He wanted Democratic votes.[17]

He won the election because of his dramatic foreign policy actions with China and Russia and the stabilization of the economy. George McGovern was also a weak Democratic candidate. The end of the war in Vietnam appeared to be in sight, but Nixon did not think that he needed a peace treaty to win the election. The other factor in his election was the weakness of the Democratic ticket and the turmoil in the Democratic Party. The Democratic candidate, South Dakota senator George McGovern, advocated withdrawal from Vietnam without any conditions, cuts in the defense budget, higher taxes for the rich, increased federal expenditures for social and environmental programs, and guaranteed incomes for the poor. McGovern was a moderate, sensible person but it was all too radical for many Americans. The AFL-CIO failed to endorse a candidate for the first time. The Teamsters Union supported Nixon after he pardoned their former leader Jimmy Hoffa, who was in prison. The original vice presidential candidate for the Democrats, Missouri senator Thomas Eagleton, was forced from the ticket after revelations that he had had electric shock treatments after several nervous breakdowns. The Democratic Party's 1972 convention was a disaster with great conflict between traditional politicians and new arrivals of women, youth, and minorities chosen under new rules that promoted quotas for representation. Frank Rizzo, the Democratic mayor of Philadelphia, openly supported Nixon. Many traditional Democratic politicians hoped for McGovern's defeat so that they might regain the control of the party at the grass roots that they had lost to reformers. An increase in ticket splitting permitted many Democrats to vote for Nixon and their own Democratic representative in Congress, and Nixon never had any hope of carrying a Republican Congress, nor did he try. Nixon won 60.7 percent of the popular vote compared to McGovern's 37.5 percent. He won majorities in every single group in the population, except among blacks. Manual workers, labor union families, people with only a grade-school education, as well as middle-class Republicans, white Southerners, and Catholics, all went for Nixon.

But all the time that he was winning, Nixon was undermining his presidency by a secret campaign of "dirty tricks" prompted perhaps by his fear of losing and the importance in his own mind of demolishing the opposition. The burglary of the Democratic National Committee headquarters in the Watergate Hotel complex in Washington, D.C., in July 1972 by men connected to the Committee to Reelect the President was the incident that would bring him down. The record reveals conversations between the president and close aides during the fall campaign about how to insulate the White House from scandal by asking the CIA to tell federal prosecutors that the issue should not be pursued any further than the burglars because of questions of national security. The investigation was on the verge of uncovering the use of illegal contributions to the CRP, which financed the burglary. Nixon was also informed at this time of the burglary of the office of the psychiatrist of Daniel Ellsberg, whom the government was prosecuting for revealing documents about the planning of the Vietnam war in the Johnson administration known as the "Pentagon Papers." The burglary was carried out under the supervision of presidential assistants. Nixon was anxious to scrape up scandal about the Kennedys. A fake memorandum, which directly implicated John F. Kennedy in the death of President Diem of South Vietnam, was produced and given to *Life* magazine, which refused to print it. Howard Hunt, one of the Watergate burglars, wore a red wig as a disguise and followed Edward Kennedy around in search of indiscretions. White House assistants hired people to disrupt Democratic rallies by canceling them or creating vocal protests. They were paid from secret funds provided by the president's personal lawyer. Someone from the White House sent a letter to a New Hampshire newspaper charging that the wife of front-runner Maine senator Edmund Muskie had used the term "Canuck," a derogatory term for people of French Canadian descent. Muskie was outraged and replied in anger, speaking from a flatbed truck on a snowy day. Snow in his eyes may have caused tears, but in any event he was derided as a man who cried, and his candidacy ended not long after. None of these things were necessary. They came solely from spite. Nixon believed that everyone did it and he should give more than he got. His close aide, William Safire, was very critical, writing later that "politics was reduced to a form of savagery."[18]

The Second Term Begins

Nixon was determined not to suffer the gradual loss of influence that second-term, lame duck presidents experience. He met with his cabinet briefly and then left the room, leaving chief of staff Bob Haldeman in charge. Haldeman immediately asked all of them to send letters of resignation to the president. White House staff members and political appointees in the departments were asked to do the same. They were not all fired, but the president had the whip hand. His plan was to reduce the size of the White House staff and send loyal people out to the departments as subcabinet officers who would be responsive to the center. Three cabinet secretaries were named assistants to the president with offices in the White House. They were to oversee the work of other cabinet officers in the broad fields of human and natural resources and community development. The secretary of the treasury, George Schultz, was given an assistant in the White House who coordinated the policy proposals of the departments concerned with economic affairs for Schultz's advice to the president about actions to take. New cabinet officers in the lesser departments went to less than impressive figures. For example, the secretary of labor was a union leader from the building trades. The president worked primarily at Camp David in the weeks after the election, meeting with people and making plans, with the assistance of Haldeman and Ehrlichman. Henry Kissinger, who was in contact with the president about the Vietnam peace treaty being negotiated in Paris noticed Nixon's dark mood after his victory as if all his "resentments had come to the surface," adding "Nixon was restless and distracted. It was almost as if standing on the pinnacle Nixon no longer had any purpose left to his life."[19] Kissinger did not know that Nixon was beginning to learn that it might not be possible to contain the secrets of Watergate. He was brooding about his own future and possible disgrace at his time of triumph.

The president prepared the outlines for a new budget that tilted to the right with cuts in expenditures, and he asserted his constitutional right to impound funds, which eventually failed from challenges in court. However, it all fell apart as Haldeman and Ehrlichman were forced by the president to resign as investigations into various aspects of the affair known as Watergate rose to public awareness and Congress prepared to investigate the presidency. Former secretary of defense Melvin Laird, a longtime Republican congressman who assisted Nixon with domestic policy in the White House briefly in the spring of 1973, abolished the new administrative structure. As Nixon's political position increasingly weakened until he resigned in August 1974, the Office of Management and Budget (OMB) ran the government, giving cues to the departments and agencies about broad policy.

The new "administrative presidency" would have failed in time because it ignored the structure of American government. Congress was not going to permit some cabinet officers to oversee others, especially without the legal authority to do so. The politics of bargaining permeates a government of divided institutions sharing powers and could not be denied. But Nixon always thought in terms of hierarchy and structured his own authority in government in that fashion. He was not comfortable with the politics of give and take.

Watergate

The interesting parts of the story are the connections with the war and Nixon's emotional responses to his critics in a number of illegal actions, including wiretaps of journalists and even his own staff. The White House denied knowledge of the Watergate burglary, and the incident was forgotten during the election campaign. However, the *Washington Post* produced a series of stories over the ensuing months that suggested clear links with the CRP and the presidency itself. Events moved quickly with a Senate investigation in 1973 that uncovered many of the connections, which the White House at the direction of the president was trying to cover up in various ways. Haldeman and Ehrlichman were forced to resign from the White House staff in the spring. Haldeman later wrote in his diary: "We never set out to construct a planned, conscious, cover-up operation. We reacted to Watergate just as we had to the Pentagon Papers.... We were highly sensitive to any negative PR, and our natural reaction was to contain, or minimize, any potential political damage. Our attempts at containment became linked to other acts within the Administration and were eventually labeled 'the Watergate cover-up.'"[20] Nixon's speech announcing their resignations denied any personal involvement. He later wrote in his memoirs that people were waiting for a yes-or-no answer as to whether he was personally involved. He made his decision "on political instinct":

> If I had given the true answer I would have had to say that without fully realizing the implications of my actions I had become deeply entangled in the complicated mesh of decisions, inactions, misunderstandings, and conflicting motivations that comprised the Watergate cover-up. I would have had to admit that I still did not know the whole story and therefore did not know the full extent of my involvement in it, and I would have had to give

the damaging specifics of what I did know while leaving open the possibility that much more might come out later.[21]

He added that the inept way that the cover-up had been handled had placed him so on the defensive that there would have been no tolerance for such a complicated explanation.

> The instinct of twenty-five years in politics told me that I was up against no ordinary opposition. In the second term I had thrown down a gauntlet to Congress, the bureaucracy, the media, and the Washington establishment, and challenged them to engage in epic battle. We had already skirmished over the limitations of prerogative and power, represented by confirmation of appointments, the impoundment of funds, and the battle of the budget. Now, suddenly Watergate had exposed a cavernous weakness in my ranks, and I felt that if in this speech I admitted any weakness in my ranks ... any vulnerabilities, my opponents would savage me with them ... therefore making it impossible for me to exert presidential leadership. Given this situation and given this choice—given my belief that these were the stakes—I decided to answer no to the question whether I was also involved in Watergate.[22]

We see here the fundamental flaw in Nixon the man and Nixon the politician. He did not trust anyone. He saw enemies rather than opponents. He surely could have saved his presidency had he acted from the outset to admit what John Mitchell called the "White House horrors" of wiretapping, burglaries, and cover-up. However, Nixon was thinking in terms of confrontation, as the statement above reveals. He had gone beyond any possibility of moderate politics.

Senate hearings into Watergate matters disclosed the existence of an extensive taping system in the White House and a special prosecutor, forced upon the president, sued for the relevant tapes. The Supreme Court decided that Nixon must surrender them. At the same time, the House Judiciary Committee voted to impeach the president after long and painful hearings. The crucial tapes revealed that four days after the break-in, Nixon directed Haldeman to tell the CIA to direct the FBI not to investigate the Watergate burglary because of national security concerns. Nixon was evidently trying to protect John Mitchell, who headed his reelection committee, and who had approved the burglary for unknown reasons. Nixon was also caught on tape authorizing payments of money to the Watergate burglars to prevent their talking about what they knew. This was enough to force the president's resignation for obstruction of justice. The House investigations uncovered a long list of misdeeds—such as, for example, the burglary in the office of Daniel Ellsberg's psychiatrist. John Ehrlichman thought that Nixon ordered the burglary himself, but there was no supporting evidence. Ehrlichman's failure to report the burglary to the authorities was the first Watergate cover-up. The burglary was done by a group set up in the White House called the "Plumbers" because they worked in the basement. But their kind of work had begun earlier when the president ordered wiretaps on members of his own staff in 1969 when the *New York Times* broke the story of the bombing of Cambodia. Eventually four reporters, thirteen staff members, and officials at the State and Defense departments were wiretapped, all without legal authorization. William Safire later wrote, "Curiously, eavesdropping is the sinister thread that traces its way from early in the administration through to Watergate."[23]

Watergate was the culmination of Nixon's political history. As Safire put it, "attack before you are attacked." It was an unfortunate fusion of the secrecy of the national security presidency and personal temperament. Other presidents have abused their powers, but the extent was far greater with Nixon. His actions were self-destructive. His distrust of his own government was so great that at the end he stood alone. He resigned on August 9, 1974.

Nixon saw impeachment as an entirely political process in which his political opponents had persuaded the public that he should be removed from office. He wrote in his memoirs that he never believed that the charges against him were legally impeachable offenses. In his view, hounding him from office was a blow to the American system of government.[24] His resignation address to the people admitted no wrongdoing, but simply said that he could not continue as president because he had "lost his political base." It rang hollow then and now.

Nixon loved to talk tough, but he was not a strong man. He shielded himself from dissenting advisers. He relied on tough lieutenants—Haldeman, Kissinger, and Connally. Above all, he wanted to be a great man in history. In January 1973, riding high after his reelection, he told Haldeman that press editorials missed the point about the president. He often referred to himself in the third person as Nixon or the president: "Why not say that without the P's courage we couldn't have had this? (peace treaty). The basic line here is the character, the lonely man in the White House with little support from government, active opposition from the Senate and some House members, overwhelming opposition from media and opinion leaders, including religious, education, and business, but strong support from labor. The P alone held on and pulled it out.... The missing link now is the 'Profile in Courage.'"[25] Despite such vainglory, Nixon was plagued all his life by the fear that he might not come up to the mark he had set for himself. He was continually on the defensive, even as he attacked before an anticipated attack. One must decide for oneself whether he was a tragic or pathetic figure.

CONCLUSION

How does Nixon measure up according to our questions about presidential leadership?

Context and Contingencies

Both the domestic and foreign affairs contexts were favorable to innovation in 1969. The Great Society had run its course politically and many of Johnson's experts were casting about for ways to rationalize and consolidate programs in the ways that Nixon was to propose. He inherited a terrible situation in Vietnam, but the nation was ready and receptive to efforts to stabilize relations between the United States and the Soviet Union, and not really surprisingly, China.

Talents and Skills

Nixon was a very good strategic thinker in foreign policy. He was prudent and measured as he worked with both Chinese and Russian leaders. This was much easier for him than it was to work with Democratic politicians in his own country, because he wanted to be on the world stage dealing with other men of power. His strategy in regard to withdrawal from Vietnam was prudent from his perspective, but critics may fairly charge that he was so imprisoned by the fear of loss of American power and prestige that he missed an opportunity to achieve a peace, with the same long-term results, much earlier.

The domestic policy proposals of Nixon's first term made sense in terms of his political position and the requirements of the programs themselves. But he became so frustrated by normal congressional politics that he lost any sense of prudence in his second term and threw down a gauntlet in a way that was sure to fail even without Watergate. Watergate made it certain. The undercurrent of emotional insecurity, which drove his passion to make a great mark, was ultimately his undoing.

Did He Make a Difference?

Nixon's boldness and determination to make a historic mark certainly found fruition in his rapprochement with communist China. Relations with the Soviets were productive in the signing of the SALT treaty, but the cold war continued, primarily in third-world nations. The Soviet leaders were as eager for arms control as Nixon, probably even more so.

Nixon's domestic policy achievements of the first term set out a path for intelligent management of the Great Society programs that unfortunately was tarnished by his disgrace. Richard Nixon was an event-making leader in the achievement of détente. That same fierce ambition to be a great president, when joined to his personal insecurity, created a crisis for the presidency and the nation.

In the final analysis Nixon lacked respect for constitutional government and was a danger to the Republic. Could one describe Nixon's actions in the Watergate affair as event making? He created a constitutional crisis of major proportions. Event making may be destructive as well as creative. His determination to win and to be a great man in history, at any cost, was at the root of both his achievements and failures.

Effectiveness

Nixon had the opportunities and the talent to be a most effective president. He was effective in his major foreign policy initiatives because he could work pretty much alone, with Kissinger's help. But this very style of the Lone Ranger battling against odds and opposition did not suit him for domestic policy leadership. His dramatic action to freeze wages and prices was primarily a political expedient taken without much consultation. His assault on Congress as his second term began had the same character. A president who lacks trust in others and tries to do it all himself will eventually undercut himself. Even without Watergate, Nixon's full second term would have been one of losing battles with Congress.

BIBLIOGRAPHICAL ESSAY

Nixon's presidential memoir *RN: The Memoirs of Richard Nixon* (1978), is much like his book *Six Crises,* more revealing of the man than perhaps he intended. He describes his strategies of leadership, the reasons for his decisions, and unwittingly gives a self-portrait of gigantic ambition, deep character flaws, and a seeming lack of awareness of how poorly his impulse for grandiosity fit democratic politics. Stephen Ambrose's three volumes of biography are very well written, and I have turned especially to the second volume, *Nixon: The Triumph of a Politician, 1962–1972* (1989). However the narrative is episodic and does not go in deeply at many points. Tom Wicker's *One of Us: Richard Nixon and the American Dream* (1991) draws on his rich experience in covering Nixon and other presidents for the *New York Times.* Wicker makes a sophisticated argument that politicians often act for politically strategic reasons rather than personal conviction, which is true. But he seems to discount moral purpose in politics as well. Joan Hoff's *Nixon Reconsidered* (1994) is a revisionist assessment, particularly of his domestic policies, which has many good points. Gary Wills, *Nixon Agonistes* (2002), is a brilliant portrait of a tragic leader. William Safire's *Before the Fall: An Insider's View of the Pre-Watergate White House* (2005) is a friendly account of Nixon from the inside, which does not spare his faults. H. R. Haldeman's *The Haldeman Diaries, Inside the Nixon White House* (1994) is a devastating picture of Nixon at his worst. Richard Nixon, *Six Crises*, unwittingly reveals the insecurity beneath the external toughness that drove the public man.

John Ehrlichman's memoir of working with Nixon, *Witness to Power: The Nixon Years* (1982), is chatty and irreverent but often insightful. There are a number of studies of the politics of welfare reform, but Vincent and Vee Burke's *Nixon's Good Deed: Welfare Reform* (1974) gives the most complete story. Hugh Davis Graham, *The Civil Rights Era: Origins Development of National Policies* (1990), is a superb study. Allen J. Matusow explains economic policy clearly in *Nixon's Economy: Booms, Busts, Dollars, and Votes* (1998). Herbert Stein's *Presidential Economics* (3d ed. 1994) is invaluable, as are the interviews with Paul McCracken and Stein in Erwin C. Hargrove and Samuel Morley, *The President and the Council of Economic Advisers* (1984). Richard P. Nathan gives an incisive insider's account of Nixon's plans for executive reorganization in *The Plot That Failed: Nixon and the Administrative Presidency* (1975). Robert T. Mason comprehensively covers Nixon's domestic politics in *Richard Nixon and the Quest for a New Majority* (2004). And A. James Reichley places Nixon in the larger context of conservatism in American history in *Conservatives in an Age of Change: The Nixon and Ford Administrations* (1981).

The best single book on American-Soviet relations is by Raymond Garthoff, *Detente and Confrontation, American-Soviet Relations from Nixon to Reagan* (1985). Jusi Hanhimaki has written a good study of Henry Kissinger as a diplomat, *The Flawed Architect* (2004). Kissinger's own *White House Years* (1979), in three volumes, is invaluable, but must be read along with other accounts. John Lewis Gaddis places Nixon, and particularly Kissinger, within the cold war theory of containment in *Strategies of Containment: A Critical Appraisal of Postwar National Security Policy* (2005). He focuses on the theories of Kissinger the scholar perhaps more than he should, because Nixon was the decision maker. William Bundy has written a good general book on Nixon's foreign policy, which, while critical, is fair: *A Tangled Web: The Making of Foreign Policy in the Nixon Administration* (1998). Seyom Brown's *The Crises of Power: An Interpretation of United States Foreign Policy during the Kissinger Years* (1979) focuses primarily on Kissinger but raises many interesting questions. Kissinger's book, *Ending the Vietnam War* (2003), which is taken from his memoirs with additions, makes a very strong, clear case for the strategy of Vietnamization and gives a full account of his negotiations with the North Vietnamese. It slides over disagreements with the president. Jeffrey P. Kimball, *Nixon's Vietnam War* (1998) covers much the same ground but does not accept the premise that the government of South Vietnam was worth saving in the end. Larry Berman, *No Peace, No Honor: Nixon and Kissinger and Betrayal in Vietnam* (2001), is highly critical of the way in which President Thieu of South Vietnam was excluded from negotiations with the North Vietnamese and how he was virtually abandoned.

There are more books on Watergate than one could read, but three books will do here: Melvin Small, *The Presidency of Richard Nixon* (1999), Michael Genovese, *The Watergate Crisis* (1999), and Theodore H. White, *Breach of Faith: The Fall of Richard Nixon* (1975).

CHAPTER FOUR

Gerald R. Ford

A Good Man

The presidencies of Gerald Ford and Jimmy Carter were periods of popular reaction against the "imperial presidency" of Vietnam and Watergate. Both presidents deliberately downplayed the elaborate trappings of office in favor of plainspoken, informal leadership. Those efforts fell short because, in the long run, many people want a president who seems larger than life. Presidents may often rise above policy reverses if they appear to be in command of events. Neither Ford nor Carter had that quality. Making scapegoats of presidents is a shallow way to deal with political reality. Rather than curb the lions, we banish the foxes. However, both Ford and Carter were initially welcomed as good men who would be democratic presidents after the storms of the recent past.

Gerald Ford became president after a traumatic scandal in government to which he was not a party. He was not tarred with Nixon's brush. People at large wanted an honest, open, democratic leader who would tell the truth and respect the Constitution. Ford was an accidental president, but he was perfect for the assignment. He had been chosen as vice president because his peers in Congress respected him for those very qualities. His first statement after taking the oath was, "Our long national nightmare is over."

The context of policy and politics was less certain. The Democrats controlled Congress. Stagflation was growing. The "détente" with the Soviet Union was stable and the Soviet leaders wanted more arms agreements. But their adventures in Africa and the Middle East worried Kissinger, who remained as secretary of state. The government of South Vietnam survived, but it was weak and on the defensive militarily. There was not much a president could do about it, because Congress would not support any military actions. The chief contingency facing the new president was what to do about Nixon.

The special prosecutor might choose to indict the former president for obstruction of justice. Ford would have to consider his alternatives in that case. He had to find economic policies to cope with stagflation. He faced no demand for domestic programs beyond the ordinary run of government business. It was not a challenging agenda. But he faced a difficult political context in which his own party was increasingly divided between a conservative movement to the right and more traditional pragmatists. The Democrats, in charge of Congress, expected to take the presidency in 1976 and were not in a cooperative mood.

Ford was a practical politician who knew how to read Congress well but was much less effective in reading national opinion. He was prudent in never trying to do too much. But he lacked a sense of how to protect himself and his objectives politically. He would rely on the goodwill of others only to be disappointed. His chief virtue was his character, and his contribution to the nation was the restoration of trust after Watergate. Character was his skill and it did engender support.

Before he moved to the White House, Ford had told journalists waiting outside his Alexandria, Virginia, home for his return from church that he and his family were going to eat waffles with strawberries and whipped cream. This was "down home" and it was Jerry Ford, the congressman from Grand Rapids who loved to talk to high school bands visiting Washington. He became the Republican minority leader in 1965 when a group of young turks among Republican House members encouraged him to challenge a tired Republican leadership. His style as leader was to listen and build coalitions in Republican ranks. His ambition was to be Speaker of the House, but he was always in the minority and finally resolved to retire from Congress before the 1976 presidential election. There was little opportunity to be a creative legislative leader, nor was that his style.

Ford was brought up in a happy family in the solid, conservative midwestern city of Grand Rapids, Michigan. He was an Eagle Scout, with a reputation that followed him through life. He was honest, reliable, and trustworthy. What you saw was what you got. He was not glib or even especially articulate, but his integrity caused people to give him their confidence. He played football at the University of Michigan and coached football at Yale while studying at Yale Law School. After serving in combat as a naval officer in the Pacific during World War II, he returned to Grand Rapids to practice law. But soon he was elected to Congress and never left, until he was nominated by Richard Nixon to the vacant vice presidency after Spiro Agnew resigned from that office on the report that he had accepted cash as payment for bribes arranged while he was governor of Maryland. When the president asked congressional leaders who could be confirmed, Ford was everybody's second choice after Ronald Reagan and Nelson Rockefeller, then governors of California and New York. Nixon was not about to appoint such strong figures, so congressional leaders made the choice for him. Nixon may have thought that since Ford was not of presidential stature, his nomination would protect Nixon from impeachment. Ford accepted Nixon's offer of the job, because it seemed to him to be a graceful way to leave politics in 1976. In fact, Nixon extracted a promise that Ford would support John Connally for the 1976 Republican nomination. Ford believed Nixon's protestations of innocence in the Watergate affair. But as the evidence began to emerge that Nixon was probably guilty, Ford refused to defend the president publicly and told him so at a cabinet meeting. It was a great irony that his selection as vice president probably helped hasten Nixon's departure.

PERSONALITY AND STYLE

David Gergen, who worked for Nixon, Ford, Reagan, and Clinton, wrote that Gerald Ford did not need to be president to be happy. He was thus like Truman, Eisenhower, and Reagan, and unlike Johnson, Nixon, and Clinton who "needed to win too much."[1] Gergen praised Ford in his belief that "truth is the glue" that holds government together and that "trust is the coin of the realm in politics." These were the views of a congressional leader in a time when trust in one's word and political accommodation across parties made the institution work. This was Gerald Ford's world. It was a world of eventful leadership. But eventful leaders must be politically skillful. We will see a number of instances in which Ford mistakenly assumed that his straightforwardness and honesty would persuade people of the rightness of his actions when, in fact, they failed to do so. He did not know how to prepare the way politically for his actions or to protect himself from political attack. Executive politicians learn these things, but Ford had made his word his bond in Congress, assuming that was enough. As an illustration of his innocence, he told Henry Kissinger that he was going to announce that he would not run for president in 1976. Kissinger persuaded Ford that he would automatically be a lame duck president. Honesty could go too far. The best illustration of Ford's strengths and weaknesses came in his pardon of Richard Nixon in the early days of his presidency.

THE PARDON

In the last days of the Nixon presidency, Alexander Haig, the president's chief of staff, informally approached Vice President Ford to tell him of the evidence on the White House tapes that incriminated Nixon in the obstruction of justice. Haig then outlined the alternatives facing Nixon. The first was to face impeachment and fight to survive a Senate trial. He could try for a congressional resolution of censure. He could pardon himself and others involved in Watergate and then resign. Or he could resign and hope that Ford would pardon him. Haig then asked if Ford had any suggestions as to what Nixon might do. Ford said that he did not but then asked Haig about the extent of the presidential power to pardon and was told that he had the power. They parted without further discussion, with Ford saying that he wanted time to think. When Ford told his aides about the conversation they were distressed, telling him that the possibility of a pardon should not have been discussed at all. Ford then told Haig that he would make no recommendation about what Nixon should do and that nothing in their earlier conversation should be considered in whatever decision Nixon made.

After Ford became president, the issue would not go away because the press was obsessed with the question of whether Nixon would be indicted by the special prosecutor, Leon Jaworski, whose office had prosecuted the Watergate offenders. The new president prepared to respond to questions about policy issues for his first press conference on August 28, 1974, but was instead bombarded with questions about a possible pardon for Nixon. He was not ready, assuming that Nixon's immediate fate was in the hands of Jaworski. When asked if he agreed with Nelson Rockefeller, who had said publicly that he thought that Nixon should be given immunity from prosecution, he said yes, but added that Jaworski should be free to take whatever action he thought proper. He would reserve his judgment about what to do until then. He used the phrase "intend to," which to him meant that he would wait until Jaworski had acted, but some interpreted that to mean that he would pardon Nixon. Ford did not initially realize that he had contradicted himself, but when he read the transcript he realized his mistake. He began to worry that his early presidency would be burdened with continuous coverage of a Nixon trial, which could take months. He had to get the question off the front pages so that he could have his own presidency. An indirect approach to Jaworski was inconclusive, and Ford soon made up his mind. He wanted to protect his presidency and thought that Nixon had suffered enough. Nor did he think that Americans wanted to see a president in jail. His principal assistants urged him to delay any decision and warned that a precipitous pardon would be met with dismay and anger. One told Ford that he trusted people too much, but the president thought his sincerity would be sufficient. Nor did he see any link between his conversation with Haig and a pardon. It was the right thing to do, he said.

On Sunday morning, September 8, the president went to church, returned to his office, and called an impromptu press conference at which he announced that he had pardoned Richard Nixon. The public response was outrage. Ford's support in the Gallup poll dropped twenty-two points from a high of 70 percent. Major newspapers condemned the action, and congressional leaders thundered. Congress very quickly passed a law keeping all of Nixon's papers under the control of the federal government. It is difficult to assess the long-term damage the pardon did to Ford. It surely cost him support in the 1976 election. In the short run, it fed into the cynicism about politicians created by Vietnam and Watergate and prompted the question of whether a deal had been made before Nixon resigned. The president took the unusual step of testifying before a joint congressional committee about his decision. This was typical Ford. Sincerity would be enough. He should have guarded his political flanks better by gradually explaining across time why a pardon might be necessary and waited to see what Jaworski would do. Sympathy might have built up for a Nixon under indictment. He acted too quickly without forethought. But most reasonable people agree in retrospect that he did the right thing. He had to clear the decks, and no one wanted to see a former president go to jail.

Executive Style

Roger Porter, who served in the Ford White House, remembered that the new president was much influenced by George Reedy's book on Lyndon Johnson, *The Twilight of the Presidency*. Reedy, who had been Johnson's press secretary, described the Johnson White House as a closed circle with too little tolerance for discordant opinions. Both Ford, and Carter after him, were determined to avoid the tightly controlled White House deliberations of the Johnson and Nixon years. The lessons for Ford, according to Porter, were not to get isolated, not to permit aides to push their own agendas, and not to give authority to the young and untested on the presidential staff. As minority leader, Ford had developed the skills of listening to a diverse number of members. His decisions as leader were usually collegial and based on the soundings he took from conversations. As president he was open to diverse streams of advice, encouraged debate, and was comfortable with the decisions he made. He discovered that he liked being president.

The first weeks were a bit chaotic, and eventually Ford recruited Donald Rumsfeld, a seasoned Republican politician, to be chief staff coordinator. Rumsfeld was never formally chief of staff, and his authority over other major players was uncertain. Three baronies were always in the mix: those of Secretary of State Henry Kissinger, Secretary of Defense James Schlesinger, and Secretary of the Treasury William Simon. In retrospect, Rumsfeld felt that Ford tolerated too many end runs, but this was Ford. He was not a disciplinarian and he always thought the best of people. There was a great deal of feuding, especially between Rumsfeld and Nelson Rockefeller, whom Ford had appointed as vice president, with congressional approval. Rumsfeld also clashed with Simon and Kissinger on occasion. To his credit, Rumsfeld ensured that the president was exposed to diverse views, for example in Rumsfeld's support for Alan Greenspan, the new chair of the Council of Economic Advisers. New cabinet appointments were of very high quality. For example, the president of the University of Chicago, Edward Levi, became attorney general. It was a government of talents, more so than with Nixon.

Domestic Policy

In his January 1975 State of the Union speech, Ford told the Congress that he would oppose any new spending for federal domestic programs. He believed that the Great Society programs were going to break the federal bank, particularly as spending for entitlement programs like Medicare, Medicaid, and Social Security grew. He and his advisers were preoccupied with the high rate of inflation in late 1974 and wanted to cut taxes and get expenditures down. Therefore there was no domestic program. This had not been Ford's plan when he promised Nelson Rockefeller that if he accepted the vice presidency, he would be in charge of domestic policy. The new president liked the idea of a grand centrist coalition that would reach across parties but did not anticipate how much Republican conservatives would oppose the Eastern Republican governor who had been a fierce rival of Barry Goldwater for the Republican presidential nomination in 1964. Rockefeller had been a policy innovator as governor of New York and hoped to do the same in Washington, but it turned out that there was no place for an activist vice president in a "steady as you go" administration. Rockefeller wanted to be assistant president for domestic policy, with the director of the Domestic Council reporting directly to him rather than through Rumsfeld. Rumsfeld would not have it, and Ford sided with his aide. Rockefeller could be the nominal chair of the Domestic Council, but once he saw that it was to be a paper-shuffling operation he lost interest and played only a marginal role in domestic policymaking thereafter.

Ford's domestic policy leadership consisted almost entirely of vetoes against congressional spending. The 1974 congressional elections flooded Congress with new Democrats as well as a new flock of Republican conservatives, many of whom would have preferred that Ronald Reagan be president. Partisan breaches were widening, and a constructive middle ground was narrowing. Ford was not hostile to education, health care, and other social programs, but he was concerned that the Great Society programs were swelling at an alarming and inflationary rate and therefore he opposed additional spending, through use of the veto. He vetoed sixty-six bills, and Congress sustained fifty-four of them with the aid of conservative Democrats and Republicans. Political scientists and journalists began to write about "gridlock" in Washington. Ford was able to pass only about a third of his proposals in Congress, a much lower level than most presidents, but it was not clear that he could have done better. The relative strength within each congressional party was shifting to ideologues in each camp caused, in part, by the growing strength of Republican candidates in the South. Ford understood Congress and knew how to work with it. The Democratic and Republican leaders respected him. But he did not ask for much, would not kneel before Democratic demands to spend, and was not a radical Republican who wished to repeal the Great Society.

Economic Policy

Economic issues were the central domestic question. Energy policy illustrates the political difficulties Ford had in finding a political center. President Nixon had created a Federal Energy Administration to develop strategies to deal with the high prices of crude oil, home heating oil, and gasoline occasioned by the OPEC cartel's oil price increases of 1973. Ford found himself caught between Democrats who wanted to keep the controls on oil prices enacted in 1971 and Republicans who wanted to decontrol prices to encourage production. In the fall of 1974, Ford's biggest concern was inflation. He hoped that the gradual decontrol of energy prices would lead to lower prices in the long run because of the conservation that would follow decontrol. He was prepared to tax oil producers in the bargain. Democrats wanted conservation, but not at the political costs of higher gasoline prices in the short run.

In January 1975 the president gave a televised talk from the White House library with a fire burning in the background. Jimmy Carter was to do the same thing in his first months as president, with as little result. Ford proposed the gradual decontrol of domestic oil prices along with a higher tariff on imported oil. The congressional response was hostile. In the spring Congress extended controls for six months, and Ford's veto of this action was sustained. Finally in December 1975 Ford signed a compromise bill that rolled back oil prices but gave him the authority to decontrol prices over a forty-month period. Congress would not act but would let the president take the heat. Secretary of the Treasury Simon, a strong free marketer, had urged Ford to refuse to compromise with Congress and push for stronger decontrol, but Alan Greenspan and energy officials argued that half a loaf was better than none; it was actually less than half a loaf, but the president was in a weak political position.

Ford's general economic outlook was that of a conventional Republican conservative. The chief role of government in the economy was to encourage business investment, balance the federal budget, and keep business taxes low. Ford was very much concerned that the growth in federal entitlements would soon reach beyond the ability of the government to pay, except through high taxes that would sap entrepreneurship and draw investment out of the economy. He was fortunate that Alan Greenspan was his chief economic adviser as chair of the Council of Economic Advisers. Greenspan, a private economic consultant in New York City, was critical of the prevailing practice of short-term solutions to long-term problems. He taught the fundamentals of limited government, balanced budgets, and strong monetary policy to deter inflation. He came to have great respect for Ford as a person who was so emotionally secure that he encouraged debate among advisers, and who would change his mind in the face of new evidence. Greenspan later said that Ford was "not really capable of abstractly articulating a philosophy" of economic action of his own. But one could see an implicit theory, and after a year he could predict how the president would decide on individual issues. He added, "I could present options and get quick decisions."[2] By the same token, Greenspan was able to sharpen Ford's understanding of his economic choices in accord with their shared values. Ford told Greenspan that he valued both him and Kissinger for the conceptual help they gave him beyond the need for immediate decisions.

In November 1974 the inflation rate was 12.1 percent over the year before, the highest it had been since 1919.[3] The Nixon adventure with wage and price controls had ultimately failed, and things were made worse by the 1973 OPEC oil shock as well as crop failures and a decline in the world food supply. In August 1974 unemployment was over 6 percent, and the Gross National Product was dropping.[4] Housing starts fell off and the stock market had declined. Greenspan's last economic forecast before leaving New York for Washington was for a mild recession in 1975. Ford and his economic advisers met on the afternoon that he was sworn in and decided that unemployment would probably rise to 6 percent that year. No one foresaw anything worse. The big concern was inflation. Ford spoke to Congress on August 12, asking for bipartisan restraint in spending, and agreed to convene a national economic summit in response to a proposal of the Senate. Similar regional meetings accompanied that White House meeting. Most of the talk was about inflation, and Bob Hartmann, the chief speechwriter, suggested the slogan "Whip Inflation Now" as a theme and "WIN" buttons began to appear on lapels. The president was determined to develop an economic program before the November congressional elections and on October 8 presented one to Congress. The main features were a 5 percent surcharge on high incomes and corporations, an increase in the investment tax credit, increased unemployment benefits, and the creation of public jobs in depressed areas. He urged a $500 billion budget ceiling, but a proposal to increase gasoline taxes was taken out as likely to be unpopular. Just as Ford announced his plans, a recession appeared. Unemployment rose to over 6 percent, the GNP declined, and the stock market dropped 200 points. Arthur Burns warned of a recession. Greenspan, who had played a quiet role to that point, not wishing to be identified with the WIN idea, began to suggest policies with which to face recession. Rumsfeld pulled Greenspan into the inner circle of advisers, and the latter convened meetings of outside economists to suggest remedies for the new problems. By late November Ford had given up hope for a $300 billion budget ceiling, and Greenspan suggested the possibility of a tax cut to stimulate the economy. It became apparent that the problem was "stagflation." Prices were climbing and the unemployment rate had increased to over 7 percent. Greenspan's intent was to bring both inflation and unemployment rates down together by reducing the federal budget slowly, with the help of tighter monetary policy from the Federal

Reserve. At the same time, capital investment would be encouraged to promote economic activity and job creation. There would be short-term uncertainties, but he thought that the economy would right itself in the long run. Of course, Ford had only two years left in his term, so how long was the long run? They began to prepare a new program in time for 1975, and on January 13 Ford gave the White House talk referred to earlier in the discussion of energy policy. He called for a three-year program of $16 billion in tax cuts to fight the recession and moderate budget restraint to cool inflation. The projected deficit for fiscal 1976 would be almost $52 billion, the highest in history. That was the most that Greenspan thought reasonable. He warned Ford that if the recession grew worse, Congress would want to spend more and that would create a deficit he could never overcome. Things were certainly bad. Inflation had climbed to over 12 percent and unemployment was beyond 8 percent.[5] The CEA's annual report predicted that the recession would continue into the spring with some leveling off in the summer. Recovery would be slow, but policy should be steady as you go. Congressional Democrats did not like these policies. They wanted to cut taxes and urged the Federal Reserve to loosen the money supply. Congress therefore increased the tax cut to $23 billion. Simon urged a veto, but Greenspan and James Lynn, director of the Office of Management and Budget (OMB), persuaded the president that Congress would not settle for less and that a stimulus was needed. Greenspan thought that the administration could live with a larger cut, if the deficit could be restrained. A veto would encourage Congress to cut taxes even more if the economy sagged. He also thought that congressional fears of a deep recession were exaggerated.

The sudden switch from a crusade against inflation to a fight against recession, while absolutely necessary, hurt Ford politically. Critics contended that the president was at the mercy of events without a clear policy of his own. An unfortunate stumble and fall at the foot of an airplane steps as he arrived in Austria became fodder for late-night comedians, despite the fact that Ford was probably the best athlete to have ever been president. Chevy Chase's imitation of Ford on the *Saturday Night Live* program always began with a stumble into the microphone. This was extremely unfair, but it played into a perception that Ford was a bumbler. People began to quote Lyndon Johnson that Ford could not walk and chew gum at the same time. Ford had failed to articulate clear themes for his presidency in the first months.

By spring the recession lifted and the economy began to improve in July. In October Ford proposed a permanent tax reduction of $28 billion to Congress, which was to be matched with $28 billion in spending cuts.

Three-quarters of the tax cuts would go to individuals and the rest to business. But Congress would only give him the tax cuts. The president vetoed the bill, and Congress replied with a smaller tax cut, which he accepted. The tax cuts did help pull the economy out of recession. There were 4 million more jobs in early 1976 than during the recession. Inflation was down to less than 6 percent.[6] Not everything was well. Productivity growth had fallen by about half since the 1950s, and real wages were down, perhaps because of the entry of increased numbers of unskilled youth and women into the labor market. The tax cuts had deepened the federal annual deficit. Ronald Reagan, running for president in 1976, attacked Ford for permitting such deficits, even though the president had achieved gradual recovery while cutting inflation—the very goals he had sought. Greenspan proposed, and the president accepted, a policy of only moderate recovery in order to keep inflation in check.

Ford missed an opportunity to articulate his moderate economic policy to Congress in his 1976 State of the Union speech. Despite the entreaties of his closest advisers, the president presented Congress with a laundry list of proposals without any overriding theme. Congressional Democrats, and many Republicans, were never happy with fiscal restraint and raised federal spending $17.3 billion over Ford's request, but recovery continued during the year. Unfortunately, unemployment rose to an 8 percent annual rate in the summer and fall.[7] Ford was determined not to inflate the economy, as Nixon had done in 1972, in order to win an election. He and Greenspan believed that the economy would stabilize in due course. But opinion surveys revealed that the public felt that Ford had failed in his promises.

The political problem of Ford's economic policies was that they were too moderate for effective presidential politics. Both he and Jimmy Carter after him had to struggle with stagflation. Democrats wanted more spending against recession. Republican conservatives wanted deep budget cuts against inflation as a way to revive the private economy. Both Ford and Carter sought to get budget deficits down as an antidote to inflation, but neither was willing to cut government spending in a radical way. There was a widening partisan political divide about what to do. The Democrats had no fresh ideas beyond wage and price controls and support for guaranteed jobs for the unemployed. That effort, in which public employment was added to employment-training programs, eventually led to considerable substitution of federal money for state and local expenditures and even to corruption in some instances. It was not long before Republican conservatives began to talk about supply-side economic theory in which tax cuts in the favor of the well-to-do and businesses were expected to stimulate investment and growth. This economic theory developed a political appeal eventually exploited by Ronald Reagan. Ford was trapped by stagflation, and his remedies, developed by Greenspan, were too sensible for the politics of the time. The public clamor was for event-making leadership without any sense of what such leadership might do.

FOREIGN POLICY

President Ford confronted the same ideological divisions in Congress and among the politically active that he had faced in economic policy. Democratic liberals, burned and angered by the Vietnam war, opposed American intervention in the third world, except for preaching about human rights, and were hostile to defense increases. Republican conservatives, often labeled "neoconservatives," saw withdrawal from Vietnam as a humiliating defeat, which increased their anticommunism. They were therefore hostile to détente and the Soviet Union. Henry Kissinger was critical of both camps, seeing them as prisoners of the traditional American view that the world could somehow be made perfect. Americans, he believed, had always been uneasy in an imperfect world of complexity in which the United States would be permanently engaged. By his account, both he and Ford saw foreign policy as a continuing process. But Ford was not a conceptual thinker and was not good at publicly articulating principles of foreign policy. Kissinger had become a substitute for the president in foreign policy leadership during Nixon's eclipse, but that could not continue indefinitely. The secretary of state cannot be a substitute for the president. As a result, as détente began to decline abroad, and support declined at home, Kissinger became a target of criticism from both left and right.

Strategic Arms Limitation Treaty (SALT)

Ford and Kissinger wanted to continue talks on arms control with the Soviets, because new weapons were emerging all the time. The United States was ahead in the number of warheads, but the Soviets had a larger number of launch vehicles for heavy missiles. This asymmetry did not bother Ford and Kissinger, so long as the striking power was equivalent. Brezhnev made clear to Kissinger in October 1974 in Moscow that he wanted an agreement. In November 1974 Brezhnev and his arms experts met with Ford, Kissinger, and Secretary of Defense James Schlesinger in Vladivostok in Siberia and negotiated a rough agreement along the lines earlier discussed in Moscow. It was not yet a treaty for ratification because details had to be worked out, but it seemed a sure thing. The agreement was to last until 1985, and negotiations for the post-1985 period were to begin after the treaty was sealed. Brezhnev proposed a pact between the United States and the Soviet Union against China that was gently rebuffed, but it was clear that the Soviet leaders feared the Chinese. Ford told Brezhnev that he had to negotiate an agreement that put both sets of forces at parity in order to win support at home, and Brezhnev agreed. The agreement set a limit of 1,320 MIRVs (warheads within missiles) on each side, as well as 2,400 launchers.

Secretary Schlesinger preferred absolute parity as did Democratic senator Henry Jackson, a defense expert, who was running for president. Ford decided to accommodate them. Two weapon systems were not included: the Soviet backfire bomber and the American cruise missile. Both sides contended that they were short-range weapons and could not be considered as transcontinental. Conservatives saw the backfire as intercontinental, which it was not without refueling. Kissinger thought it obsolete but had to deal with Jackson, who wanted it in the treaty. Ford and Kissinger did not see the cruise missile as belonging in the treaty, but the Soviets wanted it there. This impasse was not broken until the Carter administration.

The Joint Chiefs of Staff and their experts were still worried about asymmetry. Soviet ICBMs were large and could strike U.S. silos containing smaller missiles. A U.S. response with missiles from submarines might be met by a Soviet attack on American cities. Kissinger thought the Pentagon estimate of the number of Soviet missiles was exaggerated; many were obsolete, and they were not building new ones. The high count had been produced by a CIA Team B of experts on the U.S.S.R., which was intended to bring a fresh view to regular CIA estimates. Team B reported that the Soviet military were determined to fight and win a nuclear war, this at a time when Brezhnev was reducing military spending in an effort to boost the moribund Soviet economy. Senator Henry Jackson was a thorn at Ford's side every step of the way. He insisted on a Soviet guarantee of absolute numbers of Jewish emigrants from the Soviet Union each year. The Russians promised to do better, but no Soviet leader could buckle under Jackson's public threats. The Soviets canceled the trade agreement that had been negotiated in 1972, but had been held up by Jackson, and Jewish emigration declined. Ford and Kissinger could only watch and wring their hands. The increasing polarization in Washington did not help. Liberals saw the Vladivostok agreement as an arms buildup and conservatives wanted no agreement at all.

In November 1975 Ford decided to reshuffle his government. It was an abrupt act similar to his decision to pardon Nixon. He fired James Schlesinger, whom he did not like for talking down to him, and moved Rumsfeld to the Defense Department. Kissinger had held two hats as assistant for national security and secretary of state since Nixon's second term, and he lost the White House post. Ford asked Vice President Rockefeller to withdraw from the 1976 election race, and Rockefeller did so as a good soldier. Attacks from the Republican right on Rockefeller had been unceasing. Ford was trying to show the public that he was in charge of his own government, but the actual effect was to contribute to the impression that he was not fully in charge.

Kissinger soon discerned that his position was weakened, because Rumsfeld began to drag his feet on SALT. This was partly because the Joint Chiefs were so uncertain, but also because Ronald Reagan soon announced that he would run for president against Ford and attacked SALT. Kissinger traveled to Moscow in early 1976, but he was never able to negotiate an agreement because of conflicts in Washington. In February, after Reagan had attacked SALT and argued that the United States was now a second-rate military power, Ford announced that he would no longer use the word "détente." Kissinger shifted his rhetoric to "containment" of the Soviet Union. SALT was dead.

The Challenge to Détente

Détente could have continued had Ford and Kissinger been able to deliver arms control and trade agreements to the Soviets, but, by the same token, the Soviets would have had to refrain from adventures abroad. Soviet and Cuban support for Marxist guerrillas in Angola, Marxist regimes in Somalia and Ethiopia, and Marxist coups in Yemen and Afghanistan was difficult to square with détente. Suppression of Soviet dissidents was accompanied by the continued buildup of military forces. The Soviets did not see arms agreements as an inhibition on their adventures abroad. Henry Kissinger had worn out his welcome in Washington. He was, in part, a prisoner of his diplomatic style of working secretly and independently of other Washington bureaucracies, even his own State Department. He always had the confidence of the president, but Ford felt himself under increasing pressure from conservatives in his own party for a reversal of détente in favor of fervent anticommunism. He had to win the nomination and an election. Kissinger later wrote that neither he nor Ford understood the depth of the neoconservative challenge. Kissinger's realist acceptance of the necessity of working with other nations in reciprocal relations in an imperfect world was attacked as immoral. The alternative was somehow to roll back Soviet power by confrontation. It must be added that congressional liberals also distrusted Kissinger. The trauma of Vietnam had caused them to return to their Wilsonian roots by disavowing international power politics, and therefore to disapprove of the bargains that Kissinger sought to develop. Kissinger thought that his failure as a practitioner of realist politics was caught between the demands for morality without power from the one side and for power *as* morality from the other side. Americans had never been comfortable with the concept of balance of power among nations.

IDEOLOGY

We have seen the difficulties that Ford had with Republican conservatives in economic and foreign policy. Ronald Reagan almost took the Republican nomination away from him in 1976. It is important to explore Reagan's new brand of conservatism, not only to understand the political campaign but because these strands of ideas finally came to full fruition in Reagan's presidency. Jerome Himmelstein, a political scientist, has carefully examined the origins of neoconservatism and found three strands: economic libertarianism, social traditionalism, and militant anticommunism. The three strands are held together by the belief that capitalism is a moral order, supported by traditional values of work and social order. Interventionist liberal governments have disrupted this moral order by interfering with free markets and encouraging permissive social behavior—abortion, pornography, excessive welfare—and liberals have compounded the damage they have done by failure to resist the Soviet threat to the American way of life. Liberal elites in the universities and the media, especially on both coasts, are thus the scoundrels in the scheme. Himmelstein traces the union of these ideas back to the *National Review* magazine, edited by William F. Buckley, since the 1950s. Barry Goldwater's candidacy gave political expression to these ideas, and Ronald Reagan became his rhetorical heir. A conservative political movement grew out of the Goldwater campaign; for example, many present Republican officeholders were active in the Young Americans for Freedom founded on college campuses. Full political expression became possible only in the wake of the Great Society, when the white South began to turn Republican and blue-collar workers turned against affirmative action. The urban riots of the 1960s, the student antiwar movement, and the populist politics of George Wallace all contributed to defections from the Democrats.

This is not to say that all Republican voters became neoconservatives but that a large number of a new generation of Republican politicians adopted that credo. For many conservatives, Nixon and Ford were too liberal. Continuing economic problems and the difficulties of détente provided openings for the new movement. It was given expression by Reagan in 1976, and will be explored more fully in an analysis of his presidency.

ELECTIONS

Ronald Reagan campaigned for the presidency in 1976 and 1980 as an "outsider" who would clean up the mess in Washington. Reagan did not respect Ford, seeing him as neither bright nor sufficiently militant in the cause of conservatism. When he first talked about running against Ford in late 1975, the polls revealed much public dissatisfaction with the president and accepted Reagan as a reasonable alternative. Ford and his advisers underestimated Reagan for a time, as his political opponents had always done. He was seen as a lightweight who made emotional appeals. For example, in early 1976 Reagan gave a speech in Chicago in which he claimed that the federal government would save $90 billion if federal social programs were transferred to the states along with the money to pay for them. He gave the speech without any discussion among his staff. It was pulled out of a file, and it is not even clear that he had read it or thought about it. Reagan lost further ground to Ford when he said that state taxes might have to be raised under his program. Ford found it very frustrating to campaign against Reagan, recalling in his memoir: "He was a master at oversimplifying complex issues, reducing them to one-line quips, and that was very effective politically, especially among grassroots conservatives."[8]

Reagan talked for years about a nonexistent "welfare queen" in Chicago who had gotten rich from corrupting the welfare system. He charged that Ford had fired James Schlesinger as secretary of defense because Ford was afraid to tell the truth about the American military deficit in competition with the Soviet Union. He campaigned in Florida by suggesting that Social Security funds be invested in the stock market and then backed down, saying that it was only an idea. Reagan won the North Carolina primary by campaigning against the return of the Panama Canal to Panama: "We built it, we paid for it, it's ours, and we should tell Torrijos and company that we are going to keep it." Ford regarded Reagan as an entertainer and complained that "it was almost impossible to defuse his emotional appeals."[9] In addition to attacks on big government and anticommunism,

Reagan articulated new social issues in his opposition to abortion and gun control. He did not appeal to religious conservatives explicitly; they were just beginning to find their feet in politics. But in the Reagan campaign, new strategies for the organization of direct mail to conservative activists and single-issue interest groups were fully exploited. Ford's very virtue of cautious moderation was a red flag for conservative activists, who wanted something bolder. American politics were about to enter a period in what Samuel Huntington, a Harvard political scientist, calls "creedal passion," a recurrent phenomenon in American history. Ford had never run for anything but a seat in the House and he had easily won reelection. His skills were collegial rather than rhetorical. But Reagan, a movie star and governor, knew how to present himself as a president.

Ford won the New Hampshire primary with only 51 percent of the vote. Ford then won Florida after Reagan's imprudent references to making Social Security voluntary. However, Reagan proceeded to win North Carolina and then went on national television to attack Soviet adventures overseas. A series of primaries followed that produced no clear winner. The increase of the number of primaries in both parties after 1972 weakened the ability of an incumbent president to engineer his own renomination through support from Republican state organizations. The process was thrown open to voters as never before, and ideologically committed voters are more likely to participate in primaries. As the convention opened in Kansas City, Ford was ahead in delegates but short of a majority. He spent considerable time talking with delegates in efforts to win. Reagan's campaign manager, John Sears, had hit on a clever ploy to unite a ticket by persuading Reagan to choose Richard Schweiker, a liberal Republican senator from Pennsylvania, as his running mate in advance. Sears also calculated that Schweiker could bring the large number of Pennsylvania delegates to Reagan's majority, but the attempt failed and Ford gathered enough votes to win the nomination. However, conservative activists controlled the platform committee, and Ford did not challenge the platform themes of criticism of détente and the importance of retaining the Panama Canal. He did not want a floor fight on the platform and also wanted to control the vice presidential nomination. His actual choice, Senator Robert Dole from Kansas, was acceptable to both camps.

Ford entered the final event twenty points behind Jimmy Carter, the Democratic nominee. Carter campaigned against Nixon more than Ford, stressing the importance of morality in government, making the frequent promise that "I will never lie to you." He was also critical of Kissinger's balance-of-power policies and called for a reaffirmation of human rights as a major theme in foreign policy. Carter was very much a Wilsonian in the

Democratic tradition. He began his campaign in Warm Springs, Georgia, at Franklin Roosevelt's retreat but he did not stress Great Society themes in his campaign. In fact, his call for balancing budgets distressed a number of Democratic interest groups during the campaign. The Ford campaign could not label him a "McGovernite." Carter also had good support in the South, as a "born again" Baptist, among evangelicals. The Ford campaign was initially a Rose Garden strategy of being presidential in Washington with Dole out in the country attacking Democrats. But the president wanted very badly to win and he could not stay away from the fight. Reagan did almost nothing for Ford, preferring to work for conservative congressional candidates. Richard Cheney, the White House chief of staff, ran a very disciplined campaign, but Ford's campaign aides found it difficult to articulate fresh campaign themes. Ford expected to be rewarded for restoring the presidency to respectability, getting the economy in shape, and running a stable foreign policy. But his own polls showed that he was not seen as a "strong, decisive leader." The public seemed to want someone altogether free of Watergate, and Ford—perhaps unfairly—was burdened with Nixon's pardon. However, Carter did not wear well with many Democratic liberals and party regulars, who did not feel that he was one of them. Carter's strength was among white Protestants, better-educated workers, and rural and small-town voters. African Americans were solidly for him. He was not the man to renew the old Democratic coalition first created by FDR and sustained by Kennedy and Johnson.

Ford did fairly well in the first presidential debate, narrowing Carter's lead to eight points. However, the second debate was a disaster for him. In response to a question about Soviet domination of Eastern European nations, he denied that the Russians dominated these counties with the particular assertion that Poland was not under Soviet domination, even when asked the question twice. He meant to say that the Polish people did not see themselves as part of the Soviet Union. He was thinking of the hope for the ultimate liberation of Eastern Europe. But he had garbled his answer and lost the debate. The media hopped onto the issue, but Ford, not seeing his mistake, took some time to issue a clarification. The Gallup poll found that the mistake had stopped Ford's campaign in its tracks. Still, by late October Carter's campaign was slipping and Ford was behind only a few points. Ford had not done anything special, but Carter continued to slip, so that the last polls before the election showed them to be virtually tied. The election turnout was low, and Carter won the popular vote by two percentage points. Carter won 297 electoral votes for Ford's 241. The economy had slowed down during the fall and this was perhaps the crucial factor among the issues. In addition, Ford's very strengths as president, his

might have strengthened Ford as a politician of the center. He might have won reelection, but the problems that Carter confronted were a continuation of Ford's problems. Stagflation continued. Détente eroded. Ronald Reagan would have run for president in 1980. Ford and Carter were caught in a transition between the Democratic era and a Republican era to come. A strong, effective presidency became impossible for a time.

Effectiveness

Gerald Ford was the least effective of the presidents in this study in terms of policy achievement. But if one assesses effectiveness in the influence of the president on our constitutional norms and his ability to work within the institutions, even if for modest results, Ford must be remembered as most effective in his time and place in our history.

BIBLIOGRAPHICAL ESSAY

The best study of the Ford presidency is John Robert Greene, *The Presidency of Gerald Ford* (1995). Greene captures Ford's strengths and weaknesses as a political leader in a well-balanced way. James Cannon, *Time and Chance: Gerald Ford's Appointment with History* (1994), is primarily about Ford's life and career before he became president. It is laudatory but accurate as far as it goes. David Gergen's *Eyewitness to Power* (2000) has a chapter on Ford, which is insightful and sympathetic, but depicts political failures.

Ford's own memoir, *A Time to Heal* (1979), is straightforward, honest, and a bit dull. John Osborne's volume on the Ford years, *White House Watch* (1977), is high-level White House gossip filled with acute insights about Ford and his key lieutenants. Robert Hartmann, *Palace Politics* (1980), gives a picture of White House politics from the perspective of a jealous suitor for the president's attention.

There are a number of good essays on domestic and economic policy from the proceedings of the 1989 conference on the Ford presidency at Hofstra University edited by Bernard J. Firestone and Alexej Ugrinsky, *Gerald Ford and the Politics of Post-Watergate America* (1993). Of particular value are those by John W. Sloan, and Ronald F. King on economic policy. As with the other chapters in this book, I have relied on the book of interviews edited by Samuel Morley and myself, *The President and the Council of Economic Advisers* (1984). Herbert Stein's *Presidential Economics* (3d ed., 1994) is useful but limited on Ford. Roger Porter, *Presidential Decisionmaking: The Economic Policy Board* (1980), is a rich picture from one who was there, as is his chapter on Ford in Fred Greenstein, ed., *Leadership in the Modern Presidency* (1988).

One could not list all the material on foreign policy, but students should begin with Henry Kissinger's *Years of Renewal* (1999). Kissinger writes so well and so clearly that one is easily seduced. I respect Kissinger's "realist" approach to foreign policy in contrast to Wilsonian idealism and neoconservative crusading, but one need not accept all his arguments. John

Lewis Gaddis, *Strategies of Containment* (2005), is critical of Kissinger for exaggerating the possibilities of détente. William Hyland worked in the State Department and the White House with Ford and Kissinger, and his *Mortal Rivals: Superpower Relations from Nixon to Reagan* (1987) is ironic, detached, and yet sympathetic to both men as an experienced professional saw them. Raymond Garthoff, *Détente and Confrontation* (1985), is the fullest and most accurate account of Soviet-American relations in the Ford years.

Jules Witcover, *Marathon: The Pursuit of the Presidency, 1972–1976* (1977), is a very good journalistic account of Ford and presidential politics. Jerome L. Himmelstein, *To the Right: The Transformation of American Conservatism* (1989), describes the development of new kinds of conservative ideology that would bear fruition in the Reagan campaign and the Republican Party. A. James Reichley, *Conservatives in an Age of Change: The Nixon and Ford Administrations* (1981), writes from a solid, historical Republican viewpoint that sees less discontinuity in Republican politics than Himmelstein. Robert Mason, *Richard Nixon and the Quest for a New Majority* (2004), provides a good analysis of voters, party identification and changes, and elections.

CHAPTER FIVE

Jimmy Carter

The Engineer President

Herbert Hoover and Jimmy Carter have been the only two presidents to be engineers. Engineers are inclined to believe that there are correct answers to problems. This is very important when building a bridge, but politics and policy do not admit of expert solutions in the final analysis. There are too many unknowns and too many unresolved conflicts. A politician must often leap into the unknown, relying on honed skills of political calculation based on seasoning and experience.

In 1982 Jimmy Carter told a group of political scientists, meeting with him in Plains, Georgia, that when he first went to Washington he surprised people:

> I had a different way of governing, I think, than had been the case with my predecessors, and the public and the press were still in somewhat of a quandary about how we managed the affairs of the White House. I was a southerner, a born-again Christian, a Baptist, a newcomer. I didn't have any obligations to the people in Washington for my election. Very few of the members of Congress, or members of the various lobbying groups, or the distinguished, former Democratic leaders had played much of a role in my election. There wasn't that tie of interrelationship that ordinarily would have occurred had I

not been able to win the nomination by myself.... and I think they felt they were kind of on the outside.[1]

Carter's signal achievements and failures came from his "different way of governing." Carter rejected the "normal politics" of coalition building and bargaining that congressional politicians take for granted. His critics, especially in the press and among congressional Democrats, were quick to call him a naïve and inept amateur for his way of governing. Foreign leaders, among allies and foes, often had the same view. But the very same lonely determination accounted for his successes.

His policy goals were also confounding to many in the Democratic coalition. He believed the Great Society to be over and called the Democrats back to the center for fiscal probity and the consolidation, rather than the extension, of federal social programs. He was a moralist in foreign policy who presented the achievement of "human rights" around the world as his most important objective and preached to the Soviet leaders about human rights even as he sought mutual arms reductions. He wanted to be an event-making president by creating a new Democratic Party and establishing peace in the cold war. But the historical conditions were not favorable, and he lacked the coalition-building skills of a creative eventful leader.

BIOGRAPHY

Carter's first political success was winning the race for the George state senate against the attempt by local courthouse politicians to defraud him. In the state senate he developed a dislike for politicians. He saw his senate colleagues as serving the special interests that elected them instead of a common good. This gave him the idea that if comprehensive programs in the public interest were presented to the people, they would win support against special interests. When he was elected governor in 1970, this was the kind of program he presented to the legislature—the most notable being a thorough reorganization of state government. He went to the legislature and stood in the well of the state house of representatives to answer questions about his plan, causing one of them to remark that he knew more about state government than anyone in the room. He also prevailed, thus confirming his belief in homework as the foundation of persuasion.

His engineering training, his religious faith, and his values influenced Carter's approach to political leadership as a Southern progressive. His aides recalled that in his early months in the White House, he believed that if he did a great deal of study and found the correct solution to a problem, he would surely be able to persuade others to see things as he saw them. His Baptist faith told him that with God all things were possible. He also stood in a tradition of Southern progressives who sought good government on business principles, opposed the corruption of politicians, and were institutional reformers. His identity was strong and he understood it fully.

He was one of the first politicians to understand that the increased number of state primary elections created by reformers in his party would permit a candidate to run in a large number of primaries and collect delegates without winning all the contests. There was great public disillusionment with politicians in 1974, and he presented himself as an outsider who would go to Washington with clean hands. Finally, the immoralities of Watergate played on the perennial American desire for a moral politics, and this was easy for Carter.

These characteristics carried Carter successfully through the primaries and won him the nomination, despite the misgivings of many traditional Democratic politicians who wanted to hear the old refrains about what government would do for their people. The problem became more acute during the general election campaign when organized interests in the Democratic coalition wanted to know what he would do for them. The unions, the teachers, and the mayors did not see him as their man. Many traditional blue-collar Democratic voters were not sure who he was or what he stood for. Secular policy intellectuals did not know what to make of a religious Southerner who talked about morality. All of this helps explain why he almost lost the election, because he barely carried his own coalition.

CONCEPTIONS OF LEADERSHIP

Carter believed that the president spoke for the public interest and that his task was to attack unresolved national problems, whether the public demand for resolution existed or not. He, as president, would create that demand. One might call him a perfectionist who believed in the full realization of the American dream. One might compromise but not until the effort to be comprehensive had failed. He did not appear to believe that a good solution might emerge in unforeseen ways out of compromise and bargaining through a diversity of views. He had a weak sense of how to combine purpose with prudence. That kind of politics always fell short of the long-term solutions that he valued.

Carter was not curious about the motives and incentives of other politicians, especially senators, in part because he did not enjoy shoptalk as recreation with a purpose, and also because he saw senators as rivals. His apolitical stance was thoroughly political, in Carter's view, not because it sought political advantage in a game of politics, but because it would be rewarded by the public in the long run for having solved fundamental problems. He was a "trustee president," a phrase coined by the political scientist Charles Jones in his study of Carter and Congress. At the outset Carter lacked a sense of political strategy in which objectives were timed and ranked according to the need for early successes and degrees of political difficulty. Thus, he sent too much to Congress in his first year, only to see it bogged down. He refused to heed advice about prudent timing of proposals according to political considerations. And in all this he played to his personal strengths, for homework, persuasiveness, and determination. He later acknowledged the mixed character of his own style:

> A lot of my advisers, including Rosalyn, used to argue with me about my decision to move ahead with a project when it was obviously not going to be politically advantageous, or to encourage me to postpone it until a possible second term and so forth. It was just contrary to my nature.... I just couldn't do it. Once I made a decision I was awfully stubborn about it. I think if I could have one political attribute as the cause of my success to begin with, it would be tenacity. Once I set my mind on something I'm awfully hard to change. And that may also be a cause of some of my political failures.[2]

Carter's style as an executive set a premium on his ability to understand issues. A small White House staff was to assist him in that work, while the cabinet departments were to prepare legislation. Confidence that the departments would do this, particularly in cooperation with each other, soon faded, and he came to rely more on his staff. However, he never understood what staff could do for him in analyzing policy alternatives. Carter valued diversity among his advisers but wanted to mix in early and set the alternatives himself, saying, "If an issue was mine I wanted to understand it." He did the homework, and it could be a resource in his persuasiveness with others, including members of Congress. But he did not understand that he should keep himself free to think in strategic terms. He refused until late in the day to have a chief of staff who might have helped him organize his priorities more clearly. And he sometimes had difficulty reconciling the competing views of staff members, because no one was acting as a "custodian" for him in sorting out his choices. Carter wanted high cohesion and harmony among his advisers and could not always achieve it. But he did not understand that his primary task as president was to be a strategic leader who set directions and priorities. He had to turn to Vice President Walter Mondale in his second year in office to set up legislative priorities for the administration.

Carter and Congress

Carter told the editors of *U.S. News and World Report* during the campaign: "I intend to keep all my promises. It may be that the Congress would not cooperate in some of those areas. If not, I reserve the right to go directly to the people of this country and present my case there. There may be a danger with so many proposals that they will get in each other's way. But I think a compensating factor would be my inclination to capitalize on whatever mandate I get in November."[3] After his presidency, he told a group of scholars that he had expected to have more harmony with Congress than had occurred. He could agree with the Democratic leadership on some issues, but agreement did not extend that far out into the ranks. There was no loyalty to him, and he learned that he had to pick up votes issue by issue.[4]

The Democratic majorities in the two houses of Congress were ample. The Senate had 62 Democrats and 38 Republicans, while the House had 292 Democrats and 143 Republicans. But congressional reforms in response to Nixon had made presidential leadership more difficult than before. The authority of committee chairs had been weakened with the proliferation of subcommittees. The numbers of congressional staff had increased. The politics of "interest group liberalism" permeated the life of Congress more than ever as the legacy of the Great Society. The increasing cost of the entitlement programs, like Medicare, had also begun to threaten federal fiscal stability. Carter threw down a gauntlet to Congress in his criticisms of proliferating programs and budgets; he was challenging their means of political survival. Carter had run behind the congressional Democrats in the election, and they felt that they owed him nothing. Two stories illustrate the point.

As he revised President Ford's budget for fiscal 1978 in the beginning weeks of his term, Carter cut a number of water projects out of the budget altogether and held some up for further study as to their likely merit. Congress was outraged. Members had waited in line for years to get their due from the appropriations committees. It was all part of doing well at home and ensuring reelection. The Army Corps of Engineers and the Bureau of Reclamation were out in the field drumming up projects for Congress to endorse. Carter wanted to cut the budget and challenge a political way of life. There was neither advance warning, nor any attempt to use the projects as bargaining chips. He eventually had to compromise, but wrote in his memoir that he wished that he had vetoed all the projects. He recalled his concerns about fiscal discipline in 1982:

> I wish some of you could have sat in on some of our leadership meetings and just seen the stricken expression on the faces of those Democratic leaders when I was talking about balancing the budget ... which was anathema to them.... That wasn't something a Democratic president was supposed to do. So even in that early phase, I'm talking about the spring of '77, I was already getting strong opposition from my Democratic leadership in dealing with economics. All they knew about it was (economic) stimulus and Great Society programs.[5]

The second story was that of the economic stimulus plan developed in response to Carter's campaign promise to revive the economy. Once in office, he resisted the demands of Democratic groups for a large stimulus package, and indeed, was skeptical about whether it was needed at all, because it looked as if the economy was recovering. However, various spending measures were sent to Congress, along with the promise of a $50 rebate to every citizen. But Carter began to question the rebate because he was beginning to fear that inflation, rather than recession, was his long-term problem. Secretary of the Treasury Michael Blumenthal and Bert Lance, the director of the OMB, did not see the need for the rebate—nor did congressional leaders, who wanted an even stronger stimulus package. However, they agreed to try to sell it to Congress. But by early April, Carter was even more skeptical and decided to withdraw the rebate. He did not tell Blumenthal, who was defending it at the National Press Club at the very time that the announcement of the withdrawal was made. Nor did he tell Senator Edmund Muskie, who had worked hard for its passage. Carter had made a political blunder, which he acknowledged:

> From then on (after the rebate withdrawal), the basic course was set, but my advisers were right about the political damage. The obvious inconsistency in my policy during this rapid transition from stimulating the economy to an overall battle against inflation was to plague me for a long time. But I knew I had made the correct decision; for more than three and a half years my major economic battle would be against inflation, and I would stay on the side of fiscal prudence, restricted budgets, and lower deficits. Discretionary domestic spending, in real dollars, increased less than 1 percent during my term of office.[6]

These stories illustrate the amateurism of the president and his staff in the early days. These shaky beginnings damaged his reputation with Congress, the press, and the public, and were never fully eradicated. However, a more balanced assessment of Carter's leadership skills can be found in four policy initiatives: welfare reform, creation of the Department of Education, the Panama Canal treaties, and his energy program. The first two cases illustrate the difficulties of his hope for comprehensive programs, and the third and fourth reveal the success of his strategy when political conditions permitted decisive action.

Welfare Reform

Richard Nixon's plan for welfare reform foundered on the division between liberals and conservatives, the former wanting more and the latter demanding less. There was no center. Carter had exactly the same experience. But presidents often ignore, if they even ask about, the failures of their predecessors, especially of a different party. In any event, Carter wanted to do it his own way. His experience as governor had taught him that welfare programs did not induce people to work. He wanted uniform standards of payments and requirements across the states. When the transition team on income security told him that incremental changes in the existing system would be easier to pass in Congress he replied that he had promised a comprehensive bill and regarded welfare reform as a first step in presenting social policy with a "conservative" stamp. In December 1976 he told Joseph Califano, the secretary of health, education, and welfare, that he wanted a complete overhaul of the welfare program for aid to families and dependent children. There should have been, but was not, a discussion about costs of a new program, because it soon became apparent that Carter wanted a new program at current costs, and Califano believed this to be impossible.

Califano was charged with developing a bill, in cooperation with the secretary of labor, Ray Marshall. But the economists in the two departments could not agree on a plan. Labor wanted increased public service employment. The Department of Health, Education, and Welfare (HEW) was skeptical of the utility of "leaf-raking" jobs and wanted increased income payments to the "working poor." Califano had casually suggested a deadline of May 1 for a bill, and Carter publicly announced it without checking with his new secretary. In March Califano told the president that a program with national standards would be more expensive than the existing program, but Carter was not responsive. He made clear that he wanted both jobs and public assistance at existing costs. He said that he was confident that he could persuade the Congress to follow him.

When Califano and Marshall could not agree, Califano turned to White House aides for help. A compromise was finally reached in which Carter was persuaded to add the word "initial" to language about costs. In August 1977 the president introduced the Program for Better Jobs and Income. It had the same flaws as Nixon's plan. Many recipients were to receive reduced income assistance as the states were placed under one standard and the number of recipients was increased.

The bill never reached the floor of the House. Too many other Carter measures, such as energy reform, tax reform, and Social Security revision, had flooded the two finance committees in the House and Senate. Michael Blumenthal, the secretary of the treasury, asked Carter whether he was not sending up too much at one time, but Carter had replied that he wanted to move on everything at once. The politics in Congress were not congenial to welfare reform. Conservatives wanted more work and less welfare, and liberals wished to cover more of the working poor. On June 6 California voters passed Proposition 13, which restricted public spending, and congressional leaders saw this as a wind of change that would kill welfare reform. Carter should have read the Nixon experience and either pushed for modest reform or left the issue alone. But as he often said, "it is not in my nature" to fail to push for his goals.

A New Department of Education

The importance of this story is that Carter's attempt to take the Office of Education out of HEW and make it a broad department of Education and Human Development failed for political reasons that could have been predicted. At the end of the day, in 1979, he had to settle for a limited department that was a puffed up office of education and do so because he had learned about the necessity of political compromise.

Carter had made a campaign promise of a broad department, which would include early childhood education, job training, adult education, childcare, etc. His idea was to elevate education as a national priority, but he went beyond the desire of the teachers' unions in his emphasis on breadth. Senator Abraham Ribicoff, a Democrat, who chaired the Senate Government Operations Committee that would oversee any reorganization, also wanted a broad department. But Secretary Califano was very much opposed. The President's Reorganization Project, in the Office of Management and Budget, developed a plan for a broad Department of Education and Human

Development encompassing a number of programs, some of which would come from HEW. Carter discussed the plan, along with plans for a narrow department, or a strengthened Office of Education, with cabinet advisers and chose the broad option, against the advice of his own domestic policy staff. Human services and civil rights interest groups did not want to be in a new department headed by education bureaucrats and they went to work in Congress so that a stripped-down version of the comprehensive bill passed the Senate. A glorified Office of Education as a department passed into law in 1979. Carter had capitulated in order to get a department at all.

These two cases reveal the absence of strategic political thinking. Carter ran his government as a naval officer might, receiving staff recommendations and making his decisions on the basis of his own knowledge of the problem. The next two cases, the Panama Canal treaties and the enactment of an energy conservation program, were more successful. Carter had to fight very hard to win in both cases and used his skills of exposition and determination. Political support in both cases was latent, and the president was able to develop enough support to carry the day. These were not issues in which he was at odds with his own party, and he received some Republican help, particularly with the Panama Canal. Both successes came early in his term, but one sees none of the political clumsiness of other cases. Carter's success recalls his effectiveness in persuading the Georgia legislature to enact administrative reorganization. The Panama case was an appeal to the national interest. So was energy conservation, but in this case success was constrained by particular interests all the way to the end.

The Panama Canal Treaties

President Johnson had begun negotiations with the government of Panama about the transfer of the canal to Panama, and Nixon and Ford had continued the negotiations, which had faltered as Ford battled Reagan for the nomination. Carter revived the negotiations, and there was much for his negotiators to build on. There was a general fear of what might happen in Panama if there were no treaty. Violence against American residents of the Canal Zone had occurred in the recent past. The president of Panama later said that if the treaties had not passed, he would have closed the canal. But Republican conservatives were hostile to the plan and organized a massive grassroots campaign of direct mail and speakers as negotiations were begun.

Eventually, two treaties were signed on September 7, 1977. They provided for joint operation of the canal until 1999 and U.S. rights to defend the canal against attack thereafter. Carter was in his element, doing a morally right action, which was also in the national interest, as he understood it. The administration then worked the Senate intensively for six months. An organization was set up in the White House to bring opinion leaders and politicians from around the nation to the East Room, where Secretary of State Cyrus Vance and other high officials spoke week after week. Cabinet members were sent out to make speeches. Testimony before the Senate was well prepared, and Carter himself met with every senator—sometimes more than once—and kept a careful log of where each senator stood. The public was initially opposed to any "giveaway" that might weaken American power in the world, and the right wing, including Ronald Reagan, played to the public with hot rhetoric. Much of the public eventually moved Carter's way, slowly and reluctantly.

The Senate eventually passed both treaties, after hard bargaining and some concessions, by a vote of 68 to 32, just barely two-thirds. Carter had won a victory, but he may have lost a war because six Democratic senators who had voted for the treaties were defeated. Moderate Republicans felt that they dared not go to the well again for Carter. The conservatives were mobilized at the grassroots level for the next fight, which they expected to be the SALT II treaties, and Carter had not been able to mobilize much support among traditional Democratic constituencies. But Carter had won because of his conviction, determination, and great personal skill at appealing to the public interest.

The Energy Program

The Arab oil embargo and the subsequent formation of OPEC had made clear the American dependence on foreign oil. Nixon and Ford had tried without success to persuade Congress to enact measures to conserve and develop alternative sources of energy, but the increased costs to consumers had been a sticking point. The federal government continued to keep the price of oil artificially low and did nothing to discourage excessive domestic consumption. Carter decided to take the issue on, even though it had not been much discussed in the campaign. To him this was a moral question about the public welfare, which only a comprehensive plan could address. He had no patience for the deadlock of competing interests in the Congress. He turned to James Schlesinger, a former cabinet officer for both Nixon and Ford, to develop his plan. Schlesinger was to head the new energy department, but he initially worked in the White House. He was directed by Carter to develop a plan to go to Congress ninety days after the inauguration and to do it secretly. Carter did not want publicity for fear that interest groups would tear the plan apart before it could be formulated. The domestic policy staff, the head of the Council of the Economic Advisers, and the Treasury Department were told only that a plan was afoot. Schlesinger drew on individual experts in the departments and did talk with the chairmen of the two energy committees in Congress. As the complaints from Carter's economic advisers mounted, the president eventually held meetings to discuss the emerging plan. Several economic advisers warned of the inflation that would come with higher taxes at the gas pump, but Carter replied that conservation was the priority. Democratic congressional leaders also asked to be informed and, after some grumbling, they gave their support. The plan was introduced on April 20. It called for increased gasoline taxes, penalties for cars that burned excessive amounts of fuel, conservation measures in building construction, taxes to raise the price of domestic oil to world levels, tax incentives to encourage a shift to coal, expansion of nuclear energy, and an end to gasoline price controls. It was a very ambitious program with 113 interlocking provisions.

The rule of secrecy meant that there had been no effort to build a coalition in Congress behind the bill. Carter received help from Speaker Tip O'Neill, who bypassed the committees of jurisdiction and created an ad hoc committee to consider the entire package. As a result, the bill passed the House intact in August. The Senate was different. The Finance and Energy committees clashed, and oil-producing and oil-consuming states could not agree. Carter was eventually forced to agree to gradual deregulation of prices and to reduced taxes on energy. Passage finally came late in 1978. A more open process of development of the plan with congressional leaders might have produced the same result much earlier, but nothing could succeed without them. Carter was not able to persuade the public that there was an energy shortage in this first try. It was too easy to blame the oil companies. His greatest error was in not recognizing that the support of senators from the energy-producing states was necessary.

The president had a second chance in 1979, after OPEC raised prices again. The Iranian revolution also limited the supply of oil to the United States. Consumers felt the pinch in long gas lines and in the summer requirement that they get gasoline in their cars only every other day, even when traveling. Carter had learned from his first mistake and asked Stuart Eizenstat, his domestic policy assistant, to convene an interagency task force to work out a new plan. This time the relevant agencies were fully involved, and Eizenstat consulted regularly with key legislators. The centerpiece was creation of a synthetic fuels corporation to develop alternative sources of energy. Controls were lifted on crude oil prices, and Congress passed a windfall profits tax on new oil along with incentives for conservation. The people were behind the president because they could see how energy shortages directly affected their lives. Carter and his lieutenants had learned how to do things better. His desire for comprehensive policies could work when the demand was high, but he could not, by himself, create that demand. In these two cases Carter was an effective and forceful eventful policy leader. One might argue that they were event-making cases, because Carter brought his skill and will to bear effectively.

Economic Policy

Carter was caught in the same dilemma of stagflation that trapped Nixon and Ford and was no more successful in finding his way out than they had been. The most interesting aspect of his policies was his effort to keep control over federal spending and yet satisfy the demands of Democratic interest groups. He could not find support for restraint any more than Ford could.

Carter's plan was to repeat Kennedy's success in reviving a stagnant economy by stimulation of the economy through spending and tax cuts. He faced a deficit and high inflation and unemployment but hoped that a mild economic stimulus would increase jobs and reduce the deficit. However, Kennedy had not faced high inflation, because Eisenhower had fostered stable prices. Carter's economists, all Keynesians, believed that it was possible to balance inflation and unemployment by "fine tuning" the budget year to year, but this proved to be a fallacy. There were very strong pressures from business, organized labor, mayors, minority groups, and congressional Democrats for a large stimulus package. Carter was ambivalent from the beginning and resisted those pressures. But in the end he let his economic and political advisers talk him into a larger package than he wanted. He did not have an alternative plan. It was not possible for a Democratic president to take a recession early in order to wring out inflation that was only on the horizon. Americans had experienced several recessions in recent times and would not have stood for another one. There was only one plan for a Democrat—stimulate the economy to get it moving.

Throughout Carter's years the inflation rate increased from 6.5 percent in 1977 to 13.5 percent in 1980.[7] The increases were driven by many factors. Business and unions colluded in passing price increases along to the consumer. Federal entitlement programs were growing in size and indexed to inflation. Productivity at work declined as unskilled youths and women entered the labor market. The money supply was growing as a result of

Federal Reserve Board policy. Increases in the minimum wage and farm price supports from political pressures were inflationary. The value of the dollar declined in international markets. The OPEC cartel's price increases tripled the price of oil in 1979. These factors did not all come at once, but they became increasingly evident with the OPEC increase as the final nail. Any president would have been caught in these traps. These factors were not apparent in 1977, however. Carter's advisers believed that the unemployment level of 7 percent in 1977 would permit economic growth without much inflation. Carter's budget in January 1978 was expansionary, with increases in domestic programs and tax cuts. The White House was not willing to send a tight budget to Congress in an election year. But Carter continued to express his deep concern about inflation, especially since he had decided to increase defense spending at levels beyond inflation. By the fall of 1978, he had decided to introduce an austere budget despite opposition from his own cabinet, who didn't want to see their programs cut. Congressional Democrats did not want to become the party of fiscal stringency. Word about Carter's plans for the fiscal 1979 budget leaked out to the semiannual meeting of the Democratic Party in Memphis. Speaker after speaker, led by Senator Edward Kennedy, blasted the president for virtually being a Republican. Tempers were high. A breach developed thereafter between Carter and Kennedy, with liberal Democrats rallying behind Kennedy and encouraging his eventual decision to run against Carter in 1980.

In January 1979 Carter submitted a budget for fiscal 1980 that attacked inflation by cutting budgets. Painful decisions included big cuts in Medicare and Social Security. But 1979 was a hard year, especially with the price increases in energy. Unemployment rose in January 1980 to 7.5 percent.[8] The administration had created a program of wage and price guidelines earlier in the year, but the OPEC shock broke them apart as organized labor refused to cooperate. Administration economists blamed the inflation rate of 13 percent on OPEC; they had hoped to contain it at 8 or 9 percent.

The budget of January 1980 was primed for an election year, with growth encouraged in human services and urban development. There was no tax cut and increased revenues were to come from higher Social Security taxes and the windfall profits tax on oil. Defense spending went up 3 percent beyond inflation, in part as a response to the Soviet invasion of Afghanistan. But the deficit projection increased by a third over the previous year, and the financial community was not happy. Bond prices fell and interest rates rose as inflation eventually reached 17 percent.[9] Every president is a prisoner of the financial markets, and as a result, Carter tried to tighten his budget at midyear. The White House began to negotiate with congressional leaders, and in due course the current budget was reduced by $3 billion and the fiscal 1981 budget by $17 billion. Controls on credit to discourage spending were also instituted and perhaps contributed to the subsequent recession. Kennedy and Reagan—strange bedfellows—were calling for tax cuts to prevent recession, but Carter pushed Congress to balance the budget. This was undue optimism because of entitlement spending. His advisers suggested tax cuts, but he refused. He was even more insistent that inflation was the problem. He fought the 1980 election in the midst of inflation and a mild recession. Carter's war on inflation had embittered Democrats and their organized constituencies who wanted to spend and do good things for people. His economic advisers had no theory for the problem of stagflation. He supported their attempts at "fine tuning" in his budgets, but nothing worked. Carter had no policies for the political center he wished to create.

FOREIGN POLICY

Jimmy Carter repudiated the cold war politics of confrontation and called for an era of good feeling. He identified himself as a Wilsonian in his hope for universal peace. The American role was to capture the collective imagination on behalf of international cooperation, reduction of arms, and the advancement of human rights. He saw idealism as a resource for persuasion stronger than power, just as he had in domestic policy. Carter was a Baptist preacher on a world stage. World leaders were his congregation. The importance of respect for human rights was his central message. Carter was not comfortable with the cold war realism that saw conflict among nations as inherent in the world. As in domestic policy, he wanted to achieve everything at once. In 1982 he told a group of interviewers that after his election he met in Washington with his cabinet officers and Democratic and Republican leaders and during those discussions he decided to "move aggressively" on SALT talks, the Middle East, normalization of relations with China, and the Panama Canal treaties. In retrospect he said, he tried to do too much, but he would not have achieved as much with a limited agenda.[10]

Carter wanted a peaceful world in all respects, but he was not good at balancing power and morality in strategic terms because he saw the two principles as contradictory. William Quandt, Carter's principal adviser on the Middle East, remembered that one failing was "his almost total belief that if he made the right decision … people would support it because it was right."[11] And of course that goes back to a kind of moralistic streak: "You do the right thing, people will recognize it as right and they will therefore support you."[12]

Carter created problems for himself by the advisory structure he created for foreign policy. He appointed Zbigniew Brzezinski as his assistant for national security and Cyrus Vance as secretary of state. Brzezinski was a prominent political scientist, Polish émigré, and a cold warrior who wanted to wring good behavior out of the Soviets to stop adventures abroad in return for a SALT agreement. Vance was a Wall Street lawyer, who had served in the Johnson administration in defense and foreign policy roles and was an advocate of diplomacy on priorities such as SALT over linkage. Brzezinski initially played the "custodian" role as director of the National Security staff, but in time he decided that the issues were too important for him to be neutral and became an advocate. As a result, Carter was denied a "custodian" to help him in hard problems, such as the Iranian revolution where Brzezinski and Vance took opposite sides about what to do. Carter loved the point-counterpoint debate between the two and was confident that he could integrate it all coherently. But in some cases, he was overwhelmed. Issues were certainly debated but sometimes not subjected to hard, skeptical analysis. Brzezinski did not do his job. And Carter was not sufficiently sophisticated in foreign policy and recent American diplomatic history to fend for himself. He was the engineer trying to solve one problem at a time. His Wilsonian aspirations were too general to be of much help in specific cases.

The question of what to do about arms control was Carter's first policy challenge. He did not want to simply negotiate the incomplete Vladivostok agreement worked out by Ford, Kissinger, and Brezhnev in 1974. Around the White House that was called the "If Ford had won the election" option. He wanted something more ambitious. Vance and his staff wanted to complete Vladivostok, which would still require negotiation and some hard choices, before closure. The Pentagon argued for deeper cuts tilting toward an American advantage. Carter chose to send Vance to Moscow with a proposal for deeper cuts but with Vladivostok as a fallback. Vance should have put up a tougher fight for the more modest choice. No one explained to Carter that, as one Soviet diplomat later said, Brezhnev had "spilled blood" in political capital with his peers to get the Vladivostok agreement.[13] Carter kept his secrecy so tight that neither the experts in State or the CIA were brought in. It was the analogue to the development of his energy plan. He then torpedoed his own plan by making a speech to the United Nations in which he advertised his call for deep arms reductions. He told a press conference that he gave the speech because it was important to tell the American people his plan in order to strengthen his voice in Moscow. He seems to have had the idea of going over the heads of the Soviet military bureaucracy in an appeal directly to Soviet leaders. He added, "If we're disappointed (in the Soviet response)—then we'll try to modify our stance." This was an invitation to the Soviet leaders to reject both proposals.

No one seems to have told Carter how badly Brezhnev wanted an immediate agreement for the same reasons that he had wanted one with Ford. The Soviet economy was in trouble and he wanted to reduce military spending. The Soviet leadership found it difficult to shift gears in policy because they were locked into fixed, painfully negotiated positions. They had no central staffs to help them except the military, which was suspicious of any agreement. Brezhnev was prepared for a resumption of the Vladivostok talks and not for moving further. This should have been known. By the same token, the Soviet leaders were angry at Carter's preaching about the absence of human rights in their country. He even corresponded with Soviet dissidents and welcomed them to the White House. It never occurred to him that this might deter an arms agreement. As the Soviet government arrested increasing numbers of dissidents, Carter preached all the more.

Once in Moscow, Vance was met with cold, stone faces. Brezhnev complained that Carter had no right to preach about internal Soviet affairs. He quickly rejected the proposal for deep cuts. He would return to the Vladivostok table, which had been advanced by Kissinger in late 1976. They agreed to continue discussions between Vance and Gromyko. Vance later convinced Carter that this had to be done without any public diplomacy. It could not have been more badly handled.

Vance and Gromyko then spent months in negotiations until SALT II was signed in September 1979 at a Vienna meeting of Carter and Brezhnev. The agreement went beyond the Vladivostok agreement to a degree in setting limits to the numbers and types of weapons and set the path toward future negotiations. There were pitfalls along the way. The issues themselves were more difficult than had first been thought. The American announcement of the recognition of China in late 1978 may have delayed agreement; at least Vance asked Carter to delay the announcement until he could meet with Gromyko in Geneva before Christmas. But Carter was hungry for achievement and he went ahead. Senator Jackson and other critics of arms reductions attacked Carter and his negotiators, and a new group, the Committee for the Present Danger, consisting of conservative arms control experts began to publicize their opposition to a treaty, and this continued after the signing. Carter faced the same storm of conservative attack that had been directed at Ford, and Ronald Reagan was at the front of the attack.

The SALT II treaty was introduced in the Senate that fall and passed the Foreign Relations Committee but failed in the Armed Services Committee. The issue became moot after the Soviet Union invaded Afghanistan in late 1979. Carter asked Senate leaders to delay consideration of the treaty, and it was never confirmed. However, President Reagan accepted its terms, as did the Russians. So it was an achievement.

Carter's signal achievement in foreign policy, which may be called event making, was the peace agreement between Israel and Egypt negotiated at Camp David in September 1978. He used his strengths for homework and persuasion at close quarters to get two men who did not like each other— Menachem Begin of Israel and Anwar Sadat of Egypt—to sign a treaty of peace in which the Sinai land, conquered by Israel, was returned to Egypt and diplomatic relations were created. Carter was able to succeed in three weeks of negotiations by forging good relationships with both men. His first friendship was with Sadat. It was at Carter's urging that Sadat made a dramatic visit to Israel and asked for peace. Begin was harder to move, and at one point in the negotiations Carter thought that they would fail, but in a visit to Begin late in the day they spoke of their grandchildren and of their religious roots. Carter knew that Begin very much wanted the respect of the American president for his own legitimacy at home. He had done his home- work, not only on the history and geography but also on the two men. The agreement was ambiguous about the future of the Palestinians under Israeli occupation, which disappointed Sadat, and caused other Arab nations to condemn it. Carter had to continue to work on disagreements through per- sonal diplomacy in the Middle East and Washington. But the pattern was set for agreements that followed. Carter succeeded at Camp David far beyond what his advisers expected. Again, it was a matter of personal skill and will.

The three high points of Carter's foreign policy were SALT, recognition of China, and Camp David. Nothing worked after that. The Shah of Iran, a U.S. ally, was overthrown by an Islamic revolution in 1979, and American hostages were taken in the embassy and held prisoner for more than a year. The Soviet Union invaded Afghanistan in late 1979, and Carter loudly reversed his talk of peace and cooperation and reverted to cold war language and policies. Both episodes reveal a president who did not seem to be in charge. It is important to ask if he could have done better for himself, both substantively and politically.

When the Iranian revolution first surfaced in mid-1978, the key policy- makers were engrossed in SALT, issues with China, and the Middle Eastern negotiations. Subsequent decisions were in reaction to events. Vance and Brzezinski were at odds, and Carter was never fully engaged. The Shah fell, and the new Islamic regime was hostile to the United States. The seizure and holding of hostages in the American embassy in Iran was a powerful factor in Carter's 1980 election defeat. They had been held just one year on the day of the 1980 election.

The Soviet invasion of Afghanistan in November 1979 was a shock to Carter. He said publicly that his opinion of the Soviet Union had undergone a "dramatic change" for the worse. There had been a quasi-communist regime in Afghanistan for a year before the invasion, but its authority was shaky, and local insurrections were frequent. The Russians did not trust the leaders of the regime and feared that it might move into the American orbit, by U.S. design, or fall to Islamic revolution—not a comfortable thing since there were so many Muslims within the southern U.S.S.R. Carter announced that the invasion was a threat to Pakistan as well as to oil in the Persian Gulf. He was brought up short by what he felt had been his own naïveté and moved hard and fast into confrontation. He sent a message to Brezhnev that the invasion was "a clear threat to peace," and called on him to withdraw Russian forces. When Brezhnev responded that he had been invited in, Carter publicly said that he was a liar. He also said that the invasion was the greatest threat to peace since World War II. His wore his moralism and his sense of personal injury on his sleeve. European leaders thought that Carter had overreacted. But American opinion was with the president. He took a number of punitive steps: There would be no U.S. delegation to the Olympic games in Moscow in 1980; SALT II was postponed; American grain shipments to Russia were canceled; all human and technological exchanges were shut off; Pakistan was offered military aid, but declined it; defense spending was increased 5 percent; draft registration was resumed; and the construction of a naval base in the Indian Ocean was speeded up. The fear of Soviet adventurism had been aroused again. Carter's dream of universal peace was shattered.

POLITICS

Public approval of Jimmy Carter's presidency was 60 percent or more during most of the first year of his presidency, but it began to fall in September 1977 and was never to recover for any sustained time. His difficulty in taking hold of the job may help explain the decline in support. Approval dropped below 50 percent in 1978 as the economy continued to be fragile, taking another steep drop in mid-1979. By late 1979 approval was in the 30 percent range. Then it rose to 50 percent or so over the winter of 1979–1980 after the seizure of the hostages, a rally effect for the president, only to sink again throughout 1980. At the time of the election, 31 percent of a national sample approved of his presidency, and 56 percent disapproved, with 13 percent uncertain.[14] Surely the cumulative effect of the worsening economy, foreign policy setbacks, and Carter's difficulty in impressing the public that he was in charge were all important. Carter called in his best public relations expert, Gerald Rafshoon, in mid-1979 for help in reviving his popular support, and a memo that Rafshoon wrote to the president is extraordinarily revealing: "You're going to have to start looking, talking, and acting more like a leader if you're to be successful—even if it's artificial."[15]

The year 1979 started out good for Carter, with the signing of the SALT treaty and the Israeli-Egyptian accord, as well as the passage of the energy bills. But Carter made a drastic mistake in midyear when he discharged three cabinet members, including Califano. Gerald Ford had made the same mistake, and in both cases it appeared to the public that the president was not in charge of his own government. The economy was still shaky with inflation rising, OPEC had struck again, and the public seemed generally worried. At the end of the year, the hostages were taken and Afghanistan was invaded. It is quite possible that the public was weary of Carter calling for a sense of "limits" and the necessity of "sacrifice" in speech after speech. This is surely not what Americans wanted to hear. Patrick Caddell, Carter's pollster, commented that "Truth is the enemy of anyone presiding over a nation in decline."[16] This is something of a rationalization, because Carter did not have the political skill to appear to be in charge of events. He had no "star quality"—something that presidents Reagan and Clinton had, but Ford, Carter, and the senior Bush lacked. Carter's speechwriters later told a group of political scientists that they could not get Carter to play to a large audience. His persuasive skills worked only with small groups. Carter also had bad press from the beginning. One study revealed that Carter received more negative periodical press coverage than any twentieth-century president.[17] Most working journalists did not like him. It was not that he was Southern but perhaps because he was so pious. They liked to catch him in contradictions. He also did not ply his craft as they assumed a Democratic president would, being nothing like Kennedy or Johnson in welcoming politics and politicians into his net.

The Long Campaign

The year 1980 was sheer hell for Carter with Iran, the hostages, and SALT on the shelf. Then Senator Edward Kennedy ran against him in the primaries, after which Ronald Reagan took up the fight. As Carter and Kennedy fought in primary after primary, the votes for Kennedy were shown to be anti-Carter votes. Carter eventually defeated Kennedy, but the latter did not concede and only grudgingly stood with the president at the Democratic National Convention. Kennedy activists swept the platform committee in calling for increased domestic spending for jobs, job-training programs, and cities. The convention's heart was with Kennedy.

Reagan was already ahead of Carter by twenty-eight points as he was nominated, even before the Democratic National Convention. Reagan had run in thirty-five primaries, losing only six, and had worked hard for party unity, bringing moderate Republicans into his campaign organization and selecting George Bush Sr. as his running mate. His campaign message was a call for deep tax and budget cuts and increases in defense spending. Surveys showed that most voters thought that he would handle the economy better than Carter. The chief worry of voters was that Reagan was perhaps too extreme. Carter was actually ahead by two points in mid-October. But Reagan's easy, relaxed manner against an uptight president in their only television debate reassured many voters about him. He perhaps won the election by asking the television audience if they were better off than they had been four years ago? It was easy to answer no. Reagan won the debate by ten points in a *Newsweek* magazine poll. Surveys revealed that voters wanted an excuse to vote against Carter. Reagan then won the election by 51 to 41 percent of the popular vote. The turnout was low. Seven sitting Democratic senators were defeated, and the Republicans won control of the Senate and a net gain of thirty-three new House seats.

Surveys showed that there had been no shift among voters to a "conservative" ideology. Economic issues were the big worry, especially inflation. The election was a referendum on Carter. He lost support in every social group except blacks, and thus lost votes that he had won in 1976. The greatest loss was of blue-collar workers, many of whom became "Reagan Democrats." Carter lost the religious evangelical voters that he had won easily in 1976. He did not count on the creation of a new religious right coalition against him called the "Moral Majority." Republican conservative activists mobilized popular preachers like Jerry Falwell and Pat Robertson to organize the pews throughout the nation, particularly in the South. This was another step in the increasing polarization of politics.

CONCLUSION

How does Carter measure up in terms of our criteria for presidential leadership?

Context and Contingencies

Carter inherited the simultaneous inflation and unemployment that had begun in the aftermath of the war in Vietnam and had been artificially controlled by Nixon. President Ford was pursuing a steady path toward balance, and Carter and his economists continued on that road until OPEC II threw everything out of kilter. Democrats in Congress wanted more of the Great Society but took no thought for the contribution of additional spending to inflation. Carter saw an opportunity to bring Democratic policies back to a moderate center. There were opportunities for arms control, increasing rapport with China, and the Panama Canal treaties. Carter took them all. No one could have foreseen the Iranian revolution, the hostage crisis, OPEC II, or the Soviet invasion of Afghanistan.

Talents and Skills

Carter's greatest talent was also his greatest weakness. He was a problem solver who did his homework—perhaps to a fault—but lacked the inclination or ability to pull back and examine the broad political situation. His mastery of subject matter served him well in the Panama Canal fight, at Camp David with Begin and Sadat, and in the development of an energy program. His insensitivity to politics caused him to rush too many domestic programs to Congress too fast, to misjudge what the Soviets would accept in his first arms control overture, and to fail to see that recognition of China would delay SALT for several months. He did not really understand prudence because he wanted it all at once. But his lack of prudence was joined to the determination that powered his successes.

Did He Make a Difference?

He did make a difference in those contingencies in which he could bring his strongest talents to bear. His domestic policy mishaps—in welfare reform, budget reductions, failing to achieve a modus vivendi with congressional Democrats—were in part his responsibility because he threw down the gauntlet to his own party. But he would have been even more vulnerable politically had he given in to their demands. He lost the 1980 election because of inflation and the hostages in Iran plus his inability, as a public persona, to give the public a sense that he was on top of events. Carter was an eventful president who was sometimes effective and at other times ineffective. And yet there was an event-making quality to his big achievements, especially the Panama Canal treaties and Camp David, which were achieved by the force of his own capacity for homework, courage in taking on very difficult, unpopular issues, and his ambition to make a difference.

Effectiveness

In one of his books written after his presidency, Carter told the story of being on a mountain-climbing expedition in Nepal. As the party climbed, people fell away, until finally only the former president was at the summit. This story tells a lot about Carter. His great achievements, before, during, and after his presidency, were the result of his will and determination to get to the top. He was a remarkably effective problem solver who probably would have been an effective leader of industry or in the military. He founded the Carter Center in Atlanta and used his postpresidency for projects of improvement all around the world as well as at home. His postpresidency was a continuation of the ideals and purposes of his presidency. He was not a great politician but was a remarkable leader.

BIBLIOGRAPHICAL ESSAY

I have relied on my own book, *Jimmy Carter as President: Leadership and the Politics of the Public Good* (1988), for material in this chapter. But the book focuses on policymaking and is based primarily on interviews. The test for me has been whether my interpretations and assessments of Carter as president stand up in the light of subsequent studies. I have asked the same of the companion volume in the Miller Center books on the Carter presidency, Charles O. Jones, *The Trusteeship Presidency* (1988). I think that we both come off pretty well. Burton Kaufman wrote a study of Carter as president, *The Presidency of James Earl Carter, Jr.* (2d rev. ed., 2006). But Carter can hardly do a thing right in the book. John Dumbrell, *The Carter Presidency: A Reevaluation* (1993), is a good study, although not as critical of Carter as Kaufman. Don Richardson has edited a number of very good interviews with Carter that give a good insight into his beliefs, *Conversations with Carter* (1998). I would also add Kenneth E. Morris, *Jimmy Carter, American Moralist* (1996), and William Lee Miller, *Yankee from Georgia* (1978). Carter's own *Why Not the Best?* (1975), a campaign autobiography, and *Keeping Faith* (1995), reveal the man and the president.

Carter's leadership of Congress in domestic policy is analyzed by Paul Light, *The President's Agenda: Domestic Policy Choice from Kennedy to Carter* (1998). Joseph Califano's *Governing America: An Insider's Report from the White House* (1981), is descriptively good but not altogether kind to Carter. A good study of welfare reform is Laurence Lynn and David DeForest Whitman, *The President as Policymaker: Jimmy Carter and Welfare Reform* (1981). A number of good articles about policies can be found in Gary M. Fink and Hugh Davis Graham, eds., *The Carter Presidency, Policy Choices in the Post–New Deal Era* (1998). The first volume from the Hofstra University conference on the Carter presidency has many good chapters and comments from participants in Carter's administration as well as scholars and journalists: Herbert D. Rosenbaum and Alexej Ugrinsky, eds., *The Presidency and Domestic Policies of Jimmy Carter* (1993).

As in earlier chapters I have relied on Erwin C. Hargrove and Samuel A. Morley, *The President and the Council of Economic Advisers* (1984), as well as Herbert Stein, *Presidential Economics* (3d ed. 1994). Carl W. Biven has written a comprehensive study of Carter's economic policies, *Jimmy Carter's Economy: Policy in an Age of Limits* (2001).

I have again relied on Raymond Garthoff, *Détente and Confrontation* (1985), and John Lewis Gaddis, *Strategies of Containment* (2005). Gaddis Smith wrote a well-reasoned, fair account of the problems of balancing competing purposes during the years that Carter served, *Morality, Reason, and Power* (1986). David Skidmore's study, *Reversing Course: Carter's Foreign Policy, Domestic Politics, and the Failure of Reform* (1996), is an acute analysis of Carter's inability to keep détente alive. The study of arms control by Strode Talbott, *Endgame: The Inside Study of SALT II* (1979), is very rich, as is the memoir of William G. Hyland, one of the participants, *Mortal Rivals: Superpower Relations from Nixon to Reagan* (1987). Alex Moens, *Foreign Policy under Carter: Testing Multiple Advocacy Decision Making* (1990), shows how poorly Carter was served by the advisory process.

Gary Sick, *All Fall Down* (1985), is a superb story of the revolution in Iran. The second volume of the Hofstra conference, edited by Rosenbaum and Ugrinsky, *Jimmy Carter: Foreign Policy and Post-Presidential Years* (1993), contains a number of good essays and discussant comments.

Jules Witcover's study of the 1976 election, *Marathon* (1980), was used in the analysis of the Ford-Carter 1976 election in the previous chapter. The 1980 election was well analyzed in Austen Ranney, ed., *The American Elections of 1980* (1981). John C. Barrow wrote a very good monograph for his MA in history at Vanderbilt, "Evangelical Politics: Jimmy Carter and the Religious Right in the Politics of 1980." Mark Rozell dealt well with the media and Carter in *The Press and the Carter Presidency* (1988). I have again relied on George C. Edwards for *Presidential Approval: A Source Book* (1990), for opinion surveys.

CHAPTER SIX

Ronald Reagan

A Romantic with Vision

Ronald Reagan was an event-making president. There was no dark side to Reagan in comparison to Johnson and Nixon. But his very creativity, anchored in buoyant romanticism, could blind him to flaws in his dreams. He was skillful at times, in working with Congress, and Soviet leaders. But again, a romantic stubbornness could block effective prudent action.

Reagan won the presidency in 1980 because of public unhappiness with Jimmy Carter. Great Society liberalism was pretty well exhausted, as Carter had seen. A generation of new politicians had emerged from the Goldwater failure of 1964 to positions of leadership in the Republican Party, but they could find full political expression only with the disaffection of the white South from the Democratic Party, the unhappiness of blue-collar Democrats with civil rights as their lives and jobs were affected, and the appeal to patriotism in the cold war. The 1980 election was not a realigning election in which a new Republican majority could be discerned. There was no evidence of a substantial shift to the right ideologically. Enough voters were unhappy with Carter to vote for Reagan. But there were positive signs for Republicans. They gained control of the Senate with twelve new seats. The Democrats lost twenty-three House seats but kept control. New House Republicans were more conservative

148

than those departing and the Democrats they replaced. One saw growing Republican strength in the South and West. The ethnic bases of the
two parties were slowly changing. Carter won among African Americans,
Hispanics, poor whites, Jews, and working-class Roman Catholics. But
the turnout of these groups was low. Reagan's appeal was primarily to
middle-class white voters. The Democrats did not receive a majority of
the white vote after 1968 in presidential elections. They also failed to
win majorities among union voters, and the number of union members
was declining. The old New Deal coalition of the South and the big
cities was eroding fast.

These political changes did not ordain any particular policies. Republican
politicians had ideas about what to do, but the new president was the one to
set new directions. A moderately conservative Republican, like Gerald Ford,
might have different ideas than Ronald Reagan, but such a president would
have faced the same fights with militant conservatives that Ford actually
fought. Reagan was the trumpet of militant conservatism and saw himself
as moving with the grain of history in conservative directions.

Ronald Reagan was very comfortable playing a role—whether as an
actor, governor, or president—and he played that role with sincerity, as a
good actor should. If the authenticity of the character being played by an
actor is not real to the audience, then the actor has failed. Yet he was also
a very private person who did not seem to need friends, except his wife
Nancy, and was often remote from his closest advisers. He was something
of an enigma to his lieutenants and others in government, and thus carried a certain unpredictability. Critics saw him as only an actor who dealt
primarily in illusions. He was, even at his best, never a close student of
policy or programs. He saw his role as giving a sense of direction to his
subordinates and persuading the public to support his goals. Yet he was
more than a figurehead. His very strong beliefs guided his actions. He was
not a pure ideologue, because he was also a politician. He was comfortable
being both an ideologue and a politician and constantly balanced the two
attributes to his own advantage.

As a boy, Reagan acted in plays written by his mother. He continued
acting in college and further honed his verbal skills as a sports announcer.
His movie roles were usually light and comedic and expressed his natural
amiability. As head of the Screen Actors Guild he learned the skills of
collective bargaining, of which he was proud and on which he relied as
governor and president. He defeated an incumbent governor in California
by appealing to popular frustrations and promising a conservative regime,
government being the problem. But as governor of California, he found

ways to work with a Democratic legislature and accommodate himself to bureaucracy, even as he rhetorically criticized government.

We have seen Reagan's rhetorical skills in the two previous chapters. He preached his core beliefs: Government was too big; private enterprise was the key to prosperity; the world was a dangerous place; and the United States was in a race for dominance with the Soviet Union. It followed that domestic government and the taxes that sustained it must be cut back and the nation's military must be strengthened. He preached an idealized America as a "City on a Hill" whether present or future. The darker aspects of the country—poverty, racism, and a polluted environment—did not enter his rhetoric because they did not fit the vision.

He was convinced that his public approval was based on his message and saw his rhetorical skills as only a conduit for the message. This worked best in his celebratory rhetoric, such as a speech in Normandy for the fortieth anniversary of the D-Day landings. But his political rhetoric did not persuade a majority of citizens to accept his conservative ideas. He led a popular conservative movement, but it was largely Republican and never a majority. His great achievement was to create a persona that inspired public confidence. Voters are better judges of character than they are of issues. For example, he won great public support in the way in which he responded to the attempt to kill him early in his presidency. People responded to his resiliency and buoyancy. He was an All-American like his fellow actor Jimmy Stewart. However, popularity did not always guarantee public approval. Support drained from him after many people decided that he had lied in saying that he had not intended to free hostages in Lebanon by secretly selling arms to Iran. Trust evaporated. He slowly recovered support only after he recanted, and even then his reputation for staying distant from detailed decisions helped to save him.

EXECUTIVE STYLE

Reagan made his general goals clear to his subordinates and expected them to work out policies accordingly. He responded to those choices, doing little to initiate specific plans. He easily took up the routines of presidential life—meetings, speeches, playing the public role he loved—and often had to be pulled back into policy discussions. Rival advisers fought for control over his thinking, often in the process underestimating his independence of mind. But because he would not immerse himself in policy substance to any degree, when cabinet officers besieged him with competing claims he often simply withdrew, refusing to decide. However, he was also forcefully insistent on adherence to his high priorities and dealt with confrontations by relying on single advisers to help him through conflict and out the other side where he wanted to go. For example, his chief tutor in foreign policy was George Shultz, the secretary of state. Secretary of Defense Casper Weinberger continually undercut Shultz, who managed the talks with the Soviets on arms control, but the president most often sided with Shultz, because Shultz was pointing in the direction that Reagan wanted to go. But Weinberger always had his say. Reagan wanted to give hard-line conservatives a voice in government. So Reagan got what he wanted by relying on the adviser whose views were similar to his own. He was not impressive when he lacked good tutors, as the Iran-Contra affair revealed.

He had ideological blind spots. He understood that the deep cuts in taxes in his first year had created unprecedented federal deficits for years out, and he agreed to marginal tax increases for several years running but he would not confront the fundamental problem of growing deficits. He had promised to cut taxes and he would not turn on his promise. Even though he never submitted a balanced budget, he blamed Congress for the deficits. The idea of a defensive shield of rockets against incoming missiles, one initiative he took himself, delayed arms agreements, but he would never yield what many in his own government thought was an impractical idea.

The First Year: Political Triumph in Economic Policy

The inflation and decline of productivity in the 1970s opened the way for ideas about how to foster economic growth. Republican economists of all stripes favored lifting the burden of income and corporate taxes and government regulation to stimulate investment and entrepreneurship. State and local taxes had doubled in the past decade, and payroll taxes to pay for future entitlement programs were increasing. Economists argued that the rising marginal tax rates discouraged savings and investment. Candidate Reagan had been a budget balancer in 1976 who wanted to cut spending, and he never gave up this idea but he added "supply-side" economic plans to his election rhetoric in 1980. The "supply-side" idea was to cut tax rates deeply, particularly for the better-off who would invest their money, as a way of stimulating economic growth. Some "supply-side" theorists argued that new federal revenues would pay for the deficits initially created by tax cuts. Regan never promised that deficits would be overcome. He wanted to cut federal budgets to make up the difference. Nor were his ideas about what programs to cut very specific. His language was more rhetorical than precise. The "supply-side" thesis was different from the "demand-side" tax cuts of Johnson, because the cuts were distributed more widely in the 1960s and increased federal revenues did make up for temporary deficits.

Reagan and Congress

Richard Wirthlin, the president's pollster, and David Gergen, a presidential assistant, wrote Reagan a memo in January 1981 in which they asked the new president to take charge quickly and decisively. He should focus on his economic plan, put foreign policy on the back burner for a time, and avoid Carter's mistake of sending too many initiatives to Congress in the first year.

The first task was to revise Carter's budget for fiscal 1982. A Legislative Strategy Group was assembled in the White House, consisting of chief of staff James Baker; Michael Deaver, a personal assistant who handled public relations; and Edwin Meese, the counselor to the president in charge of domestic and national security policy. Baker focused on process rather than substance and was determined that Reagan win in Congress after the previous four failed presidencies. During the campaign Alan Greenspan, acting as an adviser, and Martin Anderson, a Hoover Institution economist and Reagan adviser, worked out a budget that they felt had credibility. Budgets would be reduced by 2 percent or $13 billion for fiscal 1982 and then by 4 percent or $28 billion for the following year. Anderson felt that it would be unreasonable to ask Congress for more. But David Stockman, a former Republican congressman and the new director of the Office of Management and Budget, wanted to cut $50 billion for 1982 and $100 billion by 1986. Reagan's senior White House staff supported Stockman, so he took the lead in preparation of the new budget. Neither senior White House staff nor cabinet officers were well versed in budget making, and, in any event, Stockman went to work before any of them had settled in. He had come into public view when, as a congressman, he had published an article in the journal *Public Interest* in 1975 entitled "The Social Pork Barrel." He attacked congressional Republicans for voting to reauthorize and appropriate funds for Great Society programs, despite having originally opposed them, because they were popular with constituents. Stockman was much influenced by Theodore Lowi, a political scientist who had argued that there were no longer restraints on spending in a time of "interest group liberalism." Stockman was a supply-sider, but he did not see a free ride back to prosperity. Both budgets and taxes would have to be cut. He was, as he later admitted, quite naïve in his belief that Congress would cut budgets drastically. He later admitted that he had served the president poorly by his radicalism, and he never seems to have understood that Reagan was a politician who would temper his ideology for a big political victory in his first year as president. Stockman would later present chapter and verse about Reagan's ignorance of budgets, but he also missed the point that political calculations about spending were as strong as economic ones. New presidents must win the big fights early in order to establish themselves with Congress and in the minds of the public as being really in charge, and for Reagan this meant tax cuts.

Stockman went to work on the new budget in December and eventually learned that he would have to do it all himself, with the help of a few aides and the career staff at OMB, who helped him identify weak programs. Edwin Meese did not understand what was happening, thinking that his new system of cabinet councils would make domestic and economic policy, and the president gave no specific instructions. Stockman met with the new cabinet and senior staff before the inauguration and insisted that both taxes and budgets must be cut. He reported that there was little response or understanding. Several blamed Jimmy Carter for profligate spending. Reagan's comment was that the mess had to be cleaned up. Stockman records: "His instincts were good. Yet Reagan seemed as far above the detail work ... as a ceremonial is above politics.... I was not a knight errant but I interpreted his words as a blessing to go forth and do what I thought necessary to battle with the federal dragon."[1]

Stockman had little time to sell his plans. There were only four meetings with the president before the inauguration on January 20, and the president was scheduled to speak to Congress on February 18, with just a few days to study the budget beforehand. So the new budget director acted on his own to slash and burn. He soon learned that the president learned through specific examples. For example, it did not work to tell him that a child could get a school lunch subsidy if the family income was a certain percentage above the poverty line. Rather, one said, "the kids of cabinet officers qualify." But such simplifications disguised the political costs of reductions as they added up. Reagan was never briefed on the large picture of what would happen to the budget until it was too late and Congress was in revolt. Stockman eventually met strong opposition from department heads who were protective of their own programs, but he was able to overcome many objections by drawing on the president's supposed will to cut. He got nowhere with the Pentagon, however. Secretary Weinberger insisted not only on a 7 percent increase but also on the additional 5 percent that Carter had budgeted. The president backed Weinberger. The cabinet was somewhat mollified when it was decided to put off all consideration of cuts in entitlement programs for a future time. An overture to cut Social Security for the future was palmed off by Baker on the secretary of health and human services, where it died as Baker intended, with the president escaping blame. Reagan did not personally look at Stockman's budget cuts. When cabinet officers appealed to him against Stockman or each other, he would not decide because he had no basis for doing so. Reagan could follow his own principles, as in advocating tax cuts, but he could not resolve conflicts among people. He would often suggest splitting the difference or leave it up to Stockman. Neither Stockman nor the senior staff understood the importance of preparing the president for such decisions, nor did the president ask to be educated. At one point, Stockman gave Reagan a multiple-choice test to decide which programs should be reduced, and to his great surprise the president liked them all and produced an $800 billion deficit. It became apparent to Stockman that the president was not really a budget cutter.

The president presented his budget to Congress on February 18. He proposed a deficit of $45 billion with additional cuts in expenditures of $200 billion to be made over the next three years in order to balance the budget by 1984. He promised to protect the "social safety net" for the poor. The deep cuts in taxation of what was eventually 23 percent over three years were matched, though not fully, by deep budget cuts. The projected figures on future economic growth were much overblown. Stockman had kept the initial figure for budget reductions as low as it was by positing $30 billion in "future savings" with no other specifics. So only $15 billion was really to be cut. Congressional Republicans liked the speech, and Democrats were demoralized by their election defeats. They imagined Reagan's mandate to be much greater than it actually was. But then the hard work began. Republican Senate leaders were skeptical about such deep tax cuts, knowing that budgets would not be cut enough. Senate majority leader Howard Baker called Reagan's plan "a riverboat gamble." Senator Pete Domenici, chair of the Budget Committee, balked at approving Reagan's plan, but Baker and Robert Dole, chair of the Finance Committee, talked him around. The mythical figure of unspecified future cuts seemed to make the difference, and the Senate authorized the budget by 77–20 in May, the first step in eventual passage. The House was more difficult. Democratic chairmen were not about to play along. But a coalition of Republicans and Southern Democrats, the "Boll Weevils," eventually developed a majority that guided the appropriating committees through many twists and turns. The president had run ahead of many Boll Weevils in their districts and Republicans mounted an aggressive grassroots campaign to remind their constituents of that fact, and it seemed to work. Democratic leaders eventually gave up, but at the same time pushed responsibility off on to the president should things go wrong.

The attempt by a lone assassin to kill Reagan on March 30, 1981, increased his hold on the public. His brave demeanor as he went into surgery, telling his doctors that he hoped that they were Republicans and telling Nancy that he had forgotten to duck, reinforced public confidence in the man. However, he was taken completely out of decision making in his convalescence in the spring, as doctors put him on a very limited work schedule. Presidential assistants began to think that they could do the president's work with his minimal participation, a habit that continued throughout the rest of his presidency. Congress passed the budget in June, but the actual cuts in spending were held low because of Stockman's mythical future promise. He hoped for a second round of cuts, but it never happened. It was not the nature of congressional politics to cut popular programs, so the growth in programs was slowed but not stopped. The budget passed only because Stockman gave up cuts in a number of expensive programs. By that time he was despised by Republican Senate leaders for leading them on a quixotic campaign.

Taxes

The president was far more determined to cut income and corporate taxes than he was to cut budgets. He never forgot the high income taxes he had had to pay at the peak of his movie career. The fact that he had incentives to make fewer movies each year because of high taxes fit well with the supply-side argument that high taxes discouraged incentives for investment and entrepreneurship. Economic boom times since the 1960s had brought high taxes and Reagan had a receptive audience among taxpayers. The bill on the table was the Kemp-Roth proposal to cut income tax rates by 30 percent over three years, as well as corporate tax reductions. Reagan embraced the bill despite the reluctance of Republican Senate leaders, who feared that it was too big a bite. Stockman reported that Reagan did not understand the relationship between tax reform and the budget. He never promised that the cuts would pay for themselves, but the two issues were separate in his own mind. James Baker tried to temper Reagan on taxes, but the president wanted to make tax reduction the signal mark of his presidency. He had promised tax cuts in the campaign, and when suggestions for compromise were made, he would reply, "What will the people think?" He knew that he could not violate his promises without losing public confidence. Republican congressional leaders were eventually able to win the votes for passage of his tax bills, but they did so by making big side payments in the form of tax exemptions to favorite constituencies of Republicans and Democrats in Congress. The bargaining went on all summer, and at one point Stockman suggested the delay of tax cuts until budgets were pared more stringently, but Reagan would not agree, saying that they could not publicly admit that "we were wrong." Reagan spoke on television on July 27, 1981, with a populist appeal of reducing tax burdens on all Americans, especially farmers, small businessmen, and other producers. He asked the audience to write or call their representatives in Congress before the vote for passage on July 29. House Speaker Tip O'Neill complained "we are receiving a telephone blitz like this nation has never seen."[2] The Economic Recovery Tax Act of 1981 was passed and quickly signed. The marginal tax rates were cut by 23 percent for all income brackets. Taxes were cut by $750 billion over a five-year period.

Reagan had good help from James Baker and his deputy Richard Darman, who realized that there were to be no cuts in entitlements or defense spending and that therefore the president had to win politically with tax cuts. Darman reports that he and Baker decided that political victory was more important than deficits. As the deficit problem became more apparent in the autumn, Reagan seemed not to worry, saying that if inflation went down and employment grew then the man in the street would say, "Okay, things are better."[3] Reagan's optimism influenced his advisers. He thought it most important to inspire the people with his own optimism that things would get better. Darman later wrote, "The management of illusion is part of the management of reality."[4] Words could make a difference in reviving the American spirit.

The economist Herbert Stein later wrote that if Margaret Thatcher, the contemporary prime minister of Great Britain, had been in Reagan's shoes she would have reduced the money supply against inflation, tolerated an increase in unemployment, deferred tax reductions, and cut the budget.[5] She did these things, but her authority over Parliament was greater than Reagan's authority over Congress. Senate Republicans might have gone in those directions, but there was no coalition for deep budget cuts. Reagan chose to have at least half his program rather than none at all. But from that point forward deficits grew, and no one took responsibility for them. However, prosperity also returned in time for Reagan to be reelected.

REAGAN THE POLITICIAN

What was Reagan's contribution to his political successes in 1981?

1. He provided a direction for policy derived from his campaign. He may have been weak on substantive knowledge, but everyone knew where he would and would not go.
2. Congress assumed that he had wide public support for his ideas. He did fill a vacuum in the wake of Carter's defeat.
3. He was very good at face-to-face persuasion with members of Congress. He could be both ideological and pragmatic at the same time, without feeling any contradiction.

Were there weaknesses in his style of leadership?

1. The failure to fully acknowledge the problem of deficits caused big trouble for the next two presidents, who had to find politically unpopular ways to reduce debt.
2. Reagan began the Republican mantra of "no new taxes" that carried over into future Republican administrations and congresses as the Republicans found a way to create prosperity without the pain of budget balancing.
3. He could substitute illusions for knowledge. He was not close to any of his economic advisers. The mind of the economist is one of trade-offs and hard truths, and Reagan's mind did not work that way. His senior White House staff—Baker, Deaver, and Meese—would not risk Reagan's political success by honest talk about the budget.

Paul Volker and Ronald Reagan

Jimmy Carter had named Paul Volker as chairman of the Federal Reserve Board, perhaps with hope that Volker would act against inflation, which he did with a vengeance, by tightening the money available to member banks in the Federal Reserve System. This continued under Reagan, even more so in response to the increasing deficits and caused the deep recession of 1982 and 1983 and considerable unpopularity for the president. However, Reagan never challenged Volker privately or publicly. He said that he respected the independence of the Federal Reserve Board, but it was also the case that he could accept recession because he hoped that economic recovery would come with a decline in high inflation. So he stuck it out. Reagan did not lack an understanding of the near term either in regard to taxes or inflation. His aim was recovery in time for reelection. He and Volker struck an implicit deal in which the president authorized tax increases in 1982, and Volker loosened the money supply. Reagan preached optimism and, with Volker's help, he won out.

James Baker, who persuaded the president to let him try to work something out with congressional leaders, first initiated the 1982 tax increase, which did not raise income taxes, and which Reagan justified as "tax reform." A combination of tax increases and budget reductions over a three-year period did not eliminate deficits, but recovery came and the recession eased as employment and production increased and interest rates and inflation declined. Reagan claimed credit and deflected blame for the recession on the Democrats. It seemed to ordinary people that Reagan had fulfilled his promise to restore economic prosperity. In fact, half the drop in inflation was due to the recession, but the other half was due to the drop in world food and energy prices. Reagan was lucky, but he also knew how to make his own luck. Once recovery was underway, the president would not hear of tax increases sufficient to make up deficits. His policies were working. Nor would he address the fundamental cause of looming deficits in the entitlement programs of Social Security and Medicare, which were the central problem.

A bipartisan commission, headed by Alan Greenspan, recommended increased payroll taxes and eventual increases in the retirement age to stave off trouble in the near term. Congress enacted the recommendations, but fundamental problems about entitlements were not addressed by either Congress or the president. Political support for more fundamental reforms simply did not exist.

In the late Carter and early Reagan years, American business had improved its productive capacity, absorbed the costs of environmental regulation, and labor became more productive. However, economic growth did not go beyond 3 percent per year, and savings stayed at low levels. Consumer spending brought the economy back, but manufacturing continued to decline, and the country developed trade deficits. Tax burdens on ordinary people were increased in payroll taxes for Social Security and Medicare. And total federal spending was higher in 1988 than in 1980 because of the increasing cost of the entitlements. Reagan achieved his goal of moving the economy toward greater productivity but without success in reducing deficits.

Reagan was naïvely ambitious in regard to budgets and taxes. He insisted on his priorities, but he was also sufficiently astute to see the political benefits of economic recovery in the short run with little thought of the long-run economic costs. Was this event-making leadership? Perhaps, in the sense that Reagan's very political strengths were at work. But there was no guarantee that the policies would necessarily work in the long run.

The 1984 Presidential Election

Reagan defeated former senator and vice president Walter Mondale decisively. It was a personal rather than an ideological triumph, except perhaps in the white South, where appeals to limited government, strong national defense, and conservative social values brought many longtime Democrats over to the Republicans at the presidential level. Reagan won no policy mandate for a second term, but presidents seldom do. They ask to be rewarded for a successful first term. Mondale had entered the race when the economy was weak, and recovery took the steam out of his campaign. He also promised to raise taxes, which was a fatal political mistake. Reagan won majority support in all categories of voters except blacks. Surveys showed that most voters were more moderate than either conservative Reagan or liberal Mondale on issues. There was certainly not a new Republican majority. Reagan won 53 percent of the popular vote and kept a Republican Senate but failed to carry the House. He won because he was Reagan and because of economic recovery. The Democrats made much of the deficit, but it was an abstract issue for most voters. Reagan had discovered a politics of prosperity without pain. The economy expanded without government paying the bills for its programs, at least in the short run. But his great personal appeal would probably not have saved him had the recession continued.

FOREIGN POLICY

Reagan read much about foreign policy in the years that he campaigned for the presidency, and his leading ideas as president are found in his many radio addresses before he took office. He believed that past administrations had let the Soviets gain military superiority over the United States. President Carter had canceled the B-1 bomber and delayed the MX missile and the Trident submarine. SALT II permitted the Soviets to build new weapons, and Reagan saw this as a failure of détente since the arms race continued. His idea was to build back to nuclear superiority and then use that leverage to force reductions on both sides. Secretary of Defense Casper Weinberger was directed to build up the military across the board, and the secretary spent more in five years than presidents Nixon, Ford, and Carter had spent all together. Weinberger would not permit the Office of Management and Budget to oversee allocations to the separate services within his department. Indeed, the services had to scramble to invent new missions and weapons to keep up. William Niskanen, a member of the Council of Economic Advisers, later wrote that defense budgets were only "a stapled package of the budget requests from each of the services."[6]

The Soviet leaders had hoped to work with Reagan as they had with Nixon and Ford. To them, Republican presidents going back to Eisenhower had seemed so much more businesslike and pragmatic than Democratic cold warriors. One problem was that the first three Soviet leaders Reagan had to deal with—Brezhnev, Andropov, and Chernenko—were old and ill. The unknown fact is that Reagan was amenable. He did not want to negotiate about arms for a time, but he was ready to talk. He lifted Carter's embargo on the sale of American wheat to the Soviet Union and promised to abide by the terms of SALT II if the Soviets would do the same. He wrote Brezhnev a letter in April 1981 in which he stressed their mutual obligation for world peace. Reagan could be both tough and open with Soviet leaders, trying to impress them with his sincerity. This would come to fruition in his relationship with Mikhail Gorbachev.

The administration was divided between hawks, who favored military superiority over any negotiation, and doves, who wished to move ahead in arms control with SALT. The hawks were Pentagon military and civilians and the doves were State Department professionals. Reagan wanted the buildup, but unlike the hawks, he wanted to negotiate in due time. The first year was deliberately given over to domestic policy. After the attempt on his life, Reagan was briefed but to a limited extent. Edwin Meese, who oversaw both domestic and national security policy, briefed the president regularly, but there was limited discussion of foreign policy. Secretary of State Alexander Haig could not get along with the senior White House staff, because they would never turn him loose to roam freely over policy as he wished. Haig never learned how to talk with the president. His resignation was finally accepted in 1982, and George Schultz replaced him.

One sees an example of Reagan's detachment in September 1981 when Weinberger presented him with the idea of developing the MX missile but delaying the decision about where and how to base it. Weinberger had originally rejected the MX because Carter had proposed it, but congressional experts pushed him hard to move ahead. He suggested the temporary step of basing the missiles in conventional silos, which would not protect them from attack. The alternative, considered by Carter, was to move the missiles between sites in the West by rail. The Joint Chiefs of Staff opposed Weinberger's idea because of the vulnerability of the silos. When Weinberger and Meese took the idea to the president, he approved it without any serious discussion. But he made a mess of things when the plan was announced at a news conference. A reporter asked if the silos, intended for smaller Minuteman missiles, were not vulnerable; the president replied, "I don't know but what you haven't gotten into that area that I'm going to turn over to the Secretary of Defense."[7] It was embarrassing and explains why staff tried to keep the president at a distance from reporters in casual encounters.

The other important decision in 1981 was a counter to the Soviet deployment of intermediate range missiles in Eastern Europe. Carter had promised the Europeans that he would install American Cruise and Pershing missiles in West Germany. Reagan had promised to do the same but he faced a nuclear freeze movement in both the United States and Western Europe. Weinberger came up with the idea of the elimination of all missiles in Europe, thinking that the Soviets would reject it, which they did. Negotiations began in Geneva between the two great powers. The defense hawks had seen their initiative as a propaganda ploy, but Reagan took it seriously. Almost no one understood his antipathy to powerful weapons. He went further in a May 1982 speech in which he proposed that each side reduce ICBMs by one-third. The Soviets could not accept the idea, because, having more land-based missiles, they would have had to cut more than the United States. Reagan was not well versed in the details of arms control, but his aspirations were clear from the outset.

Ronald Reagan and George Shultz

George Shultz became secretary of state in the summer of 1982. We have seen him before as secretary of labor, director of the OMB, and secretary of the treasury in the Nixon administration. He was very well suited to advise the president because he could explain things clearly and had the patience and persistence to fight his way directly to Reagan, pushing the protective blanket of national security staff aside when necessary. Jack Matlock, a career diplomat who joined the NSC staff as the Soviet expert at Shultz's behest, saw that Shultz's strengths complemented Reagan's weaknesses. He mastered details that bored Reagan. He would keep negotiations with the Soviets going when Reagan would slide away into other preoccupations. He understood Reagan's horror of weapons and thus knew that the hawks could be overruled in specific cases. Shultz fought continuing guerrilla wars with Weinberger, William Casey (head of the CIA), and successive national security advisers to the president. The president almost always went with Shultz when the chips were down.

The path to negotiation was jagged. Brezhnev died in 1982, Andropov in 1984, and Chernenko in 1985. These veteran Soviet leaders were caught in immobility between past and future. They knew that their economic system was not working and that they were spending too much money on weapons. Shultz saw during these years that a long-term strategy for arms reductions was needed, and he began to write the president long memoranda explaining the issues. He supported the strategy of "build first and then negotiate." But Shultz also saw Reagan as more radical on arms control than anyone realized. In February 1983 Shultz brought Soviet ambassador Anatoly Dobrynin to the White House secretly to talk with the president. They talked for two hours, during which, according to Shultz, Reagan talked easily and persuasively. They discussed the hard questions and began to work toward a private agreement in which the Soviets would permit a group of Russian Pentecostals to leave the American embassy in Moscow, where they had been for two years, and emigrate. The quid pro quo was that Reagan would not crow about it publicly, which would have been politically tempting to do. He did not, and, according to Shultz, the Soviet leaders began to see that Reagan would keep his word. Reagan told Shultz that he did not want the NSC staff to know the story, and one result was that he and Shultz began to talk privately free of any staffing process. This ran counter to the conventional wisdom about using staff to challenge the departments, but Reagan did not know how to use staff and he did know how to respond to Shultz.

Shultz saw Reagan as too often a prisoner of staff, but the president could also take flights of fancy, which Shultz would simply not reverse. In March 1983 he announced, without consulting Shultz or Weinberger, a plan to develop a shield of defensive missiles over the United States, which would protect it from nuclear attack. The idea of a Strategic Defense Initiative (SDI) had been in Reagan's mind since he had visited the underground North American Air Defense Command (NORAD) base in Colorado, which was the command post for the control of nuclear weapons, and had been shocked to see that the alternative to a Soviet attack was a comparable American response. There was no defensive capability. He began to meet privately with nuclear experts, including Edward Teller, the father of the hydrogen bomb, in a search for an alternative to the doctrine of mutual assured destruction.

The SDI system seemed to Reagan to be the answer to the abolition of offensive nuclear weapons, and he promised to share it with the Soviets once it was achieved. Reagan met with the Joint Chiefs of Staff to discuss SDI in late 1982. They made no commitment but began to work on the question as the new assistant for national security, Robert McFarlane, suggested. McFarlane was an SDI advocate and an aspirant to be the president's principal adviser on national security. Neither Shultz nor Weinberger were told about the nationally televised talk until just before it was given. Nor were experts throughout the administration ever consulted. Reagan used the speech in part to weaken the nuclear freeze movement, and it seems to have had such an effect, as the public responded favorably. He had to act because a resolution for a nuclear freeze had almost passed in the House in 1982. Gary Wills saw SDI, often called "star wars" by critics, as a perfect expression of Reagan's desire for a message of hope. In his view, American technology could work wonders. Experts might be skeptics, but Reagan had the audience.[9] Shultz and Weinberger were skeptical of SDI. Most administration experts saw it at best as a limited defensive weapon.

McFarlane saw it as a bargaining chip to use with the Soviets in arms talks. The Soviets did not like it, because it violated the ABM treaty against testing ballistic missiles in the atmosphere, and they knew that they lacked the technical capacity to compete. Soviet generals saw it as a means to strengthen American capability for a first strike. But Reagan believed in SDI. One could argue that it was a clever ploy to put strain on the Soviet military economy. Yet Lou Cannon, Reagan's best biographer, who covered him for the *Washington Post*, quotes McFarlane as saying of Reagan at the time: "He sees himself as a romantic, heroic figure who believes in the power of a hero to overcome even Armageddon."[10] Reagan appears to have believed that the events of Armageddon at the end of time, as described in the Book of Revelation, could occur. But he was determined to forestall it with arms control and SDI. No matter what his beliefs, he took a leap beyond the politics of international bargaining. This was how he understood himself as a leader—in short, event making.

In 1983 the United States took the first steps toward deploying missiles in Europe, causing the Soviets to leave the Intermediate Nuclear Forces talks and Strategic Arms Limitation talks, the successors to SALT. Perhaps in response, Reagan softened his public rhetoric and wrote conciliatory letters to Andropov and then Chernenko. Shultz talked with Andrei Gromyko, the Soviet foreign minister, in Stockholm in the new year and discovered that Gromyko wished to talk with Reagan informally, so a meeting in Washington was arranged. Reagan worked very hard in preparation with the intention of impressing Gromyko with his sincerity. The meetings went well, with Gromyko telling Nancy Reagan to whisper "peace" in the president's ear every night. It may be the case that the Russians saw that Reagan would be reelected and therefore that he was the man they would have to work with. In due course the Geneva talks on INF and START were reestablished. Weinberger, Casey, and the hawks protested strongly. But Reagan held to his course despite contentious White House meetings. Shultz offered to resign, but Reagan would not have it.

Ronald Reagan and Mikhail Gorbachev

Mikhail Gorbachev became general secretary of the Communist Party in March 1985 and met with Reagan in Geneva in November. It was clear that he was a reformer who spoke for a new generation of Soviet leaders that recognized that the arms race must be curtailed in order that the top-heavy Soviet economy could receive investment and develop new forms of productivity.

The illusion of central planning was entirely protective of the bureaucrats who managed it. Technology was backward across the board. Gorbachev spoke for innovators. His policies of "glasnost" for the guarantee of free expression and "perestroika" for political competition by elections within the Communist Party were startling innovations. Gorbachev had met Margaret Thatcher in London before he came to power, and she told Reagan that he was a man "I could do business with." Shultz formed the same impression after meeting him in Moscow at Chernenko's funeral. Vice President George Bush handed Gorbachev a letter from the president inviting him to a summit meeting, and an agreement was eventually reached for a meeting in Geneva later in the year. Weinberger and others pushed the president hard not to do it. They did not trust Reagan to be tough enough. But Reagan simply said, "We have to go forward." Gorbachev had told Shultz that he was opposed to the "militarization of space" but agreed to talk about arms control at Geneva, as well as regional and bilateral issues.

Reagan prepared for the Geneva meeting more than he had for any other event. Jack Matlock wrote a series of papers for him to read, and Shultz reported that: "The President's mind was engaged, not through briefing books, as through an active process that involved him in give and take, and a feel for his operational role."[11]

One obstacle to such education was Reagan's defense of beliefs that he had completely internalized such as SDI. Shultz remembered, "Once a certain arrangement of facts was in his head, I could rarely ever get them out."[12]

The talks went well. A private conversation between the two men appears to have convinced Gorbachev that the president was a sincere man and he began to like Reagan. It was the same quality that Dobrynin had seen. Reagan could sell himself with authenticity. After their private talk, Reagan invited Gorbachev to visit Washington in the next year and received an invitation to visit Moscow. The INF and START talks in Geneva were resumed. Reagan reported to Congress on his return and won support as well as public approbation.

Nothing happened immediately. Gorbachev made public commitments to the eventual liquidation of nuclear missiles, but insisted that any such steps would confine SDI to laboratory testing. But the president wanted both deep reductions and SDI. Gorbachev eventually proposed a meeting to confront the hard questions, and a meeting in Reykjavik, Iceland, was set for October 1986.

Reagan went to the meeting with neither fresh ideas nor any great personal knowledge of arms control issues. However, when Gorbachev surprised him and his American advisers with a proposal to eliminate all nuclear weapons by a foreseeable date, they were taken aback and worked through the night to respond constructively. Gorbachev's predictable price was the limiting of SDI testing to the laboratory. After much agony, Reagan turned him down. He told others that he had promised the American people that they would have SDI and he could not go back on his promise just to get an agreement. As he left the meeting site, he was reported to be very let down, saying that he had come so close to an agreement. However, Gorbachev later told George Shultz that the meeting had been a success because the two men had talked honestly and frankly to each other. The meeting was the turning point in the cold war, he said. Reagan was perhaps not aware that the Soviets saw SDI as another aggressive weapon because he himself was so sincere. He was dependent on Gorbachev for the next step.

The following February, Gorbachev separated the INF talks from START and SDI. He wanted to get missiles out of West Germany and knew that Reagan was politically strong enough to make an agreement. Reagan agreed, and the negotiators went to work and agreement on INF was reached in September. Gorbachev became a popular figure in the United States, as he charmed Washington at the signing of the INF treaty. Weinberger, Casey, and hard-line senators like Jesse Helms opposed the treaty harshly for fear that Western Europe would now be hostage to Eastern Bloc armies. But they were no match for the president. When a group of Republican senators tried to block the treaty, they discovered that he had more influence with their constituents than they did. The treaty passed the Senate 93 to 5.

Reagan's used his visit to Russia in 1987 as a platform for the moral crusade on behalf of democracy that he had always advocated. He entertained

Soviet dissidents at the American embassy, spoke for religious freedom in a visit to a monastery, visited a Jewish couple who had been denied emigration, and preached to university students that a new day of freedom was at hand. He even replied to a question that the "evil empire" of totalitarianism, a phrase that he had used often, no longer existed. It was too late for a START agreement, but the talks continued and were consummated by President Bush and Gorbachev.

Where do we see Reagan's political talent here? The first attribute was determination. He wanted to get rid of nuclear weapons. The second attribute was patience and a willingness to wait on events. George Shultz made the difference in negotiations with Soviet leaders, but Reagan empowered Shultz. This was event-making leadership because it reflected the will, skill, and determination of the president himself. But no event-making leader acts alone, and Reagan had Shultz and Gorbachev as partners. We now turn to a story in which he lacked an adviser like Shultz and disgraced himself.

Iran-Contra

The central story is clear but the responsibility for stupid actions is murky. In the winter of 1985–1986, Reagan approved a recommendation that the United States sell arms to Iran and, without his knowledge, the profits were illegally diverted to the Contra guerrillas fighting the radical Sandinista government in Nicaragua. Reagan approved the sales at the urging of Casey and McFarlane as a means of winning the future support of "moderates" in the Iranian government. The real reason, which he would never admit to himself, was the hope of freeing American hostages held by terrorists in Lebanon who were controlled by Iran. Reagan talked tough about never dealing with terrorists or terrorist governments, but he was not tough enough to follow his own words. He used his authority to set aside legal prohibitions against negotiations with terrorists, but did not tell Congress as required by law. Then his attorney general, whom Reagan had asked to get the facts on the weapons sales, discovered the diversion of funds. Congress, having the CIA in mind, had prohibited assistance to the Contras by any intelligence agency, so the operation was moved to the National Security Council. Admiral John Poindexter, McFarlane's successor, never told the president about the diversion of money, wishing to give him "deniability," and Colonel Oliver North managed both the arms sales and the diversion. They were both indicted and convicted but escaped punishment because of immunity given for their original testimony before a congressional committee. Reagan tried to keep knowledge of the initial sales secret, but it emerged in 1986.

The arms sales were strongly opposed by Shultz and Weinberger, but they withdrew from the discussions after it was clear that they had lost the debate. William Casey was the author of the plan but he died soon after the public exposure so that the full story never came out. Shultz thought that Reagan seemed not to know fully what was going on. Shultz himself was under fire from hawks for seeming to be too friendly to the Russians, and his congressional testimony that he had opposed the deal brought loud choruses that he should be fired for not supporting the president.

By all accounts, Reagan lost his grip temporarily. He fell twenty points or more in public approval and was very distressed that he had lost the trust that had always been the basis for his leadership. People felt that he had lied to them. He withdrew into immobility. A good many of his supporters, in and out of government, blamed chief of staff Donald Regan, former secretary of the treasury, for not protecting the president. Regan and James Baker had traded jobs in the second term, and the new chief, a former business executive, ran a tight ship in which he briefed the president after he had talked with aides rather than exposing Reagan to more lively talk. However, this was Reagan's style. Regan participated in the arms-for-hostages decisions and seemed to approve. The president resisted firing Regan, but Mike Deaver and, most importantly, Nancy Reagan prevailed upon him to bring in former senator Howard Baker as a new chief of staff. The sweep at the top gave Reagan new life, and Baker eventually persuaded him, again with help from Mrs. Reagan, to tell the public that although he did not intend to trade arms for hostages, the record supported the fact that it had happened. He had great difficulty changing a story once it was set in his own mind. Once he had mastered a script he would not divert from it.

Former senator John Tower chaired a committee at the request of the president to examine the affair and the Tower Report concluded that Reagan had not used the national security advisory process the way it should have been used to engage debate. It blamed McFarland, Casey, and Poindexter for monopolizing advice to the president. The difficulty with the diagnosis is that the president wanted the hostages out and persuaded himself to support the trade. He heard to the contrary from Shultz and Weinberger and ignored them. There was plenty of debate.

REAGAN AND THE PUBLIC

Much was made by the media of Reagan as the "Great Communicator." This was described as a unique quality not possessed by other presidents. To what extent was Reagan's public role an important factor in his achievement of his goals? His election victory in 1980 demoralized Democrats and gave him leverage in Congress in his first year, but it did not last. The Congress gave him only half of his economic program, and most domestic policy stood at a stalemate throughout the rest of his tenure. One exception was the enactment of a new tax code with lower brackets for all taxpayers in 1986, but the president received much help from key congressional Democrats who were also tax reformers. Reagan lost much support during the long recession of his first term, but was saved by the recovery. The fact that he stood steadfast in his hope for recovery surely strengthened him, in that people liked a man who knew what he was about despite adversity. No one wanted to go back to Carter's last days. Voters do not like presidents who twist and turn. Public opinion was with him as a cold warrior for a time, but disaffection emerged in fears that he was too bellicose and was spending too much on defense. Reagan moved in a softer direction as he engaged with Gorbachev, perhaps in response to public disquiet. He was both leading and following in arms control. The public did support SDI, and Reagan was simply lucky that Gorbachev decided to leave the issue aside. Reagan thus did not have to abandon his promise to the public to pursue "star wars." He failed in persistent attempts to win public approval for his support of the Contras. There was almost no support for American military adventures abroad, even through surrogates. After 346 peacekeeping marines were blown up in a terrorist attack in Lebanon, he withdrew the marines quickly, but responded with a quickie invasion of Grenada to squelch a Marxist government and save American lives. But his use of "rally round the flag" here was a temporary expedient.

Reagan never won support for cuts in programs for social welfare, even though the rates of growth were slowed. Indeed, spending on such programs was greater in 1988 than it had been in 1980. His one strong legacy was the introduction of antitax rhetoric as a Republican credo. He invented the idea that the nation could have prosperity while continuing to run up big deficits. As Vice President Dick Cheney later told Secretary of the Treasury Paul O'Neill during George W. Bush's first term, "Reagan proved that deficits don't matter."[13] Reagan would never challenge deficits because he could never preach hard facts to people who did not want to hear them, and that was most voters. The "Great Communicator" title was overdone. Elaborate public relations strategies were devised by Michael Deaver to fly Reagan to pseudo events around the country at which he could get favorable attention. It is not at all clear that they made much difference. Public support for Reagan's policies was shaped by the questions at stake and this varied greatly from issue to issue. The media exaggerated the effects of his rhetorical skill because that is what the media, especially television, likes to cover and can cover easily. But it was still the case that Reagan knew how to present himself day in and day out as an attractive figure in whom people could have confidence. Certainly this figure was important for a revival of confidence in the country and the future. But the dark sides of America— poverty, racism, and social problems—did not exist for the president.

CONCLUSION

How do we assess Reagan by our three criteria for presidential leadership?

Context and Contingencies

The Democrats were a spent force by 1980, and there were opportunities for new departures in politics and policy. The roaring inflation had to be stopped. The hard question was whether this might be done without recession. The Soviets had embarked on adventures to which an American response was required. Republican conservatives had a credo for action— reduce government and confront the Soviets. A moderate Republican like Ford would have been even more at odds with this partisan coalition than Reagan had been. Still, it fell to the new president to articulate and lead in new directions.

Talents and Skills

Reagan's chief talent was in the presentation of himself in public and in private. He was an actor who could play his part authentically. This was a powerful persuasive force. He gave the nation an infusion of hope for the future with his incurable optimism. He brought the same optimism to bear in his belief that the Soviet Union was sure to fail and in his actions to support Gorbachev's reforms. His other strong talent, which was also a weakness, was fierce determination. He would not yield on the problem of federal deficits but, by the same token, he persisted in his vision of nuclear disarmament and rapprochement with the Soviet Union.

Did He Make a Difference?

He made a great difference in helping to end the cold war. He could not have succeeded without his partnership with Gorbachev, who also needed him. It was a most fortunate partnership. He fostered the search for a Republican majority comparable to the New Deal coalition but did not achieve it. But he did give his party the ideas with which it would fight subsequent elections and govern. He influenced a generation of politicians and adherents in subsequent politics and policy. The politics of prosperity without pain built on deficit spending was also his contribution to his Republican successors.

Purpose overwhelmed prudence in economic policy, and the consequence was a mountain of federal deficits. Reagan's desire to be event making here was effective politically, in the short run, but it created problems for his two immediate successors and inspired George W. Bush, again with unfortunate consequences. The Iran-Contra affair illustrated how he might abandon reality for illusion, although some might argue that he knew what he was doing all along the way.

Effectiveness

Reagan was an event-making president without doubt. He wanted to be a heroic president and make a great difference. His forging of peace with the Soviet Union was effective event making. His domestic policies, in their attempt at event making, were unrealistic. On the whole, he was an effective president in the way he practiced democratic politics consistent with the Constitution. But the deceptions of the Iran-Contra scandal undermined his effectiveness as president. But there was one crucial difference between Reagan and Johnson and Nixon. Reagan did not need to be president to be a happy human being. He never confused his identity with his objectives. This detachment, which was not unlike John Kennedy's, permitted him to put events in perspective. He failed when he did not do this. In the final analysis, he was a good democratic politician and an event-making leader.

BIBLIOGRAPHICAL ESSAY

Lou Cannon, *President Reagan: The Role of a Lifetime* (1991), is invaluable for an understanding of Reagan. Cannon is a scrupulous reporter who covered Reagan like a blanket for his entire presidency. Alonzo Hamby, *Liberalism and It's Challengers* (1992), provides many keen insights. Stephen Skowronek, *The Politics Presidents Make: Leadership from John Adams to George Bush* (reprint ed. 1997), raises very interesting questions about whether it is possible for presidents to establish new long-term partisan majorities because of the great rigidity of a fragmented political system. The memoir by Edwin

Meese, *With Reagan* (1992), is disappointing because Reagan does everything right and his critics are misguided. Meese is simply an apologist who cannot detach himself from his faithful years of service, but perhaps this is all that can be expected from him. A number of edited books give many diverse insights about a number of aspects of Reagan's leadership, including H. Elliot Brownlee and Hugh Davis Graham, eds. *The Reagan Presidency: Pragmatic Conservatism and Its Legacies* (2003); Charles O. Jones, ed., *The Reagan Legacy: Promise and Performance* (1989); Larry Berman, ed., *Looking Back on the Reagan Presidency* (1990). Reagan's style of executive leadership emerged in all the many studies of his presidency. David Gergen, *Eyewitness to Power* (2000), is very good on this score. One should not discount Donald Regan's memoir, *For the Record: From Wall Street to Washington* (1988). He may not have been the best chief of staff, but he presents a good picture of trying, and not really succeeding, to work with a puzzling president. Michael Deaver's memoir, *Behind the Scenes* (1988), written with Micky Herskowitz, is very insightful. Paul A. Kowert in *Groupthink or Deadlock: When Do Leaders Learn from Their Advisors?* (2002), presents a very interesting thesis that Reagan's style of leadership required a tight hierarchy, because the president could not manage confrontation well. The key question is who was in charge of the hierarchy?

John W. Sloan has written the single best book on economic policy, which includes an incisive analysis of Reagan's style of leadership, *The Reagan Effect: Economics and Presidential Leadership* (1999). One must take David Stockman, *The Triumph of Politics: Why the Reagan Revolution Failed* (1985), with a grain of salt in his unflattering portraits of others, but he was finally honest about himself and how he failed the president. The most cogent defense of Reagan's economic policies is given by Martin Anderson, *Revolution: The Reagan Legacy* (1990), although he slides over the pitfalls of deficits far too easily. Finally Richard Darman's *Who's In Control? Polar Politics and the Sensible Center* (1996), is filled with refreshing and honest insights, including those about Darman himself and his observations about Stockman.

The best studies of Reagan's two presidential election victories are by Paul R. Abramson, John H. Aldrich, and David Rohde: *Change and Continuity in the 1980 Elections* (1982), and *Change and Continuity in the 1984 Elections* (1987). These are very detailed studies from which I borrow lightly.

There are a number of good books about Reagan's defense and foreign policies. George Shultz, *Turmoil and Triumph: My Years as Secretary of State* (1993), is an invaluable account of decisions and negotiations over time. Shultz is not kind to the hawks in the Reagan administration, but his chief contribution is to describe how he learned to work closely with Reagan to achieve the president's objectives. Lou Cannon's massive biography is also very valuable because he covers much of the same ground and does it with the objectivity of a good reporter.

Jack Matlock was at Shultz's and Reagan's side throughout the rapprochement with the Soviet leaders, first on the NSC staff and then as ambassador to the Soviet Union. He wrote many of the memos that Shultz used to educate the president. See his book *Reagan and Gorbachev: How the Cold War Ended* (2004).

Daniel Wirls gives a good picture of the defense buildup in *Buildup: The Politics of Defense in the Reagan Era* (1992). Two good but incomplete accounts of Reagan's arms negotiations are Raymond L. Garthoff, *Détente and Confrontation: American-Soviet Relations from Nixon to Reagan* (rev. ed. 1994), and William G. Hyland, *Mortal Rivals: Superpower Relations from Nixon to Reagan* (1987). A full account of the Iran-Contra affair is found in *The Tower Commission Report: The Full Text of the President's Special Review Board* (1987).

CHAPTER SEVEN

George H. W. Bush

The Patrician

An interesting critic of George Bush, the forty-first president, was his son George W. Bush, the forty-third president: "The problem with my old man is that he thinks you can solve problems one at a time, with good character, good judgment, a good team, and all that stuff. Jebby [his brother] and I understand that you need ideas, principles—based on belief."[1]

In many ways George H. W. Bush was like an English Conservative politician of the old school, the kind challenged by Margaret Thatcher, a radical who wanted to overhaul English institutions. The old school, exemplified by Harold Macmillan, believed that governing was an art based on practical reason and muddling through. To a great extent, this was the tradition of northeastern Republicans from which the elder Bush came. He took on a Texas veneer in time, trying his best to appear to be a Bible conservative, but it was not authentic, and right-wing Republicans knew it. He was, by his very nature, an effective eventful leader, except that he was not good at popular politics.

George Bush was a very good diplomat. He would have been an excellent secretary of state, and his achievements as president were in diplomacy, particularly in working with Mikhail Gorbachev to assist in establishing political stability in Russia and in concluding the START agreement. He used great skill in creating an international coalition with which to expel Iraq from Kuwait. He was not politically skillful in domestic affairs. His great political mistake was to promise not to raise taxes as he ran in 1988 and then to break the pledge in 1990, for good policy reasons as he saw it, but also alienating Republican conservatives. He lost the election to Bill Clinton in 1992 because he refused to artificially pump up an economy in recession. One may conclude—good man, poor politician, not enough political talent to be a fully effective president.

Bush's father was a Wall Street banker who had been a senator from Connecticut during the Eisenhower years. He lived in the comfortable worlds of Greenwich, Connecticut, and Andover and Yale during and after World War II, and his casual, understated, gracious demeanor revealed it. But there was another side to him. As the war began, rather than go on to Yale, he volunteered to be a navy pilot and was shot down and rescued in the Pacific. He had an adventurous side and a strong streak of patriotism: "For God, for Country, and for Yale." Rather than fall into a comfortable life on Wall Street after graduation, he and his family went to live in Midland, Texas, where Bush, with family financial help, made a modest fortune in the oil business. Eventually moving to Houston, he served two terms in the House of Representatives and twice failed to be elected to the Senate. In the Nixon-Ford years he served in a series of short-term appointments as U.S. ambassador to the United Nations, chair of the Republican National Committee, head of the U.S. mission to China, and finally director of the Central Intelligence Agency. He was out of government during the Carter years and then ran for president in 1980, losing to Reagan, who selected him as the nominee for vice president, a post he held for eight years.

Bush was not a good public politician. He separated campaigning from governing and believed that he would be rewarded by voters for policy achievement. He told his speechwriters to avoid flowery rhetoric because it did not suit him and he was right. When he tried it, he was not authentic. The prime example was his promise that there would be "no new taxes" in his acceptance speech at the Republican National Convention in 1988. He went further, imitating Clint Eastwood as "Dirty Harry," inviting the Democrats to "make my day" by trying to raise taxes. The mantra of "no new taxes" was gospel for Republicans after Ronald Reagan. Bush was ten points down in the polls against Michael Dukakis and let his speechwriters put the phrase in over the objections of his economic advisers.

By the same token, the 1988 campaign took a low road, attacking Dukakis's patriotism and his liberalism in a number of unsavory ways. But because Bush separated campaigning from governing and was not a good campaigner, he gave himself over to handlers. Surveys revealed that voters were not exercised by any great issues. His strength was with white voters, especially men, and especially in the South. He kept many "Reagan Democrats." Protestants supported him, as did the better educated and the better-off. So he won with continuity, but now he had to lead.

His governing strategy was to appear to the public as an effective leader, and, indeed, his popularity was high much of the time because the public made limited demands on government during a brief era of good feeling. People liked him and perhaps expected less of him.

EXECUTIVE STYLE

After his presidency, Bush wrote: "I was very much a believer that if you had confidence in your people, if they come together and agree, their common solution will probably prevail and work best."[2] He also wrote that he did not regard the presidency as a one-man job, saying that he had provided "steady leadership" but that he needed the strength of close advisers. He had served on the National Security Council for eight years and liked the structured, orderly procedures of fact finding and discussion. This approach to decision making was much more appealing to him than dealing with Congress or making public appeals. His ideal was to sit down with a small number of advisers and work out the problem.

Vice President Dan Quayle thought that the president was sometimes "too courteous, too forgiving" and could "let himself down with his own kindness."[3]

One risk in Bush's executive style was perhaps a failure to capture diverse perspectives. His lieutenants were, like himself, men with experience, skeptical of theories, who valued practical judgment. This does not mean that they did not argue, debate, and disagree. Bush's lieutenants were natural rivals. But they were all realists, who saw the world as it was and as it realistically might be.

Bush's close policy advisers had worked in the Ford or Reagan administrations, often both, and sometimes together. Brent Scowcroft, the assistant for national security, and James Baker, the secretary of state, were very seasoned. Richard Darman, the director of the Office of Management of Budget, and Roger Porter, an assistant for domestic policy, had worked with Ford and Reagan. Dick Cheney, the secretary of defense, had been chief of staff for Gerald Ford, and Colin Powell, the chairman of the Joints Chiefs of Staff, had been assistant for national security in the Reagan White House.

Policy Purposes

Bush would repeatedly say that he was not good at "the vision thing." It was often said of him that he had few beliefs, but simply tacked with the political winds. The first was not true, and the second was only partially true. He believed in a constructive American role in the world before and after the end of the cold war, was skeptical of domestic policy promises that exaggerated what government could do, and valued markets and the dynamism of American business. He was less firm about taxes, civil rights, and social issues such as abortion. But his own, perhaps moderate, views were increasingly out of place in a Republican Party moving fast to the right. His watchword was prudence. He would take problems as they came and do his best to combine policy and politics. He perhaps would have been most comfortable as an Eisenhower Republican like his father. He belonged to the World War II generation of Kennedy, Johnson, Nixon, and Ford. Ronald Reagan had created a new politics of the right, which Bush had to accept and work with, if he wanted to be president.

Congressional Politics

Democratic congressional leaders resolved early on that Bush would be a one-term president. They saw no sign of a policy mandate for Bush. Democrats had a majority of ten in the Senate and eighty-five in the House. And both majorities were increased after the midterm elections of 1990. The increasing ideological division of the two parties meant that liberal Democrats had gained considerable ideological unity, at the same time that conservative Republicans to the right of the new president were also stronger. There was not much middle in which to navigate. The situation was more difficult for Bush than it had been for either Nixon or Ford because of the increasing partisan polarization. Bush hoped for bipartisan government and reached out to friends in Congress, hoping for cooperation. It was not his nature to consider use of the "bully pulpit" to appeal to the public should Congress not be cooperative. There is considerable question about whether such appeals are effective, and at any rate Bush was not well equipped for the task.

There were three possible strategies that Bush might pursue in working with Congress. The first was cooperation through mutual agreement. A good example was the success of Secretary of State James Baker in winning agreement for a free election in Nicaragua. Baker won congressional cooperation for these steps, in part, by promising to limit U.S. aid for the

Contras for a temporary period and only for help in their resettlement in Nicaragua. Neither he nor Bush shared Reagan's commitment to the anti-Sandinista cause. This was the realistic pragmatism of Bush and Baker using quiet diplomacy that nullified a volatile political issue.

The second strategy was that of joining Democratic congressional initiatives to try to give them a Bush stamp. Examples were the renewal of the Clean Air Act, the Americans with Disabilities Act, and the renewal of the Voting Rights Act. Bush needed to keep only thirty-three of the forty-three Senate Republicans to sustain a veto and did so forty-three times with only one loss. He sent hints to Congress that a veto was likely if a bill was emerging of which he did not approve and would sometimes threaten a veto openly.

The third strategy was to govern as much as possible by administrative authority through executive orders and development of regulations favorable to the president's goals. He did this using the authority of the OMB to oversee and amend agency regulations, in many cases to soften them away from what was seen as undue regulation.

Each of these strategies was guided by the conscious conviction in the White House that there was little point in Bush proposing a positive Republican legislative program of his own. The Democrats would reject it, and it might be divisive among Republicans, who were split between conservatives and moderates. The old liberal Republicans, who had been strong in the congresses of the 1960s and 1970s, were almost extinct. The development of these strategies, by trial and error, was less a result of Bush's political skills than of the general reading of politics in the White House and the pragmatism that prevailed there. The president expected Congress to take the lead on domestic policy and told the leaders so privately. He did not propose spending cuts but left that to Congress. Nor did he suggest how to curb rising health care costs.

The most successful and creative Bush initiative was his proposal in June 1989 to reform the Clean Air Act of 1970. The act was controversial when it was passed because of supposed trade-offs between pollution controls and the costs to industry. Politicians from Michigan and West Virginia, with control of appropriations, had deliberately frustrated implementation of the act because of the costs to auto manufacturing and mining. The general problems were air pollution, acid rain from coal-fired plants, tailpipe emissions, and urban smog. Bush was, in fact, an environmentalist and promised to be one as president. He appointed William Reilly, a strong environmentalist, as head of the Environmental Protection Agency, and convened an early conference of environmental experts. Soon after that, he announced a plan to phase out asbestos in construction. The president set aside new land for wildlife refuges, wetlands, and new funds for national parks. He also provided money for the states for land and water conservation and helped resolve controversy about water in the Colorado River.

An Exxon tanker ran aground off Alaska with great damage to sea and wildlife not long before Bush introduced his bill, and the company was held responsible. The climate was thus right for new policy. Bush set up a working group headed by Roger Porter, and they produced revisions in the Clean Air Act in June 1989, which provided for reductions in industrial and automobile emissions, as well as regulation of coal-burning plants and toxic chemicals. The bill was conceived as a step toward reducing global warming and the depletion of the layer of ozone over the earth. The Senate responded with a stronger, more expensive bill than the president wanted, and he had to engage in veto talk when the bill came to conference between the Senate and the House. Porter, working with legislators all along the way, was finally able to broker a compromise. The support of the new Senate majority leader George Mitchell was crucial, and there were comparable House advocates. One of Bush's allies in the matter was the prime minister of Canada, Brian Mulroney, who was greatly concerned about acid rain and other pollutants for forests and fisheries in Canada. This was perhaps a source of moral suasion on Congress. Both industry and conservative Republicans were upset, but Bush went against them. It was a matter of conviction, and he was the person who broke the congressional stalemate.

The Americans with Disabilities Act of 1990 was not the president's bill, but he enthusiastically supported it and worked for it. The impetus came from advocates for the handicapped, in and out of Congress. There was widespread public support following the principles of the 1964 Civil Rights Act. The 43 million Americans with disabilities were discriminated against in employment, access to buildings, and transportation. The law, once adopted, created new requirements and opportunities for many citizens. The bill would probably have passed without Bush's active cooperation, but he was willing to again defy Republican conservatives who were worried about the cost to business. C. Boyden Gray, counsel to the president who, along with Porter, was actively engaged in bargaining between the White House and congressional sponsors, argued to conservatives that the act was significant "welfare reform" because it brought many people out of welfare into work and thus enhanced the economy. It was entirely consistent with Republican principles of moving people from welfare to work. Bush praised the law when he signed the bill in July 1990, but he received little political credit. It was a Democratic bill.

Passage of revisions to the Civil Rights Act were more difficult for both Congress and the president. Bush instructed the Justice Department to challenge all actions of the states to dilute the black vote through gerrymandering, at-large districts, or majority-vote requirements. His early speeches reached out to the black community. His support in 1989 among black voters was higher than Reagan's had been. The president was, however, opposed to legally established quotas for minorities in employer hiring and made this clear publicly. The sponsors of the civil rights bill in Congress, particularly Senator Edward Kennedy, inserted a provision for penalties on employers who practiced job discrimination, and Bush vetoed the bill in October 1990. He continued to oppose the bill but then, in an about face, signed it a year later, claiming that it was not a quota bill. The law permitted employers to assess racial balance among employees according to "business necessity." This was, in fact, a disguised quota, because lawsuits for discrimination would follow imbalance. He was opposed to quotas by conviction, but he signed the bill because a racist Republican was running for governor of Louisiana and Bush did not wish Republicans to be associated with him or racist ideas. This was a straddle but hardly immoral.

Bush had promised to be the "education president," and he asked Congress to create programs to reward superior schools and teachers and support magnet schools and science students. However, little money was pledged or available. Conservatives wanted school vouchers, merit pay for teachers, school discipline, and the teaching of values. The federal government could not do much about such things, and Bush recognized the limited role that the national government could play in primary and secondary education. Therefore, he turned to the governors and convened them to win support for an "America 2000" program in which they agreed to voluntary national tests, the involvement of business leaders in improving schools, and the creation of new, more effective schools. Secretary of Education Lamar Alexander was a tireless advocate for education, but there was no money. The deficit was exacting its price.

Bush accepted the reality of big government, but did not wish to enlarge it. In 1990 there was considerable discussion within the administration about preparing an innovative antipoverty initiative, but when the advisers could not agree, Bush dropped it. Republican intellectuals developed a number of ideas, which they called the "New Paradigm," for quasi-market programs to reduce poverty such as enterprise zones in inner cities where industry might locate, permitting tenants in public housing to purchase their homes, public school vouchers, and reducing the costs of entitlements. However, the president paid little attention, perhaps because his economic advisers saw little merit in the ideas. The president equivocated on gun control, first for it and then against it when the National Rifle Association opposed it. He would not support higher gasoline taxes, medical leave for families from work, or increases in the minimum wage. He sought to promote the interests of investors for a general prosperity and he regularly proposed, and never received, cuts in capital gains taxes. Finally, he vetoed several bills intended to permit states to liberalize abortion. He had favored choice for women in his first campaigns for Congress, but changed his view as a vice presidential candidate because Reagan asked him to do so. Conservatives never trusted him on the issue, even though he called for a constitutional amendment to overturn *Roe v. Wade*, the 1973 Supreme Court decision legalizing abortion.

By 1992 Bush had lost any support he might have had in Congress. He had won only 43 percent of his proposals as Congress recessed, which was the lowest level of support of any president since John Kennedy. It was an election year, and the Democrats expected to win. Bush had been whip-sawed between conservatives in his own party and Democratic reformers. Weakness in the center, which had bedeviled President Ford, was again a problem for an essentially moderate president. It cannot be said that Bush made a great difference as president in domestic policy. But one may argue that he was a model for moderate Republicans in how to fashion a middle path with a Democratic Congress in legislation. It was more a matter of personal moderation than of political skill. Dana Garvey, a comedian who impersonated the president on the *Saturday Night Live* television show, would say "it wouldn't be prudent." People laughed, but Bush was serious.

Economic Policy

Ronald Reagan had shown it was possible to agree to tax increases every year from 1982 to 1988 and still keep his popularity as an opponent of tax increases. Two reasons were that income tax rates were never raised and budgets were never cut drastically. The nation lived in an illusory prosperity for eight years. Reagan never reconciled the trade-offs between low taxes, the concrete benefits that people wanted from government, and the high deficits, and he received no help from Congress. Walter Mondale's defeat in 1984, after promising to raise taxes, told politicians of both parties to stop such talk.

As Bush took office, he inherited an annual federal deficit of $150 billion, a large trade deficit, and a newly discovered need to clear up nuclear wastes from federal installations that had been kept secret for years. He presented a budget in 1989 that showed that the deficit would decline and disappear by 1993 if the requirements of the Gramm-Rudman-Hollings law were implemented. The law set maximum deficit levels by each future year that, if not met, would trigger across-the-board cuts in all programs. The Bush budget proposal overestimated future revenues and did not anticipate soaring costs of Medicare and Medicaid. Alan Greenspan, chair of the Federal Reserve Board, told Bush that prices were gradually rising and that the Federal Reserve might have to act to slow the economy in the interests of price stability. The problem was that the deficit was "structural," meaning that spending did not match income, rather than "cyclical," meaning a recession from which recovery would occur. But there was no way to recover from the structural deficit without either raising taxes and/or cutting budgets drastically.

Polls during the 1988 campaign showed no great public concern about the growing federal deficit. Popular perception and economic reality are different, and voters do not worry about problems that they cannot see or feel. The deficit was an abstraction. By the time Bush was elected in 1988, many in and out of government agreed that the deficit was a problem, although there was no agreement about what to do. Richard Darman, the new director of the OMB, met with Bush and former presidents Jimmy Carter and Gerald Ford in December 1988 and Ford and Carter recommended to Bush that he seek a bipartisan package of tax increases and spending cuts. Darman met with congressional leaders about such a possibility, but Democratic leaders wanted Bush to reject his call for "no new taxes" and submit his own budget first. They also made clear that they were not going to permit cuts in entitlement programs or even consider reductions in capital gains taxes without income tax increases. Bush decided not to violate his pledge the first year. He knew at that time that he would eventually have to raise taxes. Darman told him that he could get through the first year's budget without tax increases but no longer than that. Bush placed some hope in a "flexible freeze" in which some programs would be frozen in spending but others could rise. The difficulty was that there was little agreement on which programs would be frozen. At the end of the day, the 1990 budget, after Congress finished with it, reduced expenditures by only $14 billion. Republicans were divided about taxes and not willing to cut budgets. Key individuals would admit that there was a problem but only in private. There was no bipartisan majority of the center for Bush to cultivate. So he stayed with the old Reagan incantations. The national security advisers were opposed to defense cuts, and Bush went along despite Darman's urging that defense be cut. Members of the president's cabinet were opposed to spending cuts in their own departments. But by the end of 1989, Greenspan was tightening the money supply, and Michael Boskin, chair of the Council of Economic Advisers, warned of the possibility of a recession by mid-1990. Bush's political advisers were worried that a recession might continue into his reelection year.

By January 1990, Darman, Boskin, and Secretary of the Treasury James Brady were convinced that the Reagan economic recovery was over. The economy was headed for recession. George Bush had to act with an eye to his own reelection. The deficit for fiscal 1990 was likely to be over $200 billion, with higher deficits expected in later years. It was not realistic to think of deep budget cuts with a recession threatening. Under Graham-Rudman-Hollings there would have to be a reduction of all federal programs between 20 and 45 percent at the end of the year. A coalition of the middle had to be constructed in Congress and led by the president. Bush would have to ignore the more conservative Republicans who were hostile to any tax increases. He invited negotiations with Democratic leaders in May, but they insisted that Bush publicly say that the possibility of tax increases was on the table. The president, under pressure, finally complied by accepting that "tax revenue increases" were a possibility, and serious negotiations began in June. The negotiations were carried out in secret by Darman; John Sununu, the White House chief of staff; and Democratic and Republican congressional leaders at Andrews Air Force Base near Washington. Bush did not take part. Saddam Hussein invaded Kuwait in July, and the president gave close attention to the American response throughout the rest of the year. In retrospect, it was probably unwise to begin secret negotiations without preparation of the public for what might emerge. Of course, the negotiators were on tenterhooks in relation to their own political bases in Congress and the country. There was fear that premature disclosures would sabotage any agreement. However, the congressional rank and file had no stake in the discussions, which turned out to be a problem.

The Democrats had embarrassed Bush publicly, but they also knew that they might be helping him to win reelection. However, they might also resolve the tight federal budgets for their own future claims to power. But the negotiations were very difficult. The Democratic leaders disliked Darman and Sununu, particularly the latter. Agreement was finally reached in September. The Gramm-Rudman-Hollings law was to be repealed. There was agreement to reduce government borrowing by $500 billion over five years and to cut spending by $180 billion. Entitlement programs such as Medicare were to lose $100 billion, and new taxes were to raise $150 billion, but they were to include taxes on gasoline and other commodities without any increase in income taxes. Ceilings were set for different divisions of the budget, and any increases in one part had to be offset by decreases elsewhere. The participants all thought that they had done a good job, and Bush blessed the result. He spoke to the nation on television on October 2, 1990, urging passage of the budget as a bipartisan measure. But many conservative Republicans were shocked. He had broken his campaign pledge not to raise taxes. His thought at the time was to avoid the deep cuts in programs that the Gramm-Rudman law would require, in which case much of the government would have to be shut down. He also did not want a budget crisis in the face of a possible war in the Persian Gulf. In addition, the financial markets wanted to hear a strong message about deficit reduction. Bush later admitted "I paid a terrible price."[4] The price he paid was political.

Bush spoke to the nation too late. The House rejected the budget on October 5. Both Republicans and Democrats voted against it. The Republican minority whip, Newt Gingrich, led the fight against the bill, even though he had been a full participant in the negotiations. He had failed to sell the agreement to other House Republicans and then turned against it, failing to show up for the announcement of the agreement at the White House. Gingrich continued his crusade to move Republicans to the right. The preparation of a new budget fell to the Democratic leadership of both houses, and Bush had to work with them. He had somehow lost control of the process, from delegation, inattention, and failure to clearly understand the likely political backlash from his repudiation of his pledge. He had to eventually agree to a budget that increased income tax rates on the well-to-do, cut the proposed gasoline tax in half, and reduced the cuts in Medicare. The new budget did contribute to reduction in the deficit over time. Bush repudiated the agreement during the 1992 campaign, but the horse was out of the barn politically. The fiasco strengthened the Republican opposition to tax increases.

One cannot know how much of Bush's turnaround on taxes and deficits was courage and how much was the expediency of promoting his own reelection. These are not mutually exclusive, but one can agree that it was handled badly by the president. He did not read the politics of the situation realistically and might have done better had he gotten into the pit with House Republican conservatives and argued his case. But that was not a sure thing. The problems in Kuwait were his primary concern and they were more pressing. It was easier to delegate the economic questions. He was not so much prudent as avoidant. But the budget agreement did reduce the deficit and help prepare the way for Clinton's actions to do the same.

We will discuss Bush's economic policies as the 1992 election approached later, but it is important to point out here that the president was far more successful in working with Congress in international economic policy. A signal achievement was the negotiation with congressional Democrats on the broad outlines of the North American Free Trade Agreement. Final enactment waited for Bill Clinton, but he worked from the established framework. Bush did considerable bargaining and negotiation with congressional leaders. A second achievement was the firm establishment of the president's "fast track" authority to negotiate trade agreements with other nations with a limited congressional role. This issue was worked out with Congress in preparation for the meetings of the Uruguay Round of the General Agreements on Tariffs and Trade. Bush believed strongly in free trade and was willing to bring his personal influence to bear in winning support. This was more congenial to him. Both foreign and domestic economic policy had many political pitfalls, but Bush was just more comfortable with the former.[5]

FOREIGN POLICY

Bush was very confident in his ability to conduct foreign policy. His experience was considerable and he believed that his skills at person-to-person diplomacy would be effective. Patterns of decision making among the president and his close advisers reflected his style of leadership. He knew the members of his team well and usually sought consensus among them. As he later wrote: "I was very much a believer that if you had confidence in your people, if they come together and agree, their common solutions will probably prevail and work best. Brent (Scowcroft) tried to reduce the issues to the points where he and I, and perhaps Jim Baker or Dick Cheney, could sort out any remaining problems."[6]

There was a shared worldview among his advisers, with considerable disagreement on specifics and yet little discord. They were all "realists" in the traditional sense of valuing American power in the world but prudence in its use. Crusades were out. Bush seldom convened the National Security Council, but relied on a "core group" sometimes referred to as the "Gang of Eight," whose members were the president, Quayle, Baker, Scowcroft, Cheney, Sununu, Robert Gates (head of the CIA), and Lawrence Eagleburger (deputy secretary of state). Discussions relied heavily on the streamlining of the interagency process, which was cumbersome; secrecy; the use of back channels, for example, in dealing with the Soviets; and a high degree of improvisation. One could contend that there might have been too much insularity at times, perhaps even "group think." But Bush would go against the group when his own insights told him to do so. For example, after the government of China brutally put down student demonstrations in Beijing in 1989, Bush denounced the action but in due time sent Scowcroft and Eagleburger secretly to China to assure the Chinese leaders that the United States wanted good relations. The mission was eventually exposed after Scowcroft's conciliatory words at a banquet were reported, and the president had to suffer criticism. James Baker argued against such a move, but Bush replied, "I know the Chinese.... I know how to deal with them."[7] Yet Bush would not rush into things in the case of strong dissents. Both Scowcroft and Cheney, who were more skeptical about the Gorbachev government than Baker, were able temporarily to hold up overtures. Bush was also sensitive to the politics of foreign policy, particularly in regard to Congress. He believed in consultation before action, for the most part.

George Bush and Mikhail Gorbachev

Ronald Reagan and Mikhail Gorbachev had created a domestic and international climate for reconciliation on a number of fronts, but Bush was initially cautious about Gorbachev. He was skeptical about the extent to which Gorbachev wished to reduce cold war tensions. He asked Scowcroft to oversee an interagency review about U.S. policy toward the Soviet Union. The results of the review, when they came in March 1989, were disappointing. There were no new ideas from the bureaucracy. Gorbachev, who wanted to continue as he had with Reagan, was upset and disappointed and made his views known through Eduard Schevardnadze, his foreign minister. The CIA was pessimistic about Gorbachev's chances of success in changing the Soviet regime. Bush and Scowcroft felt that they could not yet gauge the degree of Gorbachev's internal opposition. There was concern that Kennedy and Carter had moved too soon with unrealistic policies that had backfired. Scowcroft used the word "prudent" over and over in his jointly written memoir with Bush. Jack Matlock, ambassador to the Soviet Union, wrote Bush several memos recommending that the president find ways to help Gorbachev with social and economic reform at home. They were ignored at first. In the spring of 1989, the president made three speeches approving changes in the Soviet Union but asking for signs of cooperation in ways that would reassure the West that something fundamental had happened. He was particularly concerned about the Soviet puppet government in Afghanistan and support for the Sandinistas in Nicaragua. Gorbachev sent messages to reassure Bush about both cases, withdrew help to the Sandinistas, and eventually took Soviet troops out of Afghanistan. He also suggested that talks be held about setting limits on conventional armed forces in Europe.

Bush's strongest impulse was to establish good personal relationships with foreign leaders. He was playing to his strength. He called and talked with national leaders all over the world, and they were likely to comply with his reasonable requests about particular matters. He cultivated the president of France, Francois Mitterand, by inviting him to his summer home at Kennebunkport, Maine, and he felt that the close bond established there paid off in the eventual resolution of European issues. He also worked closely with Helmut Kohl, chancellor of West Germany, on all issues about West Germany in Europe. Prime Minister Margaret Thatcher of Britain was always giving him advice, some of which he took, but he knew that at the end of the day she would never challenge the United States because the relationship was the anchor of British foreign policy. By March 1989, Secretary of State Baker had established a good working relationship with Eduard Shevardnadze, and reported to the president that Gorbachev wanted continuity and also sought foreign policy successes for domestic political reasons. This sowed the seeds for new departures. Later in the summer, Baker told Bush that it was time to meet face to face with Gorbachev. Both Scowcroft and Robert Gates, director of the CIA, were uncomfortable with the idea. But Bush gradually warmed to it, because Baker wanted it, his European allies were urging him to do it, and the idea seemed popular at home. When Scowcroft warned Bush not to confuse Gorbachev with *perestroika*, the movement for political reform at home, Bush shot back, "Look, this guy is *perestroika*."[8] After considerable negotiations, an agreement for a meeting in late November at Malta on American and Soviet ships was arranged.

Bush oversaw the development of possible proposals to make to Gorbachev at Malta, despite his public claims that the meeting was only to get acquainted. Several ideas about reductions in conventional forces in Europe and interballistic missiles were worked up. The meeting was a great personal success for both men. They had met several times, but discovered that they liked each other and could talk frankly. It was agreed to begin talks on conventional forces in Europe and START and for the United States to provide some help to the Soviet economy to move toward free markets. By this time, the Berlin Wall had fallen and Bush, heeding Gorbachev's concern about a unified Germany, promised to do nothing to speed such an event. The personal relationship established at Malta was crucially important later when Bush was required to persuade Gorbachev to allow German unification and a place for Germany in NATO. Gorbachev reported that after Malta the two sides no longer felt like enemies. From that time forward, Bush was committed to helping Gorbachev stay in power, and keeping him on the track of reform.

Before the Berlin Wall fell on November 10, 1989, at the same time as the collapse of imposed communist regimes in the other captive nations of Eastern Europe, Gorbachev had told Erik Honecker, the East German leader, to reform his regime. He refused to do so and fell from power soon after. When Honecker's successor asked Gorbachev what to do, Gorbachev told him to open his borders. It subsequently became apparent that Gorbachev would not use force to protect communist regimes in Eastern Europe. In a New Year's Day address to his nation, Gorbachev announced that the cold war was over. In February he forced the Central Committee of the Communist Party to reduce its own size, adopt a multiparty system, create a new executive presidency, and begin economic reform. Bush, Baker, and Shevardnadze were worried about whether Gorbachev could survive politically, and Bush talked with him regularly by telephone to reassure him of his support. Gorbachev told Henry Kissinger, who was visiting Moscow, that he needed a long period of peace in which to carry out reforms.

In the spring of 1989, the ban on a public role for Solidarity, the reform movement in Poland, was lifted by the ruling government with Gorbachev's acquiescence. Scowcroft saw the possibility of restoring democracy to Eastern Europe, but Dick Cheney made an unfortunate public statement that Gorbachev would fail. James Baker was angry and forced a disavowal through the president's press secretary. Bush wanted to help move toward democracy in Poland, but he feared that any action to break the Warsaw Pact, the counterpart to NATO, might hurt Gorbachev at home. His general policy for Eastern Europe was to seek continued stability. When the Berlin Wall fell, Bush was relatively quiet because he thought public gloating might be harmful to Gorbachev. He told reporters, "I am not an emotional kind of guy." He wanted to sustain Gorbachev and seek incremental change in Europe. There was great fear in the White House that Gorbachev might be overthrown by hard-liners at home. It was known that the Soviet military leaders were furious about their loss of influence.

The changing picture in Europe required a broad policy review about the future of Germany, the role of NATO, and the relation of both to the Soviet Union and the new East European democracies.[9] Bush was determined to lead in the shaping of this future and recognized that he had to act in ad hoc ways because there was little time for reflection. The East German government was collapsing, and Helmut Kohl was hoping that eventual elections in that regime would pave the way for reunification. Bush could not control the pace of unification, but he hoped to stabilize it by working with Kohl so that Germany would remain within NATO. There was debate about whether to bring the allies and the Soviets into the discussions about unification, and James Baker came up with the idea of "two plus four" to work out the problems: the two Germanys, Britain, France, the United States, and the Soviet Union. The president had to work very hard to sell the British and the French on the plan because they were leery of a unified German power in the center of Europe. A more serious problem was that Gorbachev wished to delay German unification and was adamantly opposed to a unified Germany in NATO.

The communists were defeated by the Christian Democratic Party in the East German elections, and Kohl began to move toward reunification. Gorbachev eventually accepted a unified Germany but not in NATO. At the same time he dominated a Communist Party conference, warning them against obsession about the past and urging focus on reform at home. James Baker met with Gorbachev in Moscow and urged action for arms reduction and a new role for the Soviet Union in Europe. He had to admit that the United States did not have much money to lend for economic assistance because of the deficit, but added that money would be of no help without economic reform. Gorbachev and Shevardnadze came to Washington in May 1990 with a number of issues unresolved. Gorbachev said that he needed at least two years for economic reform and told Bush privately that he needed an agreement on trade for both political and economic reasons, and Bush indicated to Gorbachev that he was very much aware of Gorbachev's concerns about Germany. When the question of German membership in NATO came up, Gorbachev startled the room by saying that Germany would be free to choose to stay in NATO or leave it. Bush reaffirmed it to make sure that he had heard right. Then he noticed that the Soviet contingent were furious and began to denounce their own leader. Gorbachev seemed to retract a bit. Bush subsequently asked Baker to work up a trade agreement, which was done and agreed on. In a jovial meeting at Camp David there was agreement to work hard on conventional forces in Europe and START.

In the summer of 1990 the two Germanys negotiated treaties for unification, and the issue of Lithuania was resolved. The former satellite had declared its independence, which Gorbachev refused to acknowledge, creating an economic blockade. Bush was under domestic pressure to recognize Lithuania's independence but did not want to openly challenge Gorbachev, whom he asked not to use force. Lithuania withdrew its declaration and the blockade was withdrawn. Gorbachev thoroughly dominated a party congress during that period. He had to go forward. As Kohl told Bush, after a meeting in Moscow, "He has burned all his bridges behind him. He can't go back and he must be successful."[10]

Bush's diplomacy was effective and successful. While he was criticized for going too slow at first, he did so because he wanted stability in Europe in which change might be managed, if not controlled. He achieved his main objectives and did it through personal diplomacy with Gorbachev, Kohl, Thatcher, and Mitterand. He had talented help from Baker and Scowcroft along the way, but it was his show. This was the skilled eventful leadership.

Two subsequent important achievements were the treaty on Conventional Forces in Europe (CEF) and the START treaty, which reduced nuclear arms radically. Bush took the initiative on the CEF initially against the wishes of Thatcher and Mitterand, but he won their support at a NATO summit meeting in May 1989 called expressly for that purpose. Kohl had supported him all along. Gorbachev was eventually won over and, after much negotiation, Bush and Gorbachev signed the CEF treaty in Paris in November 1990. It called for balanced reductions of conventional forces in Western and Eastern Europe. The treaty matched current events, as former satellite states in the Warsaw Pact tore loose from the Soviet sphere. Soviet generals blocked the treaty for a time but did not prevail, and the refined treaty was signed in Vienna in June 1991. Bush did not push START talks at the beginning because of his uncertainty about Gorbachev. He believed in Mutual Assured Destruction from the nuclear balance and had never liked SDI. However, Baker and Shevardnadze working together pressed for action on START. In due course, Bush established a secret, high-level interagency group that developed the outline of START. The Gang of Eight oversaw the process, and Bush created a consensus within the group. Baker and Shevardnadze did the negotiating. The treaty was signed by Bush and Gorbachev in Moscow in July 1991. Political turmoil was growing in Russia, and Bush was anxious to support his Soviet friend in every possible way. On the way home, Bush made a speech in Kiev in the Ukraine asking for unity within the Soviet Union despite separatist sentiments there. It was later labeled by conservatives as the "Chicken Kiev" speech. Bush was perhaps behind the curve at that point, as the Soviet Union began to fall apart. The first serious warning sign appeared when Shevardnadze resigned and gave an emotional speech warning against enemies of reform. An attempted coup against Gorbachev took place in August 1991 but fell apart when Boris Yeltsin, by this time president of Russia, stood against it. Gorbachev had been about to sign a treaty in which the Soviet Union would become a union of federated states of which he would be the president. But several of the republics went their own way, and because the Communist Party no longer had an official monopoly on power—by Gorbachev's design—Yeltsin, as president of Russia, became the center of power, and Gorbachev was out of a job. Bush had been slow to support Yeltsin, but new relationships were worked out easily in due course. Bush's policies were consistent—change within stability. He was a conservative who welcomed incremental change. His personal diplomatic skills were central to the agreements that were made, especially in working with Gorbachev on German unification and France and Britain on arms control.

The Gulf War

Iraq invaded and occupied the small country of Kuwait on its borders on August 1, 1990. Saddam Hussein, the dictator of Iraq, sought Kuwaiti oil to replenish his economy after the long war with Iran. There were also old territorial claims; Kuwait had once been a province of Iraq. The United States had been caught napping because of a policy of cultivating Saddam on the chance that Iraq would be a force to balance Iranian power in the region. President Reagan had provided indirect military help to Iraq in the war with Iran, and Bush continued the relationship. Iraq was taken off the terrorist list and given credits from the Export-Import bank, but Saddam was a bad actor who made threats against Israel, bragged of his chemical weapons, and used them against Kurdish dissidents. It was a mistake for the Bush administration to continue to play up to Saddam, but concern about Iran was behind it. As the tension with Kuwait developed, American diplomats told Saddam that they had no views about border disputes but did warn against the use of force. Baker admitted that the administration should have seen that they had no effect on Saddam's actions, but concluded that the invasion could not have been stopped by American threats. Policymakers in Washington gambled on a risky policy and lost.

Saddam Hussein had violated Bush's cardinal principles—stability and predictability—and, as Bush saw it, the United States was the guardian of world stability. A quiet theme in all his subsequent actions was the idea of a "new world order," in which nations would cooperate to maintain stability with the United States in the lead. This was possible because the cold war had ended. But the idea only gradually emerged. His responses to the invasion of Kuwait were ad hoc and incremental. On August 2 he asked the U.N. Security Council to condemn the invasion and demand full withdrawal. The favorable vote was 14 to 0. The Security Council subsequently passed a resolution imposing an economic embargo on Iraq. On August 3 the United States and the Soviet Union publicly condemned the invasion and cut off all military aid to Iraq. On August 5 Bush told reporters that the invasion "will not stand." On August 6 the government of Saudi Arabia agreed to the deployment of 100,000 American troops in defense of their country. Later in August James Baker warned Bush to be careful because of the possibility of hostages, body bags, high oil prices, and recession. Bush replied: "I know that.... But we're doing what's right; we're doing what is clearly in the national interest of the United States. Whatever else happens, so be it."[11]

Colin Powell saw the "this will not stand" statement on television and realized that Bush had escalated the issue without consulting advisers. Both he and Baker were worried about the absence of forethought. This was not like Bush. Powell felt that Scowcroft was "first companion" to Bush rather than the manager of policy discussion. Bush later wrote that he did not know whether he had committed himself to using force in that statement but that he did feel that it might be necessary. His initial hope was that economic sanctions, imposed under a U.N. resolution, would be effective. He then went to work with European leaders, and the leaders of the smaller nations in the Gulf, to win support for his defensive actions. Boyden Gray, the White House counsel, had seen Bush's strong commitments before but never to this extent. Bush remembered that when he learned of the brutality of Iraq's army toward the Kuwaitis, "I began to move from viewing Saddam's aggression exclusively as a dangerous strategic threat and ... its reversal as a moral crusade." He added "It was good vs. evil, right vs. wrong."[12] At the time he was reading a history of the German invasion of Poland in 1939.

In October Bush decided that he had to act to liberate Kuwait and that meant using force. He thought that sanctions would be slow and that it would not be possible to hold a coalition together. American troops were in Saudi Arabia and they could not be kept there indefinitely. He and Scowcroft began to think about a calendar for fighting. American action would have to be in the cool months of February and March. No decisions were made to use force, but a decision was made to double the number of American troops in Saudi Arabia. This was an additional pressure to force Saddam to withdraw. Cheney was a strong advocate for war, but Baker and Powell were both reluctant. The president and his advisers decided to delay announcement of the decision to double American forces until after the November congressional elections, and Congress was not told in advance. The reason for delaying the announcement was not to complicate the elections by putting the issue before the politicians and voters. But the delay caused a firestorm in Congress.

Baker thought the failure to inform Congress was "horrible timing." Evidently, the allies felt the same way, particularly the Soviets. Baker scheduled a briefing for congressional leaders with the president. The leaders were very angry and told the president that he would have to come to Congress for approval to use force. He could not act under Article 51 of the U.N. Charter permitting states to act in self-defense. Cheney was telling Bush that he could do so and suggested fireside chats. Bush replied that he was not good at that. He believed that action, rather than words, was the best way to shape opinion.

Bush never found a consistent rhetorical theme to support American actions. Administration spokesmen talked about the defense of Saudi Arabia, the importance of preserving a balance of power in the Gulf, the need to protect U.S. supplies of oil, resistance to aggression, and atrocities in Kuwait. Bush compared Saddam Hussein to Hitler, and there was talk of a new world order. Robert Teeter, Bush's pollster, told the president that there were too many messages; he needed to simplify. But it didn't happen. The polls showed an even split in the public between reliance on sanctions and fighting. Sanctions were favored by blacks, women, highly educated people, Easterners, Catholics, Jews, and Episcopalians. Force was favored by middle- and lower-middle-income families, less well-educated workers, young males, and Southern whites. These divisions gradually shifted in favor of the use of force as events moved the nation closer to war.

Congress held extensive hearings on the issue of sanctions versus force in November 1990; it was largely a partisan debate. A parade of expert witnesses, tilted against force, passed before the various committees, but nothing was resolved. Bush decided to request the U.N. Security Council to authorize the use of force to free Kuwait, and on November 29 the council passed Resolution 678 stipulating that Iraq must withdraw from Kuwait by midnight of January 15 or member states would be authorized to "use all necessary means" to restore the integrity of Kuwait. At the time Bush thought that the threat might sink home with Saddam.

He then turned his attention to Congress. He wanted their "support" rather than their formal "approval" and would not invoke the War Powers Act, which gave him the authority to commit troops to combat under congressional supervision. Bush felt strongly that U.S. authority in the world would depend on expelling Saddam from Kuwait. There was nothing new here. The commitment to a strong American role in the world, which had been affirmed from Kennedy to Reagan, was still strong. The cold war was over, but the United States still had to lead. Bush recorded in his diary in December that the more he talked with members of Congress, the more convinced he was that he would have to act alone, which he was prepared to do, regardless of the consequences, including possible impeachment. A resolution asking for "support" was introduced in Congress on January 10. It passed on January 12 by votes of 250 to 183 in the House and 52 to 47 in the Senate; it "authorized" as well as "supported." A few Democrats sided with the president; otherwise it would not have passed. Bush worked very hard with individuals in Congress to bring them over, but it was clear that Democratic leaders had no appetite for the use of force.

Bush told advisers that he knew more about the situation than anyone, including leaders in the region. His job experience had prepared him, he had built a coalition of other governmental leaders, and he had found a purpose for which he had been in training for all of his life. He did not have Middle East experts in his advisory circle, relying rather on experienced generalists. Baker drew the distinction between scholars who used analysis and evidence and policymakers who must rely on "emotion and intuition." Bush had relied on his values and his intuition to gamble on the steps he would take.

Bush worked very hard during the crisis to bring Gorbachev on board and eventually succeeded. The Soviets had regarded Iraq as a client state and a number of Gorbachev's advisers kept pushing for delay, for special appeals to Saddam, for a conference on the Middle East that would resolve all outstanding issues in the region. Bush persisted in his path, appealing to Gorbachev in terms of their cooperation in establishing a new world order, and the appeal eventually worked. Various efforts to talk with Iraqi officials before January 15, which had been urged by the Soviets, failed. Up to the last moment Bush was fearful that the withdrawal of Iraq from Kuwait would preserve Iraq's military forces for a future fight. Military officers on the ground told him that it would be a short war to evict Iraq from Kuwait. After the deadline passed, the air attacks on Iraq's home ground began on January 17. Before the ground war began on February 23, Gorbachev was still trying to prevent it, saying that Saddam would withdraw from Kuwait, but Bush told him that Saddam had violated the deadline and action was necessary. On the day of the invasion, Bush wrote in his diary: "I'm tired, very tired, but our team operated so I haven't felt lonely in this decision. I have felt that it is only the President who can make the decision."[13] Bush spoke to the nation that night and public support was very strong. In a spontaneous burst of patriotism, yellow ribbons appeared around tree trunks all over the country. The ground war, with 500,000 coalition troops committed, lasted four days. The enemy forces were driven from Kuwait. Saddam had not committed his

of the Union address but rather called for cuts in capital gains taxes to revive the economy. As the general election approached, his economic advisers told him that the economy was improving and that a tax cut to stimulate it or additional spending would increase the deficit and thereby cause long-term damage to the economy. They believed that recovery would come in 1993. The deficit for fiscal 1992 was approaching $300 billion and adding $50 billion in spending, as some outside economists urged, would increase inflation. Monetary policy failed to revive the economy. The Federal Reserve Board cut interest rates twenty-three times from 1989 to mid-1992, but the economy did not revive. The actual economy was in no worse condition than in 1988, and the Bush recession was smaller than either Ford's or Reagan's. But Bush had no plan for revival. Popular expectations about the economic future were lower than the actual figures would suggest. Inflation was only 3 percent but the high unemployment rate of 7.87 percent worried people. The stage was set for a referendum on Bush's stewardship of the economy.

The underlying issue of a desire for change surfaced in the campaign with Bill Clinton as the agent of change and Bush as the defender of the status quo. If Reagan had been a president of achievement, Bush was a president of consolidation. However Reagan was able to hold the Republican coalition together in ways that Bush was not. Bush was slow to put a campaign organization in place. He felt sure of reelection from his foreign policy successes. However, Lee Atwater, the slash-and-burn manager of Bush's 1988 campaign, died in 1991 and Bush needed him. Robert Teeter, who did not like slash and burn, ran the campaign in the field with Bush somewhat inattentive. The Republican National Convention in Houston was a disaster. The conservative columnist Pat Buchanan, who had run against Bush in several primaries and not done badly, was given prime time for a speech that declared war on the Democrats in terms of a national "culture war." Bush's campaign staff was trying to win the Republican "base" but, as it turned out, the "base" had never trusted Bush, even though he announced that he ate pork rinds and liked country music. His acceptance speech was all about foreign policy, but public attention had shifted. Ross Perot, the Texas businessman, had entered the campaign and reserved most of his anger for Bush, primarily about the deficit.

Bill Clinton did a good job of capturing the middle ground. He presented himself as a "New Democrat" who had gone beyond the big government credo of conventional liberal Democrats. In this sense, he was Jimmy Carter's legatee. He addressed problems of health care, crime, drugs, and jobs. He stressed the importance of partnership between government and the people, for example promising "to end welfare as we know it." He used his own autobiography to illustrate that "I am one of you." His appeal was to people who "work hard and play by the rules," whose interests had been neglected. Clinton was a vulnerable candidate because of evidence that he had avoided the draft during the Vietnam war by a series of clever maneuvers and charges that he had carried on an affair with a lounge singer in Arkansas while he was governor. His standing in the polls in the early winter was low, but he fought his way through to win the nomination, campaigning as a "New Democrat." A telling illustration of his appeal was during a presidential debate when a young woman from the audience asked the three candidates how the recession had affected them. Bush did not understand the question and described how the downturn had affected others. Clinton asked the woman about her own life and how she felt. Then he described how economic distress in Arkansas affected his work as governor. He could feel people's pain, but they could feel his empathy. Bush campaigned negatively, labeling Clinton a tax raiser and warning of a runaway Democratic Congress with Clinton as president. He even called Clinton and Albert Gore, the vice presidential candidate, "bozos" at one point toward the end.

Clinton won 43 percent of the votes cast, Bush won 37.4 percent, and Perot won 18.9 percent. Studies revealed that the majority of the Perot vote was nominally Democratic but withheld from Clinton. Perot's role was to call attention to the deficit, which the new president would have to address. Clinton had the lowest popular vote of any winner since 1832. Bush did worse than all incumbent presidents except Taft in bids for reelection. The campaign did not make a difference, since Clinton was always in the lead. Clinton won because the Democrats had increased their share of union members, white working-class voters, Catholics, Jews, and white Southerners, in addition to the solid black vote. Bush won "middle America" but less so than in 1988. The mandate, if there was one, was for improving the economy. It resembled the Kennedy and Carter victories against Republican recessions.

Conclusion

How does George H. W. Bush measure up with respect to our qualities for presidential leadership?

Context and Contingencies

George Bush was elected to Ronald Reagan's third term. The economy was flourishing and the cold war had virtually ended. He inherited the large federal deficit. There were uncertainties about whether Gorbachev could actually achieve the reforms he sought. Bush faced a Democratic Congress that was more partisan than he had hoped. But the times were good for a new president.

Talents and Skills

Bush was good at diplomacy because he was astute, patient, prudent, and realistic. He worked well with Congress when these qualities could find expression. He was a poor public politician who could not speak well and separated campaigning from governing, not realizing that part of governing is campaigning. He paid a political price, as did Ford and Carter. He was intelligently prudent most of the time but could also be bold when he saw a principle at stake as he did in the invasion of Kuwait. The willingness to make hard decisions through boldness is a skill if it is not foolhardiness.

Bush created a coalition for military action through persuasion. One's judgment of the merits of his decision to fight must be made on policy grounds rather than an assessment of his personality.

Did He Make a Difference?

Bush's diplomatic abilities made a difference in persuading Gorbachev to cooperate in the unification of Germany and the inclusion of the united Germany in NATO. The negotiation of the CEF and START treaties were in large part personal achievements. Robert Gates described discussions in early 1990 about what to do about conventional forces—allied and Soviet—in Europe. Bush and Scowcroft wanted new initiatives in reductions in forces, but Cheney, Powell, and Baker were reluctant: "Out in front of everyone else on his team on German reunification, including Scowcroft, Bush now would push hard to respond to new opportunities for arms control."[15]

Bush was the prime mover in Desert Storm. It might not have happened without him. He was prudent in the decision to fight a limited war and not drive to Baghdad. The alternative to fighting was to try a blockade in hopes that Saddam would eventually withdraw from Kuwait. One may debate the merits of the decision but it was his choice and it made a difference.

There were only modest contributions to domestic policy. If Bush had been a better and more confident politician he would not have felt the need to promise not to raise taxes in 1988. One cannot know if he could have persuaded congressional Republicans to follow him in the 1990 compromise. He later disowned his own role in the compromise but it made it easier for

Bill Clinton to make the effort again in 1993. The real problem was that there is no place for a moderate conservative in an environment of polarized partisan politics.

Effectiveness

We can call Bush an effective eventful president in foreign policy. This was less the case in domestic policy, with a few exceptions, because of divided government and because he was not a good politician. But, on the whole, he was an effective, democratic leader. He contrasts very favorably with his son, the forty-third president, who, as we read at the beginning of this chapter, rejected prudence and pragmatism as timid and engaged in crusades at home and abroad.

BIBLIOGRAPHICAL ESSAY

There are a number of general books on the Bush presidency, including three biographies: John Robert Greene, *The Presidency of George Bush* (1999), Herbert S. Parmet, *George Bush, The Life of a Lone Star Yankee* (1997), and Tom Wicker, *George Herbert Walker Bush* (2004). Two good general treatments of Bush's presidency are Ryan J. Barilleaux and Mark J. Rozel, *Power and Prudence, The Presidency of George H.W. Bush* (2004), and Michael Duffy and Dan Goodgame, *Marching in Place, The Status Quo Presidency of George Bush* (1992). These books cover the same ground in many respects and all are fair and balanced. The memoir of Dan Quayle, *Standing Firm: A Vice-Presidential Memoir* (1994) is a friendly picture of Bush from a conservative who felt that Bush made a political mistake to make the 1990 budget agreement. But Quayle never makes clear how a president who sided with the Republican right could have won an election.

Descriptions and analyses of Bush's executive style are found in almost all studies of him, particularly in foreign policy. Two good portraits are William W. Newmann, *Managing National Security Policy, The President and the Process* (2003), Chapter 6, "The Bush Administration: Decision Making among Friends," and Thomas Preston, *The President and His Inner Circle and the Advisory Process in Foreign Affairs* (2001), Chapter 6, "The Gulf War." The best accounts of Bush's style are in his memoir with Brent Scowcroft, cited below. There are good discussions of the structure and politics of decision making in the Bush White House in Leslie D. Feldman and Rosanna Perotti, eds., *Honor and Loyalty, Inside the Politics of the George H. W. Bush White House* (2002). The book is one of four volumes on the Bush presidency taken from the Hofstra University conference on the Bush presidency.

A good study of Bush's work with Congress in domestic policy is David Mervin, *George Bush and the Guardianship Presidency* (1996), which makes a strong argument that not all presidents must be activists, as the presidential literature has suggested in the past, and for Bush as a guardian of continuity and stability. Charles Tiefer, *The Semi-Sovereign Presidency, The Bush Administration's Strategy for Governing without Congress* (1994), is of the same vein in its description of Bush's strategy of relying on administrative regulations to make policy, but he is less admiring of Bush than Mervin. Colin Campbell and Burt Rockman edited *The Bush Presidency: First Appraisals* (1991), in which there are a number of good chapters about domestic and economic, as well as foreign, policy. A good analysis of the passage of the Americans with Disabilities Act and civil rights legislation are in Richard Himmelfarb and Rosanna Perotti, eds., *Principle over Politics, The Domestic Policy of the George H. W. Bush Presidency* (2004). The book is also from the Hofstra series.

The best blow-by-blow account of economic policy, in all its twists and turns, is the memoir by Richard Darman, *Who's In Control? Polar Politics and the Sensible Center* (1996). Herbert Stein has been our old reliable in every chapter and he is good on Bush in *Presidential Economics: The Making of Economic Policy from Roosevelt to Clinton* (1994). John P. Frendreis and Raymond Tatalovich provide valuable economic data in *The Modern Presidency and Economic Policy* (1994). There is a good series of discussions on economic policy in Himmelfarb and Perotti mentioned above.

The best guide to foreign policymaking is the memoir by George Bush and Brent Scowcroft, *A World Transformed* (1998). Each writes his own account and then they write together in a running commentary. So far as I can tell from reading other sources, the description of situations and their own perspectives are accurate. A complementary and valuable book is James A. Baker III, *The Politics of Diplomacy, Revolution, War and Peace, 1989–1992* (1995). Michael Beschloss and Strobe Talbot have written a volume that runs in parallel with the previous two books, *At the Highest Levels: The Inside Story of the End of the Cold War* (1993). Robert Gates's chapters on Bush in his book *From the Shadows: The Ultimate Insider's Story of Five Presidents and How They Won the Cold War* (1996), is filled with insights about Bush. Bob Woodward, *The Commanders* (1991), is a story of the Persian Gulf War told largely from the perspective of Dick Cheney and Colin Powell. Robert W. Tucker and David C. Hendrickson are critical of *The Imperial Temptation: The New World Order and America's Purpose* (1992). They raise important questions that must be asked of George H. W. Bush. Similar questions are asked by Steven Hurst, *The Foreign Policy of the Bush Administration: In Search of a New World Order* (1999). There are good discussions and analyses on the Gulf War and its legacy in Meena Bose and Rosanna Perotti, eds., *From Cold War to New World Order* (2002), another volume in the Hofstra series.

Two comprehensive books, with both narrative and voting data on the 1988 and 1992 presidential elections, are by Paul R. Abramson, John H. Aldrich, and David W. Rohde, *Continuity and Change in the 1988 (and 1992) Elections* (1991, 1995). Several essays in Campbell and Rockman are useful and the same is true of Robert E. Denton, ed., *The 1992 Presidential Campaign, A Communication Perspective* (1994).

CHAPTER EIGHT

Bill Clinton

The Politician

When Bill Clinton walked into a room he would immediately be the center of attention. He knows how to seduce people to like him, in small groups and large. He wanted to be an event-making president, like FDR or LBJ, but his own style of leadership, plus the historical context in which he worked, pushed him into eventful leadership, and he was a highly effective eventful president.

Clinton's campaign strategy in 1992 was much like that of John Kennedy—get the economy moving again after a recession and advance social programs. The difference was that Kennedy spoke for an emerging progressive agenda. But by 1992 that agenda was very uncertain. Jimmy Carter had attempted to give the Democrats a new agenda, based primarily on fiscal probity, and Clinton was his legatee; two Southern governors who had learned at home how to combine liberal and conservative ideas. Clinton called himself a "New Democrat" and appealed to people he consistently called "middle class," which included working people who felt left out of the economy because of stagnant incomes, high payroll taxes, poor schools, increased costs of higher education, and a high crime rate. He promised a middle-class tax cut in the campaign. He did very well among black voters because of his rhetorical style, but offered little for the poor. In fact he promised to "end welfare as we know it." The central idea was to stimulate the economy and then use government to create opportunities for families and children. These ideas came out of Arkansas and the new South. He did not carry New Democrats into the Congress. In fact, the new Democratic members included more women and blacks and liberals, just as the Republicans kept producing more young conservatives. There were hard questions about what an effective New Democratic centrist strategy might be.[1] Was it to present fresh ideas that would reach beyond conventional liberal and conservative thought about big or little government, and, if so, what were the ideas and where were their adherents? This was Clinton's aspiration. Was it to be simply a series of managed compromises between Democrats and Republicans brokered by the president in which an ad hoc middle way might emerge? Or, was it to take a zigzag course in which the president would be liberal at some times and conservative at others, depending upon a strategy of some sort? No matter what the choice, it was sure to be confusing to voters and politicians because it would be unpredictable. The president would almost seem to be a trimmer whom no one could trust.

Democratic liberals were critical of Clinton almost from the beginning because he sent uncertain signals about his commitment to traditions of progressive reform. Carter had been the target of similar criticism. Two Southern Democratic governors were trying to find a middle way in an increasingly polarized politics. If Clinton had taken a strong liberal policy line in the campaign, he probably would have lost. It was not even clear what such a line would have looked like. Support for a national program of health insurance was very uncertain. Most congressional Democrats were protectionist in trade policy. There were no leading ideas about how to deal with the deficit while also spending new money on social programs. Carter and Clinton were telling traditional Democratic politicians that they were exhausted volcanoes, but they did not like to hear it.

POLITICAL STYLE

Bill Clinton is very elusive and difficult to capture. You think that you have him pinned down, and he does just what one least expects. The truth is that he is a package of contradictions. Almost anything that one says about him is likely to be true, but incomplete, although untrue stories are also elicited by his elusiveness. He has a somewhat larger-than-life quality. The hypotheses below are very much intertwined.

Clinton is a natural-born politician who loves to get out among the people, recognize and greet, listen and talk, show off, and get everyone to like him. He is not unique here but is just better at it than most politicians. He believes that he can persuade anyone of anything.

His mind is poor at conceptualizing. His great strength is in his mastery of complex material about politics and policy. As president he needed help in formulating political strategies in the short or long term and was continually asking his advisers to give him strategies for difficult situations. He always needed help on the big picture. His rhetoric could soar on high ideals, but strategies were often lacking.

Finally, he was undisciplined, self-indulgent, sometimes slippery with the truth, and given to grandiosity. But, by the same token, he never gave up. His political career followed a predictable cycle of self-induced crises, seeming disgrace, and then almost miraculous recoveries. He wanted to win more than anything else and would never stop trying.

These characteristics reinforced each other. They are the skills of an eventful politician who wanted agreement and was confident that he could achieve it. But politicians who are good at bargains are not necessarily moral leaders. Clinton wanted to be a moral leader and a great president in the line of previous great Democratic presidents. One must ask whether the man, or his time, was suited for that ambition.

BIOGRAPHY

Clinton was a poor boy from Hope, Arkansas, whose father died before he was born. He was often left with his grandmother while his mother studied nursing in New Orleans, and the two women, in their indulgence, gave him the sense that he was special, and he never lost it. He also saw the dark side of life with an alcoholic stepfather, and yet, much like Ronald Reagan, he pushed the dark away with fervent optimism. He wrote that his father's death made him feel that he had to live two lives, his own and the one his father had missed. This is not uncommon in children who lose their parents early. He also had a sense of his own mortality, writing "I was always in a hurry."[2] He wanted to make a mark and be recognized for it. His resilience carried him forward. If you look at his face in the photograph as he greeted President Kennedy at the White House in 1963 as a member of a Boys Nation delegation, one sees intense determination and can almost infer the thought, "I will be here some day." He is very smart and was well educated at Georgetown, Oxford, and the Yale Law School.

He was an undisciplined student who took what he wanted. He learned politics in Arkansas, through working in the campaigns of others, and eventually his own campaigns, at country fairs, pie suppers, courthouses, cafés, sale barns, radio stations, and weekly newspapers.[3] He wrote in his memoir: "All my life I've been interested in other people's stories. I've wanted to know them, understand them, feel them."[4] He wanted to help people in their lives and was optimistic that he could do so. He learned from one of his Georgetown professors that Western society had an "optimistic, progressive character," which created confidence in "the possibility of positive change."[5] The achievement of good things for people and the desire for personal glory are so deeply entangled in Clinton that it makes no sense to try to separate them. Every politician has to survive politically to do good things, but Clinton wanted to be great. His most persistent episodes of anger were when he thought that he was not appreciated or given credit for what he had achieved.

He ran a losing race for Congress in 1974 but learned that voters in Arkansas would support a government that solved problems and helped the worse-off, if in doing so it did not break the bank in taxes.[6] Here is the germ of the New Democrat idea, which was slowly developing in the aftermath of the disastrous Democratic defeat of 1972. Clinton was first state attorney general and was then elected governor in 1978 at the age of thirty-two. He tried to do too much and was defeated for reelection after a two-year term. Then he bounced back and was governor until he was elected president in 1992. His mistake the first time around was to increase taxes for driver's licenses as a means of paying for social programs. In his own words, his first term was "a policy success and a political failure." "I was always in a hurry to get things done, and this time my reach often exceeded my grasp."[7] It would not be the last time. In fact, a major contribution to the election of a Republican Congress in 1994 was the public perception that Clinton, as reflected in his plan for health care reform, was just another "tax and spend" liberal. The controversies that began with Carter and have continued after Clinton about the proper character of the Democrats as a party of reform are as yet unresolved.

Clinton's leadership skills and the political context that he faced as president were quite congruent. It was the time for a fox rather than a lion. Clinton's political skills were primarily eventful. He was a retail politician with the public and in policy leadership. Tactics were his strength rather than strategy. The times were suited to such leadership. He eventually learned to play both partisan sides against the middle to win achievements, but this "triangulation" was implicit from the first day.

EXECUTIVE STYLE

Clinton appointed experienced people to his cabinet and to the expert policy positions in the White House orbit. His personal staff was drawn from the campaign, inexperienced in Washington, and not composed of strong personalities. He was thinking, much as Jimmy Carter, like a governor who has a small staff of personal aides. There was no one comparable to James Baker or John Sununu who could help him sort out hard questions and impose discipline on the flow of information and debate. The chief of staff, Mack McClarty, was an Arkansas business executive, who had been a childhood friend of the president. The new staff had no plan for action. In part they were exhausted from the campaign, as was Clinton.

It is very difficult to estimate the importance of Hillary Clinton as an adviser to the president because the record is incomplete. But she was important. She may have taken the responsibility for an overview of domestic policy. Staff members found it difficult to speak frankly to her or even to the president if she were involved. But Clinton had great confidence in her and would brook no criticism.

In the first few months, policy meetings were like bull sessions with lots of junior people in the room. The talk was free flowing and hardly structured, with Clinton at the center of it all asking questions. Senior officials like Secretary of the Treasury Lloyd Bentsen, a veteran senator and former chairman of the Senate Finance Committee, could hardly believe it and would often leave early. Clinton was working as he had in Arkansas without any structure to speak of and relying on his own intelligence to sort out his choices. But he always wanted to hear more and would put off decisions until forced to decide. He learned by probing and questioning but did not at first appreciate what a stable staff structure could do to help him with his choices. His personal style was erratic. He was habitually late for meetings, would give vent to fierce anger often against the staff, made late-night telephone calls, and never seemed to sleep. His buoyancy was laced with egoism and often with self-pity. But everyone respected his intelligence, and this established his authority.

Two caveats are important. After a little more than a year, Clinton recognized that his own disorganization was hurting his presidency and he appointed Leon Panetta, director of the Office of Management and Budget (OMB), as White House chief of staff. Panetta was a former congressman with long experience who imposed structure and discipline, within the limits the president would permit. The second caveat is that the president relied heavily on Vice President Al Gore to force him to decisions. Mrs. Clinton seems to have played something of that role as well, although she and Gore were sometimes in competition over specific policies.

Early Days

Clinton took the White House staff and cabinet officers to Camp David in January 1993 for discussion of his priorities, which he listed as action to stimulate the economy, campaign finance reform, national service, welfare reform, and health care reform. Clinton had told Ted Sorensen, John F. Kennedy's aide and biographer, along with the historian James MacGregor Burns, that he wanted to be a great president like FDR. His conception of greatness, like that of Johnson, was to pass a lot of reform legislation. He would be liberal on a fiscal stimulus, health care, and social issues, and conservative on the deficit, crime, welfare reform, and family values. This mixed bag was not easy for others to see as a whole. And, as he later wrote: "I had always had a tendency to try to do too much, which also contributed to physical exhaustion, irritability, and my well-deserved reputation for tardiness."[8] Clinton had not rested during the transition and was exhausted as he took office. Nervous energy was no substitute for the quiet development of strategy. The result was a lack of focus and a president spread too thinly across too many proposals. There were early mishaps, which received more attention than a few early successes.

Clinton had promised an executive order to permit gays to serve in the military without penalty and was forced by the military chiefs and congressional opinion to retreat to a compromise. The first two appointees for attorney general proved to have not paid Social Security taxes for women minding their children, and a nominee for assistant attorney general for civil rights was asked to withdraw because of somewhat radical writing about black representation. Early passage of a law permitting people to leave their jobs temporarily for medical reasons passed, along with a bill to permit citizens to register to vote as they registered for driver's licenses; a gun control bill was passed, and a national service program for young people was created. These achievements were not noticed because of coverage of the mishaps because the press prefers to cover bad news.

Clinton faced two hard strategic questions of policy leadership that were to define his presidency. The first was whether to seek a middle-class tax cut as promised or to attack the federal deficit. The second question was which to do first, welfare reform or health care reform. We will consider these issues in turn.

Economic Policy

Clinton had not discussed the deficit much during the campaign, beyond promising to cut it in half in four years, and he entered office without a plan. Deficit projections from the OMB and the Congressional Budget Office (CBO) then proceeded to balloon, and he faced the possibility of a deficit of over $300 billion by the time he would prepare his last budget before the 1996 election. Democratic congressional leaders met with Clinton after the election and stressed that reducing the deficit was their highest priority. Clinton talked with Federal Reserve Chairman Alan Greenspan, who told him that increasing deficits would harm the economy in future years. A plan to reduce deficits would cause Wall Street to lower interest rates and stimulate the economy. Greenspan, by implication, would keep interest rates at reasonable levels. Clinton's economic advisers were deficit hawks. Robert Rubin, head of the newly created National Economic Council, was a Wall Street investment banker. Leon Panetta, then director of the OMB who had served as chairman of the House Budget Committee, his deputy Alice Rivlin, an economist who had been director of the CBO, and Secretary of the Treasury Lloyd Bentsen weighed in heavily on the importance of cutting the deficit. Clinton's political advisers, who had carried him through the campaign on the promise of middle-class tax cuts—particularly Paul Begala, George Stephanopoulos, and Labor Secretary Robert Reich—were horrified. They wanted the president to stick with the economic populism that had elected him. Clinton was torn because he wanted to invest in social programs like Head Start as well as cut taxes, but the economic situation was stark. Reagan had created a bias in politics against raising taxes that was not easy to confront. Meetings in the Oval Office about the budget were long and heated. The president complained that he was about to act like an "Eisenhower Republican" in trying to balance the budget. Vice President Gore pushed him very hard to decide, because the White House was otherwise paralyzed. Clinton finally decided to go with his economic advisers. The reason may have been because he understood the economic arguments, indeed, was able to dissect them in great detail. He was torn because he could do the same with his great knowledge of social programs. But he understood that his presidency was at stake. Reaganomics must be reversed if his presidency was to succeed and social programs were to be paid for. The president proposed a cut of $493 billion in the deficit over five years. There were to be some spending increases on a gradual basis, and taxes were to be increased by $247 billion. Tax increases were imposed on the highest bracket of taxpayers and a tax on pollutants from gasoline and energy production was included, to raise revenue and also as an energy conservation measure. The question was whether there was a coalition to support the plan.

Both the House and the Senate approved the initial budget resolutions in March as a general guide to the appropriating committees, but hard questions about the content of the program were not faced. In the aftermath, a fight erupted about the tax on pollutants. Oil-state senators threatened to oppose the budget if it were included, and Bentsen withdrew the idea on a television appearance, meaning to say that it could not pass the Senate. House members from energy-producing states, who had voted for the resolution, were furious; their limb had been cut. In the meantime Republicans were telling the public that Clinton was going to raise taxes on everyone. For a time, the president dropped the ball. He seems to have become discouraged, as he could not figure out what to do. He was learning how to deal with Congress in his first big fight. But toward midsummer he bounced back. His polls revealed that the public wanted him to be seen acting as a president. He worked hard to persuade members of both houses of Congress, individually and in groups. Many bargains and concessions were made by Democratic congressional leaders to buy votes. In July Clinton gave a talk in the White House Rose Garden arguing for his program that was well received. But Democrats in the Senate were divided between conservatives opposed to tax increases, liberals who did not want to cut programs, and centrists who were led by Majority Leader George Mitchell and Finance Committee chair Daniel Patrick Moynihan. Clinton left the bargaining to Mitchell and Moynihan. They replaced the tax on pollutants with a gasoline tax and cut the deficit by $500 billion. The final votes in each chamber were 218 to 216 in the House and 49 to 49 in the Senate, with Vice President Gore breaking the tie. This was the most important achievement in domestic policy of the Clinton presidency. Eventually, Wall Street and the Federal Reserve smiled, the economy grew, unemployment fell, and the stock market rose. A further budget agreement in 1997 turned a deficit of $200 billion into an eventual surplus of the same size before Clinton left office. But Clinton lost the political battle. The Republicans successfully persuaded much of the public that he had raised their taxes, and for reasons that are still unclear, he did not fight back.

Clinton's choice was a policy departure that reversed the Reagan mold. Congressional Democratic leaders created the legislative possibilities, but he had given the initial leadership. His rhetorical political skills were of limited help, but Clinton used his persuasive powers with members of Congress to good effect. He seemingly went beyond prudence, because he risked failure with Congress. But political caution, seeming prudent, in which he would have stayed with the Old Democrats, would not have been prudent in the long run. Prudence depends on prescience, and Clinton saw clearly where his and the country's interest lay.

Before the budget issue was resolved, Clinton presented a $16 billion spending bill in April, described as a stimulus package to strengthen the economy. The OMB had cobbled department proposals together for a collection of programs in urban development, education, and other human development programs. It was aimed primarily at Northern cities. Clinton made a mistake in not asking for Republican support and in rejecting compromise ideas from more conservative Democratic senators. The bill was eventually killed by a Republican filibuster in the Senate. Republicans portrayed it as a gigantic pork barrel. Many Democrats thought it should wait until budget cuts were in place. There was no public interest in a stimulus, and Republicans could cry "tax and spend." Failure caused many citizens to think that Clinton's budget had failed. The episode illustrates Clinton's uncertain grip on his job.

Clinton drew on his talents and determination in the fight for congressional ratification of the North American Free Trade Agreement (NAFTA) with Canada and Mexico, which had been negotiated by President Bush. White House advisers divided along the same lines as on the budget. Political advisers saw the opposition of organized labor and rank-and-file congressional Democrats. In their view, the treaty would take jobs out of the United States. Economic advisers saw free trade as the key to future prosperity. Lane Kirkland, head of the AFL-CIO, offered Clinton $10 million to be used by labor to support future health care reform. But if the president were to support NAFTA, then the money would go toward opposition to it. Clinton turned him down. The president gave a strong speech to Congress in support of NAFTA and brought presidents Ford, Carter, and Bush to the White House to support the plan.

His big problem was that he could not win a majority in Congress without Republican votes, and he sought them. The Democratic House majority leader, Richard Gephardt, led a large Democratic bloc in opposition. Clinton struck a deal with Newt Gingrich, House assistant minority leader, to deliver at least 100 votes. Clinton worked very hard with members of Congress and made many side agreements and compromises. He had to win. He even attacked organized labor on television. He also went to the country to reverse negative public opinion and brought it around. The key to victory may have been Vice President Gore's debate with NAFTA opponent Ross

Perot on *Larry King Live.* Gore pretty well tore Perot apart. The vote in the House was 234 to 200 with 132 Republican votes and 102 Democratic votes. The Senate supported the treaty by 61 to 38. Clinton had provided vigorous leadership and moved forward as a New Democrat. But Republican support on that scale was not repeated, and liberal Democrats were angry. Clinton put his stamp on the free trade argument that he was never to abandon. He had confronted the teachers' unions in Arkansas on education reform and was not afraid to confront labor on NAFTA. He had courage.

The budget breakthrough approximates event-making leadership, not only because it was an important policy reversal, but because Clinton made a hard decision and put his shoulder to the wheel. The NAFTA victory built on existing political momentum and was skillful eventful leadership.

Health Care Reform

Bill Clinton approached health care reform as a New Democrat. He did not think that the American people would support a government-financed system as in Canada or Britain. But a market system with increasing costs that left many people out was not enough. He conceived of a plan that would provide universal coverage and yet control inflation and would be primarily decentralized. He rejected incremental reform one piece at a time, because piecemeal changes would throw some parts of the system off course, for example, cutting Medicare costs might hurt hospitals and providers. He wanted a comprehensive plan.

He told the Congress of his intentions in January 1993 to put Hillary Clinton in charge of the planning effort. She had done the same work in Arkansas with education reform. Her assistant was Ira Magaziner, a management consultant, who was an Oxford friend of the president. Magaziner's specialty was the design of large-scale systems, with a history of uncertain results. But he was the person to design comprehensive reform, and that was what the Clintons wanted.

Magaziner had no experience in Washington and was not the kind of person to sit and schmooze with congressional politicians. He and Mrs. Clinton worked in secret with a task force of roughly 500 people. There was to be no publicity to prevent opponents from attacking pieces of the plan. But rumors traveled easily, and the press, resenting the secrecy, helped rumors along.

Donna Shalala, secretary of health and human services, was cut out of the planning, as was Secretary Bentsen. The Clintons did not trust the bureaucracy to do something original. White House economists, including Bentsen, thought that the plan would not save as much money as expected because of large administrative costs, and urged incremental reform. But they were not heeded. In a meeting in which Bentsen voiced misgivings, the president became red in the face and shouted "I am a reformer." By the same token, skeptics found it difficult to talk to Hillary Clinton. She would not listen.

The plan as it emerged after six months of work was to require all employers to pay part of the health care costs of their employees. Health care would be provided primarily by private Health Management Organizations that would be overseen in terms of costs and benefits by quasi-public organizations in each state. Federal panels would set overall prices of health care. The reform had to take a back seat to the budget fight and then again to NAFTA. But in September Clinton introduced the general plan to Congress, and Mrs. Clinton testified before five different congressional committees. Both performances were impressive. But then nothing happened. The bill was not ready and did not go to Congress until November. The president became very involved in a number of difficult foreign policy problems, and the plan was put off until January 1994, when he reintroduced it in his State of the Union address. By this time, the opposition had had an opportunity to mobilize. Clinton made a big mistake in his address. He whipped a pen from his pocket and promised to veto any bill that did not provide universal coverage. Compromise ideas that would do less were already circulating, and he wanted to steal a march on them. It was a terrible mistake because it ruled out compromise. In fact, there had been no effort to see what kind of coalition might be built in Congress. The president was peering into the dark with bravado. Clinton later admitted that he had made a great mistake. It was posturing rather than winning. But he added, the Republicans were never going to cooperate, so it did not matter.[9]

Congressional Republicans decided that the bill must be killed. William Kristol, a Republican policy advocate, wrote a memo to congressional leaders arguing that Clinton must not be permitted to go to the voters in 1994 with health care reform. The chair of the Republican National Committee, Haley Barbour, had the same worry. Senator Robert Dole, the minority leader, talked with Clinton about a compromise but eventually announced his opposition. He was running for president. Moderate Republican senators, like John Chafee of Rhode Island, tried to arrange compromises, working closely with George Mitchell, the Democratic majority leader, but it was not possible to get agreement, even on plans short of universal coverage. Newt Gingrich was already working on his plan to run against the Clintons and their plans for "big government" in a nationally unified campaign for a House majority in the fall. The Republicans did their best to block administration bills in Congress: campaign finance reform, clean water, general agreements on trade, and crime.

The insurers, hospital associations, medical groups, and all kinds of social conservatives mobilized strongly against the bill with television advertising, direct mail, talk radio, and direct lobbying. The most effective were the "Harry and Louise" television ads in which a youngish couple discussed perils ahead, all playing on fears about big government. Members of Congress listened to small business employers concerned about the costs to them. A good part of the information purveyed was false, but the Democrats did not organize a campaign in the country. At midpoint in the battle, Mrs. Clinton set up a "war room" in the White House to guide the legislative fight. That was not the way to work with Congress. The Clintons were continuing the election campaign in inappropriate ways.

Clinton's public approval went down at this time because of a sexual harassment suit filed against him by Paula Jones, a former Arkansas state employee. He was forced to appoint a special prosecutor to look into accusations that he and Mrs. Clinton had profited illegally from an Arkansas real estate deal, the so-called Whitewater affair. These events reinforced the declining support for health reform. Most people were happy with their own coverage but had been willing to accept universal coverage with reduced costs. But the fears that opponents aroused about bureaucratic schemes caused people to worry that they might lose what they had. Clinton did not do a good job rallying public opinion. He and his pollster had decided early on that they would not try to sell details but talk in terms of general principles. And yet the opponents were hitting details and were not answered. By August 1994 only 39 percent of a national sample favored the plan. The White House eventually turned its attention to persuasion in Washington.

Senator Mitchell finally gave up at the end of the summer, and so did the Clintons. The Republicans won control of the Congress in the fall elections. One of the principal reasons was the belief that the president was a "big government" man.

What Went Wrong?

Clinton later admitted that he should have put welfare reform ahead of health care. It would have solidified him with voters as a New Democrat. However, when he suggested that his health care bill be pulled in favor of welfare reform to Tom Foley, Speaker of the House, Foley said no and cited the opposition of black Democratic representatives to welfare reform.

Clinton did not accurately perceive the interests of the health care industry and the political incentives of the congressional opposition. He was back in Arkansas thinking that he could win the day by his eloquence. He was not even in the fight much of the time, deferring to Hillary Clinton. He had great confidence in her intellectual and political ability. In fact, she was stubborn and hostile to criticism. She rejected the possibility of a compromise bill early on because of her commitment to the new plan. One cannot say whether a compromise would have been possible. The Republicans would not cooperate. They tasted blood.

The political center that Clinton had hoped to create was too weak. The increasing ideological polarization between the two congressional parties was an obstacle to any bill. Major legislation like the Civil Rights Act, Medicare, the Clean Air Act, and tax reform in 1987 required large bipartisan majorities in Congress. Health reform was that kind of radical change. Democratic congressional leaders overestimated their capacity to get the votes. It had barely worked with the budget. But congressional Democrats were divided between single-payer and quasi-market plans and could never get together. Clinton thought that the president could win support for major reform by presenting himself as a reformer. This was an intellectual and personal failure. He wanted to be another FDR and could not resist the temptation.

Defeat and Comeback

When Clinton finished second in the New Hampshire primary election in 1992, he called himself the "Comeback Kid." This had happened in Arkansas, and it was about to happen again as the Republicans won control of Congress in the 1994 elections. Democrats lost eight Senate seats and fifty-four House seats. Unhappiness with Clinton for being too radical, or for doing too little, was a factor. Newt Gingrich organized a national campaign of Republicans around conservative themes. The Republican trend had been coming since 1968, but it was a shock to the president. He was confused and reclusive for a time. The deputy chief of staff, Erskine Bowles, cut Clinton's workday, giving him time to read and think with hopes that he would get more sleep. He did not do well without sleep and yet he was a night owl. He knew that he needed help with political strategy and called on Dick Morris, a political consultant, who had pulled him out of the jam in Arkansas after his loss. Morris worked secretly for some time. On the basis of polls, he concluded that Clinton must return to his New Democrat base and bless some popular Republican ideas like welfare reform and middle-class tax cuts but reject their ideas about cutting entitlements deeply. Morris used the word "triangulate," by which he meant build a center coalition from both parties. This made liberal Democrats unhappy, but it helped Clinton find his way. Gingrich, now Speaker of the House, was a man of volatile temperament given to exaggerated claims that the New Deal era was over and a new era of limited government and expansion of opportunity through the market was about to begin. Among his many rhetorical excesses, he said that Clinton was the "enemy of normal Americans." Clinton began to think that Gingrich might be his own worst enemy. He also saw that the economy was growing to give him future political support. The 1995 State of the Union message used New Democrat language. Clinton told an aide: "My first two years here I was totally absorbed in getting legislation passed. I totally neglected how to get the public informed. It was my fault and I have to get more involved in crafting my message."[10]

At the suggestion of Morris, Clinton went on the road attacking Republicans. He might have well have done so because during the first 100 days of the Republican Congress he had no role to play. Republicans were busy enacting their program. There was a big debate within the White House about whether the president should submit his own budget as an alternative to the budget the Republicans were preparing. His own staff was opposed, as were congressional Democratic leaders. It was not clear how they intended to defeat the Republican budget, except by presidential veto, but they also were afraid that the president would be too conciliatory with Republicans if there were opportunities to compromise. Clinton decided that he needed his own budget as an alternative to the Republican plan, and he was right because he later used it to bargain them down. He had an alternative to use against them. On June 13, 1995, he gave a speech promising a balanced budget in ten years. The budget would be cut by $1.1 trillion without new taxes. Middle-class taxes would be cut. There were no major cuts to entitlements.

Hard-line House Republicans insisted on a seven-year budget with cuts in entitlements. They wanted Clinton to surrender. But as time passed, polls revealed that more citizens trusted Clinton than the Republican Congress, which was seen as too extreme. By November there was no budget for fiscal 1996.

Congress passed a continuing resolution to keep the government in business along with an increase in the debt ceiling. Clinton vetoed both measures. The government shut down on November 14. Clinton then shifted gears and agreed to a seven-year budget but without the cuts in Medicare and Medicaid that Republicans wanted. The OMB had revised budget projections to provide for increased economic growth. Agreement was then reached on a continuing resolution until December 15. But if no deal was struck, large parts of the government would be closed on that date. Clinton threw a rhetorical bone to the Republicans in his 1996 State of the Union message by announcing that "the era of big government is over." But he would not back down, and in early January the opposition gave in, agreeing to a continuing resolution until March 15 and Clinton submitted his seven-year budget. Gingrich later told Clinton, "We thought you would cave." Clinton had outbluffed them. But he had also compromised on seven years.

REELECTION AND TRIANGULATION

Clinton defeated Robert Dole in the 1996 election, but he won only 49 percent of the vote. Democrats were increasingly weak in the South and among white men and the religious right. One could see the "red and blue state" divergence of later elections. Clinton did well among union members, blacks, Hispanics, women to a limited degree, Jews, Catholics, and the less educated and least paid. Dole was a weak, inarticulate candidate. He had nothing to offer the Clinton voters of 1992. The rising economy made a great difference for Clinton. The White House had spearheaded a massive advertising campaign against Republicans in the swing states in the months before the election.

The president had also hewed to the center path in working with Congress. He signed a Republican welfare reform bill in 1996, not all of which he liked, thinking that it was perhaps his only chance to do so. Much of his own White House staff and nearly all congressional liberals opposed the action. He used executive orders to curb tobacco advertising, strengthen meat inspections, and create wilderness areas. He presented small initiatives to Congress like drug testing for minors who registered for automobile licenses, to permit mothers to have longer hospital stays, and he pushed hard for free trade agreements. These were the kinds of small victories that triangulation could produce.

The important achievement of 1997 was the summer agreement for a balanced budget that went beyond the previous plan. Clinton and Gingrich stayed away from the negotiations that were carried out amicably by subordinates. By that year the federal deficit was down to $22 billion compared to the $290 billion deficit that Clinton had inherited. The federal budget would be in surplus by 1998. A good bit of this success was due to the flourishing economy. The growth rate in 1997 was 8.2 percent and unemployment was below 5 percent.[11] Clinton had listened to Alan Greenspan and Robert Rubin. Deficit reduction and the high technology boom of the nineties help explain much of the economic facts. His legislative achievements in 1998 were modest: children's health insurance, tax credits for higher education costs, putting more policemen on the streets, modification of welfare reform to include illegal immigrants, more free trade, and reform of the Food and Drug Administration.

Clinton's domestic presidency virtually ended in 1998 with his impeachment. How do we assess his political skills against the political context in which he worked? The context was one of partisan polarization. His major mistake was in the effort to do so much in health care reform. The Clintons underestimated the organized opposition that they would encounter and the fractured opinions in the Congress. Welfare reform would have been a better issue to take into the 1994 campaign. Critics of the second-term triangulation strategies did not understand that Clinton's tactical strategies were political victories, even if not ideal liberal policies. Clinton transformed himself into an effective eventful president.

FOREIGN POLICY

Clinton's achievements in foreign policy were made through the collegial work of advisers and diplomats. There were no spectacular personal triumphs. But it was not a time for such triumphs. The cold war had ended. Developments in Russia, under the leadership of Boris Yeltsin, were uncertain. Relations with China were more or less stable. The seemingly intractable tension between Israel and the Palestine Liberation Organization was still festering. A civil war among Serbs, Croatians, and Bosnians in the former Yugoslavia was growing increasingly fierce each day, but the possible U.S. role was unclear.

Clinton pushed his advisers hard to develop new concepts that would characterize and guide American foreign policy in the new era, something like the term "containment" of the Soviet Union in the cold war. George Kennan, the author of the policy of containment, advised against it. Clinton's response to the criticism was that he wanted a concept "as a politician." But no idea developed. Clinton wanted a word or words that would dedicate the United States to fostering democracy in the world. He was especially interested in such possibilities in Russia.

Clinton and his foreign policy team were not "realists" in the school of Nixon and Kissinger or even George H. W. Bush, who saw the world as it was and built alliances for stability and predictability. Secretary of State Warren Christopher had been deputy to Cyrus Vance in the Carter administration, and Anthony Lake, the assistant to the president for national security, was a strong advocate of democratization. Clinton's early approach, as set out in speeches, was a U.S. role in nurturing democracy, pushing for free trade, working cooperatively with Europe and Russia on common problems, using the United Nations for peacekeeping, and support for international agencies that promoted economic development. The credo was identical with that of Jimmy Carter. The one slogan that captured it was "enlargement and engagement." Democracy and economic growth went hand in hand, and democracies did not fight each other.

Clinton delegated foreign policy to Christopher and Lake at first, wishing to focus on domestic issues. He said that he did not see a "political winner" in foreign policy. Meetings about foreign policy were "wandering deliberations," and Clinton often did not attend. Eventually, as the new president became acquainted with foreign leaders and enjoyed talking about politics with them, he came to believe that he could make a difference through personal diplomacy. His meetings with Boris Yeltsin, the president of Russia who had pushed Mikhail Gorbachev aside, encouraged this approach. Clinton believed that Yeltsin was a democrat and wanted to help him. He had the same leverage with Yeltsin that Bush had had with Gorbachev. The Russian leaders needed Western support to keep the communist hard-liners at bay. Therefore, Clinton worked to bring Russia into Western councils, by giving the Russians a seat with the G7 of the industrial democracies and economic assistance from the World Bank and the International Monetary Fund (IMF).

Clinton later wrote that when he took office, Yeltsin was "up to his ears in alligators."[12] The Duma, the lower house of the Russian parliament, was filled with Yeltsin's enemies, both communists and reactionaries. The three Baltic states of Estonia, Latvia, and Lithuania, which had been under the Soviet yoke, were demanding independence. State monopolies were made private and run by new men who cared nothing about free markets, and organized crime was rampant. Was it realistic to think that Yeltsin could produce, or even take steps toward, democracy and markets? Perhaps not, but what choice did the West have? Russia had many nuclear weapons that were imperfectly controlled. The country could easily fall into economic collapse and political anarchy. Bush had been criticized for staking too much on Gorbachev, and Clinton faced the same criticism. Strobe Talbott, Clinton's chief adviser on Russia, remembered: "Clinton identified with Yeltsin's stubbornness, resilience, and defiance in the face of adversity and antagonism" and his capacity to "stand up to the bastards who are trying to bring him down."[13]

Clinton and Yeltsin met in Vancouver, Canada, early in Clinton's first term. They liked each other, and Clinton set up a schedule for regular meetings between Vice President Gore and Victor Chernomyrdin, the Russian premier, for a continuing discussion of issues. Issues of arms control and nuclear proliferation were delegated to Christopher and Lake. After Clinton returned from Vancouver, he pressed Lake to oversee the development of a package of economic aid to Russia. Neither congressional Democrats nor White House political advisers were happy about money going to Russia and away from domestic programs as the deficit was increased. But Clinton pushed ahead.

In the course of the next several years, Clinton persuaded Yeltsin to support Western peacekeeping in Bosnia, to accept the independence of the three Baltic states, to give independence to the Ukraine in return for the elimination of the Ukrainian nuclear arsenal, and to allow the enlargement of NATO to Eastern Europe, but without the presence of Western troops or nuclear weapons. Clinton helped Yeltsin with the integration of Russia into what became the G8 of industrial democracies and with the granting of Western aid through the IMF and the World Bank. Yeltsin's staff told Talbott that Clinton's support for Yeltsin was a powerful force for keeping Yeltsin on the negotiating track.[14] All of this was done primarily through the same kind of quiet diplomacy that George Bush had exercised. There was really no alternative. Clinton, the skilled, eventful politician, was well equipped for such diplomacy. In retrospect, he thought that he should have done more to help Russia, but, as it turned out, Russian politicians were not good at joining politics to economic reform in the direction of free markets for their own economic development. The democracy was too weak. Perhaps the trauma of dislocation in the lives of ordinary Russians was too severe for politics to ameliorate. But the achievements of integrating Russia with the West were considerable.

Balkan Wars

The nation of Yugoslavia, which had been united under Josef Tito, a communist dictator, began to fall apart after his death as provincial politicians began to attack each other. The three main ethnic groups—Roman Catholic Croatians, Orthodox Serbs, and Moslem Bosnians—had lived together peacefully for generations. The civil war that developed was not due to historical hatreds, as was often claimed. Rather, one Serbian politician,

Slobodan Milosevic, saw the opportunity to create a greater Serbia by extending Serbian control over Serbian peoples in Croatia and Bosnia. The Serbian-Croatian war began in 1991, and war began in Bosnia in 1992 as Bosnian Serb forces, with Milosevic's support, attacked Moslem populations there. The Bush administration took note but concluded that no U.S. interests were at stake. This was something the Europeans should handle through NATO, but the European community took no action. The United Nations did create an embargo on the importation of arms to Bosnia, but the Serbs had plenty of arms. Clinton had promised to do something about the situation when campaigning, but he discovered that the American public was opposed to any military action. He also did not want to embarrass Boris Yeltsin, who felt compelled to speak for his fellow Slavs in Serbia. Clinton's advisers could not come to agreement about a U.S. role, and he temporized. Eventually, the United Nations sent British, French, and Dutch peacekeepers, who were prohibited from using force. European leaders told Washington that they could handle the problem, but it became apparent that they could not.

Two choices faced Clinton and his advisers: work for a cease-fire through diplomacy or act to get the embargo lifted and permit NATO bombing of Bosnian Serb sites. The Europeans would not support "lift and strike," which would endanger their troops in the field. The president was busy with domestic issues and spent little time on foreign policy, so U.S. inaction continued until early 1994, when the Bosnian city of Sarajevo was horribly shelled by Serb forces. At that point, Clinton promised that the United States would assist in the withdrawal of peacekeeping troops if necessary. Then, in July, Bosnian Serbs captured the city of Srebrenica and murdered hundreds of Bosnian men and boys. Clinton threw his weight behind new NATO bombing and proposed a plan for peace. Richard Holbrooke, an experienced diplomat, was put in charge of the effort. At the outset, Clinton told Holbrooke that the Russians must be on board for any settlement. After months of difficult negotiations, Holbrooke was able to get the three presidents of Croatia, Serbia, and Bosnia to meet at a peace conference in Dayton, Ohio, and a cease-fire was declared in October 1994.

Clinton was determined to involve Russia in any peacekeeping required after a settlement. He and Yeltsin met at Franklin Roosevelt's home at Hyde Park, New York, in November 1994—the day after Yeltsin had hotly criticized NATO enlargement and NATO peacekeeping in Bosnia. They sat in the same chairs on the lawn overlooking the river that Roosevelt and Churchill had sat in during World War II, and Clinton persuaded Yeltsin to send Russian troops to Bosnia as peacekeepers. The question of whether they would be under NATO command was left open, but Yeltsin finally acquiesced. Clinton had played to Yeltsin's pride by meeting his request that the three presidents go to Moscow before they went to the peace conference in Dayton. They never made the trip, because Yeltsin became ill with heart problems.

Before the Dayton meetings, public opinion opposed the idea of American peacekeepers by 70 percent. The Pentagon was not happy. The House of Representatives passed a nonbinding resolution that that no American peacekeepers were to go to Bosnia without congressional approval. Clinton said publicly that the resolution would not affect the Dayton talks.

The Dayton meeting took twenty days of very difficult negotiation with very good work by Holbrooke and Warren Christopher, and it produced a peace agreement dividing Bosnia into three regions with a government representing each region at the top. Clinton embraced the agreement and worked very hard with Congress to win support for it. United States troops were to go to Bosnia for one year, a period later extended by the president.

In March 1998 Albanians in Kosovo, a province governed by Serbia, began a guerrilla war against the regime. Less than a year later, Serbia invaded Kosovo, causing devastation that left 300,000 people homeless. Even though Clinton was preoccupied with his trial in the Senate on impeachment, he led the way for extensive NATO bombing of the Serbian military. Serbia eventually withdrew, and NATO peacekeepers went in. Yeltsin was again upset, but Clinton talked him into sending Russian troops. At this point, Yeltsin was politically weak at home and was holding tight onto Clinton.

A focus on these two cases illustrates that Clinton was good at feeling his way to good outcomes, usually guided by general objectives, but with no clear initial idea about how to achieve the objective. He sometimes succeeded and sometimes failed. The foreign policy cases given below, in brief form, illustrate this point.

Three Improvisations

In his last weeks in office, President Bush sent troops to a Somalia torn by civil war in order to restore order and help aid groups feed starving people. The U.N. mission included other national armies as well. Clinton approved and continued the effort, but in the fall of 1993 twenty-eight Pakistani soldiers were killed. The question before the U.N. mission was whether to go after the warlord who had killed them. The U.N. secretary-general asked the U. S. military to find and arrest him. The mission had suddenly changed, without anyone realizing it. In October, eighteen marines on a risky daytime raid were killed when their helicopter was shot down, one dead marine was pulled through the streets and one was taken hostage. Clinton sent an experienced diplomat who secured the release of the hostage. The United States soon pulled out of Somalia. Clinton blamed the U.N. secretary-general for the tragedy and even tried to cast some blame on Colin Powell, the chairman of the Joint Chiefs of Staff. He later wrote of the raid: "I approved in principle but not in its particulars."[15] Was he paying attention?

The second case was an attempt in 1994 to restore Bertrand Aristide, the elected president of Haiti, to office after military officers overthrew him in a coup. Clinton threatened military action and would have taken it had he not sent former president Jimmy Carter and a delegation to meet with the dictators and persuade them to retire. Carter succeeded at the last minute, but critics have questioned whether the turbulent country, which has never had effective government, should have been high on the American agenda. Clinton knew that Haitian democracy was fragile, but argued that at least the United States could stop the Haitian coup leaders from "killing innocent people." He also wanted to stop the flow of Haitian refugees to American shores.

The third case was of more consequence. The secretive and isolated government of North Korea threatened in 1994 to pursue its program of development of atomic energy in order to make nuclear weapons. The American ambassador to South Korea, who knew Jimmy Carter well, angled an invitation from the government of North Korea for Carter to visit. The White House agreed, with misgivings because they could not control Carter. But he extracted promises that eventually led to an agreement that North Korea would not produce nuclear weapons and would in turn receive American help to build a light-water nuclear reactor for energy. The agreement was in time violated by the North Koreans, and Clinton may have been naïve in thinking that it would be otherwise. A Clinton biographer wrote: "It was a classic Clinton policy—a mix of blurred lines and improvisation with some good luck thrown in."[16]

International Economics

One of Clinton's most significant achievements was to provide help to the government of Mexico in 1995 when its economy was on the verge of collapse. Political instability in Mexico had caused many investors to pull out, the stock market collapsed, and inflation was very high. Robert Rubin, by then secretary of the treasury, insisted that the United States help the government of Mexico, for if it were to default on its bonds to creditors its economy would collapse with adverse consequences for the United States. He recommended a $40 billion loan. Clinton cut it back to $20 billion but then had to find the money. Congressional leaders would go along, but many Democrats were still angry with NAFTA and it became clear that an aid package could not pass before Mexico defaulted. Rubin put together funds from an executive reserve fund and loans from the IMF and the World Bank. The American public was opposed to the action, but Clinton wrote later that he had done the right thing for the long run.

The Middle East

Clinton's failures were not from lack of trying. In 1993 Israel and the Palestine Liberation Organization agreed on a plan for peace after secret negotiations in Norway. Clinton invited the respective leaders to Washington to sign the agreement in a ceremony on the White House lawn and forced them to shake hands. He had done nothing to bring about the agreement, but his intrusion into the situation committed him to further action.

For the next seven years he worked very hard with personal diplomacy to forge further agreement on plans for implementation. Three prime ministers of Israel negotiated with Yasser Arafat, the Palestinian leader, with almost no result. Clinton would call them together at retreat centers and keep them there for days, forcing all-night sessions, and achieve temporary agreements, only to see them wither away when taken home. A last major effort in his last weeks as president almost succeeded. He called Ehud Barak, the prime minister of Israel, and Arafat to Camp David, hoping to duplicate Jimmy Carter's feat with Begin and Sadat. He used all his persuasive skills and succeeded with Barak but Arafat would not finally cross the line. He had said beforehand that he was not ready to negotiate, but that was ignored. Dennis Ross, the chief negotiator for both Bush and Clinton, felt that Clinton tried to clinch deals too early before they matured.[17] Certainly Clinton believed that there was no one he could not persuade.

Other Matters

There were other achievements. The Senate ratified the START II treaty negotiated by Bush. It also voted for U.S. participation in the General Agreement on Tariffs and Trade that established the World Trade Organization. The Kyoto Accord on global warming was written with American help. Chemical weapons were outlawed by international action. Clinton supported the Good Friday Peace Agreement in Northern Ireland with limited personal diplomacy. The United States supported the work of international institutions in helping collapsing Asian economies in 1998. Terrorism appeared as the World Trade Center in New York and U.S. embassies in Africa were bombed. The question of whether the Clinton administration was sufficiently attuned to the problem of terrorism directed against the United States is complex and can only be answered in the future.

Clinton's style of leadership was much the same in domestic and foreign policy. He had general objectives but was unclear about how to achieve them. The historical context was much the same. He was trying to forge a "third way" in domestic policy and believed that politics were moving in that direction but not fast enough for him to succeed often. Clinton's aspirations for a world of democracy and free markets were a set of aspirations that were forced to confront nationalism and, at the end, terrorism. He was well suited for a politics of muddling through. His initial hopes of being a great leader gave way to a prudent, eventful approach in most cases.

IMPEACHMENT AND TRIAL

In late 1995 during the battle with Gingrich over the budget, Clinton began a casual sexual affair with a White House intern named Monica Lewinsky. Temptation was present because the government was shut down and there were few people in the White House, and she was there. The secret affair continued for some time. It finally came to light and Clinton lied about it twice to a special prosecutor originally appointed to deal with his financial affairs in Arkansas before he became president. The prosecutor had a hunting license to uncover any possible illegalities in Clinton's life. Clinton also lied to his wife, his staff, and the cabinet. His pollster and political adviser Dick Morris told the president that the public could forgive sex but not lying, so Clinton decided to lie, hoping that he would not get caught. He had always recovered from disaster before—in Arkansas, during the 1992 campaign, after 1994, and he may have assumed that he was invulnerable. Unfortunately for him, Lewinsky had a dress with Clinton's semen on it. He had asked friends to find her a job in New York, laying himself open to the charge of obstruction of justice. House Republican leaders were determined to impeach him, and after the Judiciary Committee laid charges of lying and obstruction of justice against him, the House impeached him in December 1998. Gingrich and Tom Delay, the majority leader from Texas, intimidated and threatened a number of members who favored a resolution of censure into voting for impeachment. The Senate failed to convict Clinton by a vote of 45 "yeas" and 55 "nays" in early 1999. A few Republicans saved him. The Democrats had done well in the 1998 elections, and Gingrich subsequently resigned. He had overplayed his hand again. Surveys revealed that the public thought that Clinton lacked moral character but that he was a good president and that was more important.

Clinton was a natural-born seducer and he used the skills of a seducer in politics. This is perhaps one reason why some people disliked him. He always seemed to be a politician on the make. His frequent shifts in policy positions were attributed, often by journalists and always by opponents, to his lack of a steady character. But his record shows that he was quite steadfast in his purposes but highly flexible in his methods and that he often went against popular opinion and would defy his own party. The political manifestation of his need to seduce was in the confusion he often made in mistaking campaigning for governing. He was everywhere at once in public but lacked the discipline to focus his efforts in the big fights. David Gergen, a very wise confidant and observer of presidents, believed that Clinton became president too soon before he was fully mature.[18]

CONCLUSION

How do we assess Clinton's presidency according to our key questions?

Context and Contingencies

Clinton's victory in 1992 repeated the familiar pattern, seen in Kennedy and Carter, of a Democrat beating a Republican because of a recession. The eventual period of reform carried out by Kennedy and Johnson was over, and the Republicans had redefined policy issues away from big government. Both Carter and Clinton thus faced the challenge of giving Democratic government a new definition. The deficit created by Reagan had to be challenged. Clinton could have ignored it temporarily, as his domestic advisers would have had him do, perhaps to his political advantage. But he chose to attack it. The idea of globalization presented opportunities of free trade and promotion of democracy but perhaps also the counterforces of nationalism and terrorism.

Talents and Skills

Clinton's rhetorical and tactical skills, which were sharply honed, made him a formidable political opponent. He had strong personal persuasive powers. But he lacked a strategic sense of how to achieve general goals. He was prudent for much of the time, usually by necessity, but the image of John F. Kennedy as a heroic president was probably in his mind. Kennedy, in fact, was more prudent than heroic, and an eventful leader, just like Clinton.

Did He Make a Difference?

Clinton deserves credit for pushing hard for deficit reduction and for following the advice of his economic advisers in taking steps to permit the economy to expand without inflation. Of course, the high technology boom was flowering at the same time. But deficit reduction was good for the economy. Domestic policy achievements were marginal but real. A long list of small reforms in education, health care, and the environment was topped by major welfare reform, in concert with the Republicans. Clinton learned prudence through experience. He did a good job of supporting Boris Yeltsin and pulling him into the Western alliance, often against Yeltsin's will. The passage of NAFTA and financial aid to Mexico was bold economics, but Clinton had to decide to do these things. They were in keeping with his commitment to an open international economy. He temporized on Bosnia but finally acted, to good effect, and followed through in Kosovo.

Clinton's greatest policy failure was in the inability to pass health care reform. One cannot know whether a middle course of compromise would have been any more realistic. His own conception of the "third way" for New Democrats failed him because he overestimated what a president could do. In fact, with the exception of economic policy, the New Democrat idea finally took refuge in "triangulation" as Clinton worked out tactical bargains with Congress.

Clinton worked very hard and effectively to achieve a peace agreement between Israel and the Palestine Liberation Organization. Critics said that he pushed it too hard, too fast. He was leaving the White House and wanted a great achievement. The failure caused increasingly violent conflict between Israel and the Palestinians, but one cannot blame that on Clinton.

Effectiveness

On balance, Clinton's political personality and his abilities were very well matched for the period in which he was president. It was not a time for heroes. He was often derided, particularly by liberals, for being a "let's make a deal" president. They wanted him to be a crusading liberal reformer who threw down the gauntlet to Republicans. He did not see that course as the best future for the Democrats. Clinton was supremely effective in knowing how to work with Congress, with one or two notable exceptions when he overreached. He was a transparent politician whose deceits were in his personal life rather than his public life. This tells us that presidents need not be angels in their personal lives to be effective democratic leaders.

BIBLIOGRAPHICAL ESSAY

Bill Clinton's *My Life* (2004) is more revealing on electoral politics than it is on policymaking. He is very clear on the mistakes he made in dealing with Congress. Descriptions of foreign policy are perfunctory. One hears about trips and conversations but very little about the details of decisions. The book perhaps reflects Clinton's intellectual style, lots of details but little about strategy.

The best overall study of the Clinton presidency is by John Harris, *The Survivor* (2005). Harris did a great many interviews and gives an even description of Clinton's many balancing acts. Stanley Renshon's *High Hopes: The Clinton Psychology and the Politics of Ambition* (1996), captures Clinton's complex personality very well, as does David Gergen in his chapter on Clinton in *Eyewitness to Power: The Essence of Leadership from Nixon to Clinton* (2000).

Two good books on Clinton's first years and domestic and economic policy are Elizabeth Drew, *On the Edge: The Clinton Presidency* (1994), and Bob Woodward, *The Agenda: Inside the Clinton White House* (1994). Joe Klein, *The Natural: The Misunderstood Presidency of Bill Clinton* (2002), is an apologia for some of Clinton's domestic policy failures and a good description of his successes at "triangulation." James MacGregor Burns and Georgia J. Sorenson's *Dead Center: Clinton-Gore Leadership and the Perils of Moderation* (1999) is a very strong analysis of domestic policy from a critical progressive perspective. There are a number of good books on the story of health care reform. Two of the best are Haynes Johnson and David Broder, *The System: The American Way of Politics at the Breaking Point* (1996), and the case study within a larger book by Robert Y. Shapiro and Lawrence R. Jacobs, *Politicians Don't Pander: Political Manipulation and the Loss of Democratic Responsiveness* (2000). Clinton's fight with the Republican Congress over the budget in 1995–1996 is well analyzed by Charles O. Jones, *Clinton and Congress, 1993–1996: Risk, Restoration, and Reelection* (1999), and Elizabeth Drew, *Showdown: The Struggle between the Gingrich Congress and the Clinton*

White House (1996). George C. Edwards III throws cold water on the impact of public opinion of Clinton's rhetorical skills in *On Deaf Ears: The Limits of the Bully Pulpit* (2003).

Paul Abramson, John Aldrich, and David Rohde have served us well, as in previous chapters in their two books, *Change and Continuity in the 1992 Elections* (1995) and *Change and Continuity in the 1996 and 1998 Elections* (1999). One must read Dick Morris, *Behind the Oval Office: Winning the Presidency in the Nineties* (1997), to get the inside view.

Material on Clinton's foreign policy is thin. Thomas Preston, *The President and His Inner Circle* (2001), has a very good chapter on Clinton's management of policymaking. Strobe Talbott has written a good memoir of Clinton's work with Boris Yeltsin and Russian diplomats, *The Russia Hand: A Memoir of Presidential Diplomacy* (2002). Richard Holbrooke has done the same with his account of the resolution of the Yugoslavian crisis, *To End a War* (1998). Terry L. Deibel has described Clinton's relationship with Congress in *Clinton and Congress: The Politics of Foreign Policy* (2000). Emily O. Goldman and Larry Berman give a well-balanced assessment of Clinton's foreign policy record in "Engaging the World: First Impressions of the Clinton Foreign Policy Legacy," in Colin Campbell and Bert A. Rockman, eds., *The Clinton Legacy* (1995). Finally, William Hyland, an astute foreign policy practitioner and analyst, has written a very critical book of essays on different foreign policy episodes, *Clinton's World: Remaking American Foreign Policy* (1999). The memoir by Warren Christopher, *In the Stream of History* (1998), is of no value for the historian. Madeleine Albright's *Madam Secretary* (2003), is a good book but there is very little about Bill Clinton in it.

CHAPTER NINE

George W. Bush

The Risk Taker

George W. Bush was one of three presidents who won election without winning a majority of the popular vote. His opponent, Vice President Al Gore, beat him by half a million popular votes. The contest was decided in Florida after the election when it became apparent that a number of ballots were faulty. The design of the machine ballot caused many voters who wished to choose Gore to actually vote for Pat Buchanan. A long contest in the Florida courts followed, and it became clear that Florida state officials and the legislature would declare Bush the winner in time for him to be inaugurated, as was their right under the U.S. Constitution. The U.S. Supreme Court finally resolved the question in a five-to-four majority with the conclusion that Florida had no plan for resolution of the dispute and that time constraints did not permit a total recount. Bush was made president by Republican members of the Supreme Court.

Bush ran as someone who could bring the nation together, promising that he would work in a bipartisan way as he had in Texas with the Democratic legislature. This was what voters had to go on, and the political context was generally stable with no seeming great demand for drastic policy departures. The federal budget was in surplus, the long-term issue of financing Social Security was apparent but manageable if dealt with in a timely manner, but paying for Medicare in the future was going to be more difficult. There were no dramatic foreign policy issues, aside from the failure of President Clinton to secure an agreement between Barak and Arafat about the road to peace between Israel and Palestine. The one obstacle to moderate government in the center was the continuing polarization of partisans in Congress and the country. Bush carried in a Republican Congress, but with a 50–50 tie in the Senate. Many pundits assumed, and even recommended, that the new president would govern from the center. This was even more a possibility when in the first year Vermont senator Jim Jeffords left the Republican Party and voted with the Democrats as an independent, thus putting the Senate in Democratic hands by one vote.

Government in the center was not Bush's choice. He had learned a great deal from his father's presidency, in which he was assisted by his political adviser Karl Rove, a longtime Texas politico. The first lesson was never to let any conservatives be to his right. His father had never been solid with the religious right or with the Republican conservatives who abhorred taxes. The second lesson was to be skeptical of congressional Democrats, who had done their best to make his father a one-term president. The third lesson was to use wedge issues of religion and patriotism that his father had tried only in the 1988 campaign but not thereafter.

But the most important motive in his choices was his own determination to make a difference as a conservative president of achievement. He would follow Ronald Reagan rather than his father. As governor he had set and achieved a few clear goals—education reform, juvenile justice and welfare reform, tort reform, and reduced taxes on business. He had earned political capital from his victory over Ann Richards, a popular governor, and had learned from his father's failure to strike out with new programs after Desert Storm that "you must spend political capital when you earn it or it withers and dies."[1] His job, he said, was to set an agenda and lead. He ran for president on the theme of "compassionate conservatism," which meant, in part, creating a robust, entrepreneurial economy to lift all people up and the restructuring of social programs so that people had more choices: school vouchers, consumer choice in health insurance, privatization of Social Security accounts, and the use of faith-based organizations for social welfare missions. The culture of dependency must be broken and a sense of personal responsibility must be affirmed. Given these beliefs, he could not be a president of the center, who would seek bipartisan support as a central strategy. Bush was geared to be an event-making president by his temperament and his opportunities.

His style of leadership was congruent with his purposes. One must act from convictions. He often said to others, "I'm not going to negotiate with myself."[2] Form a strong team, listen to them, let them argue, and be the decider. Do not defer or pander to public opinion. Do what you think is right. Seize opportunities and make the most of them. Take risks. Bush's self-confidence, resiliency, and willingness to act were appealing to Americans. These qualities were encased in a bravado that had little regard for prudence, a sense of fallibility, or an acceptance of tragedy. There was a two-sided stubbornness that gave him drive and purpose but that may also have shielded him from doubt and made him inflexible.

Bush was not a success in his young adulthood. He failed in the oil business, in large part because of adverse market changes, and was bailed out financially by his father's friends. He was then made the managing partner of the Texas Rangers without being a substantial owner. Two related experiences changed his life in his mid-forties. He was converted to faith by Billy Graham, a family friend, and he stopped drinking. These two decisions appear to have given him a sense of confidence that his life had a purpose. He talked about this in his campaign biography: "I could not be Governor if I did not believe in a divine plan that supersedes all human plans.... I build my life on a foundation that will not shift.... [It] frees me to do the right thing, even though it may not poll well.... I live in the moment, seize opportunities and try to make the most of them."[3]

Bush is a Methodist and, though his religious faith is serious, is not a religious fundamentalist. His appeals to the religious right were political. During his presidency, he read the Bible daily and prayed before cabinet meetings. Faith should not be denigrated, as it often is by secular critics. Bush's faith, however, is cast in the same mold as his political purposes and style. One strides out in confidence to overcome the world, without doubt.

The 2000 election was virtually a tie. Gore failed to capitalize on the prosperity brought in during the Clinton years, even though he promised to use the surplus for education and other social programs. About half the voters saw differences between the two candidates on issues, but voters in the center tilted slightly toward Bush because the Democratic vote continued to decline among whites, especially white men, which had been the case since blue-collar men began to vote for Reagan. It would have taken only a small shift to the Democrats to elect Gore. There was no clear policy guidance for the new president from the election.

Executive Style

Bush is the only graduate of Harvard Business School to be president. He explicitly followed what he believed to be good management practices in dealing with large questions, avoiding absorption in details, and surrounding himself with strong people. His actual style as an executive was somewhat unclear. He was described by his associates as asking hard questions, encouraging discussion, and demanding results. His detractors, some of whom have also worked with him, described him as not at all curious, little given to back-and-forth discussions with his senior officials, and engaging in scripted meetings with little genuine debate. It may be relevant to add that his speeches were heavily scripted with simple declarative sentences and assertions. He had great difficulty explaining his intentions when he was unscripted, as in press conferences.

Of course this is consistent with his demand for clarity and simplicity in his own work in government. It appears that full discussion often took place after Bush had decided what to do, and then the focus was on how to carry out the decisions. Bush then let his advisers compete on alternatives for action before he decided. For example, he seems not to have asked his senior officials about whether he should attack Iraq. Some were in favor and some less so. The same was true of economic policy. He wanted a big tax cut in the beginning and he got it, cutting off caveats from some economic advisers. A very small number of political advisers hovered close to him: Karl Rove; his first chief of staff, Andrew Card; and Card's successor, Josh Bolten. But the most important figure was Vice President Richard Cheney. Cheney was a logical choice by an inexperienced president. He was Gerald Ford's chief of staff, a Republican congressman, and secretary of defense under Bush's father. He had more staff and more authority than any vice president in history, and he used it—to advise, to investigate, and to guide and cut off debate. He was the president's enforcer. He was also the most conservative senior official in the Bush entourage. Bush had political experience, working for his father when he was president and as governor of Texas for six years. His shortcomings were in knowledge of national policy issues and he surrounded himself with knowledgeable people.

Colin Powell had to be named secretary of state. He was more popular than the president and could surely have been the nominee had he chosen to run. But Bush did not want Powell to dominate and, on Cheney's advice, he chose Donald Rumsfeld as secretary of defense. Rumsfeld had been Cheney's mentor, bringing him into the Ford White House, and he had headed the Defense Department briefly in the Ford administration. Condoleezza Rice, the assistant to the president for national security, had worked on the NSC staff for the senior Bush. The secretary of the treasury, Paul O'Neill, had been deputy director of the Office of Management and Budget (OMB) in the Ford administration and had worked closely with Cheney and Rumsfeld. He had left government and been a successful manufacturing executive, which Bush preferred to someone from Wall Street.

Joel Aberbach, a leading political scientist, suggests two models for leadership in the modern presidency. The first is a bargaining president who respects the pluralistic representations of national diversity in the national government and goes about creating coalitions on his own behalf. This is the norm suggested by the scholar Richard Neustadt in his book *Presidential Power*. In this conception the president and Congress are separate institutions sharing powers, and policy is achieved through bargaining and persuasion. The alternative model is one of command rather than bargaining, sometimes characterized as the "administrative presidency." The president is under great public pressure to lead and to do so strongly. There is no time for bargaining. Every part of the presidency must be subordinated to the president: budgets, executive orders, secrecy, the veto, and direct control of national security and the law supporting national security. The president then confronts the Congress with demands and seeks public support behind those demands. Nixon's attempt at the "administrative presidency" failed in 1973, in part because Watergate intruded. Aberbach places Bush closer to the second model.[4] This interpretation has merit, in part, because Bush had faithful Republican majorities in Congress for the first six years of his presidency and they deferred to him most of the time, despite unhappiness and grumbling.

Domestic Policy

Bush saw himself as a transforming president who would fulfill the vision of Ronald Reagan for a limited national government that would release the energies of private initiative in the economy and provide opportunities for the privatization of government social programs to give citizens greater discretion.

Bush's major contribution to domestic affairs was in economic policy, by deliberate design. As he entered the White House, the federal budget enjoyed a surplus estimated to be $5.6 trillion. Interest rates were low and debt was cheap, with the market high. Productivity was also high because of the high-tech boom of the 1990s. The economy grew an average of 3.8 percent a year between 1996 and 2000.[5] However, in 2000 the market dropped, federal revenues declined, and it became apparent that an economic slowdown was a sure thing. The recession in 2001 lasted eight months. Growth was at a rate of 0.3 percent.[6] Unemployment did not fall, but median income did, and consumer confidence dropped.

As a candidate, Bush had promised a $1.6 trillion tax cut over a ten-year period. It was a matter of principle for him. The Clinton administration, personified in Secretary of the Treasury Robert Rubin, believed that government needed to save the entitlement programs from which Americans would benefit: Social Security and Medicare. The surplus would be used to reduce the federal debt. The Bush view was that entitlements should be privatized to a great extent so that citizens could save for themselves and their security. He favored debt reduction but was skeptical of a large surplus for fear that Congress would spend it unwisely. Tax cuts would increase savings and induce future economic growth. These are legitimate differences without any resolution in scientific proof. The difference is between a greater tolerance for deficits in the Bush administration, which returned to the supply-side thinking of Ronald Reagan.[7]

Paul O'Neill, the treasury secretary, and Alan Greenspan, the chairman of the Federal Reserve, were longtime friends from the Ford administration. They met privately before the inauguration and found themselves in agreement on what policy should be. With a surplus of over $5 trillion over ten years, a $1.6 trillion tax cut was affordable. Government revenues were running at 20.8 percent of GDP, above the forty-year average of 18.6 percent. Continuing financing of Social Security and Medicare would be possible and $2 trillion would be left to reduce the debt and move toward the initial costs of privatizing Social Security for people under age thirty-seven. In their view, it was necessary to put "triggers" on the tax cut to pull some of it back if the surplus were to diminish.

They found little support in the White House for the triggers. Bush's economists and political advisers assumed that economic growth from the tax cuts would sustain the surpluses without triggers. They wanted optimism not caution. Bush was intent on honoring his campaign promise without qualifications. When O'Neill met with him in February 2001 to recommend the triggers, the president listened without comment and then said, "I won't negotiate with myself. It's that simple. If someone comes to me with a plan for this that has a significant amount of political backing, I'll sit down with them. But until then, it's a closed issue."[8]

Clinton had taxed the rich. Two percent of taxpayers paid 27.5 percent of the income taxes, but, of course, the less well-off paid high payroll taxes for entitlement programs. Bush wanted to give tax relief to the investing class. It was not difficult to get the Republican House to pass his bill, but moderate Senate Republicans and Democrats balked. The president proceeded to go on the stump, especially in the nineteen Democratic states that he had won in the election. He needed only a simple majority by congressional rules for finance measures, and he barely got it with a 50–50 tie in the Senate with Vice President Cheney casting the deciding vote. Some compromise was required, but the tax cut was $1.35 trillion over ten years with an immediate $85 billion rebate to taxpayers as an economic stimulus. The cuts were not permanent, however. Greenspan told O'Neill that without the triggers the "tax cut is irresponsible fiscal policy."[9] The Congressional Budget Office (CBO) concluded that the cut would require minimal new domestic and military spending.

An important part of the tax story was the administration's slippery approach to the truth. The official claim was made that the tax cut would "reduce taxes for everyone who pays taxes." The highest percentage cut was claimed to go to the lowest incomes. But such people pay so little in taxes that their gain was minimal. Ordinary people pay most of their taxes through Medicare and Social Security deductions from their payrolls. Small business owners had their taxes cut to a lower bracket but only 1.4 percent were in the top bracket. Seventy-two percent of the tax cuts were enjoyed by 20 percent of the taxpayers and 45 percent of the top 1 percent of top taxpayers. License was taken with the truth on the "Healthy Forests Initiative," which opened forests to increased logging, and the "Clear Skies Initiative," which rolled back pollution controls. The White House propaganda machine, steered by Karl Rove and Karen Hughes, White House assistants, applied this distortion of rhetoric when it suited their purposes. The great irony is that it was later used to sell the war in Iraq and it helped to reelect Bush in 2004, but it eventually exploded in a credibility gap between administration rhetoric and what people saw as the reality on the ground in Iraq.

Then came the attacks of September 11, 2001, and subsequent military actions in Afghanistan. O'Neill and Greenspan were concerned about deficits that might result from new spending for war and homeland security. O'Neill argued throughout 2002 against the ideas of White House economic and political advisers that another tax cut was necessary. But the Republicans won the 2002 congressional elections, largely on the president's claim to be the protector of national security, and there was talk again in the White House about a new tax cut. The timing was peculiar because the Congress had passed a resolution in October 2002 authorizing the president to go to war with Iraq. In early 2003 discussions heated up with plans for the elimination of taxes on dividends for stockholders and acceleration of previous tax cuts. This time the idea was proposed as an antirecession measure because the economy was still lagging. When O'Neill suggested the problem of deficits, Vice President Cheney told him, "Reagan proved that deficits don't matter. We won the midterms. This is our due."[10]

O'Neill was clearly the odd man out within the administration, and not long after that discussion Cheney called to say that the president wanted him to go, which he did, resigning immediately. His complaint about White House decision making is that politics drove economic decisions without any careful analysis. O'Neill's description of White House meetings is probably accurate. The problem, as he eventually realized, was that he was out of the loop. Arguments from the White House perspective are scattered through the editorial pages of the *Wall Street Journal* and other Republican and conservative publications. The economy needed stimulus and that could not come without big tax cuts. Unemployment was running high, and industry was working at low capacity. Supply-side tax cuts would revive the economy. Recovery did come by 2006. The difficulty was that federal deficits continued to grow.

The Congress enacted a $1 trillion tax cut in 2003, reducing the tax rates on capital gains and dividends, providing tax breaks for small business, and giving financial aid to fiscally weak states and low-income families. The 2003 "Economic Report of the President" argued that the deficit was caused by the weakness of the economy. The recession was an important factor, but other contributions were reduced taxes and increased expenditures. The president signed an expensive farm bill that Congress gave him and proposed a Medicare prescription drug plan for seniors that was said to cost $400 billion. Congress passed it and then learned that the true analysis, which had been suppressed by political executives, was half again as much. Bush was not really a fiscal conservative when it came to winning popular support. By the end of 2003, the economy was rebounding.

The 2001 and 2004 tax reductions were projected to add $1 trillion to the $3 trillion national debt over time. Annual government deficits were large, in the hundreds of billions of dollars each year. Allen Shick, a budget expert and political scientist, wrote that Bush and his advisers had been clear in their own minds about what they were doing. They believed that the bias in politics so favored spending that only large deficits could trigger radical action to curb government. They did not want to pay for the costs of war and homeland security with new taxes for fear that such taxes would be used for other purposes in due time.[11] Critics charged that a failure to increase federal revenues would deny future Social Security and Medicare benefits to citizens who had been promised them. For Bush the answer was not to refinance such programs but to change them fundamentally to privatized Social Security accounts and new forms of private competition for Medicare dollars and services. In short, Bush was far more radical than O'Neill and Greenspan recognized.

A clear sign of Bush's thinking was seen in his extended campaign in the first part of 2005 for a new program that would invest public funds in private accounts for younger adults. Rather than waiting to retire at sixty-five on an accumulation of interest on government bonds, citizens who chose the new program would be able to engage in broader investments likely to give them enhanced returns in the long run. The president went out into the country for sixty days on a campaign to sell this idea, but it did not work. The popular and congressional resistance was too strong. The trillion dollars required to set up the new accounts would have to be borrowed because of deficits. Bush showed little interest in various reform proposals to shore up Social Security, such as raising the retirement age and increasing payroll taxes. This would be just more of the same big government that he was determined to stop. By the same token, the Medicare D drug program for seniors was given to health insurance firms to run rather than Medicare itself. Medicare administration would have been cheaper, but Bush wanted competition among health plans on the assumption that costs would go down in the long run. Again, the logic is clear. Politics in the nation faces a standoff on these hard questions, and the problems are not likely to be faced without political changes that permit resolution.

The other significant legislative achievement of Bush's presidency was the No Child Left Behind Act, which requires states and localities to test elementary school students at regular intervals to assess their ability to read and do mathematical problems. This was an extension of Bush's work in Texas reflecting his firm belief that schools must no longer leave children behind in a complex economy. He reached out to Senator Edward Kennedy and other Democrats to get the votes for passage. It was necessary to reach out because education bills can be filibustered, and he needed sixty votes in the Senate.

Congressional Republicans also wanted vouchers for private schools for parents and block grants for education funds to states, but Bush compromised these ideas away to get a bill. The subsequent history has been turbulent. School systems balked at limited federal funding for the program, and many were concerned that teaching to the test is harmful to education. The controversy continues, but Bush was able to push education in the direction he wanted it to go.

A third area of domestic policy was the priority given to the production of domestic energy over conservation and abatement of pollution. Bush campaigned that he would reduce carbon dioxide in the atmosphere from industrial pollution, but once in office he deferred to Republican senators and rejected a plan by his own Environmental Protection Agency to cut emissions.

He took the United States out of the recently negotiated Kyoto treaty for worldwide limits on emissions because of the burden it would impose on the economy. However, the Senate had been hostile to the treaty, so Clinton had never submitted it for ratification. Bush did not seem to accept the existence of global warming in the beginning and met secretly with author Michael Crichton, whose book *State of Fear* denied warming altogether. He gradually came around and invested funds in research and development for improved antipollution technology. The Department of the Interior took strenuous steps to open federal public lands to oil and gas leasing. Bush's clear idea was that the United States should produce more of its own energy and reduce its dependence, particularly on foreign oil. The vice president referred to conservation as a "personal virtue" in a speech calling for more nuclear energy. Very little was done to encourage high gasoline mileage for automobiles or other forms of energy conservation. But to be fair, Congress blocked such efforts. Bush's energy policies were perhaps guided by political considerations more than anything else. The economy had to be restored.

This is a brief account of Bush's economic and domestic policies. On the one hand, Bush aspired to be an event-making president who would create an "ownership society" in place of the existing welfare state. On the other hand, he was a politician who made deals to achieve goals even if it angered his partisans. Certainly the push from the White House for Medicare D upset Republican conservatives because of the great cost. But Bush saw it differently. A program of drug benefits closely tied to the private sector undercut Democratic ideas and plans. He was a shrewd partisan who did not let anyone else define him or his presidency.

Bush's presidency seemed to be stalled in the summer of 2001 after the Democrats took control of the Senate. Bush had to make concessions on farm subsidies and steel tariffs to the Democrats as a result. The Senate Judiciary Committee blocked his nominations for appellate judges. His proposals for Social Security reform were ignored. A proposal to drill for oil in protected lands in Alaska was rejected. The idea of awarding federal grants to "faith-based" organizations to provide social services, a Bush favorite, was scuttled. The initial successes seemed behind him. The events of 9/11 changed all that.

After 9/11

Bush became a warrior president after the attacks on the World Trade Center and the Pentagon and thereby found his mission in the presidency. He was particularly suited to tell the Congress and the United Nations that the United States was at war and would not cease to be at war until the enemy was defeated. He had been a "realist," following the tutelage of Condoleezza Rice. The United States should not seek crusades abroad and should avoid "nation building" at all costs. Suddenly he found himself denouncing not only terrorists but those nations that harbor terrorists. They were as much at risk as the terrorists. He clearly had Afghanistan in mind, because the Taliban fundamentalist Islamic government had protected the al Qaeda organization of Osama bin Laden, the author of the 9/11 attack. Bush was very good as a warrior president in his self-confidence and even his swagger. He later told a friend that he believed that God intended him to lead at this time. His popular appeal could be seen as he spoke through a bullhorn to workers at the site of the destroyed buildings in New York City, promising to "smoke out the killers" and "get 'em." He courted Democratic leaders and they rallied around.

The central question was what to do about al Qaeda and the Taliban. There was little question that military action was required. Bush later told Bob Woodward: "I rely on my instincts. I just knew that at that point in time the American people were going to say, 'where is he?... Where's your leadership?'"[12]

Woodward had an inside view of the path to war in Afghanistan and reported that Bush wanted action and solutions. Once his course was set he did not let up. One acts and does not look back. There is no place for critics or doubt. Bush told Woodward that if he lacked confidence it would spread to others. Therefore he must show his support for his top lieutenants. Action was imperative, in part, because everyone was worried that another attack on the United States might come if American action was tardy.

Rumsfeld pushed the top military for a plan for Afghanistan, which, as it turned out, they did not have. They were reluctant to think of anything but large numbers of "boots on the ground," a big logistical operation. He did not want that and saw the opportunity to move toward his ideas about military force as a rapid reaction striking force, using highly focused assaults supported by precision air power. But the CIA was ahead of him with plans to reinforce the Northern Alliance in northern Afghanistan who were fighting the Taliban. Warlords throughout the country were to be paid cash to fight as well. The Taliban were warned to give up al Qaeda, and when nothing happened, U.S. forces struck.

CIA operatives began to enter the country in late September, and not long after special forces troops did the same, accompanied by air strikes. By November 12, 2001, Kabul had fallen and the Northern Alliance controlled half the country. The Taliban and al Qaeda troops were racing for Pakistan, and Kandahar in the south fell on December 7. A mere 110 CIA agents and 316 special forces troops had done the work. In due course, a government was chosen, primarily by exiles, and a president sworn in on December 22, 2001. There had been no thought in Washington about nation building, but U.S. troops stayed.

Bush had felt at the outset that he was in charge, telling Woodward on September 15: "If I have any genius or smarts, it's the ability to recognize talent, ask them to serve and work with them as a team.... When they give advice I trust their judgment." When they disagree, "the job is to grind through these problems, and grind through these scenarios and hopefully reach a consensus of six or seven smart people, which makes my job easy."[13] He would later tell Woodward that he relied on his "instinctive" reactions: "I'm not a textbook player. I'm a gut player." Woodward added, "His instincts are almost his second religion."[14]

These are the words of a risk taker who is distrustful of inaction and who wants action plans from his subordinates. They are loyal to him, and thereby he gives his confidence to them. It is a tight team. This is the style of leadership that carried the president through the war in Iraq.

War in Iraq

The initial emphasis of Bush's foreign policy was on shaking loose from Bill Clinton's commitments to engagement in international alliances and organizations in favor of unilateral approaches. The Kyoto treaty of global warming was disowned, the test ban treaty and biological weapons convention were ignored, U.S. membership in the International Criminal Court was rejected, and the treaty with the former Soviet Union for the limitation of antiballistic missiles was broken so that the United States might build its own defenses. The disposition to act unilaterally thus preceded action in Afghanistan and Iraq.

There was also an unpleasant history with Saddam Hussein's Iraq. The United States was enforcing no-fly zones in northern and southern Iraq to protect Kurdish and Shia populations from attack. United Nations inspections of Iraq's weapons had worked well until 1998, when the inspectors were barred from the country. The U.N. program of economic sanctions against Iraq was weakening. Saddam Hussein had supported terrorists in Palestine and Lebanon.

At a council of war that Bush convened at Camp David on September 15, 2001, Paul Wolfowitz and Donald Rumsfeld both suggested that Iraq might be a better initial target against terrorism than Afghanistan. Military forces could get bogged down in Afghanistan, but Iraq might break easily. Wolfowitz contended that the United States would have to go after Saddam eventually as a target in the war on terrorism. Why not now? Colin Powell and military leaders did not agree, and Bush closed the question by asking for focus on the Taliban and al Qaeda. However, Rumsfeld kept raising the issue in NSC meetings, calling for a new regime in Iraq that would be friendly to the United States and the West. There was a background to this. Wolfowitz had served in both the Carter and Bush Sr. administrations and in both cases had written or overseen the writing of memoranda advocating the overthrow of the Saddam Hussein regime. In his view, the United States must strike because "terrorism was no longer manageable."[15] The first President Bush had rejected one proposed paper, and Dick Cheney toned it down. The idea of the United States taking "preemptive" military action against a nation that threatened us was implicit in these memos. This idea reflected the thinking of "neoconservative" advocates who saw new threats to peace emerging in the world, especially in rogue states like North Korea, Iran, and Iraq. The attacks of September 11 were thus a trigger for action. This idea was expressed in Bush's State of the Union address in January 2002, in which he condemned the three nations as "the Axis of Evil."

The planning for an offensive began in November 2001 as Bush charged Rumsfeld, who in turn asked his generals to give him a plan. Bush told Bob Woodward, who had begun to write a second book, that Woodward's book would reveal a blueprint for how he made decisions: "his focus on large goals, how he made decisions, why he provoked his war cabinet and pressed people for action."[16] It was clear to Woodward that Bush wanted Saddam out of power. Bush believed that Clinton's failure to respond to a string of terrorist attacks had encouraged more terrorism. The problem was tyrants, and Saddam was the prime tyrant.[17]

There was great concern within the Bush administration that the 9/11 attacks would be followed by another attack on U.S. soil. As anthrax began mysteriously showing up in the mail of prominent people that fall, the anxiety was even stronger. Cheney and Rumsfeld feared that a state like Iraq might use terrorist networks to smuggle nuclear devices into the United States. Cheney met with the national security cabinet officers as a member and was really Bush's national security adviser. Condoleezza Rice was more of a coordinator according to reports.[18] From the very beginning Cheney was the most adamant for military action against Iraq. His belief seems to have been that in a dangerous world in which the U.S. homeland was vulnerable, every possible step should be taken to defeat terrorism. Secretary Rumsfeld had decided that the best way to shake up the military was to make crisis demands on it. He pushed General Tommy Franks, the responsible officer, for a plan for the invasion of Iraq, and as Franks proposed conventional attacks with large numbers of troops, Rumsfeld kept pushing for fewer forces. He wanted a small, lightning-fast striking force. When the army chief of staff, General Eric Shinseki, who was not in the chain of command, responded to a question at a Senate hearing that half a million troops would be required to make Iraq secure after Iraq was defeated, Wolfowitz and Rumsfeld publicly repudiated him and he was retired early.

Colin Powell was not happy about all of this. His Powell Doctrine, which he had articulated when he was chairman of the Joint Chiefs of Staff, was to strike with overwhelming force, win quickly, and have a clear exit strategy. He was not really in favor of attacking Iraq, believing that a reworked system of sanctions would suffice to weaken Saddam until the regime collapsed. Former national security adviser Brent Scowcroft and former secretary of state James Baker argued publicly against an attack on Iraq. They, like Powell, were "realists" who were not sympathetic with "neoconservative" ideas.[19]

Powell expressed his reservations to the president more than once. In one conversation he told Bush that if he conquered Iraq he would "own it," meaning that he would have to govern the country. Bush did not ask Powell whether he approved of military action, nor for that matter did he ask Rumsfeld. He was the decider, at one point telling Woodward that he did not have to explain his reasons for action to anyone. He was the president.[20]

In June 2002 the president gave an address at West Point in which he advocated the idea of preemptive military action against a group or nation that was an immediate threat to the security of the United States. The thesis was later expressed in the September publication of *National Security Strategy of the United States.* There is a fine line between preemption against an immediate threat and preventive war against a longer-term threat, but this was not clarified. Any such action must also be very sure of the evidence of an immediate threat. We now turn to that question.

Evidence That Justified the War

This is a complex story, and the many elements will have to be sorted out by historians when all the documents become available. The question was whether Iraq had developed such weapons—biological, chemical, and possibly nuclear—since the 1998 inspections had ceased because Saddam had thrown out the U.N. inspectors, and the extent of such development, if any. The charge that there were such weapons was the principal justification used by Bush and his associates for war. It would not have been possible for a president to take the nation to war against a dictator who abused his own people or supported terrorists without the threat that lethal weapons might be used against the homeland. This appeal fit easily with public fear after the 9/11 attacks. The administration tried very hard and unsuccessfully to find a tie between al Qaeda and Iraq, but rhetorically tied an attack on Iraq to the war on terrorism, which sufficed to make the link in the public's mind, as surveys revealed.

A National Intelligence Estimate of the CIA in 2000 made clear that Iraq had possessed biological and chemical weapons in 1991 and intended to develop nuclear weapons. The weapons were destroyed and not redeveloped by 1998. There was no certain evidence of the situation after 1998. The administration spoke always of weapons of mass destruction (WMDs), in which nuclear weapons were implicitly joined to the biological and chemical weapons. Evidence was cited that Iraq had tried to buy material for making uranium in Africa, but the CIA refuted this even though the president used it, citing the British, in his January 2003 State of the Union address. Other evidence presented by Colin Powell to the U.N. Security Council in February 2003 just before the United States attacked Iraq was refuted by the chief U.N. weapons inspector, Hans Blix.[21]

Paul Pillar, who was the national intelligence chief for the Near East and South Asia in the CIA from 2000 to 2005, reports that domestic and foreign intelligence agencies believed that Saddam had WMDs but that the sanctions were working and continuingly weakening Iraq. He did not believe that the Bush administration's decision to destroy Saddam was guided by intelligence. Rather the decision was driven by "the desire to shake up the sclerotic power politics and economics of the region."[22] In Pillar's view, the administration used intelligence not to inform but to justify decisions already made. The other side of the case appears to be that Cheney and others were skeptical of the efficacy of the CIA because it had failed to detect Saddam's weaponry before the 1991 Gulf War. Rumsfeld also did not trust the CIA and set up his own intelligence shop to analyze evidence. A second National Intelligence Estimate requested by Congress in 2002 judged that Saddam was unlikely to use WMDs against the United States unless attacked and that he was several years away from developing nuclear capability. Intelligence also argued that there would be attacks on an occupying force, that there were deep divisions in Iraqi society that was not fertile ground for democracy, and that political Islam would be strengthened. This analysis was overridden by Cheney, who told a Veterans of Foreign Wars convention in August 2002 that Saddam either had nuclear weapons or would have them soon.[23] This statement was said to have surprised even the president.

CIA Director George Tenet knew of the uncertainty within the CIA about WMDs, but the record is unclear about what he told the president. In March 2002 Cheney claimed in a speech that Iraq "has, in fact, reconstituted nuclear weapons," but Tenet could not provide the evidence to support the claim. Still, when Bush raised skeptical questions, Tenet is said to have insisted that it was a "slam-dunk case."[24]

Bush and his advisers saw Iraq as a future threat to the United States. They faced North Korea with nuclear weapons and Iran, which aspired to them. Why give Iraq the opportunity? It seemed irresponsible to let Saddam go that route. In January 2002 Bush had told the Congress: "America will do what is necessary to ensure our nation's security.... I will not wait on events while dangers gather.... I will not stand by."[25] In October 2002 Bush told a Cincinnati audience, "The Iraqi regime is seeking nuclear weapons. Does it make any sense for the world to wait ... for the final proof, the smoking gun that come in the form of a mushroom cloud?"[26]

The president wanted to strike a dramatic blow against terrorism and nations that sponsored terrorism. Congress was behind him and voted in October 2002 to support military action against Iraq, if the president judged it necessary. Elite opinion was behind the president, as was the mass media. Reporters did very little digging into the case for war. The public was with the president. A Gallup poll in mid-November 2002 revealed that more than three-quarters of those polled supported military action.

Deception

Bush presented himself to the public as a decisive leader in a national crisis. But he went beyond the facts in his claims, as did his colleagues, particularly Cheney. This is not unique with presidents. In the face of uncertainty they seek support, and anything less than unequivocal statements will not command support. The most important point is that purpose overrode evidence. The terrorist threat was real. The evidence was incomplete. The response was the important thing in the minds of Bush, Cheney, and others. Bush's belief in his own instincts and Cheney's dark view of a dangerous world were more important to them than evidence.

It is clear in retrospect that before he went to the United Nations for inspections in Iraq, Bush had decided that Saddam would have to be removed by force. He told the nation in October 2002 that war could be avoided if Iraq would disarm in response to inspections. But copies of a meeting of top British officials the previous July suggest otherwise. Sir Richard Dearlove, the head of M16 (the British counterpart to the CIA), told Prime Minister Tony Blair that in his recent trip to Washington he had learned from George Tenet and others that the Bush administration thought military action was inevitable "and the intelligence and facts were being fixed around the policy."[27] At that point, Bush had not decided to appeal to the United Nations. Jack Straw, the British foreign secretary, suggested that appeal to the United Nations would give legal justification for the use of force. Tony Blair agreed, and it was decided that Blair would try to persuade Bush of the need to go to the United Nations, which he eventually did.[28] Also in July, Richard Haass, the director of the policy planning staff in the State Department, had asked Condoleezza Rice what was going on about Iraq and was told to forget about it, the decision had been made. Haass later said that he would go to his grave not knowing why the United States invaded Iraq.[29]

The U.N. Security Council voted unanimously in November to install an inspection regime in Iraq, but it did not begin until the new year. In the meantime, the United States and Britain sent over 200,000 troops to the region as a stick against Saddam. From January to March the inspections yielded very little in the way of evidence that Iraq had WMDs. Bush became increasingly impatient, but Blair persuaded him to ask for a second Security Council resolution to ask for authority to use force. The effort failed, and the resolution was withdrawn on March 17. France, Germany, and Russia all argued that inspections had not been given sufficient time to work. Bush then spoke to the nation, giving Saddam a warning to leave Iraq within forty-eight hours or face the consequences. The administration had decided that it could not afford to wait. Hans Blix later said of the Bush administration: "They had a set mind. They wanted to come to the conclusion that there were weapons.... The Americans needed [Iraq to have] WMD to justify the Iraq war."[30]

Invasion

The United States attacked Iraq with land forces, supported by air power, on March 21, 2003. Baghdad fell on April 10. But the war with a Sunni and al Qaeda insurgency continued until December 2011 when Obama withdrew U.S. troops. A wave of killings between Sunni and Shia bands of militias eventually developed. On the positive side, a government of Iraq elected by a national assembly, which was itself elected, was formed. The future of Iraq is in the balance, and no one can predict the outcome. It is clear in retrospect that the U.S. government did not anticipate the internal conflicts that resulted and had no plans for reconstruction of the country. The Pentagon had no interest in "nation building" and hoped for a quick exit. The character of the society and its history were simply ignored in Washington. Both the State Department and the CIA anticipated the problems, but they were not heeded. Richard Neustadt, a leading authority on the presidency, wrote years ago that if Lyndon Johnson had made a serious effort to examine the difficulties of actually implementing an American military effort in Vietnam, he might have been more prudent.[31] The same could be said of the Bush administration. Thomas Hobbes, who lived during the civil war in seventeenth-century England, wrote that "Hell is truth seen too late."

HARD QUESTIONS

Bush's leadership style was both a strength and a weakness. He was bold and decisive and knew how to rally support. And yet he lacked prudence, did not appear to listen to naysayers, and acted too often on the basis of what he called "instinct" rather than information. Bob Woodward conducted an interview with Bush in December 2001 and asked the president whether he sought advice about the war on terror from figures outside his administration, such as Brent Scowcroft, who had advised his father. Bush replied: "I have no outside advice.... The only true advice I receive is from our war council. I didn't call around, asking 'What the heck do you think we ought to do?'"[32]

In the aftermath of the war, as no WMDs were found, Bush shifted his ground and began to speak with great passion of the importance of establishing democracy in Iraq and throughout the Middle East and the world as an American mission. This is an old American theme, but if the sole instrument to be used is military force, it will fail. Perhaps there was a failure to perceive that contemporary terrorism is not based in nations and is therefore even more insidious. Perhaps traditional "realism" is a more prudent way to see the world. A senior aide to President Bush told a journalist that he represented the "reality-based community," in opposition to those in the administration who famously opined, "We're an empire now and when we act we create our own reality."[33] This is another way of saying that one has a theory chasing problems. On July 4, 1821, John Quincy Adams told the House of Representatives that the United States would fight for liberty and independence, "but she goes not abroad in search of monsters to destroy."[34] Richard Haass, director of the policy planning staff of the U.S. Department of State, captured the uncertainty underlying this narrative:

> I just can't explain why so many people thought this was important to do. But if there was a hidden reason, the one I heard most was that we needed to change the geopolitical momentum after 9/11. People wanted to show that we can dish it out as well as take it. We're not a pitiful, helpless giant. We can play offense as well as defense. It would not have happened if there had been no 9/11. What 9/11 did was change the atmosphere in which decisions were made.[35]

The 2004 Election and Aftermath

The president won reelection against Senator John Kerry with 51.2 percent of the popular vote against Kerry's 48.4 percent. It was the narrowest popular vote margin for a reelected incumbent president since 1868. Partisan voting was very strong and turnout was high. Exit polls showed each set of partisans to be about 37 percent of the vote with 26 percent independent. Kerry had the advantage over Bush on economic issues like health care, wages, and the environment, even though the economy had largely recovered from the recession. But as the campaign developed, the fear of terrorism coupled with the war in Iraq favored Bush. He was able to persuade voters that the war in Iraq was an essential part of the war on terror. Fifty-five percent of the voters saw it that way. The following language from a Bush speech in Orlando, Florida, on October 30, 2004, illustrates the point:

> The most solid duty of the American president is to protect the American people. The president must make tough decisions and stand behind them. Especially in time of war, mixed signals only confuse our friends and embolden

our enemies. If America should show uncertainty or weakness in these troubling times the world will drift toward tragedy—and this will not happen on my watch…. We will fight the terrorists across the globe so we do not have to fight them here at home.[36]

Bush claimed that he had a mandate from his election victory with "political capital" that he intended to spend. A postelection Gallup poll raised some questions about the nature of the mandate when it asked respondents whether Bush should go his own way with a mandate or emphasize programs both parties could support because of his narrow victory. Twenty-nine percent favored his going alone, and 63 percent wanted a bipartisan approach.

The second term was an unraveling of the Bush presidency. As mentioned earlier, the campaign for private accounts for Social Security failed. The Bush propaganda machine was not effective when people knew about the issues from experience. The administration failed to cope with Hurricane Katrina, which devastated New Orleans, again a set of events that were visible and in which governments at all levels failed dramatically. A number of corruption scandals among prominent House Republicans tarnished the party with the public. Most important, the army and marines in Iraq suffered over 2,500 deaths and 15,000 casualties, without an end in sight. By mid-2005 Bush had lost the middle of the electorate. Only Republicans stood fast behind him. By 2006 a majority of citizens reported that the war had been a mistake and the president's approval rating was stuck in the thirties. The Bush administration had created its own reality in Iraq, but it was not the reality that citizens saw.

Quagmire

Inside reports suggest that Bush did not manage the war well. He does not seem to have had a role in the decisions by Paul Bremer to dismiss large numbers of civil servants in Iraq because they had been members of the Baath Party or to dismantle the Iraqi army. Richard Armitage, the deputy secretary of state, felt, according to Bob Woodward, that Bush was receiving "sophomoric briefings" on the war. Rumsfeld had created compliant chairmen of the Joint Chiefs of Staff. The secretary of defense would not participate in interagency discussions in which policy might be debated. After the 2004 election, Andrew Card, the White House chief of staff, offered to resign and suggested that the president get a new team. He argued strongly that Rumsfeld had to go. Vice President Cheney, an old ally of Rumsfeld, would not agree. Bush would occasionally hear military and CIA briefings that lacked optimism, but he said over and over that his role was to be a cheerleader for the war, inside the administration and with the public. If the president were to show doubts or to admit mistakes, the war effort might falter. Critics charged that he did not ask hard questions because he was not intellectually curious, but it is more likely that he believed in the cause so strongly that exhortation replaced questions. He held a press conference on October 26, 2006, just days before the election. He said eight times that he was committed to winning the war and had no doubts that "absolutely we're winning." He supported Rumsfeld and the military and said that no changes in strategy were planned. The public, he said, would support a conflict "with a clear path to victory." It was essential to defeat the terrorists in Iraq because if they had a base in that country they would act to overthrow moderate governments all across the Middle East and would launch new attacks on America.[37] His demeanor in the televised conference was intense and came close to frenetic. He responded to questions with long, repetitive answers in support of the war.

The 2006 Congressional Election

The Democrats won both houses of Congress in the 2006 election. The long-standing Republican strategy of bringing out the base of reliable voters did not work, because large numbers of independents voted Democratic and even one-third of evangelical Christians voted Democratic. The reasons for the change were numerous. Many voters, including Republicans, felt that the party had failed to respond to corruption in its own ranks. The war in Iraq was a principal explanation, although there was little agreement of what to do about it.

Although the economy was booming with high levels of employment, the incomes of working people had not risen proportionally. The Democrats won six Senate seats for a majority of fifty-one to forty-nine. House Democrats won twenty-eight new seats for a majority of six. The margins were still very tight, but Democratic chairmen would run the committees. A number of moderate Republicans in the North lost their seats. A number of moderate to conservative Democrats in the Midwest won new seats. The Republicans were pushed back increasingly to a conservative South.

President Bush ate humble pie in a press conference, met with Democratic congressional leaders, and promised to cooperate in passing new legislation. The central question was whether he would really do so. He passed up the opportunity to be cooperative after he first won election by a narrow margin. Would he change his spots? There was a growing atmosphere in Washington that the war would have to be somehow ended, but realistic solutions were missing. The voters seemed to be voting for a centrist coalition and cooperation between the parties.

After the election President Bush replaced Secretary of Defense Donald Rumsfeld with Robert Gates, the director of the CIA in his father's administration. Bush had publicly backed Rumsfeld strenuously up to that point, but if he had doubts, the advent of Democratic majorities made the difference. They would require a fresh face with credibility as secretary of defense, and Gates was a respected figure.

Earlier in 2006 Congress created the Iraq Study Group, a bipartisan group of ten co-chaired by former secretary of state James Baker and former congressman Lee Hamilton, who had been co-chair of the 9/11 Commission. They submitted a unanimous report in December with two reinforcing recommendations: The United States should begin a diplomatic offensive with states neighboring Iraq, including Syria and Iran, to find ways to stabilize sectarian conflicts within Iraq, and the United States should also give priority to training the Iraqi army in order to gradually relinquish its own military role. The report insisted that the government of Iraq move on a number of fronts to forge national unity among sectarian groups and regions. A temporary surge of American troops for the purpose of creating order out of sectarian civil war in Baghdad was suggested, but with no great enthusiasm. The group met with President Bush and testified before Congress, but it soon became clear that the president had other ideas. He replaced the two top generals with responsibility for Iraq and named replacements who were congenial to his new policy, which he announced to the nation on January 10. He recommended an increase of 21,500 soldiers and marines in Iraq, most to Baghdad, and 4,000 to Anbar province, where al Qaeda was strong. The mission of the troops in Baghdad was to work cooperatively with the Iraqi army to clear and hold violent sectors of the city, diminish the sectarian war, and permit the government of Iraq to seek national unity through reforms similar to those recommended by the Iraq Study Group. Bush used purple rhetoric to warn that failure to stabilize Iraq would cause the spread of violence throughout the region, with other states joining in partisan conflict with sectarian armies in Iraq. He warned that al Qaeda must be defeated to prevent the establishment of a terrorist military base in the region. His commitment to the government of Iraq was not open-ended, but he set no time limit to the U.S. role.

A firestorm of Democratic critics in Congress erupted, and administration officials were subjected to strong, critical questions in hearings in which both

Democrats and Republicans raised hard questions. The principal criticism of the plan was that a troop infusion would simply kill more Americans without requiring the Shia-dominated government of Iraq to undertake reforms. The Senate Foreign Relations Committee passed a resolution opposing the increase of troops. The implicit idea beneath the action was that the president should follow the recommendations of the Iraq Study Group. A Republican resolution supported the surge but with strong benchmarks of reform attached. Administration officials, including the new commanding general, told Congress that if the new plan did not seem to be working by the fall of 2007, new measures would have to be considered. The prospect for 2007 was for a continued verbal struggle between the president and Congress and the possibility of an Iraq in total crisis with no clear means of resolution in sight. President Bush was following the logic of his initial decision to attack Iraq, and it did not seem possible for him to reconsider in any fundamental way unless his own congressional party should tell him that he had failed. Even then, since he was not seeking reelection, he might persist. He had so raised the rhetoric of disaster from failure, as he defined it, that there was no turning back. Present judgments are dependent on past judgments. Once the furies are unleashed, it is hard to get them back in the bottle. Lyndon Johnson finally learned this about his war, which had destroyed his presidency. The wild card in the situation was public distrust of the president and opposition to the war in large majorities.

The National Security Presidency and the Law

The strongest legacy of the Bush presidency may be his approach to the formal powers of the presidency. Presidents have expanded their formal powers in wars and emergencies across history. The shock of events imposes demands on the executive from the public and Congress. Article II of the Constitution is loose and ambiguous about the extent of presidential authority in executing the law. Vice President Cheney was intent on recovering the presidential authority to act that he felt had been lost in the aftermath of Watergate. Presidential war making and budgetary authority was cut and congressional investigations undercut executive authority. The president appeared to agree with him, perhaps because Bush's leadership style was one of unilateral leadership without consultation.

Three days after 9/11, Bush won congressional approval of a joint resolution for the president to use "all necessary and appropriate force against those nations, organizations, or persons he determines planned, authorized, committed, or aided the terrorists acts that occurred on September 11, 2001, or harbored such organizations or persons, in order to prevent any future acts of international terrorism against the United States by such nationals, organizations, or persons."[38]

Bush had launched a "war" on terrorism with no stipulation as to when it might end and with legal support from his own Department of Justice for the view that there was no need for congressional or judicial review under the resolution. Presidential directives streamed forth in all directions. The National Security Agency was authorized to wiretap American citizens who might be in touch with terrorists, in some cases, without court-approved warrants. Noncitizen "enemy combatants" captured in Afghanistan and elsewhere and imprisoned were not classified as prisoners of war with the protections of the Geneva Convention. They were held in limbo. Claims of executive privilege in withholding information and documents from Congress in national security matters increased. The congressional intelligence committees were briefed about wiretapping and other matters in a very limited way, and the few who were briefed were held to secrecy under the law. Cheney tried to excise language prohibiting torture of enemy combatants from an amendment to a defense bill proposed by Republican Senator John McCain. When McCain thought that he had won on the issue with the president, Bush added a statement when he signed the law that he "reserved the right to construe [the law] in a manner consistent with the constitutional authority of the Commander in Chief." Bush and his lawyers were advocates of the theory of the "unitary executive," a doctrine that posits that the president may decide the constitutionality of laws with the same authority as the Congress and the courts.[39] Bush did not veto bills. He modified them in practice. This was a throwback to Nixon's claims of executive authority, which were never put to either a political or constitutional test because of Watergate.

The argument has been made that this is the nature of the modern presidency. Presidents who would be effective must shape the institutions in which they work so that they may be responsive to the political demands made upon them. The public demands action by the president, especially in times of crisis. The presidency, as an institution, is small and weak and much dependent upon the executive departments and agencies, which are not necessarily responsive to individual presidents who come and go. Therefore, presidents do not need the "neutral competence" of expertise in the agencies but "responsive competence" to their needs and demands.[40] Time is a luxury that presidents cannot afford, and the assembling of expertise takes time, usually with uncertainties and conflicts in the information provided. Careful analysis of problems is often too late for the decisions that presidents must make. The result in the modern presidency, according to this thesis, is centralization of more and more decision making at the top in the White House and politicization of the executive agencies to create greater responsiveness to the president and his policies. This is a long-term trend that began with the creation of the Executive Office of the Presidency in 1939 and to which each succeeding president has added. This thesis is, in part, descriptive but not wholly so. It does not admit the variation among modern presidents in this regard. Democratic presidents have worked more comfortably with the widely diverse and representative politics of Congress and executive agencies than Republican presidents. But the latter have had to face Democratic control of Congress more often. Advocates of this theory also argue that centralization and politicization are good things because they enable the president to act. However, one must ask whether policies conceived within narrow circles, perhaps in haste, are not likely to lead to great policy mistakes.

Will not such an approach also lead to political backlash in time, especially from the Congress and from others outside the government? The Bush presidency was a test case. The president's personal style, the demands of crisis placed upon him, and the constitutional powers that he invoked all reinforced the centralization of authority. The consequences will be assessed in time.

Turning Points

The departure of Rumsfeld and the seeming decline of Cheney within administration councils gave Secretary of State Rice, who had succeeded Powell in 2005, room to push policies in new directions, drawing on her great credibility with the president. An agreement was concluded in early 2007 by the group of nations that had been meeting with North Korea for a truce in the development of North Korean nuclear facilities in exchange for help in the peaceful nuclear development and financial aid. China, South Korea, Japan, and Russia all gave their good offices to achievement of the plan, but the final negotiations appear to have been moved forward by Secretary Rice, with Bush's approval. By the same token, Rice approved the decision of the government of Iraq to open formal talks with Iran, Syria, and other nations in the region, including the United States, about the stabilization of conflict in Iraq. This was a recommendation of the Baker-Hamilton commission. However, the administration was still on a collision course with Democrats in Congress about the president's decision to send additional troops to Iraq in the so-called surge. The Democrats of both houses insisted that new funding for the troops be tied to dates of eventual withdrawal in 2008. Bush saw this as a challenge to his authority as commander in chief and promised to veto such legislation. It was likely that the president would win the fight because funding was required. But if the battle in Iraq did not go well in the succeeding months, the president could find himself in great difficulty.

There were also repetitions of the "gang who couldn't shoot straight" character of the administration of the executive branch. Conditions for outpatient veterans at the army's Walter Reed Hospital in Washington, D.C., were exposed as very bad. Shortages of funds and staff were responsible with a more fundamental cause being the failure of the army to anticipate the numbers of severely injured patients that would flood the Veterans Administration hospitals. A second scandal was the firing of nine federal prosecutors by the Justice Department without seeming professional cause, but rather for political reasons. A congressional firestorm and investigations followed. Attorney General Alberto Gonzalez was in deep trouble because he denied any role in the firings and the evidence suggested otherwise. His credibility was on the line. One must ask why the Bush administration had so many embarrassments because of inept staff members. There was a shortage of talent and prudence among ideologically loyal subordinates across the board. President Bush had the remainder of 2007 to establish working agreements with the Democratic Congress and find his way in Iraq. The year 2008 would be taken up with presidential nominations and elections and Bush would be a lame duck with limited influence with Congress or the nation. He was in a race against time.

The final year of Bush's presidency was a time of waiting for something new. The president was discredited within his own party on military questions. Future policy alternatives were murky, but large sections of the public wanted fresh departures. In 2008 massive problems struck the nation in a major failure of financial institutions. These problems and the policy responses are analyzed in the following chapter.

Conclusion

How does George W. Bush stand with respect to our criteria for presidential leadership?

Context and Contingencies

The political context was not initially favorable to a president who wished to transform domestic programs toward privatization and reduce the taxing power of government. The attack on the United States gave Bush a release for his warrior energies and an opportunity to be the kind of leader that he wished to be. He seized the day with confidence.

Talents and Skills

Bush had a vision of where he wanted to go and considerable political skill in acting on that vision. He could be a compelling leader to the public when decisive action was required. His negotiating skills were not tested in the presidency because he did not have to do a great deal of negotiating, primarily because the Republican congressional majority followed him with little qualification. By the same token, he resisted negotiations in foreign policy. He showed little interest in oversight or management of the executive branch, confining his attention to the small groups who advised him on important decisions. His management of such groups was confined to immediate advisers. He was described as asking hard questions and encouraging debate, but there were also reports that he was not curious, did not read, and was generally weak on homework, relying on his lieutenants for his information. His greatest weakness as a leader was that he was not reflective or prudent. Boldness was his signature. Once his policies were set, he did not, as he often said, "argue with myself."

Did He Make a Difference?

Bush made a tremendous difference in policy. It is likely that any president would have retaliated against the Taliban and al Qaeda after September 11. The decision to go to war in Iraq was a personal choice. Advisers, including a very strong vice president, pushed him in that direction, but Bush is his own man. If advisers misled him, he permitted them to do it because their advice matched his "instincts." His assertion of presidential powers was supported by his advisers, but Bush did not seem to be a man who was tolerant of political disagreement or of checks on his authority.

George W. Bush sought to be an event-making leader who reshaped American policies and institutions in fundamental ways in response to new historical conditions. The eventful politics of bargaining and compromise fell short of his ambitions. The difficulty was that he tried to achieve major policy changes with thin majorities, an impossibility in American politics.

Effectiveness

Bush was an effective president only when he could summon such majorities, as he did in the early achievement of education reform and tax cuts.

He unified the nation after the 9/11 attacks and led an initially effective military action in Afghanistan. However, he was unable to secure Social Security reform, and the invasion of Iraq—while initially popular even in his reelection in 2004—eventually undermined his presidency.

Bush's personality does not alone explain his policies, particularly the doctrine of preemption and the war in Iraq. His single-mindedness was reinforced by his belief in the American mission in the world. In this sense, he reflected the "national conceit" that the mission of America is moral and universal. The first New England colonists brought their idealism to a new land so that a "city on a hill," as Ronald Reagan often said, would be established as a beacon to the world. The conceit was submerged in the nineteenth century because the United States had a limited foreign policy, but it was expressed in the idea of "Manifest Destiny" and the American war against Mexico. It came to full bloom during Woodrow Wilson's administration with the mission to defeat Germany in World War I in order to, in Wilson's words, "make the world safe for democracy." It resurfaced in the cold war as U.S. foreign policy divided the world into two camps, one good and the other evil. Lyndon Johnson's national security advisers, perhaps more than Johnson himself, saw the world in such stark terms and took the nation into a war in Vietnam, which was not required for American national security. George W. Bush and his neoconservative advisers saw Bill Clinton's relaxed foreign policies as weakness and proclaimed the belief that the United States had the responsibility to impose order on the world as the only "'superpower'" and returned to Wilson's dictum that the United States had to "make the world safe for democracy." Thus, we fought in Iraq to democratize a nation in the Middle East, which would be a beacon to the region and an ally to the United States in its "war" against terrorism. These are the beliefs that drove the president. They are the opposite of the "realism" of George Kennan, the author of the "containment doctrine" of the cold war period, which would deal with nations as they were, and use diplomacy to create international bargains for stability. The arguments in this study for the exercise of prudence in politics is the antithesis of Bush's messianism.[41]

Bibliographical Essay

George Bush's campaign biography, *A Charge to Keep* (1999), may have been written by Karen Hughes but it is Bush's voice. We are told that he wishes to act boldly to make a difference, that he values loyalty and teamwork, and that he has confidence in his ability to make decisions. Two favorable but accurate depictions of Bush as president are by his speechwriter David Frum in *The Right Man: The Surprise Presidency of George W. Bush* (2003), and the journalist Fred Barnes in *Rebel in Chief* (2006). Both books depict Bush as a bold leader, but neither writer idealizes him. Two good but early assessments of the Bush presidency are found in Fred I. Greenstein, ed., *The George W. Bush Presidency: An Early Assessment* (2003), and Colin Campbell and Burt Rockman, eds., *The George W. Bush Presidency: Appraisals and Prospects* (2003). There are good accounts of first-term policymaking in these books. In my view, Greenstein slights the negative sides of Bush's rush to decisions.

Paul Abramson, John Aldrich, and David Rohde provide their usual acute analysis of elections in *Change and Continuity in the 2000 and 2002 Elections* (2003) and "The 2004 Presidential Election: The Emergence of a Permanent Majority?" *Political Science Quarterly* 120, no. 1 (2005). James Campbell adds to the analysis in the same issue of the journal in "Why Bush Won the Presidential Election of 2004: Incumbency, Ideology, Terrorism, and Turnout." Gary C. Jacobson, *A Divider, Not a Uniter: George W. Bush and the American People* (2006), and George C. Edwards III, *Governing by Campaigning: The Politics of the Bush Presidency* (2006), are incisive analyses of Bush's attempt to govern with slim majorities in the country and Congress. Both books provide superb preludes to the 2006 election in which Bush's political strategies backfired.

Aside from the accounts of economic policymaking in edited volumes, the best study is by Ron Suskind, *The Price of Loyalty: George W. Bush and the Education of Paul O'Neill* (2004). Suskind writes from O'Neill's perspective, which—as I suggest in the text—is partial, but I also think quite accurate.

The bulk of this chapter is devoted to decisions about war. The literature is much richer here, although it is journalistic for the most part. However, each of the books cited below is based on extensive interviewing and fieldwork and the descriptions jibe with each other to a great degree. I have worked my way through this literature by constructing a chronological record of events and decisions, indicating at each step how different interpretations might see the history differently. The *New York Times* produced a summary of the main books on Bush and war in its issue of May 11, 2006, in the Arts section.

Ivo H. Daalder and James M. Lindsay give a good overall picture of Bush foreign policy in *America Unbound: The Bush Revolution in Foreign Policy* (2003). James Mann describes the foreign policy advisers who prepared Bush for the presidential campaign and then advised him in office in *The Rise of the Vulcans: The History of Bush's War Cabinet* (2004). Richard A. Clarke describes the early interest in Iraq even as preparations were made to fight in Afghanistan in *Against All Enemies: Inside America's War on Terror* (2004). John Prados, who specializes in providing government documents for appraisal by outsiders, has set out several cases in which he believes that the Bush people went beyond the evidence about possible WMDs in Iraq in *Hoodwinked: The Documents That Reveal How Bush Sold Us a War* (2004).

Todd Purdham drew on the work of *New York Times* reporters to write a narrative of how the United States went to war in Iraq, *A Time of Our Choosing: America's War in Iraq* (2003). John Western has an excellent chapter on the selling of the war to the public in his book, *Selling Intervention and War* (2005).

Bob Woodward did a tremendous amount of interviewing within the administration for his two books *Bush at War* (2002) and *Plan of Attack* (2nd ed., 2004). He interviewed all of the top policymakers, including the president, often more than once. He intended, and I think that he has succeeded, in describing the views of key decision makers. He does not pass judgment. His third book, *State of Denial* (2006), is less flattering of Bush, and seems to rely on fewer informants than the other two books, perhaps because neither the president nor vice president cooperated in the third effort. I think that Woodward is an objective journalist and he is describing a war gone bad. Two comprehensive and critical books are George Packer, *The Assassins Gate: America in Iraq* (2005), and Michael R. Gordon and Bernard E. Trainor, *Cobra II, The Inside Story of the Invasion and Occupation of Iraq* (2006). These books deal extensively with the war, but their accounts of initial policymaking confirm other accounts. James Bamford, *A Pretext for War* (2004), covers much the same ground. Thomas Ricks, *Fiasco: The American Military Adventure in Iraq* (2006), is a very well-researched account of the difficulties of fighting a war in Washington and Iraq.

Finally, Francis Fukyama takes the neoconservatives in the Bush administration to task for their single-minded obsession with Iraq as the enemy and their seeming belief that democracy can be imposed by force in such nations. Fukyama, once a neoconservative, now calls for a "realist idealism" in which the United States should seek world order through international alliances. See *America at the Crossroads: Democracy, Power, and the Neoconservative Legacy* (New Haven, CT: Yale University Press, 2006).

CHAPTER TEN

Barack Obama

Transformational or Transactional Leader?

President Obama was caught in his first term between two models of presidential politics. The first is that of a partisan majority leader who relies on his party's majority in Congress to enact a program that has general party and public support. The second is that of a leader without a strong partisan majority, in or out of Congress, who seeks bipartisan coalitions through bargaining, compromise, and agreement between his own party and the opposition. Due to wide partisan disagreement between the parties, neither of these models has been reliable for Obama, because both depend on considerable agreement in the center of politics and policy to work. Presidential majorities have been most effective when legislative victories have reached beyond their own parties. Such issues usually embrace a wide consensus. However, the present polarization denies either possibility.

Obama has had to struggle with intransigent Republicans, who have blocked many of his legislative proposals. Some Democrats cooperated with this effort to an extent because of their own electoral uncertainties. Other Democrats have supported his programs, despite their wish to be more radical. This politics has followed the gradual polarization of parties in the nation in part by virtue of state legislative gerrymandering after each census to increase the number of safe seats for each party in the federal House of

Representatives. Reinforcement has come from the ideological separation of the national parties. Republicans have driven moderates from their parties as they have abandoned New England and parts of the Northeast and moved south. Grassroots conservative groups have challenged moderate Republican representatives and senators in primaries, often winning, and to some extent have pushed against leaders in both houses who might be more moderate but fear to do so. Democrats have not moved to such extremes, but their loss of the House of Representatives in 2010 weakened the strength of the center path in Congress. Presidents Carter and Clinton had to resort to bargaining with Democrats and Republicans even as polarization impended, thus revealing the weakness of liberal reform after the Great Society. Such shifting back and forth is confusing to voters, particularly Democrats, and Obama's shifts have created uncertainties about his purposes, as was the case with Carter and Clinton.

BIOGRAPHY

The appeal to the center from a reforming perspective was consistent with Obama's early life and his political personality as it developed in adulthood. He was born of a white American mother and a black Kenyan father and grew up in Hawaii. His father left his mother when Obama was a small boy in order to attend graduate school at Harvard. In due course he returned to Kenya and a divorce followed. His mother, Ann, now a graduate student in anthropology, then married an Indonesian, and when Obama was six, they moved to Indonesia. Obama attended school there for four years and then, so that his mother might do anthropological field work in Indonesia, he returned to live with his grandparents in Hawaii. They were Kansans who had moved to Seattle, and then subsequently to Hawaii. Obama met his father for a few days when he was ten, and there was no contact after that. Barack Sr. died in an automobile accident a few years later. Obama attended Punahoe, an exclusive private school, on a scholarship. His interest was primarily in playing basketball, and he was a good but not motivated student. His biographer, David Maraniss, reported that in these years Obama was like a writer who studied his environment and absorbed it without commitment. Maraniss compares him to the character in Walker Percy's book *The Moviegoer*, who learns by going to the movies and observing, rather than acting. Obama wrote later that, while at Punahoe, "I had no idea who my own self was" and that "I learned to slip back and forth between my black and white worlds."[1]

At Occidental College in Pasadena, California, Obama continued to learn to put himself "in the shoes of others," according to Maraniss. Many of his friends were minorities, often from abroad. He participated in a student rally about racism in South Africa and found that he was a good speaker. He could find the right words and connect with the audience. His race might have helped, but he realized that that alone was insufficient were he to continue in that vein.[2] He transferred to Columbia University for his final two years and appears to have devoted himself to his studies, playing little part in university life. He worked for a time in New York and then moved to Chicago to become a community organizer. He attached himself to a veteran organizer and began the hard path of working with workers and their families who had been displaced by the closing of a steel plant in the city. He worked on issues of unemployment, welfare, schools, and problems faced by displaced families. He learned how to work with local politicians. His style was to avoid confrontation. Maraniss depicts him as a "realist" who hoped to keep lines of communication open and not burn bridges.[3] He joined a black church to find legitimacy for his work and gradually found a genuine faith in the tradition of the black gospel.

Obama decided that a career in law would give him more power for action than a life of organizing, but before entering Harvard he decided to discover what he could learn from and about his family in Kenya. The trip and his conclusions are told in a book he wrote after his first year at Harvard Law School, titled *Dreams from My Father*.

Obama's father was dead, but he met several half brothers and sisters, his grandmother, and various aunts and uncles in Kenya. He learned of his father's alcoholism, strong temper, and unsteady career path, and of two subsequent wives, one white American and one African. It is not clear why he called the book *Dreams from My Father*. He was not praising or even commemorating his father. Perhaps he hoped to record his father's unrealized ideals or describe his own aspirations. In any event, he did not find a personal identity in Kenya. He went with "great emptiness," but there was no "illusionary wholeness." His solution was to find himself in a fully American identity of unity amid diversity. He began to believe that America needed a new kind of politics based on "shared understandings that pull us together as Americans."

Obama was elected president of the *Harvard Law Review* in his second year of law school. He successfully guided the review during years of controversy at Harvard, when both faculty and law students were divided in their positions on the possibility of objectivity in the law versus radical claims that law was shaped and biased by interests of many kinds. He steered his way among these conflicts by trying to be fair to all sides, listening to both and managing a balance of articles in the journal. This role came naturally to him. Years later, one may ask whether a mediator role is appropriate in a U.S. president, but it was reasonable that he tried, because it had worked in Chicago and at Harvard. These were his first political successes.

Obama joined a law firm in Chicago and taught constitutional law part-time at the University of Chicago Law School. He met his wife, Michelle, when she was assigned by the firm to oversee his work. Maraniss records that, during the Columbia years, a white girlfriend with whom he was very close saw that he was moving toward the black world and predicted that he would someday find that a "lithe, bubbly, strong black lady was waiting for him."[4] That was Michelle.

In due course he entered politics as an Illinois state Senator. He was attracted to Bill Clinton's "Third Way," which rejected excessive ideology in favor of a pragmatic center. He also began to feel that a "cross-pollination" was taking place in which Americans were looking at new ideas not rooted in their fixed opinions.

Beliefs

A teacher at Occidental, Roger Boesche, taught history according to a "passion for community" in politics as an antidote for exaggerated American individualism. This influenced young Barack. Louis Kloppenburg sees Obama as a "civic republican" who wishes to balance individuality and community, not in the sense of a set of absolute values, but through accommodation. Obama looks back into American history to affirm the ideas of William James and John Dewey that reject "certainty history" in favor of discussion and debate. Community is invoked to balance individualism. All victories in politics are incomplete, but little is achieved by confrontation. He reaches beyond being a utilitarian toward a republic of moral purpose.[5] Persuasion is the best path to agreement. Obama wrote of how the elimination of the death penalty was worked out in the Illinois legislature through careful discussion among contending parties. There may be a certain naïveté in this hope. For example, President Obama hoped initially for discussion of a national health care plan by the same method. He believes in politicians using values for leadership, but they also use values for disagreement with him, something he has learned as president. Obama asks for "authenticity" in political leaders and cites the "empathy" for others that his mother and grandmother showed. This word got him into trouble when he later said that he hoped that his nominees for the Supreme Court would have "empathy" in the effects of their decisions. He saw an "empathy deficit" in the country as he was beginning to run for president. The Constitution was a "conversation," a framework for argument without any authoritative answers. Finally, in opposition to a good many "liberals," Obama has argued that liberals must acknowledge the value of religious faith for their politics and purposes.[6]

THE 2008 CAMPAIGN

Obama values compromise in legislatures, but he is not a natural legislator. He wants to lead. His abilities and desires push him to the center of the stage. Once elected to the Senate in 2004, he found it frustrating because the legislative process was slow and cumbersome. Harry Reid, the Democratic majority leader, took him aside in June 2006 and advised that he run for president because he would not enjoy life in the Senate. Obama took the advice and began running in 2007. He had a very hard fight, primary after primary, against Hillary Clinton, the initial front-runner. He won, but not without wounds and anger among Democrats, which were not fully healed until he persuaded her to become secretary of state. He was able to carry blue-collar states and women against John McCain in the general election. He won 53 percent of the popular vote and carried majorities among women, independents, political moderates, African Americans, and Hispanic people, and he did better with white voters than Bill Clinton. McCain won white men and women, evangelical Christians, conservatives, and older voters. Obama won a number of swing states. Had there been no financial meltdown, as there was in the fall, Obama still would have won. Voters were unhappy with wars in Iraq and Afghanistan, and the economic crash sealed the fate of Republicans. It also presented Obama with a major recession that he had not anticipated.

Obama and his advisers searched the evidence of past presidential victories to assess the possibility of a presidency of Reconstruction, as set out by Yale political scientist Stephen Skowronek.[7] There have been five such presidents according to Skowronek's thesis: Jefferson, Jackson, Lincoln, Franklin Roosevelt, and Reagan. These presidents were able to reconstruct politics and institutions to point to new directions for national policy. The cycle pointed in a progressive direction for the first four and then shifted toward conservative paths with Reagan. There has been no clear pattern since Reagan, and Skowronek has questioned whether the cycle will continue, because of the polarization of parties and the glut of interest groups that clog the functioning of government. Obama's rhetoric during the campaign moved toward reconstruction in health care and financing, regulation, education, and energy renewal, but always reached back to the center and national unity, as past presidents of Reconstruction have done successfully. It takes at least two successive victories for Reconstruction to prevail. Reelection has not moved Obama in that direction because partisan polarization is so great.

LEADERSHIP STYLE

Although he clearly wished to be a transforming president, Obama also wished to build a coalition of Democrats and Republicans for his programs. He was still the "moviegoer" to an extent. One sees a combination of detachment and commitment, as in earlier parts of his life. He wished to rise above diversity to find unity. And yet Obama is not comfortable with the politics of schmoozing with other politicians that Bill Clinton so enjoyed. He has not called members of Congress to talk informally and get acquainted. He has perhaps relied too much on his own intellectual capacity as a persuasive power. He has left the glad-handing to Joe Biden, his vice president, who is a natural politician. For example, Obama met with Senate and House leaders in a daylong televised seminar on his health care bill as it began to move forward in Congress. One might easily say that he was the smartest man in the room; he certainly held his own against one critic after another. But was that really the point? One could not see any persuasion at work. He does not enjoy fund-raising and is not comfortable with business leaders, many of whom have resisted his calls for regulations on businesses, especially banks, and other agents of the deep recession. He keeps decisions closely within his own staff and his own thinking. David Brooks, the *New York Times* columnist, described the new president as self-confident and not emotionally needing to be president, but asking whether he might be "an island of rationality in a sea of tumult." He might be an "observer" rather than a "leader," because more aggressive actors would not cooperate with him. A "lack of passion will produce a lack of courage."[8] And yet the president showed considerable courage in proceeding with a major reform of health care and the decision to kill Osama bin Laden. Obama the observer will often act decisively once he has made up his mind. He has developed this style because he has been an outsider all his life. In being required to balance different worlds, he must observe before he is ready to act.

He is not like a standard American politician. We know who the Bill Clintons are; we have seen them in high school when they run for class president. But who is this man who grew up in Indonesia and Hawaii? He can be eloquent. He saved his candidacy for the presidency in a March 2008 speech in Philadelphia, responding to charges that the minister of his church in Chicago was a racist. Obama gave examples of racism in American life and recalled that his white grandmother expressed fear of black men on city streets. We have to rise above such matters, he insisted as he disowned his minister.[9] The speech was an example of Obama's recuperative capacity. His inaugural address in January 2009 traced many important themes and was mildly phrased, but there was no big story in it. He did not take advantage of the recession to call for a fundamental reform of economic life. He needed, but lacked, a story.[10]

The new vice president, former senator Joe Biden, was an experienced politician and a former chair of the Senate Foreign Relations and Senate Judiciary committees, with a great knowledge of Congress and considerable expertise in foreign policy. He was to be an assistant president. The new president moved quickly to appoint his White House staff, before looking to cabinet and subcabinet appointments. This is important because White House appointments may be an afterthought if too much attention is given to the cabinet early on. Thereby, Obama made it clear that he intended to run the policies of importance to him from the White House. Rahm Emanuel, a Democratic congressman from Chicago, became White House chief of staff. David Axelrod, a public opinion and voting expert, also from Chicago, became an important political adviser.

Lawrence Summers, a Harvard economist and secretary of the treasury with Clinton, was to head the National Economic Council, through which advice is pulled in to the president. Summers had advocated deregulation of financial markets when he worked for Clinton but now favored increased regulation. His former assistant at treasury, Tim Geithner, left the presidency of the New York Federal Reserve Bank to become secretary of the treasury. Peter Orzag and Christine Rohmer, two respected economists, were to manage the Office of Management and Budget and the Council of Economic Advisers, respectively. There were respectable advisers with perhaps more radical ideas, such as temporary nationalization of the banks, but Obama hoped to buttress the banks as a path to economic recovery. By appointing Hillary Clinton secretary of state, the president healed party rifts and brought Bill Clinton to his side. By the same token he persuaded Robert Gates, the incumbent secretary of defense, to stay on, which Gates did for two years. Cabinet and subcabinet appointments were made carefully and with much study by Obama. The professional quality was high.

Economic Policy

The new president faced a broad and deep economic recession on the verge of a depression as he entered office. Millions of people were losing their homes because mortgage companies had sold homes that many new homeowners could not afford. As payments could not be made, especially as unemployment rose, homes were repossessed and sat empty. It was falsely assumed by borrowers and sellers that prices would keep going up. National investment banks had sold a number of securities in financial markets that were not sustainable, even in the short term. Again, it was assumed that rewards would keep soaring up, but many of these instruments were not sustainable, and when they faltered investors suffered and banks found themselves in deep trouble. Investment banks were in the business of making money for their partners, as they served investors, but their commitments were overextended. In 2008, Bush policy makers decided to buy the "toxic assets" of the investment banks in default, but they could not be priced and the idea then shifted to federal investment in fragile banks to prevent bankruptcy and a collapse of the financial economy. Banks were to repay the government, but they had little money in the short term to lend money to businesses for private finance of recovery.

It then became apparent that General Motors and Chrysler were on the edge of bankruptcy and might disappear altogether. The new administration acted to invest in both companies, force them into a managed bankruptcy, and give them new corporate managers.

The rescue of the banks and auto companies was unpopular with the public, particularly as unemployment increased, because they appeared to be saving the villains responsible for the crisis. It was difficult for the government to argue that the economy would have been worse without such actions. One cannot prove a negative in politics. The turning point against Obama came in March, when it was discovered that bankrupt AIG (American International Group), an international insurance company, had given their officers millions of dollars in bonuses according to their individual contracts with the company. This smelled, even though contracts had to be legally honored.

The president sent an economic stimulus program of $787 billion to Congress in February 2009. It included tax cuts of $288 billion, and $224 billion in aid to state and local governments for education, health care, unemployment, and support for jobs in the public sector that would otherwise be lost. Another $275 billion went toward job creation from federal contracts, grants, and loans to local governments. The program passed, but no House Republicans voted for it, and it passed the Senate only with concessions to two Democrats and three Republicans. Congressional Republicans called for tax cuts for businesses to revive investment. The party had sworn to "no new taxes" for a long time. Obama perhaps mistakenly let Democratic congressional leaders write the bill in order to win quick passage. As one might expect, pork for constituencies was piled on. The creation of public employment was rejected because it would take months to get public works going and the private sector was thought to be the best source of good jobs. Economists friendly to the administration, especially Paul Krugman of the *New York Times*, thought that the stimulus was far too modest, but it was not clear that Congress would have done more, as the struggle for passage revealed.

Obama sent a ten-year budget to Congress that reflected his long-term priorities. He set aside $634 billion for health care reform. Global warming was to be arrested through taxes on carbon emissions. Middle-income taxes were reduced and the affluent were to pay more. There was to be new support for research and development in wind and solar energy. The budget predicted 3 to 4 percent in economic growth in the next four years. The inherited $1.2 trillion deficit was pushed up to $1.8 trillion. Projections revealed increased interest payments on the national debt of $806 trillion annually by 2019. Obama planned to reduce future deficits through control of rising health care costs, along with economic growth. Health care reform thus became crucial for deficit reduction in the president's eyes.

Health Care Reform

The American health care system treats the insured very well but at high cost compared to other industrial nations, and about 20 percent of the population, 50 million people, were without insurance as Obama began to innovate. The costs of medical care were about 16 percent of the national economy, and rising. The population over age sixty-five is covered by Medicare, which is increasing in cost as the baby boomers begin to retire. Medicaid, which is administered by the states and paid for through federal-state matching, is only for the very poor and does not include the working poor. Big businesses may provide health insurance for the employed, but many small businesses cannot afford to do so. The industrial democracies, except for the United States, have widely varying systems of national health care, and they are cheaper than our own medical costs. Attempts to create national health insurance have failed politically, most notably in the Clinton administration.

Obama's close advisers tried to talk him out of a comprehensive plan, arguing that economic recovery came first. This perhaps made political sense if the tools for economic recovery had been certain. A national New Deal might have required much public employment and would have uncertain results. High employment came for the New Deal only with World War II. The president's economic advisers may have been too bent on half measures, but politics was also not favorable. More importantly, perhaps, the president wished to strike a big legislative victory such as a President of Reconstruction might achieve.

Obama was mindful of Clinton's failed strategy of sending a full program to Congress that was never considered, so he provided an outline of principles and asked key congressional committees to put flesh on the bones. His principles included a mandate that all citizens buy health insurance, and a "public option" by which one might buy insurance on a competitive basis, under stated guidelines, as an alternative to more expensive plans. His idea was to cut the subsidies that Bush had given to private insurers in order to reduce public health insurance. The White House negotiated with insurance and pharmaceutical companies to support his program, which would bring them more customers. Major unions and companies agreed to reductions in health costs in coming years. These agreements were worked out privately and, when later revealed, appeared to many citizens to be backdoor deals, something they disliked about Washington. The American Medical Association agreed not to oppose the plan. Former Republican senators Howard Baker and Bob Dole signed on. Unfortunately, Senator Edward Kennedy, who was dying of cancer, was not in the fight.

The summer of 2009 saw the development of grassroots politics, in opposition to the administration, focused on spending and deficits. It consisted of a number of local Tea Party groups that mounted virulent attacks against national government power, especially the power to tax, and the health care program in particular. Tea Partiers were, by and large, right-wing Republicans who had had enough. They did not press the moral and social causes that inspired religious evangelicals. These groups had a new lease on life as well, even though they had been politically active for some years.

The Democratic majority in the House passed the bill without a single Republican vote, and attention shifted to a subcommittee of the Senate Finance Committee, chaired by the chair of the full committee, Senator Max Baucus, a Democrat from Montana. Aside from Baucus, the members were three Democrats and three Republicans, each representing small rural states. None of the Republicans were friendly. Senate leaders of their party were against the bill; indeed, their majority leader, Mitch McConnell of Kentucky, said publicly that the Republican goal was to make Obama a one-term president.

The committee could not resolve hard questions, about the public option, about federal payment for abortions, about long-term costs. After the attempt at bipartisanship, the president's public appeals worked mainly with Democrats. The Gallup poll in September reported that 39 percent of those polled opposed the plan and 37 percent favored it. They were, by and large, following the views of their representatives in Congress. Those fifty and over were most opposed, and women, lower-income people, the highly educated, and easterners were most favorable. A slight majority of the upper-income classes were against reform, while middle-income people were divided.

The subcommittee reported the bill to the full Finance Committee with three Democratic votes and one Republican vote. The full committee sent it to the Senate with all Democrats voting yes and all Republicans voting no. The bill passed with a filibuster-free sixty votes. However, in January, Scott Brown, a Republican, was elected senator for Massachusetts to replace Edward Kennedy. The House and Senate bills were different, and a compromise at final passage would open the Senate up to a Republican filibuster. Obama asked the House to adopt the bill that had passed the Senate and it did so, enabling congressional passage of the bill.

Under the Affordable Care Act, all citizens would be obliged to buy health insurance, with subsidies for the poor and small business employers. Medicaid was expanded above the poverty line. Seniors would receive discounts on drugs within Medicare. The full bill would not be implemented until 2014, but bans on preexisting medical conditions by insurance plans were eliminated and young people under age twenty-six could stay on their parents' medical insurance beginning immediately.

There was great complexity in the regulations that would have to be written and uncertainty about the eventual cost. Republicans immediately promised to abolish the program as soon as possible. Several state attorney generals sued the federal government, arguing the unconstitutionality of the law because it forced citizens to buy insurance.

Economic and Social Policy

The president's economic advisers bet wrong on the near future of the economy. They predicted growth and reduction of unemployment for 2010 and 2011 that did not occur. Most voters, aside from public employees, did not see the stimulus as a good thing. The tax cuts were modest and not greatly noticed. The hard question for the new government was whether to emphasize job creation, deficit reduction, or some combination of both. Obama wanted a combination, while Republicans in Congress wanted economic stimulus through tax and budget cuts. Most Democrats resisted budget cuts and were lukewarm about tax increases. Obama wanted both tax increases and long-term budget cuts. The political center, which might have backed the president in Congress, was weak. Policy was stalled through disagreement. By the end of 2009 the number of foreclosures was rising, the use of food stamps was increasing, state and local budget gaps between income and expenditures were growing, and unemployment was rising.

A president who sought middle ground between two polarized parties was getting nowhere. It became harder as public unhappiness grew. The negative messages of cable and radio talk shows, dominated by conservatives, cast a pall over opinion. Some economists began to talk of a "new normal" in modern economies of a declining, poorly educated labor force. Recovery from a deep recession was thereby handicapped. Tax cuts for businesses were also not as effective as hoped. The safety net of temporary unemployment insurance and other welfare measures was built on the now faulty idea that unemployment would be only short term. Republican congressional leaders wanted deep tax cuts for businesses as a remedy, but it was not clear this short-run idea would work, especially if consumers had weak purchasing power. The Federal Reserve Bank in Washington kept interest rates as low as possible, as long as inflation was low. And yet business owners were in no mood to invest in new ventures, nor were banks eager to make new loans in such an uncertain economy.

The presidential party collided with a disillusioned public in 2010, as Republican support grew at the expense of Democrats. Many Democratic reformers were also unhappy about the lack of action on energy innovation, reduction of emissions, and immigration reform. The health care fight consumed the energies of the president and his political allies in 2009, and congressional Republicans blocked majority votes short of sixty at an unprecedented rate, frustrating the president. Obama did manage to secure some reform of Wall Street practices in the Dodd-Frank bill in July 2010, but there was concern among critics of the practices of investment banking that the rules would be too weak; regulators would fall short, and investment firms, which lobbied against the bill designed to reform them, would find new ways to misbehave. Focus groups revealed concerns about social breakdown of principles in government, business, labor, and the media.

The Republican victory in taking command of the House of Representatives in 2010 was thus a blow for the president and his party, but they should have seen it coming. The Republicans would have 242 seats in the new House, and the Democrats would be a 193-vote minority. The vote may have simply been a punishment for Congress, which ranked low as an institution.

Obama's critics from the left wished that he would have come out swinging as a fiery crusader in early 2009 with massive employment programs and major reforms of the banks, plus fights for new energy policies to explore and conserve resources. Some moderate critics would have had him postpone major health care reform in favor of getting the economy back into shape, which might have prevented public anger about these issues. Obama may have been too intent at the outset to enact a major reform beyond an electoral mandate. And yet, the Republican Party has become a "movement" of believers in the creed of small, limited government, no tax increases, and fixed opposition to abortion and same-sex marriage. Republicans were divided between economic and social conservatives, but they all voted the same way. Obama was caught in a trap created by the Constitution. Neither a party majority nor divided party control produced effective government. The former was too weak and the latter produced gridlock. His hopes for bipartisan government of the center were impossible. This had not been true in the past. Congress has been productive in either situation, but only within a broad center politics. Polarization is not compatible with the structure of the Constitution. This fact does not require identical political parties. Party control of government may shift according to national politics; it has always done so. But government by one party without cooperation of the opposition is not possible. Legislative majorities must reach to a shifting center.

The Budget Fight of 2011

The big story of 2011 was the failure of the president and Congress to agree on a budget agreement that would increase revenues, lower tax rates, and reduce the federal deficit over the long term. The cause of the failure was the inability of the president and House Republican leaders to agree on revenue increases. The president wanted a repeal of the tax cuts for the wealthy created by President Bush and congressional Republicans, additional tax increases, and a plan for long-term reductions in federal spending. Republicans would not agree to any tax increases. Most House Republicans had signed a no-tax-increase pledge. The eighty Tea Party members of the

House majority pushed hard against veteran Republicans who were conservative but not so hidebound. Republican congressional leaders chose the need to renew the federal debt ceiling, usually a routine matter, to force the president to agree to cuts in programs. The date for default on the federal debt was August 2, 2011. Democrats in Congress were opposed to the radical budget cuts that Republicans favored. Failure to raise the debt ceiling would mean interest on the debt and cuts in Social Security, Medicare, and other valued programs. President Obama hoped to bring the two parties together on a middle course. President Clinton had left a $137 billion federal surplus along with a booming economy. President George W. Bush created a $1.2 billion deficit that came with large tax cuts, but did not pay for wars in Iraq and Afghanistan or an additional drug benefit in Medicare.

In the spring and summer, President Obama and House Speaker John Boehner had private conversations about a compromise that would reduce tax rates, permit long-term budget cuts, close tax loopholes, increase tax revenues, and specify future cuts in entitlement programs. However, Boehner could not persuade his fellow House Republicans to agree. He accused the president of wishing to increase tax revenues at the last minute, adding up to $1 trillion of new revenue. It is not at all clear what happened between Obama and Boehner, although there is no question that Boehner could not persuade his party to agree. He may have been concerned about keeping his job because the Republican majority leader, Eric Cantor, quietly opposed any agreement. Obama was also worried about making too many concessions on domestic program budgets for fear of opposition by congressional Democrats. Independent voters had been important for Obama's 2008 victory, but by 2011 many of those voters were disillusioned by economic conditions and unhappy with the president. The center would not hold. The ideas of politics as the art of the possible had been forgotten with party polarization.

Failure led to an accommodation in the Budget Control Act passed on August 2. Default was prevented. The Joint Select Committee on Deficit Reduction was created to face facts again and find a remedy. The twelve-member bipartisan group of six senators and six representatives was selected by the four majority and minority leaders. The recommendation of the committee was to be presented to Congress, requiring a simple majority vote without amendments. The committee failed to agree on a plan because key Republicans voted no. Failure meant that by the end of 2012 there would be a trigger of $1.2 billion automatic spending cuts, equally split between national security and domestic programs, with the big entitlement programs excepted. Members gave different reasons for failure, but the big party difference was that too few Republicans would raise taxes and too few Democrats would cut spending.

FOREIGN POLICY

Obama was critical of President Bush's tough stance toward the world, which seemed to promise the use of American influence and power to extend democracy to nations that denied it. He gave a speech in Cairo in early 2009 in which he promised a foreign policy that respected the wishes and practices of other nations without abandoning the American commitment to democracy. He called for peace between Israel and the Palestinians, called for limiting nuclear weapons, and invoked the human rights of women, with implications for Arab practices. He quoted the Hebrew Bible, the Koran, and the New Testament's Sermon on the Mount: "Blessed are the peacemakers for they shall be called the sons of God."[11] The new president also appeared to soften the past treatment of terrorists in detention by promising to close the prison in Guantanamo Bay, Cuba, and bring the worst offenders to trial. Neither of these was achieved. Congressional resistance to prisoners in mainland jails was hostile, and plans to try the men who planned the 9/11 strikes in civilian courts were not acceptable anywhere. The administration increased the use of force against terrorism in a number of ways, particularly the use of unpiloted drones in Afghanistan and Pakistan as part of military operations and to kill terrorist leaders.

Obama followed up the speech in Cairo with overtures to the government of Iran asking for talks on the development of Iranian nuclear weapons. There was no response, and Iran continued to talk with a quartet of Russia, France, Britain, and the United States, without a positive outcome. The result has been an allied tightening of economic and other sanctions against Iran that has created considerable hardship for ordinary Iranians but produced little in the way of conflict resolution.

In 2012, Obama had difficulty with Prime Minister Benjamin Netanyahu of Israel, fearing threatened Israeli attacks on the sites of nuclear production in Iraq, insofar as they are known. Any such attack was delayed until after the 2012 election, but the question was still put off and not resolved. Obama moved quickly to create international treaties to limit the testing of nuclear weapons, with some success. The United States and Russia signed a treaty for the mutual reduction of nuclear weapons from a stockpile of 2,200 weapons down to 1,500. The chief worry has been the effect of Iranian weapons on other nations in the Middle East who might want their own nuclear arsenal. Not all of these states have that capacity. Obama has publicly pledged that Iran will not be permitted to acquire nuclear weapons, but has not said how he would prevent it. He may have backed himself into a corner. Would the United States attack an Iran that had such weapons? If Israel were to strike Iran, what would Obama do? Iran is unlikely to attack Israel knowing that its own destruction would follow. The mullahs are not suicidal. The president is relying on sanctions to bring Iran around, but there is great uncertainty. Pakistan and India each have nuclear weapons, and the long-standing tension between those nations is dangerous. In particular, Pakistan has provided support for the Taliban in Afghanistan for fear of undue Indian influence in that country. This has complicated the American fight against the Taliban in Afghanistan. Most of the Taliban guerrillas are based and protected in Pakistan. To say the least, Pakistan has not been an active partner in the American war against the Taliban.

The administration has been successful in withdrawing American military forces from Iraq. The country is more or less stabilized, with a residue of terrorists and hostile relations between a Shia majority and Sunni minority, which ruled the country for decades during and before the regime of Saddam Hussein. The most serious problem facing the president has been Afghanistan. The Bush administration drove the Taliban and al Qaeda from Afghanistan after the 9/11 attacks on America, but the leaders of al Qaeda were not captured, and regrouped their forces in Pakistan. The Bush administration then took their eyes off Afghanistan and invaded Iraq in 2003. Chapter 9 on the Bush presidency describes the American invasion and occupation of Iraq. Whatever the merits of that campaign, it permitted the Taliban, with al Qaeda help, to reenter Afghanistan and threaten the fragile government that the Americans had installed in Kabul.

The new president had been in office one month when the Pentagon generals called for more American troops in Afghanistan. The secretaries of defense and state agreed, and Obama sent 17,000 men and women. His reluctance was clear, but the war was going badly. The central government in Kabul was weak and had limited authority in a tribal society. The traditional culture was corrupt, and the war had added new forms of stealing. President Hamid Karzai stole the 2009 presidential election by about 1 million votes, but the United States had no way to force him out. Obama hoped that the United States might withdraw in 2011, but that was uncertain. The fight was against al Qaeda in theory, but the United States was actually fighting the Taliban.

In September 2009 the president decided to use the National Security Council system to develop plans for the near future. He sought fresh ideas, but they were not easy to extract from players with fixed positions. The Joint Chiefs of Staff gave him familiar choices, ranging from adding 20,000 to 40,000 troops. He rejected the smallest number and turned to Robert Gates, the secretary of defense, for advice. White House advisers for national security opposed higher numbers. Gates was a realist who believed that the Taliban might be contained but not defeated. Containment depended on whether Afghanistan could develop an army strong enough to enforce it. A consensus was reached for 30,000 troops. American forces would depart Afghanistan in 2014, leaving only support forces. The president insisted that all participants sign support for the plan. The top generals dragged their feet every step of the way and attempted to change the president's mind over and over, but he resisted and won out.[12]

Two years later, Obama judged the incursion to have been successful and announced in June 2011 that 10,000 troops would be withdrawn from Afghanistan by the end of the year, with another 20,000 of the original surge withdrawn in 2012. The United States would no longer fight big battles and keep mobile forces ready to attack as needed. The military considered such action premature, but many Republicans and much of the public wanted an end to the conflict.

American forces were withdrawn from Iraq, by order of the president, in December 2011. The military had hoped to leave some forces, but the government of Iraq would not sign an agreement that would protect American forces from criminal charges by the Iraqi government. In any event, the president had made it clear that he wished to bring the two adventures to a close.

The Arab Spring

In late 2010 and early 2011, a number of popular demonstrations and revolts in the major Arab countries of Egypt, Tunisia, and Libya erupted. New regimes appeared after much violence. The United States provided military support, as did NATO, and used air naval forces to help bring down the Libyan dictator, Muammar Gaddafi. Subsequent American policies supported new quasi-democratic regimes in these countries. President Obama called for Egyptian president Hosni Mubarak to resign in the face of rebellion in the streets, and supported new regimes in Tunisia and Libya. The future of these regimes was uncertain, but Obama developed a strategy of support without visible interference. The Middle East continued to be a tinderbox, however, as revolts in Syria led to a violent civil war, which had not been resolved as 2012 closed.

Obama's actions in the Middle East suggest that he is a "realist" in the sense that he does not seek military adventures. He is always an idealist in his hope for the resolution of conflicts that will permit the United States to lead toward conciliation. One sees the same restraint in his economic policies: move slowly and gradually toward one's goals, building support along the way. There have, however, been exceptions. He ordered the murder of Osama bin Laden by a small team of Navy Seals in May 2011 when bin Laden's hiding place in Pakistan was discovered. The operation was successful. Bin Laden was living in a town filled with Pakistani army barracks and the United States did not inform the Pakistanis in advance, which led to bad feeling for some time. The president has been quite willing to use drones to kill Taliban and al Qaeda leaders in Pakistan once they are found, another thorn in the side of the Pakistan army and its intelligence service, which protects the Taliban. The problem of the political weakness of Pakistan's government, the power of its military, and the corruption of the society and government may not be something that any Western nation can do much about, yet it casts a pall over the future of a stable Afghanistan.

POLITICS AND POLICY

President Obama has faced the most partisan polarization of any president in modern history. There was no overlap in ideology between activist members of the two parties. There was less such polarization among the electorate, particularly among Democrats, about half of whom hovered around the middle. Republicans clustered more to the right of center and a further right. Adherents of the two parties are increasingly separated by residence, religion, ethnicity, age, and gender. Partisans have increasingly developed feelings about adherents to the other party. Trust in government varies depending on which party has the White House. If the House of Representatives had fifty more centrist Republicans, the president would have had a better chance of winning passage for many of his programs. Fifteen more centrist Republicans in the Senate would have permitted easier passage of Obama measures, perhaps even overrides of Republican insistence on sixty votes for every Democratic victory.

Obama and Speaker of the House John Boehner met in 2011 and seriously discussed the possibility of a "grand bargain" between parties on budget issues, in which tax rates would be lowered, some deductions would be limited, and a long-term agreement on budget cuts, including Social Security, Medicare, and Medicaid, would be established. However, the agreement broke down after a few days. One interpretation was that Obama insisted on adding tax increases. The other view was that Republicans, rank and file, would not agree. It was clearly a failure for the president. Obama's presidency lacked the strong popular support that had animated the progressive politics of the two Roosevelts, Wilson, and Lyndon Johnson. He inherited the politics of the middle way from Carter and Clinton, but Republican opposition was fiercer than for those presidents. Critics of the president argued that he should have escalated the fight on his own behalf, but that was not his nature. It is a moot question whether it would have worked.

The 2012 Presidential Campaign

A number of debates and elections took place before Mitt Romney won out against his fellow Republican candidates, none of whom could have beaten Obama because they were strong conservatives. It was an eccentric group, most of whom took extreme ideological positions to which Romney chose to adhere. For example, he was forced to disavow the health care reform program he had established when he was governor of Massachusetts, which Obama copied for his own program. Romney promised to wipe out the Affordable Care Act of 2011 his first day in office. Romney's principal campaign argument was the need to cut all taxes across the board in the hope of stimulating investment in the economy, particularly by "job creators." Obama continued to call for raising taxes for all those who made more than $250,000 a year, with continued cuts for all others. New revenue would finance health care, education, and energy reform. The question of whether either set of plans would pay for new programs or resolve long-term deficits was never seriously debated. Rhetoric substituted for reason. Foreign policy was ignored.

The key to victory would be the swing states of North Carolina, Virginia, Florida, Nevada, Ohio, and Pennsylvania. Obama was ahead in those states with the rest of the country quite even until the first debate on October 3. Romney took an aggressive stance and carried the day against a passive president who never seemed to realize that he was onstage. He surely underestimated his opponent. He recovered in the next two debates, but lost ground in opinion polls.

Victory

The president won 332 electoral votes to Romney's 270. He won the popular vote with a rounded 62 to 58 million votes. Obama carried all the swing states, except North Carolina and Indiana. Republicans won 52 percent of men, 59 percent of whites, and 53 percent of those with incomes over $50,000, in addition to voters over sixty-five. Democrats won majorities among women, African Americans, Hispanics, Asians, and those from eighteen to thirty-seven, with a tie among thirty-four- to sixty-four-year-olds. These margins perhaps forecast the future of a white Republican minority and a varied and cosmopolitan Democratic majority. Republican polls underestimated the new majority.

Democrats won the Senate with fifty-five seats, including two independents. The Republicans won 233 House seats and the Democrats 195, with one or two outstanding. There are no Republican House seats in New England, and Republicans dominated safe Southern seats. It is difficult to imagine how the margins might be changed. One can see little incentive for House Republicans in safe seats to compromise with Obama. He cannot threaten them.

Politics Continues

The president and Congress faced a "fiscal cliff" after the election, because the Joint Select Committee on Deficit Reduction had failed to reach agreement. Domestic and military budgets were to be cut in half after Congress convened unless agreements on alternatives were made. Once again, Obama and Speaker John Boehner spoke in moderate terms of an agreement. The president called for a repeal of the Bush tax cuts for those taxpayers who earned more than $250,000 a year. There would have to be reductions in tax loopholes. New revenues would go toward deficit reduction and new programs. Tax rates would be lowered for all taxpayers. Deficits could not be faced without tax increases. Boehner said publicly that he was willing to raise new revenue through reducing tax rates and deductions without raising taxes. Tax increases would not be sufficient to pay for programs without big budget cuts. Both assumed that reform of entitlements had to be faced, though perhaps not immediately, although many Republicans insisted that Medicare, Medicaid, and Social Security would have to be cut now to forestall future bankruptcy in those programs. It was clear that Obama would have to find a new personal style of close talk and bargaining in working with congressional leaders. Compromise would be necessary, but neither side dared give up too much for fear of losing support on their left and right wings. And yet each side had to allow the other a partial victory in order for an agreement to be made. This was primarily Obama's responsibility. He had to offer the Republicans a face-saving proposal in which he could also win.

The president sent Vice President Biden to negotiate with Senate leaders on the last day of 2012. After intense negotiations, agreement was reached with minority leader Mitch McConnell to increase income and estate taxes on the rich. Unemployment benefits were extended for one year, as were Medicare payments to doctors. Spending cuts were delayed for two months. The plan passed the Senate with support from both parties. This pressured House Republicans to go along. Many resisted, but the Democrats threw their weight against a split Republican group to win passage.

Hard questions remained. The federal debt question was delayed. Spending cuts would have to be made, along with enough revenue to fund the government and Obama initiatives. Partisan issues were still deep.

CONCLUSION

Obama has been a perplexing president to many. He is cut from a different cloth from other modern presidents, not especially because of his race, but because of his personal history in Hawaii and Indonesia and his emotional detachment. Where does he stand? He is a progressive communitarian who values both the individual and the community. He is also a cautious progressive who sees reform as a gradual process, except when he wishes to take a big leap, as with health care reform. He may have made a mistake when he overloaded his legislative agenda in his first two years in office, initiating health care reform, regulatory reforms, and fresh departures in energy reform. It was too much for Congress and the public to accept, especially when the economy was so bad. He wanted to return the nation to its original ideals in a "redemptive" sense that would exceed the politics of bargaining. He called for collaboration between president and Congress that far exceeded the possible and underestimated the deep party polarization in the other branch. He relied on previous political success in this regard and had to face a rude awakening. He was determined to redeem the nation through moral appeals without an initial consideration of how to build winning coalitions out of diverse interests. He has had difficulty combining his rhetorical talents with the importance of sitting down with Congress and senators to do the gritty work of fashioning bills and laws. He does not enjoy this kind of work and relies on others to do it.

Obama had hoped to be a transforming president, like FDR, but the day for such presidents may be past, at least for some time. Democratic presidents have been reaching for, and failing to achieve, such goals since Lyndon Johnson. Johnson's dominance of Congress followed from a weak opponent in Barry Goldwater in the 1964 election and a presidential landslide. No such majority can be achieved in the present polarization of parties. Effective transactional leadership is more difficult than ever, but that is the best strategy. We return to our criteria for presidential leadership.

Context and Contingencies

The historical and political context has not been favorable to creative presidential leadership. Obama faced severe economic problems, but the recession was not nearly as awful as the depression that Franklin Roosevelt faced. Financial and business collapse was far more severe in the 1930s. Unemployment was much higher, but opposition to reform was much weaker, allowing FDR to have his way with Congress in his first term. Obama faced a much stronger antipathy to the power of the federal government, which had been building during the Reagan and Bush years. A conservative community of ideas and institutions had been marshaling its forces against government and was ready to fight big government with both barrels firing.

Talents and Skills

Obama is very intelligent and has a historical perspective that permits him to look ahead and see new possibilities. He articulates his hopes and dreams for the nation with eloquence. The reverse side is that he does not enjoy and is not good at close-order bargaining even with his allies, much less his opponents. Some of this ability, had he possessed it, might have permitted greater agreement on his major initiatives, although one cannot be sure. Congressional Republicans not only rejected his overtures as partisans, they also stood in ideological opposition.

Inexperience also mattered. Obama relied on Democratic congressional leaders to put the stimulus bill together, thus pandering to their constituency interests unduly. Too little was asked of congressional Republicans.

Did He Make a Difference?

Obama won two presidential elections and achieved major health care reform. He expanded AmeriCorps and increased money for national forests.

The Department of Education began a series of challenges to the states to improve the quality of public education. New regulations of financial institutions were passed into law, but not yet fully implemented. Innovative departures in energy development were begun but seemed to stall along the way because of the great costs and limited political support. Pay discrimination for women was banned and health insurance for children was increased. The most important problem was that unemployment fell only slightly. Obama has been unable to close the prison at Guantanamo. He failed to reconcile Israel and the Palestinians (though the principal responsibility remained with the two sets of leaders). The U.S. military withdrew from Iraq and will surely do so from Afghanistan by 2014. The regime of Afghanistan is weak, the government is corrupt and inadequate, and the Taliban, supported by Pakistan, may return. The gamble is that the regime will be able to hold together sufficiently to control the Taliban. New Arab regimes may be able to balance stability and provide some degree of authoritarian democracy, but their future is still uncertain. U.S. relations with Russia and China may stay stable, an Obama objective. There will be less aspiration to oversee the world through American intervention than in the Bush years.

Effectiveness

Obama has been a talented, eventful president with considerable achievement when he might have been a failure. He has stayed on a pragmatic even keel. That is all one could ask of a president in his time.

Obama's second inaugural address was a clear call for progressive policies on social justice and equality couched in an appeal to national unity. He sought unity behind progressive reform in line with his electoral victory and the victories of other progressive presidents. Second-term presidents have at best two years to achieve goals before they become lame ducks themselves. At this writing, Obama is on his way to making the most of that brief time with a renewed focus on major policy initiatives in the areas of immigration, gun control, and international security.

BIBLIOGRAPHICAL ESSAY

This chapter relies less on published material than previous chapters, because the scholarly research on Obama has necessarily been more limited. There are a few very good books, however. David Maraniss's biography, *Barack Obama: The Story* (2013), is a fine depiction of Obama's family origins and his life up until he went to Harvard Law School. Maraniss analyzes layer after layer of a young life so we see the adult man that Obama became. Obama is the "moviegoer," an acute observer of the life around him. The inner restraint and calm so evident in the mature politician is made clear. Yet also evident is the way he may act forcefully once it is clear to him what he wants to do. We can see why Obama is not a natural bargainer and coalition builder, even though he is a pragmatist who prefers to achieve his goals one step at a time. We see here the complexity of personality that may create the difficulties that others find in trying to understand him. He sees the many-sided world of life and politics, but not all those sides see him wholly. This is the single best portrayal of Obama currently published.

Obama's own books, *Dreams from My Father* (2004) and *The Audacity of Hope* (2008), are illustrations of James Kloppenberg's thesis of Obama's deep anchoring in both American idealism and pragmatism, as set forth in *Reading Obama: Dreams, Hope, and the American Political Tradition* (2012). He explains why Obama has confounded liberals by being a communitarian and thus able to incorporate a realism of uncertainty and compromise into his liberalism. At the same time, his conservative critics, who are too sanguine in their economic and moral individualism, do not understand his affirmation of community, which would restrain the disruptive effects of their ideologies. This may be one reason why Obama is hard for many Americans to understand, because our political culture lacks a communitarian dimension.

Stanley Renshon has written the most arresting thesis about Obama, depicting him as seeking "redemption" for his parents, himself, and the nation according to a strong idealistic conception of American purpose. In *Barack Obama and the Politics of Redemption* (2011), Renshon finds a leader who is driven by passion to realize the American dream as formulated by Lincoln and other prophets, and yet he understands the need to be practical always tugging at his coattails. Crisis presents a national leader with the chance to articulate and fulfill the dream anew. A president must perceive where he is in history and then seize the day for bold action. Renshon's concern is that Obama may reach for greater achievement than was practically possible and thus risk failure. He wrote before the first term was over and Obama was reelected. He would have the president temper his ambitions and depart from grandiosity in order to save his presidency. These concerns are applicable to a second term, and we will watch Obama accordingly.

Stephen Skowronek expresses the same concerns from a historical perspective. He does not think that Obama could be a transforming president because the historical situation will not permit it. *Presidential Leadership in Political Time* (2011) describes the conditions for the achievement for Presidents of Reconstruction. They have been Jefferson, Jackson, Lincoln, Franklin Roosevelt, and Reagan. These presidents challenge a declining party regime and offer new conditions for politics and policy. They are able to fashion new national political coalitions that will last some time until they are undercut by challenges as well, not from Presidents of Reconstruction, but from less ambitious regimes. It is unlikely that Obama can achieve Reconstruction, because partisan politics are too polarized and the representation of organized interests is so strong and yet fragmented. Potential national partisan coalition is far distant. The Republicans after Reagan have tried repeatedly and failed to do so. One can see the possibilities of a new national coalition in Obama's 2012 election arising from a group of minorities against a shrinking older white Republican majority, but only time will tell.

Jonathan Alter's *The Promise: President Obama, Year One* (2010), is the best journalistic study of Obama as president. Alter reports events accurately and is restrained in his interpretations and judgments. One hopes that he will complete his study.

In *Bending History: Barack Obama's Foreign Policy* (2012), Martin Indyk et al. have written good interpretive essays covering foreign policy up to the past year. They describe a president who reversed the bellicose rhetoric of George W. Bush about U.S. power to push the world toward democracy. Yet Obama has increased some forms of military technology, particularly deadly drones, against al Qaeda leaders with little restraint. We have thus managed to kill many Afghans and Pakistanis, causing difficulties with the governments of Afghanistan and Pakistan, who have been uncooperative in our wars against al Qaeda and the Taliban. The broad thesis of the book is that Obama's foreign policy around the world has been cool and practical without any great strategic imagination. But the world is not friendly to American aspirations, in any event.

Bob Woodward gives a blow-by-blow description of the president's military decisions about the American role in Afghanistan in *Obama's Wars* (2011). Very close detailed attention is given to the process, managed through the National Security Council, in which the president sought and received advice about alternative military paths for Afghanistan. The central struggle was between the high military and White House advisers, the hawks and the doves. The hawks wanted to send 40,000 fresh troops and the doves sought a lower figure, perhaps half as many. The doves, particularly Vice President Joe Biden, were skeptical about whether the Taliban could be completely defeated and thought in terms of various fallback strategies. The president was unhappy with the generals because they kept returning with the same advice, even after being turned down. Finally, Obama and Secretary of Defense Robert Gates settled on a moderate commitment, with clear plans for a future withdrawal. Woodward, relying on interviews, presents a rich description of bureaucratic politics.

Presidential Leadership Revisited

Character: "Unhappy the land that has no heroes."
Galileo: "Unhappy the land that has need of heroes."
—*Bertolt Brecht,* Galileo

Democracies embody a dilemma. They sometimes need leaders who are event-making leaders, most often at critical times in history. The most successful event-making presidents have respected and worked with constitutional institutions and not overreached to any great extent, the three exemplary examples being Washington, Lincoln, and Franklin Roosevelt. Eventful leaders, however, match the logic of American constitutional institutions even better because they make no attempt to overpower checks and balances as some event-making presidents do. The dilemma presents itself, however, if eventful leaders are politically ineffective. Then the popular clamor for heroes and greatness swells. American myths reinforce the clamor. Just look at the faces on Mt. Rushmore. An even greater danger occurs when Congress and even the Supreme Court sense the clamor and subordinate themselves unduly to the leadership of presidents. Effective government depends upon healthy constitutional balance. James Madison wrote in Federalist Papers 10 and 51, respectively, that "enlightened statesmen will not always be at the helm" and therefore constitutions must make sure that "ambition must counteract ambition."

Making a Difference

We have compared ten presidents with a number of questions in mind. The first question is whether presidents make significant differences in historical events? The approach has been to examine important actions of presidents in history that may be attributed to their creativity. Making a difference may be for good or for ill, depending upon the consequences. Event-making leaders who have made a significant difference are Johnson, Nixon, Reagan, and George W. Bush.

Event-Making Presidents

Domestic reform, following on John Kennedy's leadership, would have taken place without Johnson, but he added a tempo and velocity that was unique in his leadership of Congress. His political skills were especially important in 1964 when Congress passed the civil rights bill, the tax cut, and the antipoverty law. There is much debate about whether Johnson was a prisoner of politics in his decision to intervene in Vietnam, but I believe that he had leeway and decided to intervene as an act of will.

Nixon certainly made a difference as he worked to create a "détente" with China and the Soviet Union. His decision to fight on in Vietnam for four years was also an act of will. The pathos of Watergate was a direct extension of his lack of trust in normal, democratic politics.

Reagan helped to end the cold war, working with Mikhail Gorbachev. He created a new pattern of politics by presenting a conservative alternative to liberalism that influenced a new political generation and redirected the Republican Party. His default was his sacrifice of prudent economic policy to both ideology and political advantage. The Iran-Contra affair was a serious constitutional crisis which, unlike Watergate, was a direct abuse of governmental power in behalf of public policy.

George W. Bush's concerted domestic strategy was to fulfill the Reagan promise by creating a coalition of the right on the principle of a majority of 50 percent plus one in Congress and among the public, and he achieved a semblance of that goal until the congressional elections of 2006 when the Democrats captured congressional majorities. His response to the tragedy of 9/11 unified the nation and the subsequent short-term victory in Afghanistan was a mark of leadership. The decision to fight in Iraq was a matter of choice rather than necessity, as were the mistakes made in the execution of both wars. The subsequent management of war from Washington, both in the White House and the Department of Defense, was so slipshod as to verge on incompetence. Excessive tax cuts in wartime, which contributed to an increasingly uneven distribution of wealth among Americans, were unwarranted. Demands for excessive power over the conduct of national security affairs strained the limits of constitutionality. The failures of the administration in its lackluster response to the tragedy of Katrina, the hurricane that demolished New Orleans, reinforced the increasing public concern about incompetence. The backlash came in the 2006 congressional election, when the Republicans lost control of Congress, in part because of the unpopularity of the war in Iraq and the president who made it.

Eventful Presidents

John Kennedy was a practical reformer who moved prudently toward domestic policy goals that he would surely have achieved, to a considerable extent, had he lived and been reelected president. He floundered about Vietnam but he did not flounder alone. He did make an extraordinary difference in his management of the Cuban Missile Crisis. His intelligence, detachment, and prudence made all the difference as he made one practical decision after another, often against the strong advocates of massive air strikes or the invasion of Cuba. His critics who advocated stronger military action were proved wrong when he got Khrushchev to back down and remove the missiles. If Khrushchev had not been cooperative, Kennedy might have taken stronger action, but it would surely have been prudent and contained.

Gerald Ford's contribution was simply to be himself. He restored an era of good feeling. His domestic and foreign policies were conventional and reasonable but he was undermined by challenges from the right and the left with no center to stand on.

Jimmy Carter had major achievements, particularly the Panama Canal treaties and the Camp David agreement between Israel and Egypt. A more skillful politician, wise in the ways of Washington and with a stronger public persona, might have survived into a second term, but he was a Democratic president as the Democratic coalition was collapsing.

George H. W. Bush was a good president but a poor domestic politician, and his significant foreign policy achievements were undercut by his failure to understand electoral politics.

Bill Clinton wanted to be an event-making president in the worst way, but learned that he would have to settle for less, and adapted well, with a good many achievements. His flaws of character tarnished his presidency and, perhaps, precluded some policy achievements. But the times were not ripe for heroic leadership.

Barack Obama intended to be a transforming president who would lead an era of reform. His one major achievement was health care reform, which just scraped through after the 2010 congressional election almost killed it. Partisan polarization thereafter weakened his leadership in Congress.

How do these conclusions match the conventional idea that presidents make a difference only at the margins? The four event-making leaders reached beyond the margins in their crucial decisions. The six eventful presidents varied in this regard but Kennedy, Carter, Clinton, and Obama all made important differences in single events in ways that cannot be dismissed as at the margins.

National security policy has afforded a greater scope for presidential action, for better or for worse. The Cuban Missile Crisis, the Vietnam War, "détente," Camp David, the resolution of the cold war, Watergate, Iran-Contra, and the war in Iraq have been major policy events. Policy achievements in domestic affairs are more likely to follow from eventful leadership because the constitutional constraints on presidential action are greater.

The fact that abuses of power occur most often in national security policy might cause one to shift the responsibility from presidents to the policy arena itself, which thrives on secrecy and closed circles of decision making. But this makes the character of presidents even more important. Hard questions about the lack of critical oversight by Congress and the courts on the national security executive must also be posed. The myths of presidential "greatness," combined with the invocation of American nationalism, reinforce such passivity.

SKILL IN CONTEXT

What was the relationship between skill and context in making a difference for all of these presidents?

Event-Making Presidents

Johnson, Nixon, Reagan, and George W. Bush brought considerable skills of political leadership to relatively favorable historical and political contexts. Johnson took advantage of rising reform politics, and his great skills of legislative leadership were perfectly matched to the task. However, he was not well prepared for the decisions he would face about Vietnam. He thought that he could use force to bargain with the leaders of North Vietnam, much as he had with opponents at home, but this belief was based on ignorance. At the end of the day, his prolonged refusal to reconsider his policies in Vietnam put the nation through an ordeal that damaged the comity of American politics and policy for a generation.

Nixon's chief skill was the ability to think strategically, in the sense that he could see a big picture of more stable relations among the great powers, particularly in his wish to open relations with China. He initially wanted Soviet and Chinese help in getting out of Vietnam. This failed, but in the process he began to see the possibility of stable relationships with the two major powers. The time was ripe for the stabilization of great-power relations that he blessed with the term "détente." However, his political strategic thinking was also weak in his refusal to try to work out an early compromise with North Vietnam on the status of the South. And his ambitious plans in 1973 for reorganizing American government were politically unrealistic and constitutionally questionable. Nixon's abilities were not accompanied by an understanding of democratic politics. He knew only about elections, not about accommodation and compromise. He destroyed his presidency as a result.

Reagan's skills were perfectly suited for his opportunities. He knew how to set broad goals, sell those goals to the public, and find subordinates to implement them. The decline of the Democratic coalition, unhappiness with Jimmy Carter, and the surge of conservative ideals among Republican politicians were all backdrops for innovative leadership. He knew what he wanted from the Soviet Union and had a clear plan to get it, through an arms buildup and then through negotiation. He was lucky to find Gorbachev as a partner. Otherwise little would have happened, and we might see Reagan differently. Reagan was a romantic and he often lost touch with practical things; in his economic policies, in his support for the Contras in Nicaragua, which led directly to the Iran-Contra scandal, and his dream of a Strategic Defense Initiative.

George W. Bush did not find his presidential legs until September 11, 2001, when terrorists destroyed the World Trade Center and attacked the Pentagon. He turned himself into a warrior president, which seemed to fit his personality quite well. In the eyes of his critics, he carried the warrior role beyond the norms of democratic politics. He came out of Texas like a thunderbolt determined to put a "revolutionary" stamp on politics and policy. As a result, he was the most divisive president of modern times and may never have discovered that his strategy for presidential leadership was hollow. Some of his close advisers saw the American defeat in Vietnam as a sign of national weakness that could be redressed in Iraq. They eventually found themselves in the same kind of unwinnable war that Johnson faced.

Eventful Presidents

The six eventful presidents reveal variegated patterns of the relation of skills to context.

Kennedy was a man of practical reason well suited to the emerging climate of domestic reform. He entered office as a cold warrior but, after the shock of the Cuban Missile Crisis, sought a way out of cold war tensions. His very rationality could not seem to comprehend the baroque character of Vietnam.

Ford had the skills of a congressional politician that actually served him well as president in his openness and common sense. But the partisan fevers of the times overwhelmed him as president.

Carter's skills of intelligence, homework, and diligence achieved some signal victories, but he was going against the political grain in every instance. He tried to turn his coalition around, but the ship was too large and too resistant.

George H. W. Bush was an underrated president. He guided a talented and experienced foreign policy team to work out long-term agreements on disarmament with Soviet leaders and did so without fanfare. This was quiet and effective leadership but there was an element of Reconstruction. He was working within the grain of existing politics.

Clinton's courage in taking on the deficit was a significant achievement. Personal political skill was required for persuasion, and he used it effectively. He had the good sense to follow the advice he received about both domestic and international economic policies, but clarity of mind about the problems was more important than any particular political skills. His tactical skills were most useful to him as he bargained to wring compromise agreements out of congressional Democrats and Republicans, to the complete satisfaction of neither.

Obama is not very good at coalition building, but party polarization has been a much stronger impediment to legislative success.

EFFECTIVENESS

We have described the individual political skills of each of the ten presidents. Is it possible to develop general standards for effectiveness in presidents? I suggest five benchmarks:

1. The first is to have a policy vision and the ability to read the historical context realistically in terms of that vision and set one's goals accordingly. One must have a broad policy vision, but it must match what is politically possible.

2. A related quality is prudence, the ability to know how far one may push and when to trim or pull back. This is a personal virtue. Michael Oakeshott, a British political theorist, makes a distinction between those who operate by faith that their goals can be achieved and those who are skeptical that any goals can be achieved. The golden mean is somewhere in the middle in a balance between faith and skepticism, and the middle is not always obvious. One must have the prudence to sense it.[1]

3. A third sign of effectiveness is the personal ability to persuade others to join in one's purposes and to accommodate the purposes of others. All the standard political abilities—of rhetoric, coalition building, and bargaining—belong here.

4. A fourth is "emotional intelligence" in which the ability to read others, by observation and listening, is joined to personal emotional security so that conflict and issues are not personalized.[2]

5. I would add a fifth attribute—not a skill, but a strong personal commitment to constitutional government. By this I mean that the president and his lieutenants would respect constitutional limits on their actions. But I also mean a respect for Madison's insight in Federalist 10 that the new government would not work unless the representatives of the people distilled the conflicts they represented into a national interest. The logic of the Constitution requires collaboration out of conflict. We must insist that presidents act as unifiers, in that sense, rather than dividers.

Presidents must lead forcefully. They dare not be passive. But they must also understand that the larger the coalitions they can build behind their policies, they greater they will ensure the long-term achievement and endurance of those policies. Good policy is not made by narrow coalitions. This is not always possible, as the histories in this book attest. But the lesson for me is that presidents confronted with strong partisan disagreement should not attempt to force fundamental change. By the same token, presidents with large, temporary majorities must be careful not to ask for too much, because the foundations of their achievements may not be solid.

Of all these skills and benchmarks, prudence is the hallmark of effective presidents. Abraham Lincoln, our greatest president, moved prudently at every step of the way in winning and keeping support for the war and in gradually advancing the freedom of the slaves. The result was practical reason and moral greatness. How did the ten presidents match these criteria for presidential effectiveness?

All but perhaps Ford and George H. W. Bush had general policy visions that they brought into the presidency with them. Ford might have developed one in a second term, and Bush swept into office as Reagan's legatee. Kennedy and Clinton get high marks for the ability to read the historical context clearly. They were well anchored in the politics of give and take, and at matching goals to possibilities. Carter was initially less realistic about politics in Washington and then was overtaken by events. Obama presumed more cooperation from Republicans than was possible.

The event-making presidents exaggerated what might have been achieved. Johnson was astute enough to understand that his influence in Congress would be temporary and he drove that influence to the hilt. He was a political realist. But he did not know how to read the situation in Vietnam clearly, even though he may have read it more clearly than his immediate aides. Again, Nixon's strategic vision was strong, but his lack of appreciation for the limits of presidential action in American politics destroyed his presidency. George W. Bush was determined on his domestic and national security visions. His realism in calculating his leverage to dominate others worked for a time but collapsed in his second term. Ronald Reagan comes off better than the others. He was a good democratic politician who could work with opponents. This ability worked with Gorbachev and permitted him to override opposition among Republicans. His failing was in his belief that a conservative policy coalition could be created, when in fact only a conservative movement was reinforced.

The eventful presidents were generally more prudent in their leadership than the event-making presidents. They had less latitude with which to act. But as individuals they did not make claims to greatness as the event-making leaders did. Kennedy, Clinton, and Obama, who would have liked to be great Democratic presidents on the model of Franklin Roosevelt, came to understand that they would have to be less than that to be effective leaders.

Johnson, Nixon, and George W. Bush were realists in the ability to calculate the main chance but not prudent in their personal or their political makeup. Reagan stands alone here. His rhetoric was far more extreme than his actions.

Only a few of these men were highly persuasive as persons. Johnson, Reagan, and Clinton had extraordinary qualities of persuasiveness. Nixon and George W. Bush were good with their own political coalitions, but each man relied on levers of official power more than persuasiveness to achieve their goals. The other eventful presidents did not have outstanding persuasive skills, and this suggests that such skills are fairly rare.

The eventful presidents all get high marks for emotional intelligence. I would not give such marks to Johnson or Nixon. George W. Bush is a self-confident person and seems to be well grounded emotionally. His more extreme actions would appear to be based on beliefs rather than defensiveness. Of the four, Reagan was the most emotionally healthy.

Finally, and this is becoming a repetitive pattern: Johnson, Nixon, and George W. Bush were quite ready to run up against and over the Constitution when it served their purposes. Johnson's sins were the least. The Gulf of Tonkin Resolution was misused, and too much was claimed for it, and the president and his aides misled the public about the war. But these were violations of constitutional morality rather than law. Nixon broke the law pure and simple. George W. Bush made extreme claims to executive authority that raised a number of constitutional questions, many of which were not resolved during his presidency. Reagan's lapse in the Iran-Contra matter permitted two violations of the law. The law required him to inform the Congress when he sold weapons to Iran, a terrorist nation, and he did not do so. The diversion of funds by his staff to the Contras was illegal and he claimed not to know. But he did know that the same staff was raising private funds for the same purpose.

EVENTS, EFFECTIVENESS, AND DEMOCRACY

American democracy does not require that all presidents be event-making. The three great presidents in our history—Washington, Lincoln, and Franklin Roosevelt—served in times of great national crisis. Their talents were crucial to the resolution of those crises. Our four event-making presidents resolved serious problems but also created them in their ambition to make marks for greatness. I do not think that constitutional democracy requires event-making presidents except in times of great national crisis. Great leaders then fight their way to the top and are recognized as such.

Perhaps it is time to cast aside the belief that presidents must be "great" in favor of the idea that they should be good political leaders who know how to work with others within our institutions. We need a normative conception of presidential leadership, one that does not focus on presidential power, as so much popular literature does, but calls for the ability to lead through persuasion and focuses on policy goals. We must value "democratic character" in our presidents and must devalue vainglory and exaggerated promises, and look for emotional security. The primary task of the American president is to teach the American people about reality. Politics is about competing conceptions of reality and false conceptions do us harm in the end, whereas approximations of reality bring us closer to our goals. I see the ability to achieve a balance between purpose and prudence as the most important virtue of any president. It may be thought necessary at times to leap beyond prudence to achieve great goals. But such leaps may be disasters. Prudence is not the same thing as caution or reluctance to act. It is the virtue of acting with uncertain knowledge with the realization that one may be mistaken and the detachment that permits correction and adjustment if the action proves to be folly.

This insight does not match our political culture in which our national mythologies have idealized presidents. Presidents stand in the shadows of exemplars from the past. The mass media both idealizes and destroys presidents, according to false standards for presidential greatness. The public is more realistic in that presidents are assessed by the effectiveness of their policies, and this is as it should be, but the public may also be swept up into unrealistic judgments by the manipulations of the mass media by politicians and the rhetoric of presidents. The mythology of the heroic presidency is too strong to be replaced by a more workaday conception. The best one can do is write and talk about presidents in realistic terms as an antidote to myth.

One wonders if we learn from history. During the lifetime of this author, two tragedies have been imposed upon the nation by presidents: the wars in Vietnam and Iraq. Both wars were justified as necessity when, in fact, they were actions of choice. Once commitments were made, they could not be undone because the doctrine of necessity became a trap. Presidents find it difficult to admit major mistakes without repudiating their presidencies. Rhetoric and reality diverge and doctrine is misused as patriotism in partisan ways. Presidents eventually fail from the tragedies they create and the uncertain search for effectiveness in the presidency begins anew.

Notes

Notes to Chapter One

1. Erwin C. Hargrove and Samuel A. Morley, eds., *The President and the Council of Economic Advisers: Interviews with CEA Chairmen* (1984), 175.

2. John Lewis Gaddis, *Strategies of Containment: A Critical Appraisal of American National Security Policy during the Cold War* (New York: Oxford, 2005), 208.

3. William Taubman, *Khrushchev: The Man and His Era* (New York: W. W. Norton, 2003), 531–532.

4. James Blight, *The Shattered Crystal Ball: Fear and Learning in the Cuban Missile Crisis* (Lanham, MD: Rowman and Littlefield, 1990), 7.

5. Robert S. McNamara, with Bryan Van De Mark, *In Retrospect: The Tragedy and Lessons of Vietnam* (New York: Times Books, 1995), 70.

6. Charles E. Bohlen, quoted by Michael Beschloss, *The Crisis Years, Kennedy and Khrushchev, 1960–1963* (New York: Harper Collins, 1991), 73–74.

7. Ibid.

Notes to Chapter Two

1. Carl Albert, June 10, 1969, in Robert Lester, *Oral Histories of the Johnson Administration* (Austin: University of Texas, LBJ Library, 1963), 6.

2. Ibid.

3. Erwin C. Hargrove and Samuel Morley, eds., *The President and the Council of Economic Advisers: Interviews with CEA Chairmen* (Boulder, CO: Westview Press, 1984), 278. Personal communication, Wilbur Cohen, 1987.

4. Joseph Califano, *The Triumph and Tragedy of Lyndon Johnson: The White House Years* (New York: Simon and Schuster, 1991), 338.

5. Paul Conkin, *Big Daddy from the Pedernales: Lyndon Baines Johnson* (Boston: Twayne, 1986), 194.

6. Michael Beschloss, ed., *Taking Charge: The Johnson White House Tapes, 1963–1964* (New York: Simon and Schuster, 1997), 529–530.

7. Michael Beschloss, ed., *Reaching for Glory: Lyndon Johnson's Secret White House Tapes, 1964–1965* (New York: Simon and Schuster, 2001), 120–122.

8. Ibid., 227.

9. George Meany, August 4, 1969, in Lester, *Oral Histories of the Johnson Administration*, 7.

10. Joseph A. Califano Jr., June 11, 1973, in Lester, *Oral Histories of the Johnson Administration*, 25.

11. James H. Rowe Jr., September 16, 1969, in Lester, *Oral Histories of the Johnson Administration*, 4.

12. Beschloss, *Taking Charge*, 350.

13. Hargrove and Morley, *The President and the Council of Economic Advisers*, 177, 223–224.

14. Beschloss, *Taking Charge*, 177–178.

15. Ibid., 178.

16. Ibid., 435.

17. Jonathan Rosenburg and Zachary Karabell, eds., *Kennedy, Johnson and the Quest for Justice: The Civil Rights Tapes* (Charlottesville, VA: Millar Center, 2003).

18. Russell Riley, *The Presidency and the Politics of Racial Inequality* (New York: Columbia University Press, 1999), 233.

19. Beschloss, *Taking Charge*, 211.

20. Clinton Rossiter, speech at Brown University, October 1964.

21. Beschloss, *Taking Charge*, 346.

22. George McT. Kahin, *Intervention*, 1986, 374–376.

23. Yuen Khong, *Analogies at War: Korea, Munich, Diem Bien Phu, and Vietnam Decisions of 1965* (Princeton, NJ: Princeton University Press, 1992), 97.

24. John Burke and Fred I. Greenstein, with Larry Berman and Richard Immerman, *How Presidents Test Reality: Decisions on Vietnam, 1954 and 1965* (New York: Russell Sage Foundation, 1989).

25. Robert McNamara, *In Retrospect: The Tragedy and Lessons of Vietnam* (New York: Times Books, 1995).

26. Leslie Gelb with Richard Betts, *The Irony of Vietnam: The System Worked* (Washington, DC: Brookings Institution, 2000).

Notes to Chapter Three

1. Tom Wicker, *One of Us: Richard Nixon and the American Dream* (New York: Random House, 1991), 2.

2. H. R. Haldeman, *The Haldeman Diaries: Inside the Nixon White House* (New York: Putnam, 1994), 59.

3. Richard M. Nixon, *RN: The Memoirs of Richard Nixon* (New York: Grosset and Dunlap, 1978), 424.

4. Haldeman, *The Haldeman Diaries*, 424.

5. Murray Weidenbaum, personal communication.

6. Stephen Ambrose, *Nixon: The Triumph of a Politician* (New York: Simon and Schuster, 1989).

7. Erwin C. Hargrove and Samuel A. Morley, *The President and the Council of Economic Advisers: Interviews with CEA Chairmen* (1984).

8. Nixon, *RN*, 518.

9. Haldeman, *The Haldeman Diaries*, 424.

10. Ibid., 326.

11. Nixon, *RN*, 602.

12. Ibid., 607.

13. Ibid., 736.

14. Ibid., 615.

15. Ibid., 588.

16. Ibid., 670.

17. Mason, *Richard Nixon and the Quest for a New Majority Majority* (Chapel Hill: University of North Carolina Press, 2004), 161.

18. William Safire, *Before the Fall: An Insider's View of the Pre-Watergate White House* (New York: Doubleday, 2005) 313.

19. Henry Kissinger, *Ending the Vietnam War: A History of America's Involvement in and Extrication from the Vietnam War* (New York: Simon and Schuster, 2003), 382.

20. Haldeman, *The Haldeman Diaries*, 326.

21. Nixon, *RN*, 978.

22. Ibid., 850.

23. Safire, *Before the Fall*, 475.

24. Nixon, *RN*, 976.

25. Haldeman, *The Haldeman Diaries*, 472.

NOTES TO CHAPTER FOUR

1. David Gergen, *Eyewitness to Power: The Essence of Leadership, Nixon to Clinton* (New York: Simon and Schuster, 2000), 141.

2. Alan Greenspan, quoted in Erwin C. Hargrove and Samuel A. Morley, *The President and the Council of Economic Advisers: Interviews with CEA Chairmen* (Boulder, CO: Westview, 1984), 416.

3. Ibid., 411.

4. Ibid., 410.

5. Ibid.

6. John Robert Greene, *The Presidency of Gerald Ford* (1995), 79–80.

7. Hargrove and Morley, *The President and the Council of Economic Advisers*, 412.

8. Gerald Ford, *A Time to Heal* (New York: Harper and Row, 1979), 346.

9. Ibid, 380.

10. John Robert Greene, *A Nice Person Who Worked at the Job: The Dilemma of the Ford Image in Gerald R. Ford and the Politics of Post-Watergate America*, Bernard J. Firestone and Alexei Ugrinsky, eds. (Westport, CT: Greenwood Press, 1993), 269.

NOTES TO CHAPTER FIVE

1. Steven H. Hochman et al., "Interview with Jimmy Carter," November 29, 1982. Miller Center Interviews, Carter Presidency Project, in Don Richardson, ed., *Conversations with Carter* (Boulder, CO: Lynne Rienner Publishers, 1998), 226.

2. Jimmy Carter interview, Carter Presidency Project, vol. 19. Jimmy Carter Library, Atlanta, Georgia, 70, 72.

3. Jimmy Carter interview with the editors of *U.S. News and World Report*, September 13, 1976, quoted in Richardson, ed., *Conversations with Carter*, 23–24.

4. Hochman et al., in Richardson, ed., *Conversations with Carter*, 227.

5. Carter Presidential Project, vol. 19. Jimmy Carter Library, Atlanta, Georgia, 69.

6. Jimmy Carter, *Keeping Faith: Memoirs of a President* (New York: Bantam, 1982), 77–78.

7. John P. Frendreis and Raymond Tatalovich, *The Modern Presidency and Economic Policy* (1994).

8. Burton Kaufman and Scott Kaufman, *The Presidency of James Earl Carter, Jr.* (Lawrence: University Press of Kansas, 2006), 167.

9. Erwin C. Hargrove and Samuel A. Morley, *The President and the Council of Economic Advisers: Interviews with CEA Chairmen* (Boulder, CO: Westview, 1984), 493.

10. Hochman et al., "Interview with Jimmy Carter," 225.

11. William Quandt quoted in Herbert D. Rosenbaum and Alexj Ugrinsky, eds., *Jimmy Carter: Foreign Policy and Post-Presidential Years* (Westport, CT: Greenwood, 1994), 62.

12. Ibid.

13. Alexander Moens, *Foreign Policy under Carter: Testing Multiple Advocacy Decision Making* (Boulder, CO: Westview, 1990), 79.

14. George C. Edwards, *Presidential Approval: A Sourcebook* (Baltimore, MD: Johns Hopkins University Press, 1990), 111, Table 6.1.

15. John Anthony Maltese, "'Rafshoonness': The Effort to Control the Communications Agenda of the Carter Administration," in Rosenbaum and Ugrinsky, eds., *The Presidency and Domestic Policies of Jimmy Carter* (Westport, CT: Greenwood, 1994), 442.

16. John Dumbrell, *The Carter Presidency: A Reevaluation* (New York: Manchester University Press, 1995), 50.

17. Richardson, *Conversations with Carter*, 3.

NOTES TO CHAPTER SIX

1. David Stockman, *The Triumph of Politics: Why the Reagan Revolution Failed* (New York: Harper and Row, 1986).

2. John W. Sloan, *The Reagan Effect: Economics in Presidential Leadership* (Lawrence: University Press of Kansas, 1999), 145.

3. Richard Darman, *Who's in Control? Polar Politics and the Sensible Center* (New York: Simon and Schuster, 1996), 101.

4. Ibid., 120.

5. Herbert Stein, *Presidential Economics: The Making of Economic Policy from Roosevelt to Clinton* (Washington, DC: American Enterprise Institute, 1994), 232–233.

6. William Niskanen, *Reaganomics: An Insider's Account of the Policies and the People* (New York: Oxford University Press, 1988), 300.

7. Ibid., 33.

8. Lou Cannon, *President Reagan: The Role of a Lifetime* (New York: Simon and Schuster, 1991), 169.

9. Gary Wills, *Reagan's America* (New York: Penguin, 1988), 424–427.

10. Cannon, *President Reagan*, 290.

11. George Shultz, *Turmoil and Triumph: My Years as Secretary of State* (New York: Scribners, 1993), 576.

12. Ibid., 601–602.

13. Ron Suskind, *The Pride of Loyalty: George W. Bush and the Education of Paul O'Neill* (2004).

NOTES TO CHAPTER SEVEN

1. David Mervin, *George Bush and the Guardianship Presidency* (New York: St. Martin's Press, 1999), 21.

2. George Bush and Brent Scowcroft, *A World Transformed* (New York: Knopf, 1998), 35.

3. Dan Quayle, *Standing Firm: A Vice Presidential Memoir* (New York: HarperCollins, 1994), 93–94.

4. Bush and Scowcroft, *A World Transformed*, 380.

5. Steven Hurst, *The Foreign Policy of the Bush Administration: In Search of a New World Order* (New York: Cassell, 1999), ch. 8.

6. Bush and Scowcroft, *A World Transformed*, 35.

7. Thomas Preston, *The President and His Inner Circle, Leadership Style and the Advisory Process in Foreign Affairs* (New York: Columbia University Press, 2001), 195.

8. James A. Baker III, with Thomas M. Defrank, *The Politics of Diplomacy: Revolution, War, and Peace, 1989–1992* (New York: Putnam, 1995), 168.

9. The following section on Bush and Gorbachev relies heavily on Bush and Scowcroft, Baker, and Michael Beschloss and Strobe Talbott, *At the Highest Levels: The Inside Story of the End of the Cold War* (Boston: Little, Brown, 1993), and Robert M. Gates, *From the Shadows: The Ultimate Insider's Story of Five Presidents and How They Won the Cold War* (New York: Simon and Schuster, 1996).

10. Bush and Scowcroft, *A World Transformed*.

11. Baker, *The Politics of Diplomacy*, 277.

12. Bush and Scowcroft, *A World Transformed*, 374–375.

13. Ibid., 418.

14. Robert W. Tucker and David C. Hendrickson, *The Imperial Temptation: The New World Order and America's Purpose* (New York: Council on Foreign Relations, 1992).

15. Gates, *From the Shadows*, 486.

NOTES TO CHAPTER EIGHT

1. Paul J. Quirk and William Cunion, "Clinton Domestic Policy: The Lessons of a 'New Democrat,'" in Colin Campbell and Bert A. Rockman, eds., *The Clinton Legacy* (New York: Chatham House, 2000).
2. Bill Clinton, *My Life* (New York: Knopf, 2004), 7.
3. Ibid., 87.
4. Ibid., 45.
5. Ibid., 78.
6. Ibid., 228.
7. Ibid., 263.
8. Ibid., 477.
9. Ibid., 577.
10. Elizabeth Drew, *On the Edge: The Clinton Presidency* (New York: Simon and Schuster, 1994), 66.
11. John Harris, *The Survivor: Bill Clinton in the White House* (New York: Random House, 2005), 260–261.
12. Bill Clinton, *My Life*, 504.
13. Strobe Talbott, *The Russia Hand: A Memoir of Presidential Diplomacy* (New York: Random House, 2002), 285.
14. Ibid., 268.
15. Bill Clinton, *My Life*, 552–553.
16. John Harris, *The Survivor*, 129.
17. Ibid., 415–416.
18. David Gergen, *Eyewitness to Power: The Essence of Leadership from Nixon to Clinton* (New York: Simon and Schuster, 2000).

NOTES TO CHAPTER NINE

1. George W. Bush, *A Charge to Keep* (New York: William Morrow, 1999), 186.
2. Ron Suskind, *The Price of Loyalty: George W. Bush and the Education of Paul O'Neill* (New York: Simon and Schuster, 2004), 28.
3. Bush, *A Charge to Keep*, 6.
4. Joel Aberbach, "The State of the Contemporary American Presidency: Or, Is Bush II Actually Ronald Reagan's Heir?" Chapter 3 in Colin Campbell and Bert Rockman, eds., *The George W. Bush Presidency: Appraisals and Prospects* (Washington, DC: Congressional Quarterly Press, 2003).
5. Suskind, *The Price of Loyalty*, 5.
6. John P. Friendreis and Raymond Tatalovich, *The Modern Presidency and Economic Policy* (Itasca, IL: F. E. Peacock, 1991), 229.
7. Allen Schick, "Bush's Budget Problem," Chapter 4 in Fred I. Greenstein, ed., *The George W. Bush Presidency: An Early Assessment* (Baltimore: Johns Hopkins University Press, 2003), 95.
8. Ron Suskind, *The Price of Loyalty*, 117.
9. Ibid., 162.

10. Ibid., 291.

11. Shick, "Bush's Budget Problems," 80.

12. Bob Woodward, *Bush at War* (New York: Simon and Schuster, 2002), 168.

13. Ibid., 74.

14. Ibid., 342.

15. Bob Woodward, *Plan of Attack* (New York: Simon and Schuster, 2004), 426.

16. Ibid., 343.

17. Ivo H. Daalder and James M. Lindsay, "Bush's Foreign Policy Revolution," in Greenstein, *The George W. Bush Presidency*, 125.

18. James Risen, *State of War: The Secret History of the CIA and the Bush Administration* (New York: Free Press, 2006), 64; Woodward, *Plan of Attack*, 164.

19. Michael R. Gordon and Bernard E. Trainor, *Cobra II: The Inside Story of the Invasion and Occupation of Iraq* (New York: Pantheon Books, 2006), 102.

20. Woodward, *Plan of Attack*.

21. John Prados, *Hoodwinked: The Documents that Reveal How Bush Sold Us a War* (New York: New Press, 2004), 93–99, 102.

22. Paul R. Pillar, "Intelligence Policy and the War in Iraq," *Foreign Affairs* (March/April 2006): 16.

23. Ibid., 18.

24. Todd S. Purdum, *A Time for Choosing: America's War in Iraq* (New York: Times Books/Henry Holt, 2003), 89; Woodward, *Plan of Attack*, 239.

25. Ibid., 21–22.

26. James Bamford, *A Pretext for War* (New York: Doubleday, 2004), 325.

27. Con Coughlin, *American Ally: Tony Blair and the War on Terror* (New York: HarperCollins, 2006).

28. Mark Danner, *The Secret Way to War: The Downing Street Memo and the Iraq War's Buried History* (New York: New York Review of Books, 2006), 7, 9–11.

29. George Packer, *The Assassin's Gate: America in Iraq* (New York: Farrar, Strauss, and Giroux, 2005), 46.

30. Bamford, *A Pretext for War*, 360.

31. Richard E. Neustadt, *Presidential Power and the Modern Presidents: The Politics of Leadership from Roosevelt to Reagan* (New York: Free Press, 1990).

32. Packer, *The Assassin's Gate*, 390.

33. Ivo H. Daalder and James M. Lindsay, *America Unbound: The Bush Revolution in Foreign Policy* (Washington, DC: Brookings Institution, 2003), 4.

34. Nicholas Lehmann, "Remember the Alamo: How George W. Bush Reinvented Himself," *New Yorker* (October 18, 2004): 158.

35. Ibid., 157.

36. Mark Danner, "How Bush Really Won," *New York Review of Books* (January 13, 2005): 150.

37. Jim Rutenberg, *New York Times*, October 26, 2006.

38. John Owens, "Presidential Power and Congressional Acquiescence in the 'War' on Terrorism: A New Constitutional Equilibrium?" unpublished paper, Department of Politics, Essex University, Great Britain, 13.

39. Elizabeth Drew, "Power Grab," *New York Review of Books* (June 22, 2006): 10.

40. Terry M. Moe, "The Politicized Presidency," in John E. Chubb and Paul E. Peterson,

eds., *The New Direction in American Politics* (Washington, DC: Brookings Institution, 1985).

41. William Pfaff, "Manifest Destiny: A New Direction for America," *New York Review of Books* (Febraury 15, 2007).

NOTES TO CHAPTER TEN

My Vanderbilt colleague David Lewis helped me sort through "fiscal cliff" quandaries while I was in the hospital with a broken ankle, and I am grateful to him.

1. David Maraniss, *Barack Obama: The Story* (New York: Simon and Schuster, 2012), 564.

2. Barack Obama, *Dreams from My Father: A Story of Race and Inheritance* (New York: Three Rivers Press, 2004), 82.

3. Maraniss, *Barack Obama: The Story*, 535, 555–575.

4. Ibid., 26, 33, 507.

5. James T. Kloppenberg, *Reading Obama: Dreams, Hopes, and the American Political Tradition* (Princeton: Princeton University Press, 2010), 42–45, 101–109, 153–156.

6. Barack Obama, "Speech on Faith and Politics" (Washington, DC, 2006), Keynote at the Call to Renewal's Building a Covenant for a New America Conference. *New York Times*, June 28, 2006, 28.

7. Stephen Skowronek, *Presidential Leadership in Political Time: Reprise and Reappraisal*, 2nd ed. (Lawrence: University of Kansas Press, 2011), ch. 6.

8. David Brooks, "Thinking about Obama," *New York Times*, October 17, 2008.

9. Barack Obama, "A More Perfect Union Speech" (Philadelphia, March 18, 2008). http://obamaspeeches.com.

10. Barack Obama, "Inaugural Address" (January 20, 2009). http://obamaspeeches.com.

11. Barack Obama, "Speech in Cairo" (June 4, 2009). http://obamaspeeches.com.

12. Bob Woodward, *Obama's Wars* (New York: Simon and Schuster, 2010), ch. 25.

NOTES TO CONCLUSION

1. Michael Oakeshott, *The Politics of Faith and the Politics of Skepticism* (New Haven, CT: Yale University Press, 1996).

2. Fred I. Greenstein, *The Presidential Difference: Leadership from Franklin D. Roosevelt to George W. Bush*, 2nd ed. (Princeton, NJ: Princeton University Press, 2004). Greenstein's comparative analysis of presidents creates a framework by which presidents are assessed according to their capacities as effective leaders. He draws conclusions about the attributes of effectiveness. I did not follow his framework in writing my narratives but expected that we would agree at the end of the day. In fact, my conclusions match his very well. I add other factors in my analysis of the ingredients of effectiveness in keeping with my historical and normative approach.

Index

Mitchell, John, 77, 99
Mitterand, Francois, 186
Model Cities program, 36, 45–46
modern presidency, 250–251
Mondale, Walter, 129, 159, 180
moral dimension of leadership, 7, 41–42,
  127, 138–139
Moral Majority, 144
Morris, Dick, 212–213, 222
Morse, Wayne, 36
Moyers, Bill, 40, 43, 53
Moynihan, Daniel Patrick, 71, 72, 207
Mubarak, Hosni, 273
Mulroney, Brian, 178
Muskie, Edmund, 76, 91, 96, 130
mutual assured destruction, 162, 189
MX missile, 160–161

Nathan, Richard, 72
National Association for the Advancement
  of Colored People (NAACP), 78
national crises, 2–3
National Economic Council, 206
National Intelligence Estimates, 241–242
National Review, 118
National Security Agency, 250
National Security Council, 83–84, 166, 174,
  184, 272–273
national security presidency, 249–251
National Security Strategy of United States,
  240–241
National Welfare Rights Organization, 73
negative income tax, 72
neoconservatives, 115, 117–119, 239
Netanyahu, Benjamin, 271
Neustadt, Richard, 5, 56–57, 58, 231, 244
New Deal, 10–11
New Deal coalition, 149
New Democrats, 195–196, 200–201, 224
New Frontier, 11
New Paradigm, 179
new world order, 190, 192, 194
Nicaragua, 166, 176–177
Niebuhr, Reinhold, 194
Niskanen, William, 160
Nixon, Richard M., 2, 3, 40, 66–103, 231,
  290; 1972 election and, 94–97; ambition,
  68, 69, 70–71, 100; biography, 68–69;

civil rights and, 77–79; context and
  contingencies, 101; debates Kennedy, 11;
  détente and, 83, 86, 87–88, 287; domestic
  policy, 70–71; economic policy, 79–82;
  effectiveness, 102; environmental policy,
  76–77; Ford pardons, 107–108; foreign
  policy, 82–94; lack of trust, 68, 69, 80,
  99; as president, 70–75; revenue sharing,
  74–75; search for Republican center and,
  76–82; second term, 97–98; Strategic
  Arms Limitation Treaty and, 84, 85,
  86–87, 92; as strategist, 71, 84; talents
  and skills, 101, 261; as vice president, 69;
  Vietnam War and, 70, 88–94; Watergate,
  69, 94, 284; welfare reform and, 71–74
Nixon Doctrine, 83
No Child Left Behind, 235–236
North, Oliver, 166
North American Free Trade Agreement
  (NAFTA), 184, 208–209, 224
North Atlantic Treaty Organization
  (NATO), 218–219
Northern Alliance, 238
North Korea, 84, 220
nuclear waste, 180
nuclear weapons, 271–272

Oakeshott, Michael, 263
Obama, Barack, 5, 257–281, 285, 287; 2008
  campaign, 261–262; 2012 campaign,
  275–276; accomplishments of, 278–279;
  beliefs, 260–261; biography, 258–260;
  budget fight of 2011, 269–271; context
  and contingencies, 278; economic policy,
  264–265, 267–271, 276–277; effectiveness
  of, 279; fiscal cliff and, 276–277; foreign
  policy, 271–274, 279; health care reform,
  260, 262, 265–268; leadership style of,
  262–264; partisan politics and, 257–258,
  269, 274–275; political style of, 277;
  social policy, 267–271; talents and skills,
  278; tax policy, 268, 269, 276
Obama, Michelle, 260
O'Brien, Larry, 40
Office of Civil Rights, 77
Office of Economic Opportunity, 43
Office of Management and Budget (OMB),
  76, 98, 113, 152, 177, 208

JUN 2 0 2016

CPSIA information can be obtained
at www.ICGtesting.com
Printed in the USA
LVOW04s1955060616

491420LV00016B/1073/P